CITY OF WALLS

CITY OF WALLS

Crime, Segregation,
and Citizenship in São Paulo

TERESA P. R. CALDEIRA

University of California Press
BERKELEY   LOS ANGELES   LONDON

Title page illustration: Avenida São João, São Paulo. Photograph
by Cristiano Mascaro.

University of California Press
Berkeley And Los Angeles, California

University of California Press, Ltd.
London, England

© 2000 by the Regents of the University of California

Library of Congress Cataloging-in-Publication Data

Caldeira, Teresa Pires do Rio.

    City of walls : crime, segregation, and citizenship in São Paulo /
Teresa P. R. Caldeira

      p. cm.

    Includes bibliographical references and index.

    ISBN 0-520-22142-7(cloth : alk. paper) —ISBN 0-520-22143-5
(pbk. : alk. paper)

    1. Crime—Brazil—São Paulo. 2. Segregation—Brazil—
São Paulo. 3. Social classes—Brazil—São Paulo. 4. São Paulo
(Brazil)—Race relations. 5. São Paulo (Brazil)—Social
conditions. 6. São Paulo (Brazil)—Politics and government.
I. Title.

    HV6895.S3 C35 2000
    364.981'61—dc21   00–028713
                                               CIP

Manufactured in the United States of America

9 8 7 6 5 4 3 2 1 0

10 9 8 7 6 5 4 3 2 1

The paper used in this publication meets the minimum requirements
of ANSI/NISO Z39 0.48-1992 (R 1997) (Permanence of Paper).

To Jim,
explorer of cities, real and imagined

CONTENTS

MAPS, ILLUSTRATIONS, AND TABLES

MAPS

FIGURES

PHOTOGRAPHS

TABLES

ACKNOWLEDGMENTS

This book has lived with me for a long time. I started to think of the relationship of violence, democracy, and the city in the early 1980s in São Paulo, when I was studying social movements on the periphery and listening to people talk about the increase in crime. Just after I wrote the first article on what I would later call "the talk of crime," I took a leave from my jobs in São Paulo and came to the University of California at Berkeley for doctoral studies in anthropology. Since then, I have moved back and forth. This book is situated in these constant displacements. It owes a great deal to many people and institutions who have supported me along the way and whom I can finally acknowledge.

Various institutions funded the research for this book. Fieldwork in Brazil between 1989 and 1991 was funded by an International Doctoral Research Fellowship from the Joint Committee on Latin American Studies of the Social Science Research Council and the American Council of Learned Societies, with funds provided by the William and Flora Hewlett Foundation and the Andrew W. Mellon Foundation; a fellowship from the Inter-American Foundation Doctoral Fellowship Program; and a grant from the Ford Foundation. At UC Berkeley, I was able to pursue my graduate studies with the support of a Latin American and Caribbean Fellowship from the Inter-American Foundation and a Doctoral Fellowship from CNPq (the Brazilian Conselho Nacional de Desenvolvimento Científico e Tecnológico). The two institutions in which I worked as a research associate and a professor in Brazil for more than a decade provided me not only with leaves of absence for my studies at UC Berkeley but also with the best conditions for research and writing. They are the Centro Brasileiro de Análise e Planejamento (Cebrap) and the Universidade Estadual de Campinas (Unicamp), especially the Department of Anthropology. I am grateful to all these institutions for their support, and especially to my colleagues at Cebrap and Unicamp.

I presented the first version of this work as my doctoral dissertation in anthropology at UC Berkeley. There I had the privilege of working with Paul Rabinow, my dissertation adviser. In addition to offering stimulating seminars and thought-provoking comments on my work, he gave me the freedom to follow my own ideas. I am especially grateful for that freedom and for our continuing dialogue. I am also grateful to Nancy Scheper-Hughes for her critical readings and continuous support. I want also to acknowledge the support at Berkeley of Todd Gitlin, David Collier, and Albert Fishlow and the Center for Latin American Studies.

My work has been strongly influenced by a group of leading intellectuals and scholars in São Paulo with whom I have had the privilege of working. I would like especially to mention Ruth Cardoso, who transformed me into an anthropologist and who continues to guide me, and Vilmar Faria, José Arthur Giannotti, Guillermo O'Donnell, and Juarez Rubens Brandão Lopes. I hope this study reveals some of what I have learned with them about combining rigorous research with a passion for public discussion and commitment to social change.

Many people helped me obtain data and material, granted me interviews, and became interested in my work. I was especially lucky to have João Vargas as my research assistant in Moóca. I cannot thank him enough. In addition to sharing with me the enthusiasm of discovering the neighborhood, he helped me enormously in collecting and organizing statistical material and newspaper advertisements. I am grateful to Fundação Seade in São Paulo, and especially Dora Feiguin and Renato Sérgio de Lima, for helping me with crime statistics. I want to express my respect and admiration for all the people and institutions who fight for human rights in Brazil. I thank them for their generosity in sharing with me their insights, concerns, and information, and for letting me use their archives. Particularly, I thank the Comissão de Justiça e Paz da Arquidiocese de São Paulo and the Núcleo de Estudos da Violência of the Universidade de São Paulo and its directors, Paulo Sérgio Pinheiro and Sérgio Adorno. Most of all, I am grateful to the residents of São Paulo who trusted me and agreed to talk to me even when they were afraid. This is a study not only about their fear and the social transformations it generates but also about the hope that those who fight for human rights and democracy sustain even in the face of strong opposition.

The dissertation was transformed into a book as I shifted jobs and moved from Brazil to the United States. I acknowledge the indispensable support of the Department of Anthropology, my colleagues, and the School of Social Sciences of the University of California at Irvine. I am grateful for a Faculty Career Development Award granted by UC Irvine that allowed me time to concentrate on the revisions. I finished the book during a year in residence at the International Center for Advanced Studies of New York University, as a fellow of the program "Cities and Urban Knowledges." It was a year of stimulating discussions and much creativity, for all of which I would like to thank especially Thomas Bender, the center's director.

Many colleagues and friends discussed this book or parts of it with me and generously shared suggestions and information. I especially thank Sonia Alvarez, Marco Cenzatti, Paul Chevigny, Margaret Crawford, Guita Debert, Jim Ferguson, Farha Ghannam, Maria Filomena Gregori, Liisa Malkki, George Marcus, Bill Maurer, Maria Célia Paoli, and Gwen Wright.

The friendship of Danielle Ardaillon, Esther Hamburger, and Sonia Mendonça has been fundamental for me. Cecília de Mello e Souza and Ricardo Meth shared with me the everyday life of Berkeley, and I thank them for their generosity and friendship.

During my constant movements between São Paulo and California I have always had the support of my family. I thank my father Jorge Alberto, my sister Marina, and my brothers Cafu and Eduardo for their care, for looking after numerous things that I cannot manage from afar, and simply for always being there.

Finally, the most complex acknowledgment: my fellow anthropologist James Holston has been my toughest reader and best critic. With him I have explored cities and ideas, carried out fieldwork, and discussed passionately the arguments that shape this and other studies. I thank him for his engagement with my work, for his perseverance, and for countless other things.

Olivia entered our lives in August 1998 as I finished revising the manuscript in São Paulo. To research and write on violence produces many anxieties. Yet what sustained my study of urban violence and segregation is the dream of a different city life that I wish for her.

ABBREVIATIONS

BNH	Banco Nacional de Habitação
CID	common-interest development
MRSP	metropolitan region of São Paulo
MS	minimum salary
MSP	municipality of São Paulo
OM	other municipalities of the metropolitan region
PM	Polícia Militar
PNAD	Pesquisa Nacional por Amostra de Domicílios
PT	Partido dos Trabalhadores
ROTA	Rondas Ostensivas Tobias de Aguiar, a division of São Paulo's military police
SEADE	Fundação Sistema Estadual de Análise de Dados

INTRODUCTION
Anthropology with an Accent

I

Violence and fear are entangled with processes of social change in contemporary cities, generating new forms of spatial segregation and social discrimination. In the last two decades, in cities as distinct as São Paulo, Los Angeles, Johannesburg, Buenos Aires, Budapest, Mexico City, and Miami, different social groups, especially from the upper classes, have used the fear of violence and crime to justify new techniques of exclusion and their withdrawal from traditional quarters of the cities. Groups that feel threatened by the social order taking shape in these cities commonly build exclusive, fortified enclaves for their residence, work, leisure, and consumption. The discourses of fear that simultaneously help to legitimize this withdrawal and to reproduce fear find different references. Frequently they are about crime, and especially violent crime. But they also incorporate racial and ethnic anxieties, class prejudices, and references to poor and marginalized groups. The circulation of *& Urban* these discourses of fear and the proliferation of practices of segregation invariably intertwine with other processes of social transformation: transitions to democracy in Latin America, the end of apartheid in South Africa and of socialism in Eastern Europe, and immigration in Southern California. Nevertheless, the forms of exclusion and enclosure under which current spatial transformations occur are so generalized that one feels tempted to treat them as a formula adopted by elites in large cities everywhere.

This book focuses on São Paulo and presents a comprehensive analysis of the ways in which crime, fear of violence, and disrespect of citizenship rights have intertwined with urban transformations in the last two decades to produce a new pattern of urban segregation. This was the period of democratic consolidation following the military regime that ruled Brazil from

1964 to 1985. The increase in violent crime in São Paulo since the mid-1980s generated fear and a series of new strategies of protection and reaction, of which the building of walls is the most emblematic. Both symbolically and materially, these strategies operate by marking differences, imposing partitions and distances, building walls, multiplying rules of avoidance and exclusion, and restricting movement. Several of these operations are accomplished in the everyday discourses that I call the talk of crime. The everyday narratives, commentaries, conversations, and jokes that have crime and fear as their subject counteract fear, and the experiences of being a victim of crime, and simultaneously make fear circulate and proliferate. The talk of crime promotes a symbolic reorganization of a world disrupted both by the increase in crime and by a series of processes that have profoundly affected Brazilian society in the last few decades. These processes include political democratization and persistent high inflation, economic recession, and the exhaustion of a model of development based on nationalism, import substitution, protectionism, and state-sponsored economic development. Crime offers the imagery with which to express feelings of loss and social decay generated by these other processes and to legitimate the reaction adopted by many residents: private security to ensure isolation, enclosure, and distancing from those considered dangerous.

The talk of crime works its symbolic reordering of the world by elaborating prejudices and creating categories that naturalize some groups as dangerous. It simplistically divides the world into good and evil and criminalizes certain social categories. This symbolic criminalization is a widespread and dominant social process reproduced even by its victims (the poor, for example), although in ambiguous ways. Indeed, the universe of crime (or of transgression or of accusations of misbehavior) offers a fertile context in which stereotypes circulate and social discrimination is shaped, not only in São Paulo but everywhere. This universe of crime and fear is obviously not the only one generating discrimination in contemporary societies. But it is especially important because it stimulates the development of two novel modes of discrimination: the privatization of security and the seclusion of some social groups in fortified and private enclaves. Both processes are changing concepts of the public and of public space that used to be dominant in Western societies until very recently.

The privatization of security challenges the state's monopoly of the legitimate use of force, which has been considered a defining characteristic of modern nation-states (see Weber 1968:54–56; Tilly 1975; Elias 1994 [1939]). In recent decades, security has become a service bought and sold on the market, fueling a very profitable industry. By the mid-1990s, the number of guards employed in private security outnumbered police officers three to one in the United States and two to one in Britain and Canada (U.S. House 1993:97, 135; Bayley and Shearing 1996:587). Citizens of these and many other countries increasingly depend on private security not only for protection from crime but also for identification, screening, surveillance, and isolation of undesired people, exactly those whose stereotypes are elaborated in the talk of crime.

In São Paulo, the privatization of security is escalating, but security guards do not yet outnumber police officers. Nevertheless, the trend acquires a perverse and worrisome characteristic in the context of the distrust of the institutions of order: the police forces and the justice system. Even under democratic rule, the police in Brazil frequently act outside the boundaries of the law, abusing, torturing, and executing suspects, and the justice system is considered ineffective by the population. As a result, an increasing number of residents of São Paulo are opting for types of private security and even private justice (through either vigilantism or extralegal police actions) that are mostly unregulated and often explicitly illegal. Frequently these privatized services infringe on, and even violate, the rights of citizens. Yet these violations are tolerated by a population that often considers some citizenship rights unimportant and even reprehensible, as evidenced in the attack on human rights that I analyze in later chapters.

This widespread violation of citizenship rights indicates the limits of democratic consolidation and of the rule of law in Brazil. The universe of crime not only reveals a widespread disrespect for rights and lives but also directly delegitimates citizenship. This disrespect for individual rights and justice represents the main challenge to the expansion of Brazilian democracy beyond the political system, where it has been consolidated in recent decades. Moreover, the privatization of security equally presents a challenge for consolidated and traditional democracies such as the United States, as their citizens increasingly choose private policing and private enclaves and, by doing without public services and authorities, delegitimate them.

The new pattern of urban segregation based on the creation of fortified enclaves represents the complementary side of the privatization of security and transformation of notions of the public in contemporary cities. Although segregation has always been common in cities, its instruments and rules have changed over time. They have also obviously varied in different cities, helping to shape each one's particular identity. However, it is possible to identify patterns of spatial organization and segregation and their instruments that constitute repertoires from which the most diverse cities borrow. Examples of widely used models include the Laws of the Indies,[1] corridor streets, Haussmann boulevards, the Garden City, and the CIAM (Congrès Internationaux d'Architecture Moderne) modernist city. The fortified enclaves transforming cities such as São Paulo exemplify a new way of organizing social differences in urban space. It is a model that segregates middle and upper classes around the world. It generates another type of public space and of interaction among citizens. This new model does not use totally new instruments in either its design or its location. Walls are old indeed, various design features are modernist, and the enclaves are usually located in the suburbs, where the middle classes have isolated themselves for decades. However, the new model of segregation separates social groups with an explicitness that transforms the quality of public space.

Fortified enclaves are privatized, enclosed, and monitored spaces for residence, consumption, leisure, and work. They can be shopping malls, office complexes, or residential gated communities. They appeal to those who fear the social heterogeneity of older urban quarters and choose to abandon those spaces to the poor, the "marginal," and the homeless. Because access to enclaves is privately controlled, even if they have collective and semipublic uses, they deeply affect the character of public space. In fact, they create a space that contradicts the ideals of openness, heterogeneity, accessibility, and equality that helped to shape both modern public spaces and modern democracies. Privatization, enclosures, policing of boundaries, and distancing devices create a public space fragmented and articulated in terms of rigid separations and high-tech security: a space in which inequality is an organizing value. In the new type of public space, differences are not to be overlooked, taken as irrelevant, or left unattended. Neither are they to be disguised to sustain ideologies of universal equality or of peaceful cultural pluralism. The new urban environment that enforces and values inequalities and separations is an undemocratic and nonmodern public space. That this type of space often emerges at the moment when a society undergoes political democratization, the end of a racist regime, or social and ethnic heterogenization indicates the complexity of the links between urban forms and political forms. Moreover, it indicates that the built environment may be the arena in which democratization, social equalization, and expansion of citizenship rights are contested. Therefore, this book explores how social inequality is reproduced in contemporary cities and how this reproduction intersects with processes that, in theory, should eliminate discrimination and authoritarianism. However, the fact that private and fortified enclaves are as much a feature of Los Angeles and Orange County as of São Paulo and Johannesburg should prevent us from classifying the new model as a characteristic of postcolonial societies. The new model seems to have spread widely. The challenges it poses to democracy and citizenship are not restricted to newly democratized societies.

II

This book is about São Paulo, the city where I grew up, spent most of my life, have done anthropological fieldwork since the late 1970s, and worked as a researcher and professor for fifteen years. Its first version was written in California, where I did my doctoral studies in anthropology and now work as a professor. I wrote it in Los Angeles and in La Jolla, and I started to revise it during my commute between La Jolla and Irvine, in the heart of Southern California. I finished the revisions in New York City and back in São Paulo, where I spend about three months every year. My thinking about violence, urban public life, and spatial segregation is marked by my experiences as a resident of these cities, and especially by the struggles and tensions provoked by the confluence of these different experiences and the knowledge they generate. Displacement is at the heart of this book, both as lived experience and as epistemological and critical device.

The struggle over language is probably one of the most frustrating parts of this displacement. I am a native speaker of Portuguese, the language in which I studied up to my master's degree, wrote my first book, and conducted the research for this one. Yet I wrote this book in English. In writing it I faced daily the realization that, more than my words, my thinking was shaped in a certain style and in a certain language. When I write, I can hear the repetitive and eventually exasperated complaint of one of my copyeditors: "What is the subject? Do not write in the passive voice! Can't you learn it?" Useless to explain that a sophisticated academic style in Portuguese is frequently structured in the passive voice and often with an ambiguous subject; pointless to come up with an interpretation of the meaning of the different grammar choices in each academic style. I was no longer writing in that most taken-for-granted language and was no longer allowed the freedom and the security of unconscious constructions. But, obviously, the question was not of words and grammar alone: it was epistemological and methodological. Anthropology and social theory have what one might call an "international style," that is, a corpus of theory, method, and literature shared by practitioners worldwide. Although this corpus offered me a reference point as I went back and forth between Brazil and the United States, I became acutely aware that academic questions have strong local and national biases and that the discipline is, in fact, plural: there are anthropologies, not anthropology. What American academic discussions emphasize as relevant and exciting is not often among the central concerns of my Brazilian colleagues, and vice versa. At a certain point, the perception of the local framing of questions was so acute that I considered writing two books, or at least two introductions, one for each audience, in Portuguese and English, each addressing different questions. I concluded, however, that this approach also was an impossibility, since my thinking and my perception had already been transformed and shaped by my simultaneous immersion in both contexts and could be squeezed into one or the other mold only artificially and with some loss. My languages, my writing, my thinking, my critiques all had acquired a peculiar identity. I came to realize that as my English has an accent, so does my anthropology; it persists no matter from what perspective I look at it or in which language I write it.

III

And Polo said: "Every time I describe a city I am saying something about Venice. . . . To distinguish the other cities' qualities, I must speak of a first city that remains implicit. For me it is Venice."

Italo Calvino, *Invisible Cities*

Had I written this book in Portuguese for my Brazilian colleagues, as I did my first book (Caldeira 1984), it would add to the list of studies by anthropologists about their own society, the norm in Brazil and in many of the so-called "national anthropologies" (in contrast to the "imperial" ones).[2] But I wrote this book in English, and I was thinking of my American colleagues in addition to my Brazilian ones. This does not automatically make it a work in the "Euro-American style," however, since I continue to be a "native" investigating my own society and did not experience any of the estrangements and oddities of traveling abroad to do fieldwork. Otherness was definitively not an issue framing my research methodologically, although it was certainly one of its central themes.[3] To talk about my fieldwork among fellow citizens in Brazil as an "encounter with the other" or to invert things and conceive of my experience in graduate school in the United States and of what I learned there as "other" would require some rhetorical and symbolic acrobatics I find little sense in undertaking. In this study, there is no otherness, in the sense that there is no fixed other; there is no position of exteriority, as there are also neither stable identities nor fixed locations. There are only dislocations.

At a certain point in Italo Calvino's *Invisible Cities*, Marco Polo declares that he has told the Great Khan about all the cities he knows. Then the Great Khan asks him about Venice, the only city Polo has never talked about. He smiles: "What else do you believe I have been talking to you about?" To the Great Khan's argument that he should have made his model explicit in his descriptions, Polo replies: "Memory's images, once they are fixed in words, are erased. . . . Perhaps I am afraid of losing Venice all at once, if I speak of it. Or perhaps, speaking of other cities, I have already lost it, little by little" (Calvino 1974:86).

Anthropologists of the "Euro-American style" usually proceed like Marco Polo: they describe the foreign cities they have visited to people who have never been there, without talking about their own societies and cultures. Like Marco Polo, they frequently make invisible comparisons to their own cultures, the constant hidden references in relation to which the unknown culture can be described as different. For classic anthropologists and Marco Polo alike, this procedure guarantees that their own cultures and cities remain untouched—preserved, perhaps—by their analysis. Like Marco Polo, classic anthropologists transform into method the silence about their own society and the selection of all other cultures around the world as the object of their detailed descriptions and analyses.[4]

Marco Polo's position, however, is not accessible to all. It requires an empire of cities to be described, an emperor eager to know about them, and a nostalgic describer interested in maintaining the image of his or her native city intact. For colonial, postcolonial, and "national" ethnographers, silence about one's native city is often neither a possibility nor a choice. Usually, they do not go abroad because they have neither resources for nor interest in doing so. Instead, they are interested in their own societies and, more important, in their own nations. In contrast to the anthropologies marked by the constitution of empires, peripheral anthropologies are frequently associated with processes of nation-building and therefore are concerned with the internal predicaments of their own societies.

Nation-building engages anthropologists in paradoxical ways. One dimension of this engagement is the role of the intellectual. In Brazil, as in other postcolonial countries, intellectuals have a prominent role in public life. They think of themselves first as public intellectuals, working to influence public debates, and only second as academics.[5] As a consequence, many Brazilian anthropologists study what is politically relevant to them. Moreover, most public intellectuals (including anthropologists) conceive of their work as a civic responsibility. This view shapes their relationships with their fellow citizens and with the subjects of their research. When public intellectuals study their own cities, they tend to write as citizens, not as detached observers. This means that they talk not only to fellow intellectuals but to the broadest public they can reach. It also means that even when they write in a scientific and authoritative tone, and in spite of all the inherent powers of a professional and social elite, their view of their society is more liable to contestation both by other social analysts and by fellow citizens. Theirs is only one perspective in a public debate, although it is usually a powerful one. Their position is thus different from that of specialists in foreign cultures talking to an academic audience in a debate among specialists about distant places.

When I write about São Paulo in Portuguese for a Brazilian audience, then, I write as a public intellectual and as a citizen, and therefore I approach the city in a certain way. The cities of which we are citizens are cities in which we want to intervene, build, reform, criticize, and transform.[6] We cannot leave them untouched, implicit, unspoken about. Maintaining the imagery of one's city untouched is incompatible with a study (or a project) of social transformation. The cities that remain crystallized in images we are afraid of touching are not cities we inhabit as citizens but cities of nostalgia, cities we dream about. The cities (societies, cultures) we live in are, like ourselves, continuously changing. They are cities to make sense of, to question, to change. They are cities we engage with.

My engagement with São Paulo as one of its citizens—which marks anything I write about it in Portuguese for the Brazilian public—is significantly displaced, however, when I write in English. The position of the public intellectual writing as a citizen concerned with the predicaments of her society is not available to me in American academia. Because the role of intellectuals in the United States does not include the same public perspectives, this type of engagement is not available to other American anthropologists either. In American academia, one's concerns as a citizen are frequently divorced from one's subjects of study, in spite of all the efforts of feminists and minority scholars to unite the two. From the Brazilian concept of public intellectuals, I retain the critical intention. However, writing in English, I lose the public space for engaging in debates with the other citizens of the city. And although I still translate and publish the same works in Portuguese, an undisguisable American accent changes the way in which I am read in Brazil, too.

IV

As "national anthropologists" study their own societies almost exclusively, they can work with the "international style," and its methodological requirements of otherness and comparison, only in problematic ways. The position of researchers trying to be strangers to their own culture is intrinsically dubious. Yet the imperative of otherness has been maintained fairly uncritically as a methodological device in national anthropologies, even when it cannot be effectively practiced.[7] This paradox exposes two types of power relations framing the practice of national anthropologies such as the Brazilian. On the one hand, the fact that national anthropologists study "themselves" and not "others," and yet insist on the construction of otherness without criticizing it, indicates the power of the international style in shaping the discipline on the periphery. On the other hand, the fact that national anthropologists have long been successfully investigating their own societies and cultures reveals that otherness is less an immutable requirement of method than an effect of power.

Intellectual historians (Corrêa 1982; Martins 1987; Miceli 1979; Peirano 1980) have shown that Brazilian intellectuals, including anthropologists, have usually engaged in nation-building by studying various subaltern social groups who, at different moments, present challenges for the nation. Often claiming to constitute a vanguard, intellectuals identified the Brazilian other to be known (and brought to modernity) as the poor, the black, the Indian, the members of ethnic minorities, and the working-class organizers of social movements—in short, those whose membership in the modern nation might be problematic. As "national intellectuals" are usually members of a social elite, it is evident that the "self" about which these studies frequently keep silent is the elite, secure in its position of leadership.[8] Otherness becomes again a matter of power relations, but in this case the relations are internal to the society of anthropologists.

In contrast with this tendency to a certain kind of silence in national anthropology (as well as in international anthropologies), I assume that my data and knowledge are produced interactively in relationships framed by the social positions of those involved. In Brazil, my middle-class and academic position framed my relationships with people of all the social groups I studied. It framed the detailed answers of working-class people who felt obliged to attend to my requests for interviews and who talked about crime in their neighborhoods even when their fear and insecurity justified refusal and silence. Refusals increased as I talked with people farther up the social hierarchy, who felt confident in saying no to a middle-class person. Interviews with upper-class people were hard to obtain and required introductions.[9] Thus my position equally framed the silence of upper-class people and their frequent dismissal of some of the questions that all working-class people answered: elites assumed I shared their own views and knowledges, and answered my requests for further explanations with "You know what I mean!" Finally, my social position shaped my interactions with politicians and businessmen, who gave me the attention a university professor commands even when they strongly disagreed with me on matters such as human rights.

My research for this book contrasts with the national style in another important way: it is comparative. If Euro-American anthropologies tend to avoid the national self, national anthropologies tend to focus too much on their own nation. Instead of becoming internationalized, they become parochial. National anthropologists read broadly and are well-trained in all international discourses, which they absorb and transform as they look at their own societies. Although they thereby look to the center, they rarely look to the side to make comparisons or to conduct research in other societies. Thus, Brazilian anthropologists do not write or teach about other countries, even about their neighbors in Latin America. This localism significantly narrows the scope of their discussions.[10] As a result, their research tends to emphasize uniqueness. Moreover, localism prevents Brazilian anthropologists (and other national anthropologists) from establishing a critical dialogue with the international literature and the production of the knowledge they consume. This isolation helps to maintain the international style in a form unmodified by local anthropologies. In fact, the strong epistemological critique generated by recent American anthropology has not changed the relationship between national anthropologies and the international ones, even if it has changed the individual relationships of some international anthropologists with the people they study. Rather, international anthropologies still tend to treat national anthropologies as native information, as data, and do not accord it a status equivalent to that of the knowledge produced in the international style and published in the international languages.[11]

V

Although I engaged with São Paulo's problems as a citizen and produced the most comprehensive study I could of the city's current violence and spatial segregation, my intent is not to highlight its unique and national character. Rather, it is to understand and criticize processes of social transformation and segregation that São Paulo exemplifies. This book is about São Paulo, then, but it is also about Los Angeles, Miami, and many other metropolitan regions that are adopting walls, separations, and the policing of boundaries as ways of organizing differences in urban space. These regions are obviously different, but difference does not preclude their use of similar instruments and common repertoires. The combination of fear of violence, reproduction of prejudices, contestation of rights, social discrimination, and creation of new urban forms to keep social groups apart certainly have specific and perverse characteristics in São Paulo, but they are manifestations of processes of social change taking place in many cities. Therefore, the comparison with Los Angeles has theoretical interest and furthers our understanding of widespread processes of spatial segregation. Moreover, comparison keeps me in check, forcing me to relativize São Paulo's uniqueness and to frame its analysis in terms that make sense to those studying other cities. As I write about São Paulo while living in Southern California and thinking of Los Angeles, and also while living in São Paulo and thinking about Los Angeles, São Paulo does not become "the other" or strange to me. Yet it is certainly not the same as if I had never left. Because of this displacement, my Brazilian colleagues may think that I end up doing what Marco Polo feared: losing São Paulo as I speak about other cities. But I think not. São Paulo already changed for me when I studied its periphery, and it continues to change as I study it in new ways.

VI

My research, conducted in São Paulo from 1988 to the present, relies on a combination of methodologies and types of data. Participant observation, usually considered as the method par excellence of an ethnographic study, was not often viable for this study, for a number of interconnected reasons. First, violence and crime are difficult, if not impossible, to study through participant observation. Second, the unit of analysis for the study of spatial segregation had to be the metropolitan region of São Paulo. An urban area of sixteen million inhabitants cannot be studied with methods designed for the study of villages. I could have studied neighborhoods, as anthropologists have frequently done in cities and as I have done in earlier research on the city's periphery. However, I was primarily interested not in the ethnography of different areas of the city but in the ethnographic analysis of experiences of violence and segregation, and those could not be studied equally in different neighborhoods. Whereas working-class neighborhoods still have a public life and are relatively open to observation and participation, in middle- and upper-class residential neighborhoods social life is interiorized and privatized, and there is little public life. Because observers in these neighborhoods are suspect and become targets of the private security services, participant observation is not viable there. To rely on participant observation in poor areas and on other methods on the rich areas would mean to "primitivize" the working classes and disregard the relationships between class and public space. Finally, because I was interested in a process of social change that could be only marginally captured through direct observation, I had to use other types of information.

It was necessary, then, to use a combination of methods and types of data, bringing to my anthropology the perspectives of the other social sciences. To understand violent crime in contemporary São Paulo, I analyzed crime statistics. To evaluate these, I had to study the history of the civil and military police forces and uncover how their practice is entangled with the reproduction of violence. To understand changes in patterns of spatial segregation, I reconstructed the urbanization of São Paulo using demographic and socioeconomic indicators produced by different state agencies and academic institutions. To understand the new style of closed collective residences, I analyzed real estate advertisements in newspapers.

Although these and other methods and sources of data provided information about broad processes of change, they could not tell me much about how Paulistanos were living out these processes. For that understanding, I relied on open-ended interviews with residents. I also used newspapers as a source of public debates on human rights and capital punishment. Finally, I interviewed public authorities, human rights activists, journalists, and people involved in the provision of security either in private enterprises or in fortified enclaves. I also draw on my own experiences and memories as a resident of São Paulo to discuss some of its transformations. Most of the interviews were conducted in the years 1989 to 1991. In chapter 1 I discuss the specificity of this period in Brazilian history.

I conceived this research as a cross-class investigation of experiences of fear and crime and their relations with processes of social change. This cross-class perspective is central to my research for three interconnected reasons: because this is a study of social and spatial segregation; because social inequalities are acute in São Paulo; and because violence is a widespread phenomenon that both cuts across class lines and emphasizes class differences. To focus on only one social group or on one area of the city would limit severely the understanding of phenomena that fundamentally affect the relationships between groups and the ways in which the spaces and the possibilities of interactions between people from different social classes are structured in the city. Moreover, to capture the diversity of experiences of violence and crime and understand how associated measures of protection help to reproduce social inequality and spatial segregation, I needed to investigate them in different social contexts.

Although I could have conducted interviews all around the metropolitan region, I decided to concentrate on three areas of the city occupied by people from different social classes. To conduct interviews that would reveal in-depth information about experiences of fear and violence, and especially to be able to interpret them, I needed to observe people's everyday lives and the spaces in which they lived. This was more easily done by concentrating my interviews in a few areas of the city, which I came to know well. This study is not, however, an ethnography of these areas. It is rather an ethnographic analysis of experiences of violence, the reproduction of social inequality, and spatial segregation as expressed in some areas and by the residents of São Paulo who live there.

The first area in which I did research was the poor working-class periphery, created through "autoconstruction." This is the process through which workers build their own houses in precarious neighborhoods distant from the center of the city (see chapter 6). Workers thus simultaneously become property owners, urbanize the outskirts of the metropolitan region, and are politicized. In demanding their "rights to the city," the new homeowners of the periphery have affirmed their citizenship rights and organized most of the social movements of the 1970s and 1980s, contributing to the political changes that led to the overthrow of military rule and to democratization. Most of my research on the periphery was conducted in Jardim das Camélias, in the eastern district of São Miguel Paulista. I have been doing research and following the organization of social movements in this area since 1978 (Caldeira 1984). Because of my familiarity with the area, I draw on observations and interviews with its residents from earlier studies, although for this research I conducted new interviews about violence. Moreover, I use interviews and observations from other neighborhoods in the periphery of São Paulo during the years 1981 through 1983, when the concern about crime started to increase. These interviews were part of a research project on the expansion of the periphery and the political mobilization of its inhabitants, in which we paid special attention not only to the process of democratization but also to the problems shaping everyday life on the periphery.[12]

The second area in which I did fieldwork was Moóca, a lower-middle-class neighborhood close to downtown. Moóca became an important part of São Paulo at the beginning of the twentieth century, when it was one of the first areas to be industrialized. However, it is no longer an important industrial area. Although its landscape is still marked by decaying warehouses and industrial buildings, most of the traditional textile and food factories have closed down. Moóca's deindustrialization began in the 1950s, when new industries were placed in other municipalities or on the periphery. The industrial workers who settled in Moóca around 1900 were European migrants: mostly Italians, but also Spanish, Portuguese, and eastern Europeans. Most of their children never became industrial workers but instead took jobs in commerce and service. By the 1960s, Moóca had become a lower-middle-class neighborhood. The deindustrialization of the area was accompanied by a displacement of residents who rose socially and moved to other parts of the city. This out-migration, which has continued for four decades, reduced the local population. Currently, although Moóca still retains its warehouses and factories and many of its old working-class houses, and although its population still cultivates an Italian accent and ethnic identity, two new and contradictory processes are reshaping the neighborhood. On the one hand, many old and large houses have been transformed into *cortiços*, a type of tenement occupied by workers who cannot afford to own a home, even through autoconstruction. On the other hand, the construction of a subway line has led to reurbanization and gentrification. The construction of luxurious apartment buildings, mansions, and a more sophisticated commerce cater to a richer part of the population that prefers not to move out and to wealthier residents from other neighborhoods who are moving in. All these processes have produced a social heterogeneity and a social tension previously unknown in the neighborhood. This tension is clearly expressed in the talk of crime.[13]

Finally, I did research in upper- and upper-middle-class neighborhoods in the western part of town, specifically in Morumbi and Alto de Pinheiros. Until the 1970s these were areas with a small population, many green areas, and immense houses on large lots. After the mid-1970s, they were transformed by the construction of high-rise apartments, many built on the model of the closed condominium. Morumbi represents most clearly the new pattern of urban expansion that I describe in chapters 6 and 7. Today rich people who used to live in traditional central neighborhoods move to Morumbi to live in fortified enclaves. Morumbi is also more socially heterogeneous than those traditional areas because the rich enclaves are adjacent to some of the largest favelas (shanty towns) of the city, where its poorest residents live. As a consequence, Morumbi expresses most clearly the city's new pattern of spatial segregation. Alto de Pinheiros pioneered the construction of closed condominiums in the 1970s, but the pace of construction was slower, and today it has fewer favelas than Morumbi.

I conducted all interviews on condition of anonymity. In marked contrast to other research projects I have done, in which residents were eager to talk to me and to see their words and ideas in printed form, in this project I faced resistance and reluctance toward discussing crime and violence. Many times people initially asked me not to tape-record the interviews, although they always gave me permission to take notes. In most cases they eventually gave me permission to record as well. When people fear the institutions of order, and when they feel that their rights are not guaranteed by the justice system, this reaction is understandable. I decided not to use fictitious names to identify the interviewees: since I cannot acknowledge their real names, I prefer to omit names altogether as a sign of the fear in which they live. This rule of anonymity does not apply to state officials, members of human rights groups, journalists, and private security businesspeople, who talked to me in their capacity as public figures and in full knowledge that I could make their statements public.

VII

This book is divided into four parts. Part 1 focuses on the talk of crime. In chapter 1, I analyze the structure of narratives of crime and the way in which they symbolically reorder a world disrupted by experiences of crime. I also give an overview of Brazilian political, social, and economic transformations in the 1980s and 1990s. Chapter 2 focuses on some of the specific themes articulated by the talk of crime: the economic crisis of the 1980s and 1990s, the end of the era of progress and social mobility, the images of the criminal and of the spaces of crime, and conceptions of the spread of evil and its control by strong authorities and institutions.

Part 2 deals with crime and the institutions of order. In chapter 3, I analyze statistics of crime to demonstrate the significance of violent crime after the mid-1980s. Chapter 4 traces the history of the Brazilian police forces and shows their routine abuse of the population, especially of those in subservient social positions. Chapter 5 continues the analysis of police abuse, demonstrating how it escalated during the transition to and consolidation of democratic rule in the early 1980s. These abuses are associated with the population's distrust of the justice system and their adoption of private and violent measures of security (which help to boost a private industry of security). Moreover, this association has contributed to persistent violence and to the erosion of the rule of law. The abuses by the police, the difficulties of police reform, the discrediting of the justice system, and the privatization of security generate what I call a cycle of violence. This cycle constitutes the main challenge to the consolidation of democracy in Brazilian society.

Part 3 analyzes the new pattern of urban segregation. It indicates how discourses and strategies of protection intertwine with urban transformations to create a new model of segregation based on enclosures and a new type of public space. Chapter 6 presents the history of São Paulo's urbanization during the twentieth century and its three patterns of spatial segregation, with special attention to recent transformations. Chapter 7 focuses on the fortified enclaves that constitute the core of the new mode of segregation. I explore especially its residential version, the closed condominiums. I also show the difficulties of organizing social life within its walls and demonstrate that an aesthetic of security has become dominant in the city in the last twenty years. Chapter 8 analyzes the changes in public space and in the quality of public life that occur in a city of walls. The new pattern of spatial segregation undermines the values of openness, accessibility, freedom of circulation, and equality that inspired the modern type of urban public space and creates instead a new public space that has inequality, separation, and control of boundaries as organizing values. I use the comparable case of Los Angeles to demonstrate that the pattern of segregation inspired by these values is widespread.

Part 4 has one chapter, in which I focus on a crucial aspect of the disjunction of Brazilian democracy: the association of violence, disrespect for civil rights, and a conception of the body that I call the unbounded body. I ground my arguments on the analysis of two issues that surfaced after the beginning of democratic rule in the early 1980s: a widespread opposition to defenders of human rights and a campaign for the inclusion of the death penalty in the Brazilian constitution. In these debates, a dominant theme is the limit (or lack of limit) to violent intervention in the criminal's body. I show that notions of individual rights are associated with conceptions of the body and indicate that in Brazil there is a great toleration for manipulating the body, even violently. On the basis of this association, I argue that this toleration of intervention, the proliferation of violence, and the delegitimation of justice and civil rights are intrinsically connected.

PART 1

The Talk of Crime

CHAPTER 1
Talking of Crime
and Ordering the World

As violent crime has increased in São Paulo in the past fifteen years, so has the fear of crime. Everyday life and the city have changed because of crime and fear, and this change is reflected in daily conversation. Fear and violence, difficult things to make sense of, cause discourse to proliferate and circulate. The talk of crime—that is, everyday conversations, commentaries, discussions, narratives, and jokes that have crime and fear as their subject—is contagious. Once one case is described, many others are likely to follow. The talk of crime is also fragmentary and repetitive. It breaks into many exchanges, punctuating them, and repeats the same history, or variations of it, commonly using only a few narrative devices. In spite of the repetition, people are never bored. Rather, they seem compelled to keep talking about crime, as if the endless analysis of cases could help them cope with their perplexing experiences or the arbitrary and unusual nature of violence. The repetition of histories, however, only serves to reinforce people's feelings of danger, insecurity, and turmoil. Thus the talk of crime feeds a circle in which fear is both dealt with and reproduced, and violence is both counteracted and magnified.

It is in such everyday exchanges that opinions are formed and perceptions shaped: that is, the talk of crime is not only expressive but productive. Narratives, says de Certeau, go ahead of "social practices in order to open a field for them" (1984:125). This is especially true of crime stories. The fear and the talk of crime not only produce certain types of interpretations and explanations (usually simplistic and stereotypical); they also organize the urban landscape and public space, shaping the scenario for social interactions, which acquire new meanings in a city becoming progressively walled. Talk and fear organize everyday strategies of protection and reaction that restrict people's movements and shrink their universe of interactions. Moreover, the talk of crime exacerbates violence by legitimating private or illegal reactions—such as hiring guards or supporting death squads and vigilantism—when institutions of order seem to fail.

In this chapter I analyze a particular narrative of crime shared with me in an interview. As with everyday conversation, the interviews, conducted in moments of intense preoccupation with crime, were frequently punctuated by the retelling of crime stories. Although I was interested in the stories, I rarely had to solicit them: they emerged spontaneously in the middle of conversations, particularly in discussions about the city and its transformations and about the economic crisis. I look at how a narrative of crime replicates the experience of violence and how, by doing this, it reorganizes and resignifies not only the individual experience but also the social context in which it occurs. Narration, says de Certeau, is an art of speaking which is "itself an art of operating and an art of thinking" (1984:77). Narratives of crime are a specific type of narrative that bestow a specific type of knowledge. They attempt to establish order in a universe that seems to have lost coherence. Amid the chaotic feelings associated with the spread of random violence in city space, these narratives attempt to reestablish order and meaning. Contrary to the experience of crime, which disrupts meaning and disorders the world, the talk of crime symbolically reorders it by trying to reestablish a static picture of the world. This symbolic reordering is expressed in very simplistic terms, relying on the creation of clear-cut oppositional categories, the most important of which are good and evil. Like other everyday practices of dealing with violence, crime stories try to recreate a stable map for a world that has been shaken. These narratives and practices impose partitions, build up walls, delineate and enclose spaces, establish distances, segregate, differentiate, impose prohibitions, multiply rules of avoidance and exclusion, and restrict movements. In short, they simplify and enclose the world. Narratives of crime elaborate prejudices and try to eliminate ambiguities.

Crime narratives cut through and connect the most diverse themes. I deal throughout the study with the most important of these: economic crisis, inflation, poverty, the failure of the institutions of order, city transformations, citizenship, and human rights. In this chapter I focus on how narratives of crime are structured and how they operate, and I discuss the relationship between violence and narration. I also offer an overview of political, social, and economic transformations in Brazil during the 1980s and 1990s.

CRIME AS A DISORGANIZING
EXPERIENCE AND AN ORGANIZING SYMBOL

The narrative that follows was told to me in 1989 by a woman whose parents migrated from Italy to Brazil in 1924. They settled in Moóca, at that time an industrial neighborhood inhabited mainly by European immigrants, and opened a tailor's shop. The woman was born and spent her whole life in Moóca, witnessing its various transformations, whereas some of her siblings have left for "better places," as she put it. She is a housewife and was an elementary school teacher before she married. When I interviewed her, she was in her late fifties.[1] Her husband is a real-estate agent and her son a dentist.

I chose this narrative for two reasons. First, it synthesizes various themes that appear in the other interviews in more dispersed, and sometimes more inarticulate, ways. Second, it is one of the most dramatic narratives of crime that I collected, one that justified changes in her family and everyday life. The discussion of these crimes lasted for two-thirds of our interview. I did not ask her about the crimes: the comments came out as she described the changes Moóca had undergone during her lifetime. I quote extensively from this interview because I want to convey the ways in which the narrative is organized and the talk of crime weaves into its logic highly divergent themes.

I quote a few parts of the narrative, with some elisions either because of repetition or because of a change of subject (she talked, for example, about changes in the Catholic church, the history of her family in the neighborhood and their migration, her trips to Italy, her family's attachment to music, her son's achievements, her support for an authoritarian government, and her views of radio and television programs). The bracketed phrases, summarizing or explaining parts of the narrative, are my own interpolations. My own questions during the interview are set on their own lines. I use these conventions for quotations throughout the book. Each quote has a number: the first digit identifies the chapter and the second the quote. All translations from Portuguese are my own.

1 . 1

> Moóca has had a lot of progress. The best thing in the neighborhood
> is progress. It has had progress in schools, progress in houses. The
> most beautiful houses used to be on Avenida Paes de Barros; they
> were called *palacete*.[2] [Paes de Barros is the street on which she lives.]
> The street was residential; today it is commercial. The change started
> about fifteen years ago. Only chic people used to live on Paes de

Barros. Moóca's elite today lives in the new neighborhood, Juventus. The neighborhood has had a lot of progress. It has new hospitals, the João XXIII, the São Cristóvão. There is also the university. The São Judas University started on Clark Street: it was a large shed. . . .

I have my roots here, I was born here, I have friendships here in the neighborhood. What has spoiled Moóca a lot are the favelas.[3] The one in Vila Prudente is a city. It has more than fifty thousand people! . . . There are also a lot of *cortiços*.[4] There are a lot of *cortiços* in Moóca since the people from the north came. There are three hundred *cortiços*, each one has fifty families with only three toilets—how is it possible to live like this? What is damaging is this, the poverty. Here we have the middle class, the rich class, and, far down, the poverty of the *nordestinos*.[5] The neighborhood became worse since the crowd from the north started to arrive. . . . This was about fifteen years ago. Now there are too many of them. Gorgeous houses, beautiful houses of Moóca were sublet, and today it is impossible to enter them, they've torn them down. For the last fifteen years Moóca has been slipping in this respect. Moóca has had a lot of progress, but it slips back because of the poor population.

But before, were there not poor residents in Moóca?

Before, there weren't. We used to go out wearing hats, the teachers used to wear hats. I used to wear gloves and hats. From when I was fifteen to when I was eighteen, I used to go out in the street wearing a hat. The Praça da Sé, rua Direita[6] . . . it was so chic! Today we don't go there, it's not possible, you know how it is. . . .

[We started discussing what should be done in relation to poverty and the poor residents.]

They should receive more support from the government. They have infested everything, they should go back there.[7] The government should give them houses there in the northeast so they wouldn't need to come here. . . . Today here in Moóca one cannot even go out of the house. It has been six years since I've been robbed, and six years since everything seems to have lost its color. Here in Moóca, there isn't a person who hasn't been robbed. . . .

[She then spoke of the case of a private guard at the local supermarket who had been killed a few days ago during an armed robbery. He was a father of five and had been working there for less than three months.]

The worst thing in Moóca is that people are afraid. There is too much crime, too much robbery. It has been more dangerous in the last eight years. Extremely dangerous. Nobody goes out at night, nobody wears a necklace, anything.

Who are the criminals?

People who rob are *nortista*.[8] They are all people who live in favelas. People from the neighborhood and from outside. It doesn't make any difference if you want to do something. You fill out a police report, but nothing is solved. When I was robbed, I filled out the police report, I had a friend, a lawyer, it didn't make any difference, they haven't found anything. . . .

Today nobody wants to live in a house because of the lack of security. I used to live on Camé Street, with electronic gate, intercom, a Doberman inside the house. One day, at 7 A.M., my husband went out to go to the garage. A guy came, jumped on the top of him, covered his face, and stabbed him in the heart. Since that day my husband has never been healthy any more; he has a heart condition. . . .

[After the robbers attacked her husband, they entered the house and asked her for money and jewelry, probably knowing that her husband used to be an occasional jewelry dealer. She immediately gave them a big box of jewelry: "We gave everything." The robbers started to direct her and her son to the maid's room in the back of the house, but on the way she managed to open the dog's kennel. The Doberman attacked the robbers, who fired a few shots without hurting anybody and then ran away. I asked her to describe them.]

They had "good face."[9] One was short, kind of dark, you could see he was from the north. The other had a white face, but was certainly *nortista;* he should have been from Ceará. . . .

[From her specific case, she returns to considerations about changes in the neighborhood.]

In Juventus there are gorgeous houses, but all with fences. In the streets there are guards in guard houses. In Moóca, everybody stays locked in: the robber stays out, and we are all locked in. And not even this helps. My house which was robbed had an electronic gate, an intercom. The robbers entered the neighbor's house—a house which was also mine and was rented—and jumped over into my house and hid in the garage. In Juventus, all houses are closed, but if you talk with their residents, they're going to tell you about many robberies. Moóca's residents are sad because of the lack of security. It's not only Moóca, it's all around São Paulo. The schools look like prisons. Before it was wonderful, the children used to play on the streets, people would stay at the doors talking, there was more friendship, people used to visit each other. Today people live in fear in Moóca. Today, if you ask on the street, each one has a story to tell: if his house wasn't burglarized, he has had a necklace taken, a ring, a wallet. . . .

[She recalls a theft of which her sister has just been a victim: she was walking home from the street market with her purchases when someone took her wallet. Many times, she says, people will take your shopping cart filled with food.]

Moóca is infested.

[The discussion turned to possible solutions.]

There can be a solution. It should come from the government. The government should give assistance to the poor. The neighborhood became ugly with the cortiços. And the poor are like that, when they cannot buy the things they need, they rob. It is also the lack of culture. Moóca has had a lot of progress, has grown a lot, has had progress in houses, buildings, but it has an amount of cortiços that never seems to end. The government should close the exportation, stop this migration of people from the north. If you knew what my husband says when he goes by a favela! He is so disgusted. I am too. I've lost my health since I was robbed. I left the house on the same day, I sold everything there, I threw everything away. . . . My husband, you don't know what he says. When he sees a cortiço, a favela, he says that a bottle of kerosene and a match would solve everything within a minute. . . .

Moóca has had a lot of progress, but has regressed as well. The cortiços spoil Moóca's beauty. Today people sell their houses and move into apartment buildings.

[She explains that the house that had been robbed was a remodeled one in which her family had invested for years. It had a swimming pool and a barbecue area.]

We had those things not to be snobbish, but to give comfort to the family. Today's problem is that one cannot have the privilege of enjoying the fruits of one's sacrifices.

[She likes the last phrase, tells me to write it down, and repeats it. Then she continues to talk about her house, which she decided to sell just after the second robbery.]

Because I sold everything, I lost everything. I sold from one day to the other, I sold for nothing and on top of that there was the Plano Cruzado on the day after I sold. When we realized it, the money had already turned into nothing.

Moóca regresses because of the *cortiços*. This migration of people to here should be stopped, they should give them conditions to stay there. But people are also lazy. They don't want to know anything about work. The worst is the favela; bandits are inside the favelas. They earn little money, but if you enter inside a favela, you see a lot of televisions, videos, stereos, from where? Everything stolen. . . .

I'm going to tell you right away: I'm in favor of the death penalty for people who deserve it. Here in Moóca we're in favor of the death penalty. I know that the [Catholic] Church condemns the death penalty, but, in my opinion, there must be a real punishment for someone who does wrong. For example, a person who has a two-hundred- or three-hundred-year prison term, he is not going to have so many years of life! If it were the death penalty, another person wouldn't do the same. It's nonsense this story which says that the wrong person could be punished, that would be injustice. It would be an example. People should see the right thing, with consciousness. People who are sentenced to so many years of prison, how are we going to support the bum in prison at a cost of four hundred cruzados a day? In Moóca everybody is in favor of the death penalty. . . .

[At this point her maid enters the living room to serve coffee and cookies, and the woman asks her if she is in favor of the death penalty. The maid says she is.]

She is a Pentecostal and she too defends the death penalty; I'm the sister of a priest, and I defend it as well. There wouldn't be so many children on the street, because there are mothers who put children in the world without thinking, either because of poverty or because of shamelessness.[10]

[At this point she is talking passionately and comments:]

The more irritated I become, the more beautiful my vocabulary becomes. When I'm mad I can speak as well as a lawyer. Formerly, I used to speak even better, but I lost the habit. I'm not accustomed to speaking so much anymore. I'm mad! I've changed so much because of that robbery! I've lost the desire to do things. Before I was happy— we were happy and we didn't even knew it. The house was clean, beautiful, everything in order.

[She starts to tell the story of the robberies again.]

Two months before the robbery, my maid had gone to Minas. One day, at 4:00 P.M., the house was in order, and I was at home dressed up, feeling very vain, very well dressed, wearing diamond earrings [the same ones she was wearing during the interview], and the matching ring that I still had at that time. I sat down to relax. Sometimes I used to sit down at the piano. . . . The bell rang. Let me tell you: it was a young white man, wearing a work coat! If I get nervous, I can't speak. If I listen to a story like that, I'm able to climb a podium and inflame São Paulo. It was a young man of my height, a medium height, around twenty-two years old, thin, with a blue work coat with the logo of the Perfumaria Abaeté on the pocket, with a pad and a pencil. He called me over the intercom and said that he had a delivery to make. I asked, "Aren't you mistaken?" He said, "No, it's here." He had a package this big [she shows the size of a shoe box], well wrapped, with a ribbon and a card. He asked: isn't this the residence of José?[11] Yes, he is my son, but nobody has bought anything. He got mad, "We work, we're employees, and people don't want to receive the merchandise." I thought, "My son is young, maybe it was a fan, a girlfriend." It was my luck that instead of opening the door through the intercom, I went down the marble staircase. I took the box, it was heavy. I got the pad to sign, and then he pulled a gun, this big [she indicates twenty to thirty centimeters], and he said, "Go up the stairs!" Another guy appeared, a darker one, with a razor. I started to scream. They sat me down, then pushed me while I was kneeling, and threw me into the garage. I got a bad knee to this day, a bad kidney. . . . "I'll give you everything, don't do anything to me!" But with the scream my neighbor thought that Maria José, who was my maid and a scandalous type, had come back from Minas and she opened the door. That was my salvation. They ran away. Exactly two months after, they came back. . . . I stayed two months in bed, urinated blood, took an X ray of my knee, had to do a painful treatment. . . . I don't go out at night, I don't visit anybody. Today I live in an apartment. . . . You never get rid of that trauma. My son is twenty-eight, and the fear my son has! I was so happy. I was happy and I didn't know it. I was an active person, I was moving around all the time, I used to do work for the poor. . . .

In Moóca everybody has fear, and because of that everybody leaves. The sophisticated population goes away and the *nordestinos* keep arriving; we are giving up space for them. . . .

When I was robbed for the second time, I had my brother-in-law, my husband's brother, in my house. He had been in Brazil seventeen days. He had a heart attack and died. He had been at my house for eight days when the robbery happened. He was sleeping. He had come to rest and to take care of himself. I tell my husband that it wasn't because of the robbery, but he doesn't think so, he thinks he was frightened. . . . One of the robbers had a knife and he held it to my son's eyes. My son's office is full of bars, closed windows, closed doors—can one live like this? . . .

Nowadays people only meet at funeral services. The circle of friendship, of fellow countrymen, is fading away. Friendship is getting distant because of the fear of going out at night. Look what a nice little sentence! The Moóca that I once knew was so different! People could live, go out without this dreadful feeling. When the population was smaller, there was more tranquility. The *nordestinos* infested Moóca, made Moóca ugly.

Most narratives of crime introduce the episode by stating the exact time at which it happened. They also always give details about the place, circumstances, and routine character of what was going on just beforehand, creating a precise mark of rupture through the elaboration of small details. They represent an event that had the power to interrupt the uneventful flux of everyday life, changing its quality for ever—an event that stands out because of its absurdity and gratuitousness.

This traumatic event divides history into "before" and "after." This orderly division makes crime assume exactly the reverse meaning in the narration that it had in the experience: to be a victim of violent crime is an extremely disorienting experience. Violent crime imposes a disorder on lived experience. Life does not go on as it used to. Many people repeated to me, "You never lose that fear." It is a common belief that those who have been victims of crime hold different views about crime and violence, and even about society and the city, from those who have not. Although the interviews were not totally conclusive in this regard, they showed very clearly that the experience of violence always provokes changes. Usually an experience of violent crime is followed by reactions like enclosing the home, moving, restricting children's activities, hiring private guards, not going out at night, and avoiding certain areas of town, all actions that reinforce a feeling of loss and restriction as well as the perception of a chaotic existence in a dangerous place. Experiences of crime are also followed by talk of crime, numerous retellings of the event, and conversations in which it is discussed repeatedly.

Yet as the story is told and retold, crime, instead of being disruptive, structures the narrative by establishing static temporal marks and by lending its categories to other processes. As the narratives are repeated, the neighborhood, the city, the house, and the neighbors all acquire different meanings because of the crime, and their existence may be realigned according to the marks provided by crime. In the above story, the arrival of the *nordestinos* in the neighborhood occupies a position equivalent to that of a crime, dividing local history into before and after. What crime does for the narrator's biography, the arrival of the *nordestinos* does for the neighborhood.

In the narratives, crime organizes the structure of meaning and, by doing so, counteracts the disruption caused by the experience of violence. However, this use of crime as a divider between good and bad times simplifies the world and the experience. For the sake of rhetoric, the division between before and after reduces the world to an opposition of good and evil. In making this reduction, people usually present simplistic accounts of experiences and tend to create caricatures. The before becomes too good; the after becomes too bad. In the above case, before the assault the victim "was happy but did not know it." Descriptions of previous happiness are romanticized: the house with the marble staircase, swimming pool, and barbecue; the diamonds worn on an ordinary afternoon; the relaxing interludes at the piano; in short, comfort, order, and status, all interrupted by the fateful doorbell. After the assault, life is hell: everything has lost its savor, she and her husband have lost their health, her son is full of fear, they have lost money and status. They sold their nice house overnight and moved into an apartment building. They do not consider this a comfortable way of living; they cannot show off their status or benefit from their many years of sacrifice to build a respectable residence and a good social position. It is also interesting to note that the two episodes of crime, two months apart, are retold in the above narrative, but they symbolically merge in various moments to justify the changes in everyday life. Although the circumstances and actions of each are different, they are introduced in the same way and are said to have provoked similar effects (health problems and loss of status and money), and they sometimes become a single unified experience.

The reductions made at the level of narration go to the point of distorting facts to make them fit. The woman considers that with the move to the apartment she lost not only comfort and status but also money, and she blames the loss on the Plano Cruzado, a 1986 economic and monetary reform aimed at controlling persistent high rates of inflation. At this point the narrative becomes confused. She claims that they lost money because they sold their house one day before the plan took effect. However, she also says many times that the assault took place six years previously and that she has been living in the apartment for six years. That would place the attack in 1983, for this interview took place in September 1989. Her husband and her sister, with whom I also spoke, later confirmed that they had moved six years earlier, which means that she probably added the Plano Cruzado to her narrative to underscore the assertion that her individual loss was caused by the country's economic crisis, not by their personal failure. Moreover, it associates the experience of living under permanent high inflation— a situation where the value of cash is volatile and people don't know what their assets will be worth tomorrow—with the disruption of values and assets that robbery causes. Because she had exchanged property for cash, she lost. By associating in her narrative the moment of crime with the occurrence of the economic plan and the collapse of her world, the narrator reveals how crime, economic crisis, and social decay interconnect in the perceptions of São Paulo's residents: that is, how biography and social conditions intertwine. It is crime, however, that provides the language for expressing other experiences like inflation and social decay, and not the other way around.

Biography and social conditions coincide in another way in this narrative through the intervention of the universe of crime: changes in the neighborhood and in the city space are given the same structure of meaning as the experience of crime, for they also have a before and an after whose threshold is related to crime. Before, there was progress; afterward, regress. Before, there were sophisticated streets where women walked with gloves and hats; afterward, there were only places no one would consider going to. Before, the neighborhood was small, elegant, filled with friendly acquaintances, children playing in the streets, outdoor conversations, nice houses, comfort, and no visible poverty; afterward, the neighborhood expanded to encompass fear, poor residents and *cortiços*, fences and crime, apartment buildings, and people imprisoned in their dwellings. Before, there was intense local sociability; afterward, encounters with friends occurred only at funerals. In this case, the trauma was the "invasion" (like a home robbery) of the neighborhood and of the city by poorer residents, the *nortistas* who live in the *cortiços* and favelas. Many residents of Moóca repeat the same history about the neighborhood: between the mid-1970s and the beginning of the 1980s, old houses started to be transformed into *cortiços*, and an immense new population arrived. The new residents, considered to be poorer, are identified as criminals by most of the people I interviewed. Their arrival is equated to an infestation.

Two main reductions are embedded in this history of the neighborhood. First, it ascribes all the changes to the arrival of new residents, who are accused of being criminals (in the same way that the narrator reduces to a single crime the factors that have changed her life). Again, crime offers a simplified code for other social changes. In recent decades, Moóca has certainly gone through a series of transformations. The old food and textile factories, from the first phase of São Paulo's industrialization, started shutting down in the 1950s as industry shifted to other parts of the metropolitan region, where heavy industries with more modern technologies were developed. Moóca's economy slowed down, and with this change the neighborhood lost part of its industrial character. This shift was accentuated by a sharp transformation of the urban environment: new avenues were opened, and the construction of a subway line led to the demolition of numerous old buildings, both residential and commercial.

Moóca has also been losing population since the 1950s. As the economic and social dynamics of the city changed, especially during the prosperous 1970s, those residents of Moóca who could afford it moved to areas of the city more closely identified with the middle classes rather than stay in a place seen as industrial, ethnic (mostly Italian), and in economic decay. Old residences have in fact been abandoned, but this has less to do with crime than with socioeconomic transformations, which include both the upward mobility of long-term residents and economic decay. As better-off residents moved out and the local industries declined, various buildings were indeed transformed into *cortiços* through a process typical not only in Moóca but in all old industrial districts.[12]

However, the neighborhood also changed because of gentrification. As old residential areas became zones of commerce, a new gentrified area, Juventus, started to be built in the 1980s, with plenty of apartment buildings. Members of the middle classes who have stayed in the older part of the neighborhood, like the narrator, felt the transformations deeply, as they radically changed everyday life and its pattern of sociability. The point I want to stress, however, is the way crime offers a language for expressing the feelings related to changes in the neighborhood, the city, and Brazilian society more generally. These changes are seen as regressive by old residents, and the association of change with the invasion of the neighborhood by "criminals" expresses their views in a compelling way. Crime is bad, there is no doubt about that; to associate neighborhood changes with criminals is to attach a clear negative value to them.

The second reduction is that embedded in the category of the *nordestinos*, who are characterized as ignorant, lazy, dirty, promiscuous, immoral. In a word, they are criminals. These derogatory terms have been used in Brazil since the time of the Conquest to describe the native, the African slave, the worker, and the poor, and I analyze them further in chapter 2. In Moóca, these undesired neighbors are all considered to come from the impoverished northeast: like many of the residents' parents, they are migrants, but not from Europe. It is clear, however, that the *nordestino* of the narrative is an essentialized category meant to symbolize evil and explain crime. It is simplistic and caricatured—which does not mean that it doesn't affect social relations. It is a product of classificatory thinking concerned with the production of essentialized categories and the naturalization and legitimization of inequalities (see chapter 2 and Malkki 1995:256–67). It is revealing, though, that Moóca's residents have selected migrants from the northeast as the target of their prejudice. Although the talk of crime constantly elaborates essentialized categories and prejudices, the target of the categorical thinking varies. Bias against the *nordestinos* exists everywhere, but whereas in Moóca they are insistently targeted as the criminals, in other neighborhoods the main target of criminalization varies. Probably this tendency relates to the fact that most of Moóca's families are descended from migrants and that residents of the city usually see the neighborhood as a place of migrants. Because the label *migrant* also applies to the residents I interviewed (like the narrator above, a daughter of Italian migrants), and because they feel that there are social differentiations in the neighborhood that must be maintained, they feel compelled to distance themselves from these more recent migrants. In other words, the classificatory principle at work here is that the category closest to the narrator, but still different, must be most emphatically distanced and condemned. Categorical mixture produces cognitive anxiety and leads to abhorrence, as Mary Douglas reminds us in her study of classification: "Uncleanness or dirt is that which must not be included if a pattern is to be maintained" (1966:40). To distinguish themselves from the newer migrants, the older ones treat them symbolically as polluting and associate them with crime and danger.

Many of those living in Moóca today are only second- or third-generation residents, but they feel that the place is theirs. They display a local identity and territorial sense that is generally unknown in the other areas where I did research. Moreover, they feel that they have risen socially in comparison to their parents, a process that the economic crisis put in jeopardy. The newcomers, migrants like themselves but who came later and are poorer, are therefore targeted to express the boundaries of their community and to enhance the older residents' social superiority. Newcomers are marked not only as foreigners but also as invaders who are destroying the place that Mooquenses and their parents conquered and built for themselves. Treated as contaminating, the presence of the *nordestinos* is said to spoil the whole environment: they have "infested" the neighborhood, repeats the narrator to punctuate her story. Their poverty threatens the social status of all residents. *Nordestinos* represent the process of social decay that many in the neighborhood are going through or are afraid of. At the same time, that association allows the old migrants to maintain that they are not as poor as the *nordestinos*, those who are "far down"; they are better off, they have proper houses (until they lose them either to crime and fear or to inflation).

In sum, the *nordestino* is for Moóca's residents a synthesized image of everything reprehensible and therefore criminal. *Nordestinos* represent the threat not only of crime but also of social decay. As a synthesis of evil, the category of the *nordestino* does not correspond to reality, although it is a powerful expressive tool. However, because of the distance between the image and the reality, there is always a tension between its general use in the talk of crime and details of such narratives.

The talk of crime and the elaboration of categories of the criminal are simultaneously a kind of knowledge and a misrecognition. This is not a characteristic exclusive to the talk of crime but one it shares with other types of classificatory thinking, such as racism. Analyzing racism as a kind of knowledge, Étienne Balibar argues that "the racist complex inextricably combines a crucial function of *misrecognition* (without which the violence would not be tolerable to the very people engaging in it) and a 'will to know,' a violent *desire for* immediate *knowledge* of social relations" (1991:19, emphasis in the original). This combination generates great ambiguity when people try simultaneously to organize thought and narrative using these categories and to account for the details of specific experiences. Although ambiguity can be avoided when the task at hand is simply to state the categories and elaborate a general discourse on crime, it is unavoidable when people are dealing with specific details.

This type of ambiguity is clear in the case I have been analyzing. The woman concludes that the men who robbed her, despite being white, with a "good face," could only be from the north, probably from Ceará, one of the poorest states of Brazil. In neither robbery did the criminals exactly fit her images of a *nordestino* or criminal. In one case, she even mistook the robber for a worker and had to warn me that he was a young white man! But in her comments on crime she insists on using the image of the *nordestino*/criminal anyway, for it is inconceivable to her that the situation could be otherwise. She has to stick to the available stereotypes to make sense of the assaults and of the changes in her life and neighborhood. The categories are rigid: they are meant not to describe the world accurately but to organize and classify it symbolically. They are meant to counteract disruption at the level of experience, not to describe it. This does not mean that description is impossible: the robbers were white and good-looking, and she mistook one of them for a worker. But this misperception is part of the disorganization of the world, of the experience of violence and social decay that I reintroduced many times by asking for details. In the organized narrative, the criminals must be nonwhites from the northeast, from *cortiços* and favelas, the proper place for criminals. Misrecognition is inherent to the symbolic reordering of the world. It is part of the labor of resignifying a reality that is not making sense, that has been disrupted and is changing.

Sometimes the narrator acknowledges the simplified and even absurd nature of her categories and opinions. For example, she distances herself from the most extreme prejudices against favelados by saying that the idea of burning them all was her husband's, not her own. Later on, she moderates her defense of the death penalty and her reviling of *nordestinos* by reflecting on her rage and the passionate quality of her speech: "When I am mad I can talk as well as a lawyer," she reminds me. A lawyer is also a stereotypical character, one associated with corruption, manipulation, and the masterful and deceptive use of words. In sum, the talk of crime deals not with detailed description of criminals but with a set of simplistic categories: a few essentialized images that eliminate the ambiguities and categorical mixtures of everyday life and gain currency at moments of social change. The talk of crime is made up not of balanced views but of stereotypes, even if their simplistic character is acknowledged. The talk of crime elaborates prejudices. However, because this misrecognition may be acknowledged, the talk of crime is also ambiguous, with slippages that reveal possible doubts in the speaker's mind.

These ambiguities persist in crime narratives in the form of alternations of clear-cut categories with commentaries that attempt to account for aspects of reality that do not fit stereotypical description. They are especially apparent in the numerous commentaries about the poor. The poorest people in the area are always associated with criminals and spoken of in the most derogatory terms, even by poor people themselves. However, everybody recognizes that poverty is excessive and has recently worsened: Brazilian society is becoming more unequal than ever before. Even the woman I have been quoting acknowledges that living conditions for the poor are deteriorating and that state policies to combat poverty are ineffective. She counts her philanthropic labor as part of the "before," that is, the period when she was happy and her life was in order. Her piety and her understanding of social conditions, however, practically have to be silenced if her history is to make sense and if she is to present it to me as a strong case. They are silenced so that the stereotypes may rule.

Crime supplies a generative symbolism with which to talk about other things that are perceived as wrong or bad, but for which no consensus of interpretation or vocabulary may exist. It also offers symbolism with which to talk about other kinds of loss, such as downward mobility. Moreover, crime adds drama to the narration of events that themselves may be undramatic—for example, a forty-year process of change in a neighborhood—but whose consequences can be distressing. In the talk of crime, fear of crime mixes with anxiety about inflation and social position; the individual condition intertwines with the social situation and with transformations in the city, public space, and the neighborhood; biographical experiences mirror social conditions. In fact, it is the recurrent translation and continuous reflection of these different levels through the common vocabulary of crime and its categories that dramatize the evaluation of society's predicaments.

VIOLENCE AND SIGNIFICATION

Violence always poses problems of signification. The experience of violence disrupts meaning, a disruption that narration tries to counter. But narratives can also make violence proliferate. Theoretical discussions of violence frequently have embedded in them theories of language and symbolism as well as discussions about the construction or destruction of a cultural order. I consider some of the most prominent of these discussions, which may be divided into two perspectives. First are authors who analyze violence from the perspective of cultural order and who consider that violence jeopardizes language and, conversely, that symbolic clarity helps to control violence. Second are those who argue that narration mediates violence and enables it to proliferate. My intention is not to develop a general theory of the relationship between violence and signification but to highlight the particular fea-

tures of the narratives of crime and to indicate how they relate to the reproduction of violence and to other social processes, especially democratization. As narratives of crime deal with the disruption caused by crime (or
by one of the processes of disruption that crime symbolically expresses),
they produce a certain type of signification. These narratives are simplistic,
marked by prejudices and stereotypes. They contradict democratic discourse
and initiatives, the sorts of practice Brazilian society was trying to consolidate before crime became the talk of the city. Moreover, although the clear
distinctions of the talk of crime do reorder experiences disrupted by violence, they are not effective in controlling violence. Instead, they reproduce
fear and violence.

In his ambitious study *Violence and the Sacred* (1977), René Girard offers what he calls a scientific theory of the transformation of violence into
culture, or, more exactly, of the generative mechanism able to control violence and signify the passage from nonhuman to human (1977:309, 311).
Making a case for the primacy of social order, Girard describes social
processes of widespread reciprocal violence (such as private vengeance) as
"sacrificial crisis," which he defines as

> a crisis of distinctions—that is, a crisis affecting the cultural order. The
> cultural order is nothing more than a regulated system of distinctions
> in which the differences among individuals are used to establish their
> "identity" and their mutual relationships. . . . Order, peace, and fecun-
> dity depend on cultural distinctions: it is not these distinctions but the
> loss of them that gives birth to fierce rivalries and sets members of the
> same family or social group at one another's throats. . . . This loss forces
> men into a perpetual confrontation, one that strips them of their dis-
> tinctive characteristics—in short, of their "identities." Language itself
> is put in jeopardy. (Girard 1977:49, 51)

Thus a sacrificial crisis is a kind of war of all against all in which men
(this is Girard's language) lose their distinctions as they are leveled by violence. His solution to this crisis is a sacrificial substitution in which society unanimously agrees on an act of violence against a single victim, the
surrogate victim, who symbolically stands in for all the potential victims
(Girard 1977:81–82). Analyzed by Girard through the myth of Oedipus, the
surrogate victim transforms generalized violence and chaos into social order. His sacrifice combines both bad and good violence, the violence that kills
and the violence that restores order. The unanimous violence against the
surrogate victim initiates a constructive cycle, that of sacrificial rites and religion. In this cycle, the generative violence (the unanimous one) is constantly evoked through repetitive rituals, keeping reciprocal violence under

control and allowing culture to flourish. For Girard, "the original act of violence is the matrix of *all* ritual and mythological significations" (1977:113, his emphasis). The purpose of rituals is to consolidate the difference between good and evil and to select a certain form of violence and mark it as good and necessary in opposition to the other forms, which are deemed bad.

Girard's theory relies on the unproven assumption that violence is inherent in human beings, that both aggressiveness and revenge are innately human, and that violence is contaminating and communicable. Moreover, it assumes that violence is paradoxical in its nature: it is like blood, a substance that can "stain or cleanse, contaminate or purify, drive men to fury and murder or appease their anger and restore their life" (1977:37). Violence can be controlled only through violence, that is, by the good and legitimate violence that directs evil violence into the "proper channels" (1977:31). To control violence, therefore, society must maintain the distinction between good and bad violence. "As long as purity and impurity remain distinct, even the worst pollution can be washed away; but once they are allowed to mingle, purification is no longer possible" (1977:38). According to Girard, this distinction can be maintained only by an authority of wide legitimacy that, by sanctioning violence in a culturally enclosed form, maintains the distinctions between good and evil, legitimate and illegitimate violence, the judicial system and vengeance. It is thereby able repeatedly to perform the controlled rituals (good violence) necessary to reproduce order and symbolism.

Girard's theory of sacrificial crisis and its control is certainly not at odds with Mary Douglas's analysis of matter out of place. In both cases, danger is controlled and social order maintained by clear categorizing. Douglas equates disorder with dirt and sees the efforts to avoid it as creative and helping to unify experience. "I believe that ideas about separating, purifying, demarcating and punishing transgressions have as their main function to impose system on an inherently untidy experience. It is only by exaggerating the difference between within and without, above and below, male and female, with and against, that a semblance of order is created. In this sense, I am not afraid of the charge of having made the social structure seem overrigid" (1966:4). Douglas likens rejecting pollution to rejecting ambiguity, anomaly, and disorder. "Reflection on dirt involves reflection on the relation of order to disorder, being to non-being, form to formlessness, life to death" (1966:5). Thus, for Douglas, efforts to create order and distinctions (which counteract danger, pollution, and, we could add, violence) are fundamental cultural enterprises.

Elaine Scarry's analysis, although opposing violence and language as Girard's does, makes a different argument, for she is not as concerned with the question of social order. Her analysis of torture starts from the assumption that "physical pain does not simply resist language but actively destroys it, bringing about an immediate reversion to a state anterior to language, to the sounds and cries a human being makes before language is learned" (1985:4).[13] Torture also "mimes (objectifies in the external environment) this language-destroying capacity in its interrogation, the purpose of which is not to elicit needed information but visibly to deconstruct the prisoner's voice" (1985:20). The structure of torture is the structure of unmaking. For Scarry, the main issue of torture is not truth but power. This structure is opposed to that of making, creating, signifying—in short, of language.

While authors such as Girard and Scarry oppose violence and language, there are others who argue, conversely, that narrative helps violence circulate and proliferate. In his study of terror and violence during the rubber boom in the Putumayo region of Colombia, Michael Taussig argues that terror is mediated through narration (1987:127). For him, the colonial encounter was an encounter shaped in a space of misunderstanding, and it created a culture of terror based on imagining and reproducing fear. Through the colonial work of fabling, reality became uncertain, and it was violence that structured social interactions. Acknowledging the imbrication of violence and narration, according to Taussig, has implications for the work of the anthropologist: since terror is fed through narration, it becomes difficult to write against it (see Taussig 1992). Nonetheless, he does write against violence and tries to find a way to produce estrangement from it. Moreover, he suggests that terror may have unexpected effects, as its symbolism helps to give contemporary shamans their power to heal. The imbrications of violence, order, and signification thus become substantially more complex.

Allen Feldman's (1991) analysis of political violence in Northern Ireland also reveals the complexity of these imbrications. Like Taussig, who considers that the culture of colonialism is inscribed in the body and that meaning is produced in the bodies of the dominated, Feldman argues that Northern Ireland's political culture is based on the "commodification of the body" (1991:8). For him, the primary political instrument in Northern Ireland is the body, which is simultaneously victim and perpetrator of violence and through which social transformations happen and history is visualized (1991:9). "The manifold formation of the body by violence, political technologies, and jural ritual renders it into an inscribed text and an inscribing agent, into a defiling and defiled instrument, a 'doing' and a being 'done.' This ambivalent construction of the body and its establishment as a political form are coeval with the institutionalization of violence as a mechanism that perpetuates itself by exchange and mimesis" (1991:144–45). Feldman argues that oral narratives reassemble the body that has been fragmented by violence. In the process, however, narratives exert the same effect as political violence: they testify to the emergence of political agency (1991:10–16). "Many of the texts transcribed in this book can be understood as a cultural-political project on the part of their authors and myself, to locate narrative in violence by locating violence through narrative" (1991:14).

Analyzing the reproduction of sectarian violence in Northern Ireland, Feldman shows not only how each political character and space become implicated in violence and are then recreated in narration, but also—in direct contradiction to Girard—how actions that are supposed to counteract violence, such as sacrifice (for example, a hunger strike), can end up reproducing it instead. This happens because in Northern Ireland political signification is always attained through violence and the body. A sacrificial act therefore cannot break the cycle of reciprocal violence by resymbolizing it, as Girard theorizes, but rather reinforces the same symbolism and perpetuates violence. Because the "reciprocal production and exchange of sacrificial objects" (1991:264) is not strange to the political culture, an act of sacrifice is unable to establish a difference between the illegitimate violence that kills and the legitimate violence that heals. It only repeats the same meaning and therefore adds to the "circularity of violent mimesis" (1991:264). By pointing out how violence assimilates that which was supposed to stop it (sacrifice and narration), Feldman presents us with a cultural formation destined to repeat itself endlessly. In his scenario there is no possibility of change or resignification, as everything stays within the cycle of mimetic violence.

Taussig's and Feldman's analyses of the role of symbolism in the reproduction of violence, as well as my analysis of the effects of the talk of crime in São Paulo, show that the problems of signification posed by violence are not simply a matter of stabilizing distinctions and trying to establish order. The talk of crime and the increase in violence in contemporary São Paulo indicate the existence of intricate relationships among violence, signification, and order in which narration both counteracts and reproduces violence. Indeed, the talk of crime makes violence proliferate as it counteracts it and symbolically reorders the world. The symbolic order engendered in the talk of crime not only discriminates against some groups, promotes their criminalization, and transforms them into victims of violence but also makes fear circulate through the repetition of histories, and, more important, helps delegitimate the institutions of order and legitimate the use of private, violent, and illegal means of revenge. If the talk of crime promotes a resymbolization of violence, it does so not by legitimating legal violence to counteract illegal violence but by doing exactly the opposite.

As narratives of crime operate with clear-cut oppositions and essential-ized categories derived from the polarization of good and evil, they resig-nify and order the world in a complex and particular way. Moreover, this specific reordering of the world both counters disruptions caused by vio-lence and mediates and exacerbates violence. Beyond maintaining a sys-tem of distinctions, narratives of crime create stereotypes and prejudices, and they separate and reinforce inequalities. In addition, inasmuch as the categorical order articulated in the talk of crime is the dominant order of an extremely unequal society, it does not incorporate the experiences of dominated people (such as the poor, *nordestinos*, and women); rather, it criminalizes and discriminates against them. Thus the experiences of these groups must find alternative means of expression, which are frequently am-biguous: they both reaffirm and deny the categorical order. Finally, the talk of crime is also at odds with the values of social equality, tolerance, and re-spect for others' rights. The talk of crime is productive, but it helps pro-duce segregation (social and spatial), abuses by the institutions of order, contestation of citizens' rights, and, especially, violence itself. If the talk of crime generates order, it is not a democratic, tolerant egalitarian order but its exact opposite. Democracy (as I argue in chapter 8) is about openness and the indeterminacy of boundaries, not about enclosures, rigid bound-aries, or dichotomies.

In the field of crime, barriers are embedded not only in discourses but also, materially, in the city's walls, in the residences of people from all so-cial classes, and in technologies of security. Prejudices and derogations not only are verbal but also reproduce themselves in rituals of suspicion and in-vestigation at the entrances of public and private buildings. As people's thoughts and actions are shaped by the categorical reasoning of the talk of crime, its influence spreads, affecting social interactions, public policies, and political behavior. The symbolic order of the talk of crime visibly mediates violence. In contemporary São Paulo, support for private and violent solu-tions has fueled the phenomenal growth of private security enterprises (both legal and illegal). Additionally, it has generated indifference to the illegal and brutal actions of a police force that in 1992 killed 1,470 suspected crim-inals in São Paulo. The new constitution, approved after the end of the mil-itary regime, is mocked by many as "protecting bandits" because it sets out rules for the detention of suspects and limits police powers of search and seizure. People who defend the human rights of prisoners are considered to be advocating "privileges for bandits." If the fear of crime and the spread of violence are real in São Paulo, and if crime is supplying a language in which to talk and think about many other destabilizing processes, it is also the case that a much more segregated city and unequal society is taking shape, one in which the notions of justice and citizenship rights are contested despite the democratic political system.

In São Paulo in the 1980s and 1990s, and especially when I did most of the interviews (in 1989 and 1990), crime was not the only destabilizing process. This period was marked by multiple processes of transformation and considerable instability. These various processes, though obviously connected and in dialogue, did not have coincident meanings. Some were restrictive and resulted in loss and deterioration (high inflation, economic depression, unemployment, violence). Others, however, especially political democratization, were expansive and generated freedom and respect for rights. In this context, crime offered not only a language with which to make sense of other destabilizing processes but also, through its peculiar symbolic ordinations, an arena in which many citizens resisted democratization. Although this resistance was significant at some points, and although the city of walls created by the strategies of security is fundamentally antidemocratic, the resistance did not prevent democracy from taking root or citizenship from expanding. However, it did challenge democratization and exposed some of its limits and disjunctions.

Because my primary focus is on crime, the fear it provokes, the symbolism it creates, and the defensive reactions it generates, this book deals mostly with what one might call a dark side of social reality. It not only refers to violence but also enforces authoritarianism and segregation, stirs up prejudices and racism, and naturalizes social inequalities. To focus on this universe and to expose its power is not to belittle São Paulo's citizens' capacity to resist domination or disdain their efforts to consolidate democracy. Rather, it means exposing in all their complexity the processes that hinder democratization and present severe challenges for its consolidation beyond the political system. For democracy to take root in Brazilian society, it will have to counter the processes of violence, discrimination, and segregation that the universe of crime articulates. Thus, violence and crime exist in Brazilian society in a tense dialogue with democratic consolidation.

FROM PROGRESS TO ECONOMIC CRISIS, FROM AUTHORITARIANISM TO DEMOCRACY

A generation of Paulistanos grew up believing that their city was destined to be "the locomotive of the country." From the 1950s on, the motto that accompanied the city's intensive industrialization and urbanization was "São Paulo não pode parar!" (São Paulo cannot stop). Until recently, progress seemed indeed to be São Paulo's—and Brazil's—destiny. However, the 1980s have been labeled "the lost decade": instead of growth, there was deep recession. High inflation, associated with poor economic performance and the impoverishment of the population, reversed the picture. At the beginning of the 1990s, the belief in progress gave way to pessimism and frustration, feelings that were expressed in discussions about crime. I summarize here the main changes that have transformed Brazilian society and São Paulo over the last twenty years. I do not offer a complete history but highlight a few of the main events to provide context for my subsequent analysis.

Brazilian government policies from the 1950s to the 1980s were framed by national developmentalism. The idea was to promote rapid import-substitution industrialization and expand the national market. This was to be achieved by attracting foreign capital, providing state incentives, and giving the state a central economic role. Although aspects of this agenda had been put in place during the presidential administrations of Getúlio Vargas (1930–1945 and 1950–1954), it had its most emblematic expression under Juscelino Kubtischek. He took office in 1956, presenting the "Target Program" aimed at promoting fast economic growth: "Fifty years in five" was his slogan. The creation of Brasília was to symbolize and help to promote Brazil's leap from backwardness to modernity.[14]

The metallurgic industry (especially automotive industry) was the core of the new industrialization, which was based in São Paulo. In 1907, São Paulo state's industrial production represented 16 percent of the national production; this percentage grew to 32 percent in 1919, 38 percent in 1929, 49 percent in 1950, and 55 percent in 1960 (Brant 1989:19). In 1970, the state of São Paulo contributed 58.2 percent of the national value of industrial transformation (Rolnik n.d.:27). Although various other regions have increased their production considerably, and although the economic crisis and a recent process of deindustrialization have considerably affected its position, São Paulo remains the industrial center of the country.

As expected, industrial growth was associated with intense urbanization. The population of the metropolitan region of São Paulo grew at a rate of around 5.5 percent a year between 1940 and 1970. Internal migration was responsible for 50 percent of this increase: it brought more than one million new inhabitants to the region in the 1950s and two million in the 1960s (Perillo 1993:2). Construction and transformation were intense, and the local government repeated that "São Paulo cannot stop!"

By the early 1960s, however, some sectors of the Brazilian elite were diagnosing a national crisis associated with high inflation (although it pales compared to that of the 1980s and 1990s) and especially with political mobilization, as industrial workers, peasants, and students all around the country began to demonstrate and press their demands. The struggles between the traditional elite and the new political forces culminated in the 1964 coup inaugurating military rule, which lasted until 1985. The military forcibly shut down all political organizations and opposition but did not interrupt developmentalism: it too wanted to make Brazil into a modern country. Under military rule, the GDP (gross domestic product) grew by as much as 12 percent annually in the early 1970s. Economic progress was based on foreign debt and direct state intervention in the economy. This intervention was responsible for, among other things, the creation of a new infrastructure of roads and satellite communications and the expansion of public facilities and services, such as a national system of health care and social security. However, everything was done without the political participation of the masses and without distribution of wealth. During the "miracle years," as the early seventies came to be known, the military announced that it was necessary to grow first and "divide the cake" later. In spite of persisting inequality, Brazil changed rapidly, and despite the political repression, the population took pride in their "miraculously" modern country.

Although São Paulo presents the most obvious case of industrialization and urbanization, the trend was nationwide. Brazil's urban population, which in 1950 represented 36 percent of the total population, represented more than 50 percent (around eighty million people) by 1980. Half of this urban population lived in thirty urban centers with more than 250,000 inhabitants. By 1980, Brazil had nine metropolitan regions with populations over one million, which had grown by an average of 4.5 percent a year between 1940 and 1970. In these metropolitan regions is concentrated around 30 percent of the Brazilian population, which in 1996 reached 157 million, 78 percent of which was urban.[15]

The economic expansion of the 1970s and the consolidation of a "system of cities"—a complex pattern of territorial division of labor between the countryside and the cities and between cities (Faria 1991:103)—are associated with complex changes in economic production.[16] Its most dynamic sector has been durable consumer goods for the internal market, which is associated with increased production of intermediate and capital goods. Despite cyclical crises, this more dynamic sector was able, until the early 1980s, to create a considerable number of new jobs. As a result, an increasing number of workers were drawn into the world of formal labor contracts and wages. At the same time, a national market for labor and goods was constituted (Faria 1991:104). The same economic dynamism, however, fostered the expansion of an informal and poorly paid labor market (personal and domestic services, marginal construction industry, etc.) based on intensive labor and low productivity and on the proliferation of subemployment. Finally, the economic expansion of the 1970s aggravated an already unequal distribution of income: at the end of the 1970s, the poorest 50 percent of the population received only 14 percent of the total income. Summarizing the urban social structure created during the 1970s, Faria argues (1991:105) that it was constituted by three broad segments: first, occupational groups of very high or high incomes, few in number but with high purchasing power and political and social influence in a society that became more authoritarian and elitist during the 1970s; second, significant contingents of blue- and white-collar workers incorporated into the most dynamic and modern productive sectors; and finally, a mass of poor subemployees.

The consumer market that resulted had important peculiarities. National industrial growth was based on the expansion of the internal market. Considerable numbers of people were integrated into the consumer market on the basis of a vigorous credit policy that, as Wells shows (1976), gave the lower strata access to durable goods (such as televisions) and clothes. This policy accounts for the presence of televisions in slums and helps explain how it was possible to expand the internal market while maintaining an unequal distribution of wealth.

Indeed, the combination of growth and inequality marked all the achievements of the 1970s. According to Faria (1991:107–8), health services, social security, and basic education expanded, but they did so at the cost of a reduced quality of services and of extremely low salaries paid to the professionals providing them. Moreover, because civil society's control of these services was feeble, they were offered in a distorted way: for example, basic medical services were lacking despite high investment in a few sophisticated technologies, and the administration of social security funds was corrupt. In areas requiring high public investment, such as housing, public transportation, and basic sanitation, the results were even worse.

In sum, from the 1940s to the end of the 1970s, both Brazil and the metropolitan region of São Paulo changed in dramatic but paradoxical ways: significant urbanization, industrialization, sophistication and expansion of the consumer market, and diversification of the social structure were accompanied by authoritarianism, political repression, unequal distribution of wealth, and a hierarchical pattern of personal relations. In other words, Brazil became a modern country through a paradoxical combination of rapid capitalist development, increased inequality, and lack of political freedom and respect for citizenship rights. São Paulo epitomizes these paradoxes. With its sixteen million inhabitants, industries and skyscrapers, high-tech offices and favelas, sophisticated subways and high infant mortality rates, satellite communications and low literacy levels, the metropolis of São Paulo has become a symbol of a poor but modern industrial consumer society, heterogeneous and deeply unequal.

Despite their imbalances, industrialization and growth have helped sustain many promises: progress, social mobility, and Brazil's entry into the consumer market and into the modern world itself. When GDP was growing up to 10 percent per year, when per capita income was growing 6.1 percent a year, when the majority of migrants were becoming property owners and building houses in the country's largest city, when these houses were being decorated with all kinds of mass-produced goods (above all television), and when the children of these families were receiving education and health services (even if these services were bad), it was possible to believe that Brazil was indeed becoming modern, that the future would be better, that the new generation would be better off, and that political participation and greater equality would come with time.[17] Although the elite remained uncomfortable with the working classes' incorporation into this modern society, it was acceptable as long as their own enrichment was guaranteed.

Faith in promises of progress and growth was sustained until the economic crisis of the 1980s, when demographic, political, economic, and social changes began to transform Brazilian society. They brought to an end the pattern of development, urbanization, and growth of previous years. The demographic changes that became clear in the 1980s are said to mark a "demographic transition" in Brazil. From the 1940s to the 1960s, Brazil enjoyed a decline in mortality rates and consistently high fertility rates (around 6.0 children per woman). As a result, the average rate of population growth was also high (around 3.0 percent per year), and the age distribution of the population was young. In the 1970s, fertility rates started to decline. Initially limited to the richest and urbanized areas, by the 1980s this trend was apparent throughout the country. As a result, the total fertility rate dropped from 5.8 in 1970 to 4.3 in 1975 and to 3.6 in 1984, a decline of 37 percent in fifteen years. Estimates for 1990 indicated a rate of at most 2.9 children per woman.[18]

Vilmar Faria offers an interesting explanation (1989) of this sharp decline in the absence of any public policy of population control. According to him, the change in reproductive behavior was an unexpected effect of four government social policies that followed urbanization: the national health system, the social security system, the telecommunications system (which allowed the diffusion of the mass media), and direct financial credit for individuals. The change was possible at least in part because of the increased availability of medical services, which affected especially women and their perceptions of their bodies. However, it cannot be understood without the assumption of significant changes in women's perceptions and attitudes and a complete reassessment of the value of large families. These changes in values can be traced back to urbanization and especially to the exposure of the majority of the population to the mass media, which, in Brazil, became the main disseminator of the model of a modern middle-class family, with a working wife and few children.[19]

As a result of the drop in fertility rate, population growth declined in the first half of the 1990s to 1.9 percent. A second result was a change in the age distribution of the population, which became older. A third was a change in the pattern of urbanization. During the 1980s and, especially, during the 1990s, there has been a significant decline in the rate of urban population growth. This trend is especially clear in the nine biggest metropolitan regions, where growth rates dropped from 4.5 percent in the period from 1940 to 1970 to 3.8 percent during the 1970s and 2.0 percent during the 1980s. After growing only 1.2 percent a year during the 1980s and registering significant emigration for the first time in history, São Paulo, the city which could not stop, the paradise of migrants, had a population growth of only 0.4 percent between 1991 and 1996.

The 1980s were also years of such severe economic crisis that they became known as the "lost decade." Brazil's GDP dropped 5.5 percent, and the real minimum wage decreased 46 percent between 1980 and 1990 (Serra 1991). Between 1940 and 1980, GDP had grown 6.9 percent annually (4 percent in per capita terms). Between 1980 and 1992, it grew only 1.25 percent annually, and per capita income dropped 7.6 percent (PNUD-IPEA 1996:73). One of the main components of the economic crisis was the persistent high inflation shown in table 1. Successive plans to deal with inflation failed until the mid-1990s—including the famous Plano Cruzado in 1986 and the Plano Collor in 1990. Moreover, they had severe effects on the lives of citizens. High inflation forces people to live on a day-to-day basis and give up long-term planning. Even the most basic budgeting has to be suspended, for salaries and rents may be readjusted every month, and prices can vary daily. In addition, the economic recession generated unemployment and few opportunities for recovery. It was impossible to be sure about one's social place, and it became difficult to think of future progress and upward social mobility: decline became a more realistic bet.

According to some analysts (for example PNUD-IPEA 1996:73–76), the failure of economic policies in the 1980s and 1990s was at least partially due

TABLE 1   Yearly Inflation, Brazil, 1980–1998

Year	Inflation (%)	Year	Inflation (%)
1980	99.7	1990	1,585.2
1981	93.5	1991	475.1
1982	100.3	1992	1,149.1
1983	178.0	1993	2,489.1
1984	209.1	1994	929.3
1985	239.1	1995	21.9
1986	58.6	1996	9.1
1987	396.0	1997	4.3
1988	994.3	1998	2.5
1989	1,863.6		

SOURCE: IBGE: INPC *(Índice Nacional de Preços ao Consumidor)*.

NOTE: Values refer to the annual variation of consumer prices, measured in December.

to their failure to promote the necessary structural changes to initiate another pattern of development. These analysts acknowledge that the previous pattern—based on import substitution, heavy state intervention in the economy, and foreign indebtedness—reached its limits in the 1980s. Inflation was controlled only after 1994 with the Plano Real elaborated by the minister of the treasury, Fernando Henrique Cardoso. Elected president in 1994 on the basis of the plan's success, Cardoso has adopted policies that are transforming the previous pattern of growth. Cardoso's administration has adopted an aggressive program to privatize public enterprises (including telecommunications, energy, and oil, whose national monopoly was the symbol of Brazilian nationalism in the 1950s), is attempting radical reform of the social security system, and is trying to control public debt. He was reelected in 1998, but his second term started in the midst of an economic crisis associated with public indebtedness and currency devaluation that brings back to Brazil the specters of the IMF, international concern, instability, and the risk of inflation.

Although definitive analysis of the direction of changes in production is still lacking, available data for the state of São Paulo indicate some important transformations.[20] Since the 1980s, São Paulo's share in the value of industrial transformation has dropped. From 58.2 percent in 1970, it dropped to 49.6 percent in 1984 and to 41 percent in 1991 (Rolnik n.d.:27; Leme and Biderman 1997). The effects of the economic crisis were especially severe in the city of São Paulo and in the most industrialized areas of the metropolitan region, exactly those that had boomed in the previous pattern of development. During the 1980s and 1990s, the industrial center of the country was closing down industries and restructuring its economy.

The social consequences of the economic crisis were devastating. After a decade of inflation, unemployment, and recession, poverty grew to alarming dimensions in the early 1990s.[21] Recent research demonstrates that the effects of the crisis were especially harsh among the poor and aggravated the already unequal distribution of wealth.[22] Rocha shows (1991:37) that the proportion of poor people in the nine metropolitan regions matched the oscillations of the economic crisis: it peaked during the recession of 1983 (38.2 percent) and hit its lowest rate during the recovery year of 1986 (22.8 percent). For the whole country in 1990, the poverty rate was 30 percent (Rocha 1996:1).[23] Although this level is lower than that of 1980 (34 percent), in comparison to the long period of social mobility and diminution of poverty of the 1970s it reveals a strong reversal of expectations. In a context of crisis and inflation in which hopes of upward mobility were dashed, dissatisfaction became widespread, especially in the metropolitan areas, where the proportion of poor people is higher than in the smaller cities (see Leme and Biderman 1997 for an analysis of the state of São Paulo). The interviews I analyze in chapter 2 clearly demonstrate this reversal of expectations.

In 1995, Brazil had a GDP of U.S.$536 billion and a per capita income of U.S.$3,370. Its GDP is now among the ten highest worldwide. Nevertheless, its distribution of wealth is among the most unequal. The proportion of income appropriated by the richest 20 percent of the population grew from 54 percent in 1960 to 62 percent in 1970, 63 percent in 1980, and 65 percent in 1990, while the proportion appropriated by the poorest 50 percent dropped from 18 percent in 1960 to 15 percent in 1970, 14 percent in 1980, and 12 percent in 1990 (Barros, Mendonça, and Duarte 1997). Recent studies have shown that the highest concentration of wealth occurs at the top of the distribution, especially in the richest 1 percent; the difference between the lower deciles is not accentuated and is comparable to other Latin American countries. In the 1990s, according to the results of the PNADs, the proportion of income in the hands of the richest 1 percent of the Brazilian population has grown from 13.0 percent in 1981 to 17.3 percent in 1989 and 15.5 percent in 1993.[24] A recent study by PNUD (Programa das Nações Unidas para o Desenvolvimento) comparing fifty-five countries showed that, measured by the ratio of the average per capita income of the richest 10 percent and of the poorest 40 percent of the population, Brazil had the greatest inequality. While for the majority of these countries (including all de-

veloped countries and all other major Latin American countries) the income
of the richest 10 percent is on average up to ten times higher than that of
the poorest 40 percent, in Brazil it is almost thirty times higher (PNUD-
IPEA 1996:17). The metropolitan region of São Paulo is one of the better-
off and has one of the best distributions of wealth of the country. In 1990
the poor constituted 17 percent of the population of the state (the second
lowest proportion in the country; PNUD-IPEA 1996:182). Nonetheless, the
GINI coefficient—a standard indicator of inequality—grew from 0.516 in
1981 to 0.566 in 1989 and to 0.5748 in 1991 (Rocha 1991:38; and 1991 census).[25] In the state of São Paulo, the richest 1 percent holds 13.8 percent of
the wealth (Leme and Biderman 1997:192).[26]

Some groups, like women and people of color, are more adversely affected
by poverty than others. In 1996, women represented 41.6 percent of the active economic population, according to the PNAD. They worked mostly in
the service sector (around 70 percent), and their average income was only
55.3 percent that of men. Although women are slightly more educated than
men, their incomes are consistently lower than men's in all occupational
categories and at all educational levels (PNAD 96). Lopes shows (1993) that
the effects of the economic crisis were worse for households headed by
women. This type of household has increased considerably in the last years:
in 1960, 10.7 percent of the total number of households were headed by
women; by 1989, that number was 20 percent (Goldani 1994:309–10). In
1989, 33 percent of the households headed by women were living below the
poverty line, compared with 23 percent of the total number of households
(Goldani 1994:320). The situation is especially severe for black women.
Households headed by women are more common among black households
than among white households (21 percent compared to 14 percent in 1989).
Moreover, in the same year almost half (49 percent) of the households
headed by black women were below the poverty line (Goldani 1994:309,
320). Although many people like to think of Brazil as a "racial democracy,"
any reading of socioeconomic indicators shows a pervasive discrimination
against the black population. On average, the income of people of color is
only around 65 percent of that of the white population (PNUD-IPEA
1996:22).[27] Moreover, Lopes (1993) shows that 68 percent of the urban
households below the indigent line had either a black or a *pardo* head of
household, while black or *pardo* households represented only 41 percent of
all urban households.

The other change in Brazilian society during the 1980s was political democratization. The end of the 1970s and the early 1980s were marked by a
significant expansion of political citizenship and rights. Starting in the mid-

1970s, the working classes, especially in São Paulo, began to organize a series of political activities that substantially affected politics and the dominant authoritarian rule. A new type of trade union movement emerged in ABCD, that is, the area of the metropolitan region of São Paulo with the greatest industrial concentration and which symbolizes the model of development prior to the economic crisis. This movement rejected the trade union structure organized since the time of Getúlio Vargas, and it had a new leadership that the state and the elite were unable either to coopt or to repress. At the same time, a series of neighborhood-based social movements emerged in the poor urban peripheries, frequently supported by the Catholic Church, advancing the idea that they had "the right to have rights." Movement participants were often new property owners who realized that political organization was the only way to force city authorities to extend infrastructure and services to their neighborhoods. They discovered that being taxpayers legitimated their "rights to the city." They directed their demands to a local administration that, anticipating future elections, wanted to expand the services offered to the population and was trying to obtain international aid to fund some of them (for example, health services and sanitation). In the early 1980s, when the military federal government allowed the reorganization of political parties, representatives of the trade union movements and the social movements, together with representatives of minority movements (such as women, blacks, and homosexuals) which had also bloomed in that period, founded Partido dos Trabalhadores, the Worker's Party (PT), probably the first political party in Brazilian history that was not created or commanded by the elite.

While the economic crisis deepened, there was still hope in political transformation. The social movements and the political opening in fact significantly enlarged political citizenship rights. For a while, the resulting enthusiasm was shared by all social classes and was synthesized in the desire for the military dictatorship to end. The movement "Diretas Já" (Direct Elections Now) captured this hope. Even before the population could vote, the expansion of citizenship was celebrated in the streets and squares in 1984. On January 25, the anniversary of the founding of the city of São Paulo, around three hundred thousand residents of all social classes congregated in the Praça da Sé to demand their right to vote directly for president. Equally large demonstrations followed in all major cities. In mid-April, the crowd in São Paulo's streets was calculated at one million: it was the largest political demonstration the city and the country had ever known. However, following the old elitist pattern, on April 25 the National Congress voted to deny the population the right to vote, deciding that the next president would be elected by the National Congress, which had as its members one third of the Senate directly appointed by the military regime. The newly elected president, Tancredo Neves, who had the support of the population, died before taking office. Vice President José Sarney, the former leader of the military-dominated political party, took office. (He had been appointed in a political alliance aimed at defeating the right-wing candidate in the National Congress election.) Although Sarney enjoyed some popularity because of a new policy he adopted to freeze inflation (the Plano Cruzado of 1986), his government ended amid economic disaster and numerous accusations of corruption. In 1986, Brazilians elected a Constitutional Assembly that wrote a new democratic constitution, promulgated in 1988. The term of the Constitutional Assembly was one of the most democratic periods of Brazilian history: thousands of groups all around the country mobilized to send in petitions and lobby for their demands.

In 1989, when Brazilians could at last vote for president, Brazil had eighty-two million registered voters. The society and the polity they represented were radically different from those represented by the fifteen million voters who had last elected a president in 1961. This time, the electoral campaign took place primarily on television, present in almost 60 percent of households. The two candidates who advanced to the second round were both young (in their early forties) and represented what could be called new styles of doing politics. The winner, Fernando Collor de Mello, was a new conservative, a young politician from the northeast oligarchies who grew up in Brasília, had been governor of the small northeast state of Alagoas, and was adept at using the mass media. He campaigned against administrative corruption and state intervention in the economy and for the elimination of trade protectionism and neoliberal politics. His opponent was the leader of the PT, Luís Ignácio Lula da Silva, a migrant from the northeast who had been a metal worker in the ABCD region and was its most important trade union leader in the 1970s. Lula campaigned for socialism, a better distribution of wealth, agrarian reform, and the political organization of workers. The fact that he defeated a series of famous national politicians and could run in the second round testifies to how much the country had changed. But it had not changed enough.

Brazilians elected the mass-media product of the conservative oligarchies, believing that he could bring modernization and an "appropriate" image of Brazil to the "modern nations of the world," as I was told by one of the people I interviewed. However, hopes for an easy modernization were soon dashed. By March 1990 it was clear that inflation was out of control. The day after Collor took office, he adopted a radical economic plan—the Plano

Collor—intended "to kill inflation with a single bullet." This plan froze all existing bank accounts over Cz$50,000 (around U.S.$1,250) for one and a half years, leaving the economy with no liquidity. The plan failed to defeat inflation; rates continued to rise after a few months. Instead it provoked immense repercussions in people's everyday lives. In addition to the effects of inflation itself, which totally devalued the frozen bank accounts and was accompanied by a decrease in real wages, the Plano Collor enhanced a feeling of loss of social position even among the upper middle classes. The interviews show very clearly that the Plano Collor became a crucial symbolic divider of before and after, better and worse.

In mid-1992, inflation was again greatly elevated, reforms to control administrative expenditures had not been undertaken, state enterprises had not been privatized, and a series of allegations of federal corruption implicating the president led the National Congress to investigate and finally to impeach Collor. Millions of citizens demonstrated in support of this act. Collor was replaced by his vice president, Itamar Franco. The most important event of his administration was another plan to control inflation, the Plano Real, which was launched in 1994 and has been largely successful, holding inflation rates at the lowest level since the 1950s. This success helped to elect Fernando Henrique Cardoso, the treasury minister in charge of the plan, to the presidency in 1994. He had 54.3 percent of the votes in the first round, the second largest margin of any presidential candidate in Brazilian history. His closest opponent was again Luís Ignácio Lula da Silva.[28]

The increase in violent crime since the mid-1980s obviously adds insecurity to already intensified anxieties over economic uncertainty, inflation, unemployment, social movements, and political transformation. Discussions about fear of crime reveal the anguish produced when social relations can no longer be decoded and controlled according to old criteria. Although there are certainly many positive aspects to the disintegration of old power relations in Brazil, it is also clear that many social groups have reacted negatively to the enlargement of the political arena and the expansion of rights. These groups have found in the issue of crime a way of articulating their opposition.

The universe of crime—including the talk of crime and fear, and also the increase in violence, the failure of the institutions of order (especially the police and the justice system), the privatization of security and justice, and the continuous walling and segregation of cities—reveals in a compelling way the disjunctive character of Brazilian democracy. James Holston and I have developed the concept of disjunctive democracy in order to account for the contradictory processes that mark Brazilian society and to indicate the sphere in which the expansion of rights is more problematic.[29] One of the main contradictions marking contemporary Brazil is that between expansion of political citizenship and delegitimation of civil citizenship. On the one hand, the country has seen regular and free elections, free party organization, new political leadership, and routine functioning of the legislative body at all levels, along with freedom of expression and the end of media censorship. On the other hand, violence—civilian, state-sanctioned, and state-related—has increased considerably since the end of military rule. This increase in crime and violence is associated with the failure of the justice system, the privatization of justice, police abuses, the walling of cities, and the destruction of public spaces. In other words, in Brazil political democracy has brought with it not respect for rights, justice, and human life, but their exact opposites. The talk of crime not only expresses and articulates other negative processes of change, but it also represents the limits and challenges to Brazilian democratization. In fact, the universe of crime indicates the disjunctive character of Brazilian democracy in a double way: first because the increase of violence itself erodes citizens' rights, and second because it offers a field in which reactions to violence become not only violent and disrespectful of rights, but also help destroy public space, segregate social groups, and destabilize the rule of law.

In this book I focus on those parts of Brazilian society where democracy takes root only reluctantly or not at all. I focus on violence and on the various dimensions of the delegitimation of justice and civil rights. This is the sphere in which democratization is challenged and where resistance to transformations that might lead to a more egalitarian society are explicitly articulated. Because I insist on the disjunctive character of Brazilian society, I never assume that the dark social processes I analyze constitute the primary or only mark of that society, or even the only attempt at creating order. However, I argue that the field of violence and crime counteracts democratic tendencies and helps sustain one of the most unequal societies in the world.

CHAPTER 2

Crisis, Criminals, and the Spread of Evil

The talk of crime extends its particular logic to countless themes. Discussions of crime almost always lead to reflections on the state of the country. Economic crisis, inflation, and unemployment were repeatedly associated with violence by people who were losing their hope of social mobility. They talked about their individual difficulties and experiences of decay and violence, but they also discussed the situation of the country and asserted that the project of modernity that had prevailed until then was simply coming to an end. Long before discussions about the exhaustion of the national-developmentalism model, the end of the Fordist phase of capitalism, industrial restructuring, neoliberal policies, and the new international order emerged from a restricted academic circle to become themes of public debate, the sense of the end of an era was palpable among the people I interviewed from 1989 to 1991.

Views of the socioeconomic context in which violence increases and about the future of the country were expressed in similar ways by interviewees from different social groups. Experiences of violence, however, tend to be class-specific. Although all social groups are victims of crime, they are victims of different types of offense, with the working classes being the most victimized by violent crime. These different experiences obviously mark their perceptions of crime. Nevertheless, Paulistanos from different social groups—at least the ones I interviewed—share certain conceptions about crime and evil. They seem to think that the spaces of crime are marginal ones, such as favelas and *cortiços*, and that their inhabitants, potential criminals, are people from the fringes of society, humanity, and the polity. They also see crime as a phenomenon related to evil, something that spreads and contaminates easily and requires strong institutions and authorities to control it. This control is seen as a labor of culture against the forces of nature.

I analyze the explanations of crime, which indeed offer assessments of the country's transformations, and the views about crime and criminals that were expressed in interviews with residents from different social groups in São Paulo. My analysis deals only with those themes relevant to understanding the interconnections of violent crime, urban segregation, and citizenship. I pay special attention to the tensions, ambiguities, and contradictions that surface in people's talk as a result of two particular situations. First, generic statements inspired by the clear-cut categorizations derived from the opposition of good and evil must coexist with more detailed explanations that deal with everyday, nuanced, and ambiguous experiences. Second, people dealing with stereotypes that discriminate against them do not question the stereotypes but instead disassociate themselves from the images and try to associate them with others, usually neighbors. When interpreting the interviews, I did my best to understand what each person told me. However, I present not individualized opinions but a summary I derived by juxtaposing all the interviews.[1] In my narrative, I cite the interviews in two ways: as examples, in which one quotation stands for many similar ones, synthesizing commentaries and images found in more fragmentary ways throughout the material; and as specific instances I consider especially revealing about a certain point. Needless to say, the purpose of undertaking a qualitative analysis is to capture some of the richness of meaning embedded in social practices that defies large categorizations and broad descriptions. I turn to other methodologies to understand different dimensions of the universe of crime.

LIMITS TO MODERNIZATION

Between 1989 and 1991, when I conducted the interviews, São Paulo's residents still thought of their city and country in terms of the ideology of progress that had been forged in the previous decades. However, at that time of high inflation and economic recession, the dream of uninterrupted progress was only a reminder of lost possibilities: the "country of the future" seemed to be losing its way. If there had been progress before, nevertheless the present reality was marked by regression. The interviews reveal a reversal of expectations and the frustrations and anxieties that accompany it. They indicate how people were trying to deal with the negative changes in their lives, which they perceived as permanent. These discussions about the economic crisis, the social decline it produced, and the reversal of expectations were the context for the increase in crime that everybody perceived.

From the unemployed worker living on the periphery to the Morumbi businessman, most people experienced the late 1980s and early 1990s with pessimism, uncertainty, and disillusion. Most could not recall another time when things had been so bad, not even the military years, which people remembered as a time of political repression tempered with economic prosperity. A few, usually from the upper classes, were able to maintain their belief in progress and their optimism by looking at the possibilities of a new international order. Most, however, found more grounds for distrust. First, there was the palpable reality of high inflation and unemployment, which provoked strong feelings of uncertainty, perplexity, and disorientation in people from all social groups.

2.1

Inflation is this: you buy something today and tomorrow you don't know if it's possible to buy it. You eat today and tomorrow you don't know if you're going to eat. Who loses? The people, the poor, always.

Unemployed salesman, age thirty-two,
single, lives with a married sister in Moóca

2.2

Inflation and this disorganization in the system made us lose our points of reference. We do not have references any longer as to what is better: if it is better to pay an employee more or to give him a basic basket,[2] or security, or health service. We have lost the reference. . . . I think that one of the reasons provoking the increasing criminality is this inflation, which is inhuman and which so affects the class with lower income. The Plano Collor—I voted for Collor—took away the purchasing power of the consumer. It was meant to diminish poverty, to take from the rich and give to the poor, but I think that the opposite happened, the poor are poorer and the rich are richer. . . . Hyperinflation completely erodes the concepts of morality. Your values change. . . . I think that under hyperinflation everybody loses everything; nobody wins anything. . . . Inflation makes you lose your concepts. Inflation makes you pay very little for your employee, inflation brings money to the rich, it concentrates income, so I think it is immoral. It is like robbery, and robbery for me is immoral.

Real estate developer, mid-forties, owner of his own
company, lives with his wife and three children in Morumbi

It was a commonsense opinion that the remedies for dealing with high inflation had been consistently ineffective, culminating with the Plano Collor. This plan affected everybody, and the interviewees all agreed that despite its intentions, the plan accentuated social inequality and made the distribution of wealth even more iniquitous.

2.3

Look, however incredible it may seem, and it may have been an illusion, but at the time of the Brazilian miracle under Delfim Neto, inflation was not going up so fast. It think it was a more stable inflation. I think that it was a better time. . . .

I think that the generation of people in their fifties who got the Plano Collor is a generation which is economically finished. It has no more chance. Because people who had money for traveling or who saved to buy an apartment for their children or even who saved to buy their own home had their money impounded. It is very difficult to recover from that; it was a hard blow indeed. . . . Nowadays, the amount of wealth in the country has increased, but the distribution is very bad. But what I think has really increased is the number of poor people. Rich people have a few children; those who have children like guinea pigs are the poor. So, I think that poverty increased much more than wealth. People say Brazil is the eighth economy in the world. But the distribution of income is worse than in African countries, worse than in Senegal, I read. People say it's a shame! It's incredible!

Real estate agent (female), age fifty-six, divorced, started working in 1990, lives with one daughter in Alto de Pinheiros

The Plano Collor was considered to have been especially devastating for the middle classes, whose savings lost almost all their value during eighteen months of high inflation, while bank accounts were frozen. However, even working-class people, who saw virtues in a plan that for the first time affected the rich, recognized that their own purchasing power decreased after its implementation. Moreover, working-class people's interviews were full of comments about the increase in unemployment and the desperate situation of families whose members had lost their jobs.

The highest level of frustration related to the government and to politicians. The majority of the interviewees thought that the government had betrayed people's expectations, misled them with unfulfilled promises, adopted policies that contradicted the rosy pictures painted in electoral campaigns, and accommodated the interests of a minority of rich and powerful people. They felt that politicians had been ineffective in addressing the country's problems. Some people thought that there was no real leadership anymore, and that the government was as unstable and volatile as inflation. Some turned their hopes, even confusedly, to the idea of a strong government, "constant and durable," as one said.

2.4

> Brazil is in chaos. Because we are living from various lies, and one of the biggest is inflation. . . . Brazil needs, for example, a president who would rule with an iron hand, democratically, someone who could be reelected and reelected until things get straightened out.
>
> *Accountant, age sixty-three,*
> *lives in Moóca with his wife, a housewife, and one son*

In Brazil the idea is entrenched that a good president, especially one who works for the poor, has to be strong. This image has been associated, especially by working-class people, with Getúlio Vargas, the dictator who ruled Brazil from 1930 to 1945 and was elected president in 1950. Many workers excuse Vargas's authoritarianism by arguing that he had to be strong to control the powerful—*os tubarões*, literally the sharks—and that he was the first ever to rule in favor of the workers, by creating labor legislation that is still largely intact.[3] Not surprisingly, the military rulers and their ministries were sometimes mentioned in association with a period when things were better: Delfim Neto, an economic minister during the military dictatorship, is defended by a PT voter in quote 2.3. Given that the distressing economic situation of the early 1990s was caused by the first elected president, to many the military regime did not look so bad.

The appeal to a strong, perpetuating authority embodies a threat to the democratic order, an order that even people looking for an "iron hand" seemed to be ambiguously seeking to preserve. What this ambiguity reveals is a greater concern with solving an immediate problem (sometimes by adopting the most common solution, for authoritarianism was the norm in Brazil throughout the twentieth century) than with analyzing the longer-term consequences of the solution. But it also reveals the ambiguous relationship of Brazilians with democratic rule.

Disenchantment with leaders and their broken promises combines with frustrations about the country's progress and its threatened modernization. Although the belief in progress went virtually unchallenged until very recently, in the interviews people observed that progress is an illusion and not a promise, that the country was never able to live up to expectations and never would be. A young resident of Moóca expressed this skepticism in a compelling way:

2.5

I cannot see how our country is going to unite with the rest of the world. You can't get it; it's totally undefined. I think that [the situation] is optimistic, from one perspective, because I recognize that we are a new history. . . . Our sadness, let's put it this way, is that we are seeing on the movie screen other countries prospering, and we want to be like them. We narrow the gap. We think we're on the same level. But no, it's an illusion. That's a movie screen, that's in a time way ahead of us, and we have to work a lot to make a country out of this.[4] . . . It's necessary to have a second, true independence of Brazil. . . . It could never really come into its own, have its own epoch, because it was never really independent, and this already gives you a sense of insecurity. . . . Brazil has never had a good period; if it had, it was an illusion and has already gone by. Maybe the Vargas period created an illusion like that. But this was just a short period of fullness, because his power was limited; as great as it may have been, it was only for a moment. What we need is a constant power, lasting. It does not help if a powerful man arrives and does something wonderful for the country and suddenly . . . it is the same thing as building a castle in the sand, building a wonderful castle on the top of drifting sand, soft sand, and water. This is simply an illusion. If someone tells me that there have been better periods, I would say that it is true, but it only lasted for the time it took to photograph that castle, because soon after the water came up. And if we can only have that castle for a second, then I think it is better not to have any. There are many people who talk about that era, I agree, but I understand the illusion that the person has lived; I haven't lived it, I have only seen that photograph.

Unemployed college graduate with degree in communications,
majoring in radio, age twenty-three, lives with his parents in Moóca

It is certainly common in postcolonial and developing countries to think of development in terms of an exterior model of modernity of which the local reality is an imperfect, incomplete, underdeveloped, or at least special version. In this sense, anxieties about copy, identity, independence, and the modern are inherent to the project of the nation and its development.

They are widespread not only among citizens but also in social science theories and public policies.[5] Even at the height of popular belief in progress and social mobility, in the period from 1950 to 1980, the gap between the ideal of development and the Brazilian reality offered a background for discussions about the future. One of the formulaic ways to deal with this gap has been to assert that "o Brasil é o país do futuro" (Brazil is the country of the future). However, Brazilians have always treated this observation with irony. This ironic view is expressed, for example, by an old Brazilian joke that various interviewees mentioned. According to the joke, there was a time when the country stood on the brink of an abyss, but it finally made some progress and took one step forward. . . . Formulaic images about the potentialities of the country are also reiterated in a skeptical way.[6] Although the ambiguity produced by simultaneously affirming and doubting the possibility of progress is common in Brazil, it seems to have deepened recently, as people have come to realize that development never lives up to the alleged possibilities. On the one hand, there is the theme of illusion, beautifully articulated in quote 2.5.[7] Both the model of development on the movie screen and the alleged periods of Brazilian growth captured in imaginary old photographs are like sandcastles, illusory and impermanent. On the other hand, playful jokes are giving way to straight pessimism and sometimes even despair.

2.6

Brazil is each time—I don't say less viable—but it is a country which is not giving a good projection of the future for the Brazilian people. We're worried. As a young person, I'm worried because I'm not an alienated young person. I think that this new government will face a series of difficulties because we're a country of the third world, we're a country which, culturally, we are from the third world. We have a very big external debt; we have a bad quality of life, of health, of nourishment. We have even general type of problems, you know, of how to position ourselves facing the developed world. It is a country that, okay, it's rich, it's a country which has a lot of land, has a lot of future, people say it's going to be the granary of the world. But my father used to say that, and my grandfather used to say that, and I am seeing that time passes by and things stay the same and even worse. There has never had so much misery in Brazil, I think, as we have today.

Middle-rank civil servant, age thirty-two, single,
with a college degree, lives with his parents in Moóca

The anxieties originating in the colonial predicament still frame thoughts about the future of the country, leading to the repetition of the question: "What is going to be the place of Brazil in the international order?" As the national-developmentalist approach began to show signs of exhaustion, some people expressed their pessimism. But there were also optimists, people enthusiastic about Collor's initial moves toward redefining Brazil's position in the international order and adopting neoliberal policies that contradicted the old model based on import substitution, protectionism, state sponsorship, and closed markets.

2.7

I think that things are going toward internationalization. I think that the national state is being surpassed. Everything is very interconnected, one nation doesn't survive without the other. I mean, that old spirit of "let's close the borders and stimulate the internal market" doesn't exist anymore. Knowledge spreads very fast, and this happens through a synergy among nations; if one closes up, one gets left behind. . . . I don't think that Brazil has lost the train of history. I do think that we have lost ten years, unfortunately, but I think it is possible to recuperate. I am an optimistic guy. I don't share the pessimism, I vibrate with everything which is going on politically, all these changes. . . . I think we are in the right path. I didn't vote for Collor. I voted for Lula in the second round.

General director and co-owner of a chemical factory, Morumbi, age thirty-seven, two children; his wife is a housewife

2.8

Look, I don't think it's easy, but I think that this is the first step toward something new. We couldn't keep being something old-fashioned in the contemporary world, it was necessary to shake things up. . . . I think there is a whole new mentality that has to be introduced in the country. We cannot continue to be so outside of the world. I don't know how, but maybe we're going to succeed. Sometimes I have the feeling that we're starting to get better. I think that people are starting to talk in more international terms, something wider. I think people have already understood that it cannot be as it used to be. . . . It's not easy. Our mentality is something, I don't know, a little primitive even. This lack of a notion of economy, this thing of not knowing how to consume properly. As long as we do not understand—I am talking about all of us, the people—that we have to save, that we have to consume properly, it will be difficult. . . . I think that the worst is the consumption of the little people [i.e., the poor], people who don't have a notion of anything. . . . I think that while it does not change, it's going to be hard to keep up [with the rest of the world]. But I think that step by step we make progress.

[Later the speaker argued that São Paulo is a special place. She explained that if one travels in the interior of the state of São Paulo, its development is surprising. During the first days after the Plano Collor, "when it was that national misery," she had to fly to Minas. Looking down from the airplane, thinking that nobody had money at that moment, she saw all the cultivated land, "that fantastic thing," and she thought:]

Brazil is a phenomenon, it cannot sink. São Paulo is very different from the rest of Brazil. . . . People in São Paulo work, they are not idle; they are working and getting ahead in their lives. There is no way this can stop, I think. There is nothing that can make this part of the country stop. People want to work. As long as we don't get rid of this mentality of the government as protector, it's not going to work. This idea that everything is the government, the government must provide, the government must do, the government. . . . This is a disaster. What we need is the free market, to work, to get ahead in our lives.

Housewife, age fifty-two, Morumbi, with two children;
her husband is an executive of a multinational corporation

The few people who were optimistic about the country in 1990 and 1991 were from the upper classes. They were able to see a new formula of progress, of incorporation into a world economy and into modernity (represented by Collor), one that maybe could ignore the backward aspects of the country (the poor, the northeast) and focus on strengthening the direct connections of the modern and hard-working São Paulo with the exterior. But this elite discourse of modernity was frequently entangled with the expression of deep social prejudices. The country's backwardness is commonly blamed not only on the government but also on the people, at least the poorest of them—the so-called "little people." Recognition of Brazil's immense social injustice and of the devastating effects of inflation on the poorest people does not prevent some middle- and upper-class people from asserting that the poor themselves are at least partially to blame for their situation and for the problems of the country. Quote 2.8, to which I return below, expresses this elitist position: it highlights the country's potential and the exceptional situation of São Paulo, attributing to the poor attitudes that prevent this potential from being realized. The upper-class optimism was not, however, shared by other social groups. What the upper classes saw as signs of improvement looked more like an illusion to those for whom the current crisis had meant anything but progress.

GOING DOWN SOCIALLY
AND DESPISING THE POOR

> My salary is only for eating. It is not even enough to go to the amusement park to take Maria to play on the Ferris wheel.
>
> Auto mechanic, age twenty-two, married, lives
> in Jardim das Camélias with his wife Maria and two brothers

The same feelings of pessimism and uncertainty expressed in comments about the country mark discussions about individual experiences. For the individual, social decline was increasingly the reality. This trend occurred among all social groups, but it was obviously expressed in different ways and associated with different hardships according to social class.

Just before Christmas 1990, I interviewed three brothers in Jardim das Camélias whom I have known since 1978, when they were boys. In December 1990, the eldest (A) was twenty-two, had just married, and was working as an auto mechanic, making Cr$35,000 a month (almost three times the minimum wage), or U.S.$230; his brother (B) was sixteen and was an unskilled worker in a textile factory, making Cr$18,000. The third brother, (C), was nineteen and looking for a job: he had just returned from Bahia, where the family had moved a couple of years ago. The interview revealed not only their poverty and the restrictions on their everyday lives but also their lack of hope for a better future. This pessimism can be best fathomed in relation to another set of interviews I held ten years earlier with a group of young men in their late teens and early twenties in Jardim das Camélias: all of them believed in progress and thought that in a couple of years they were going to be better off, although they believed that it would require great personal effort, including hard work and years of study (Caldeira 1984:168–72). In 1990, however, people growing up in Jardim das Camélias felt they could do little to improve their lives. Even if they worked very hard—as they do—and if they studied—as they did—they would accomplish little. For them, the opinion—unanimous ten years before—that São Paulo was a good place because it offered jobs and social mobility was no longer valid. It might still be a good place to find a job, but the salaries did not allow participation in consumer society, as they had a decade ago, or social mobility. Salaries were being used up on food and transportation, and the young men spoke sadly and ironically about the possibilities offered them: as one said, he could not even take his young wife to the amusement park once in a while. Building a house of their own was out of the question.

In the late seventies, when I started doing fieldwork in Jardim das Camélias, it was an exciting neighborhood in which everybody believed in progress. People were building their own houses and organizing all sorts of neighborhood associations and social movements to obtain better services and infrastructure (Caldeira 1984, 1987, and 1990). They supported democracy, some were enthusiastically organizing a local branch of the PT, and many others participated in electoral campaigns for candidates of different parties (Caldeira 1987). They obtained most of their urban infrastructure and neighborhood services in the 1980s and thus helped to urbanize the periphery (see chapter 6). Most people managed to enlarge and finish their autoconstructed houses. Nevertheless, their children, in their late teens and early twenties, who are now getting married and who have been on the job market for a while (usually working-class people start working between the ages of fourteen and sixteen), felt they did not have the opportunities their parents had had. As they repeated to me many times, they could not see any results from their efforts. Over the past few years, as one of them said, all they saw was that "those who were rich, became richer; and those who were poor no longer have a way of going up." To compound their feelings of hopelessness, they realized that their neighborhood, the calm and peaceful place where they grew up playing in the streets, was becoming dangerous. Some of their friends had already been killed on the same streets where they used to play together. The parents of the three young men I interviewed in 1990 were among the most active and enthusiastic leaders of the local associations in the late 1970s and early 1980s and were among the founders of the local branch of the PT. In the mid-1980s, however, feeling that things were getting too difficult and violent, they moved back to their native Bahia. Since then, each of their seven children has returned to São Paulo in search of better opportunities.

The brothers' description of the country's economic situation was bleak: "Nobody has money, employers are all ending in bankruptcy, they are firing employees; the Plano Collor screwed a lot of people," said the eldest brother. Although two of them were still employed, they did not expect to keep their jobs for long. One was sure to be fired before the end of the Christmas season. Especially compelling and sad were their reports on trying to find work (despite their youth, all of them had tried many jobs already), their long hours of work and commuting, their attempts to lower their expectations, and the continuous frustrations of their hopes. They were knowledgeable about the possibilities of consumption the city offered and wanted to partake on at least a modest level, one compatible with a dignified working-class life; but they knew they were excluded. They felt they were victims of injustice, a feeling they expressed by using images taken from the universe of mass culture and referring to Rambo, Sylvester Stallone's film persona, as an advocate of workers' rights. Their knowledge of urban culture, seen against the marks of their exclusion from it, conveys the injustice they suffer. Their interviews were so persuasive that further interpretation is superfluous.

2.9

A: My salary is only enough for eating. It's not even enough to go the amusement park to take Maria to play on the Ferris wheel. If I spend on transportation to the park, then I won't have money to go to work the day after. So I stay at home, it's better, I stay at home. . . . I don't think the movies are worth it either. Someone who has a video can rent a movie for [Cr$]150 and spend the whole day watching the film he wants. What I really like is to watch Rambo movies. I could spend the whole day watching Rambo.

Why do you like Rambo?

A: Because he's a violent guy. Have you ever seen him in the United States?

I've only seen his movies.

A: When you go to the United States, if you see him, tell him that there is a guy here who wants his autograph.

I would tell him, but I think it's going be difficult to meet him—only on television . . .

A: I watch Rambo because his role is to defend, to seek to have rights respected,[8] to defend the good, defend the poor and the good, destroy greed. You see that he goes after greedy people and ends up well. It would be good if people would get these rich men like that, would get these very greedy men and shoot them. If it happened, Silvio Santos would be dead, Roberto Marinho would be dead, because they are all greedy, all rich, all these rich people are greedy. In order to have just a little something it's necessary to be greedy. . . .

Do you think that today a person who works their whole life has a chance of moving up socially?

A: I think that someone who works their whole life doesn't have a chance of going up socially.

C: Before it was possible; today it's not.

Before when?

C: Ten, twenty years ago. Now you make a little money and you show it, the robber comes and takes it. You can't even spend it.

B: It's not worth buying good things anymore. You make twenty thousand, and you go to buy a pair of pants, it's almost fifteen thousand.

A: You work a month to buy a pair of pants!

B: Shoes, if you're going to follow the fashion, you have to make around a hundred thousand to wear the label people are talking about.

C: You have to win the lottery.

A: A guy makes some money, a reasonable amount, more or less. He will want to buy some good furniture for the home. One day he goes out, and when he comes back the crooks have taken everything. You have to go out and ask a neighbor to keep watch over your house.

How do people manage to follow the fashions?

B: Many people buy stolen clothes. Where I work the guys buy stolen things. Many stay in fashion because of that, because working in the factory you can't do it.

C: If there were a fashion of going around naked . . .

A: If the government approved that, I would go around naked in order not to get my clothes dirty.

C: Then I would put a label on it [his naked body]: imported.

Would you like to buy some clothes with a fashionable label?

B: I don't have this thing of showing off labels, but I would like to go around looking more handsome, a few more beautiful clothes, some well-made clothes.

C: There is no way you can be handsome.

B: I would have to make a hundred thousand to go around as I want. Making eighteen, it is only enough for the monthly transportation expenses. Just in transportation I spend like seven thousand. Then there is food to take everyday, there are expenses, and so it's impossible to dress right . . .

What rights do poor people have today?

A: What rights? None. Only the right to go to work, to come back home and sleep in order to go to work the next morning. The poor man spends four hours in the traffic to get to work, two hours to go, two to come back.

Do you think that if Lula were elected he would defend you more?

A: He would. He would give a more dignified life for all of us. We all want not only to eat, but to have a nice house, nice furniture, a car, nice clothes, nice everything, to have enough money to help our family. We don't have money to eat, let alone to help the family! This time of Collor is the worst. . . . I think that if Lula had won he would do something for us, because he has already suffered what we suffer, and Collor has never suffered, neither Collor nor the others who came into power, everybody was born in a golden cradle.

C: They all turn into the same thing when they reach the top.

People from other social groups I interviewed, in Moóca and especially in Alto de Pinheiros and Morumbi, live in conditions vastly different from the poverty of Jardim das Camélias. However, they also feel they are worse off than previously, that they are declining socially, that social inequality is greater, and that prospects for the future are not encouraging. Although the degree of pessimism varied, the descriptions of worsening social conditions were essentially the same. People described a feeling of restriction and of being unable to go out and enjoy what the city had to offer; they had a sense that salaries evaporated and that levels of consumption had decreased. Restriction refers not only to consumption but also to sociability and use of public space. Crime adds to and enhances these perceptions: even the very little that people can afford might be stolen.

Moóca residents, who in general considered themselves middle-class and felt that their possibilities for social mobility were diminishing, were anguished about maintaining their social position and frequently concluded that theirs is the social group most affected by the economic recession.

2.10

> We're all going down in class and nobody is doing anything. And it is clear that the poor and the middle class are doing worse: the rich continue rich, in good shape.
>
> *Teacher in a nursery school and a decorator of churches for weddings, Moóca; in her forties, single, lives with her widowed mother*

2.11

> The middle class has disappeared. Today there is only the poor class and the millionaires. I used to consider myself middle-class, but today I consider myself poor-class. Today I don't consider myself middle-class because . . . if I didn't have this house, today I wouldn't have any means whatsoever to buy another one . . .
>
> *And what about the lower class, the people who live on the periphery?*
>
> For them I don't think it is so bad because we, the middle class, we must be presentable. You cannot go around any way you like. That's not their case. In general, there are four, five people working in the family, they manage to survive. They aren't living, they're surviving. I think that who is really suffering the most is the middle class, which must maintain a certain appearance: you must have a reasonable house, you're not going to live in a *cortiço*. It's difficult, really. For the rich class, things are good. Look at the apartments they're building today, all have four, five suites, five-car garages, all like that, rooms for everything.[9]
>
> *Widow in her fifties, Moóca, who shares her house with her sister, also a widow, so that her nephew's family can live in her sister's house without paying rent*

In spite of some elements that still guaranteed a decent quality of life, such as a house of their own, people were convinced that they were declining socially. In such a situation, concerns with social position become acute. To highlight the deterioration of their own social position, people who think of themselves as middle-class may rhetorically associate themselves with the poor. But this exercise is not long-lasting, and the marks of distinction in relation to those below are asserted right away. Quote 2.11 exemplifies one of the most common ways used to differentiate the poor: they are considered to be closer to the necessary, preoccupied only with surviving, and lacking other concerns such as appearances and style.

These assumptions about the poor are obviously not exclusive to the Brazilian upper and middle classes. There is, for example, a long tradition in aesthetic studies which maintains that poor people's taste is a function of necessity; in fact, that poor people have no aesthetic perception because they focus only on need. A recent, elaborate version of this view is presented by Bourdieu (1984, especially chapter 7), who claims that the working classes are confined to the "choice of the necessary." The dialogue of the Jardim das Camélias brothers (quote 2.9) and many other interviews with working-class people about their home decor and style of dress demonstrate that they understand fashion and style, and that they articulate aesthetic judgments in their consumption choices.[10] If they do not display their taste and knowledge more often, it is because they are overexploited and impoverished, not because they lack aesthetic sense or desire to consume. To describe the poor as being limited to the necessary is just another prejudice against them, one that is very common among those who think of themselves as better off. Moreover, to locate the poor close to necessity, to identify them with need, nature, and a lack of reason or sophisticated culture can be a way of associating them with crime, which is often identified with the same traits.

But the question of appearances, introduced in quote 2.11, has another twist. One reason why the middle classes were especially sensitive to recent transformations is that they were having difficulty maintaining the right appearances and distances. Before it was easier, mostly a matter of the right clothes and a cozy home in a peaceful neighborhood. But with the neighborhood changing too fast, the consumer market broadening, the economic crisis reducing people's purchasing power, the new democratic practices transforming political life, and the old beliefs in future achievements being shaken, people felt uncertain about their social position. One way of dealing with this uncertainty was to emphasize and elaborate social differences. Therefore, discussions about social decline become discussions about social difference and the maintenance of one's own place in the social hierarchy.

Social distance is marked in various ways. It can be created materially, through the use of fences and the careful distinction of the single-family house from *cortiços* and favelas. Enclosure offers the additional feeling of protection, which is crucial in times of fear of crime. But derogatory conceptions of the poor also fulfill the function of social distancing; they form a kind of symbolic fence, both marking a boundary and enclosing a category, and therefore avoiding dangerous categorical mixtures. In quote 2.11, the speaker, who thinks that the middle classes are disappearing, portrays the poor as people who are used to indignity and who accept their position outside society and the consumer market. When this image is contradicted by the poor and they display signs of participating in society and the consumer market, those who want to keep them out can react strongly. Irritation toward poor people's consumption was expressed many times in the interviews, especially in side commentaries by upper-class people. In quote 2.8, the speaker criticizes "the little people" who impede the country's progress. She continues:

2.12

> I think that the worst is the consumption of the little people, people who don't have a notion of anything, . . . creatures who leave a faucet open and go inside to do I don't know what and leave the faucet on. I see this inside my home. I'm talking to you about an everyday thing. You can enter the kitchen, and there is the faucet on. Now, if I arrive, I feel that the creature [i.e., the maid] comes back to turn off the faucet because I have already said, "Look, water doesn't come from the sky, it's something expensive." . . .
>
> *Do you think that there is something squandered?*
>
> A lot. More from the little people than from the others.
>
> *But wouldn't these be the people with less to squander?*
>
> They are, but you cannot imagine how much they squander, it's something phenomenal! You would say, "But how do they squander if they don't have much?" But if they have it, they squander it. What they have, they squander. They don't know how to preserve, to save, they don't know. . . . Now, in the south of the country it is completely different. In the south you're going to find people who know how to save, who buy their houses, who come from nothing and keep saving and buy their own house.

The ideas that the poor do not know how to consume properly, waste resources, and have a "squandering mentality" are widespread among the upper and middle classes. They are obviously contradicted by the reality of any of Brazil's urban peripheries, where the working poor have built and decorated houses on their own, urbanizing their neighborhoods without financing. However, those who consider themselves better off frequently deny the poor the characteristics and behaviors associated with capitalism and modernity, such as rationality, knowledge, saving, planning, and getting the most out of resources. Such arguments are applied not only to poor individuals but also to poor regions. Paulistanos argue that São Paulo is the best, and the south is almost as good, but the north and the northeast are as hopeless, as the poor people there do not know how to save and or work efficiently. The interviewee of quote 2.3, for whom the Plano Collor was immensely detrimental, still owns a five-bedroom house with a swimming pool in an upper-class neighborhood; but she lost all her savings and had to start working at age fifty-five. She had extremely critical things to say about social inequality in Brazil, but she also thinks that the poor are to blame because they "have children like guinea pigs." She thinks that dramatic social inequality is associated with the increase in violence. However, commenting on consumption by the poor, she goes on:

2.13

> This is something revolting. If you go to any shack, either in Rio de Janeiro or here, close to the freeways, in those favelas, you see a television antenna in every little house. They don't have refrigerators, but they have television. A refrigerator would be more useful, but they don't have a refrigerator and have a television. They are following the way the rich live, and that the television displays.

The image of the television in the favela shack is a formulaic way of signaling the irrationality and extravagance of the poor. It is an image used, as we see here, even by those who are critical of Brazil's social inequality and the arrogance of rich Brazilians. It is invoked again and again to indicate poor people's alleged inability to manage their little money wisely. If they had spent money on a refrigerator, the interviewee reasons, that would be acceptable because it is closer to necessity; and of all there is to buy, food is the most necessary. According to this view, poor people should not dare to enter the world of consumer goods and imitate the lifestyle of those who are better off, which they see on TV. Television best symbolizes this transgression not because of its price—a TV costs less than a refrigerator—but because of the access it allows to information. Through television the slum residents have access to the same symbolic universe as the wealthy; they can become aware of the immense social inequality of a society where anyone can buy a television on credit, but the lifestyle it displays is the province of the elite. On television, probably the only form of leisure poor people can still enjoy on a daily basis, they love to watch Rambo, and they imagine that one day he will declare war on Brazil's "greedy men." And maybe it is not by chance that the greedy men cited as an example by the brothers of Jardim das Camélias were Roberto Marinho and Silvio Santos, the owners of the two most powerful television networks.

Irritation with poor people's participation in middle-class consumer markets was also expressed in upper-class discussions about the deterioration of living conditions in the city. This following quotation records conversation among three women (M, O, and P) who live in detached houses in Morumbi. They think that they have been affected by the economic crisis, but the terms in which they present their social deterioration constitute a display of the immense inequality separating social classes in São Paulo.

2.14

M: Before, we used to have more money too! I used to eat shrimp every Saturday, shrimp, lobster. . . . Now, in order to buy shrimp. . . . For me it's harder. I work the same, my husband does too, but nowadays . . . I charge in dollars in order to avoid readjusting for inflation every month. But I feel that before, we used to make more sophisticated food, we used to live on my husband's salary, and today his salary is not enough for half a month. Seriously. The money factor makes you apprehensive, more irritated.

O: I felt [a difference] since the Plano Collor.

M: I think that before social differences were not so great, they weren't felt as much as today; today it's bigger. The former upper class, from ten years ago, the high is not as high anymore, it's more like middle; and we, the middle, we have obviously fallen down in relation to what we used to be. So those who were high still want to affirm themselves, and in this process there is a lot of aggressiveness. . . .

O: For you to have an idea, go take a look at a simpler neighborhood, the little houses, very small little houses, then you see that gates are like this, this big, in order to fit the Del Rey, the Caravan.[11] The family spends the whole year there, saving everything, but the big car is there in front of the house to show off that they have this year's car. They don't travel, don't go on vacation, don't do anything, everybody hysterical inside the house, in a word, what is this? It's to show off! I'm amazed!

P: It's self-proclamation. It has always been like this. That person who cannot have, he wants to live by appearances . . .

O: What horror! What horror! I think it's ridiculous.

P: There is a young man who works in the factory [her husband's factory], a production foreman, it was very funny, because he was doing well, he was making money in profit-sharing—if the company would make more money, that was divided—and he made good money. He lives—he is from Ceará—he lives with his wife and four children in a bedroom-living-room-kitchen-bathroom of his own, and he has a good lot, my husband has been there. When he got that money, instead of building another room onto the house or improving the house, what did he do? He traded in his VW Beetle for a new Voyage. So you still see the mentality of keeping up appearances. They trade appearances for a better level of life, but I think that this has always been that way. This brings out a lot of aggressiveness . . . you want something and you can't get it, and I think that this, indirectly, when they get that big car to drive in the traffic, they think they're the greatest, put all those repressed things out.

M, O, and P are all in their late thirties, each with two children. O and P are housewives and married to businessmen; M works as a sports instructor in an elite club and is married to a upper-echelon public servant who also has his own business.

Upper-class people may have trouble purchasing luxury items at the rate they once did, but they think they should be able to do so. But consumption by the poor is reprehensible if it appears to transgress the imagined boundaries separating social groups and keeping them in their "proper" place. How dare an employee buy the same type of car as his employers? How dare he look like his bosses and be taken for someone of another class in traffic? The disgust that upper-class people feel about the incorporation of workers into consumer society, even in modest ways, is quite evident. If poorer people spend money on something considered upper-class, they are "ridiculous," it is "such a horror"—even when the poor are demonstrating their incorporation into capitalist relations.[12] Policing the boundaries of social belonging is a crucial operation of the talk of crime, and it is undertaken not only by the elite but by all social groups: the poor themselves disparage the residents of favelas and *cortiços*.

Prejudices against the poor do not preclude upper-class people from recognizing that working-class living conditions may be close to intolerable. However, they always find a way of blaming the poor for their own poverty and of dismissing arguments to the contrary. The three women just quoted agree that income inequality in Brazil is absurd, and they contrast it to some European countries. However, they partake of the common prejudice that workers are lazy and unwilling to work hard, and that is why people like their husbands are not willing to pay them better. Moreover, they share the prejudice that the poor remain so because they have children like "guinea pigs." They could not bring themselves to believe my reports of decreased fertility rates even among the poor, and of my own research in Jardim das Camélias, which indicated that poor women were not having more than two or three children. They continued to insist that the decrease in population was "basically from the middle class up" and that the population continued "to grow in the poor class." Thus the unequal distribution of wealth is partly justified by the myth of the large population increase among the poor.

The prejudice that poor women "have children like rabbits" is widespread, and even when the decrease in fertility rates is admitted, as in the mass media, common explanations reinforce the view that the poor are dominated by irrationality and necessity. One explanation held mysterious international organizations responsible for sterilizing poor women who could not understand what had been done to them. Another blamed increasing poverty for diminished fecundity. In the last twenty years, I have talked to countless women in Jardim das Camélias who do not want to have large families anymore. This is not for strictly economic reasons but because, like any middle-class woman, they want time for themselves to do other things, including getting better jobs than being maids (Caldeira 1990).[13] They do not want to be prisoners of necessity, and many of them have chosen to be sterilized after the birth of a second or third child. They consider it a true liberation. They have learned—and television with its portrayal of upper-class women's behavior and family patterns has taught them a great deal in this matter—that to control their sexuality and fertility can offer immense liberation not only from the burdens of nature but also from male dominance. But people from other social groups—including intellectuals who believe themselves to be writing on the women's behalf when they attack, in newspapers, the few clinics that offer birth control for the poor—refuse to accept such a transformation. Family planning is considered sophisticated modern, middle-class behavior; the place of poor women is still considered to be on the side of nature and necessity. The other argument, that fertility rates have decreased because severe poverty causes infertility, similarly renders poor people prisoners of both their social condition and its "natural" consequences.

It is difficult for anyone in any social group to accept changes that represent a deterioration in their living standards. However, for the upper and middle classes it is also hard to accept some of the changes of the last decades that, in spite of the recession, have meant the incorporation of the working classes into consumer society and into political citizenship and what can be considered modern patterns of behavior. People from the upper classes doubt not only the capacity of poor people to make consumer choices and control their fertility but also their ability to vote rationally. Just as they are irritated by poor people's televisions, they are irritated with their incorporation into political citizenship through social movements and franchising. The idea that the poor do not know how to vote is traditional in Brazil and has served to justify more than one authoritarian coup; it is invoked every time an unfavorable electoral result has to be explained. It emerged, for example, in the late 1980s, when Lula was running for president against Collor, and when Luíza Erundina, the PT mayor of São Paulo at the time of the interviews, was elected.

By jeopardizing social positions across the social spectrum, the economic crisis feeds a sense of uncertainty and disorder. A context of uncertainty, in which people feel threatened socially and see transformations occurring, seems to stimulate the policing of social boundaries. One way of undertaking this task is to elaborate prejudices and marks of distinction. The most explicit and passionate derogations arise when proximity and the threat of mixture have increased. This happens when an employee buys a car similar to his employer's; when new migrants come to live close to old migrants who consider themselves better off; when someone living on the periphery has to prove that she is better off than a neighbor living in a favela; and so on. In other words, proximity leads to the refinement of separations in order to sustain a perception of difference. The context of increased violence and fear of crime intensifies uncertainties, but at the same time it provides a context in which derogations and separations may proliferate almost unchecked.

THE EXPERIENCES OF VIOLENCE

Most people I interviewed had already experienced violence either directly or indirectly (a friend, family member, or someone close by had been a victim). However, their experiences—and fears—varied a great deal. In Moóca and Morumbi, crimes against property, mostly burglary and robbery, are the most common. The elite are deeply concerned about kidnapping, of which rich businessmen have frequently been targets in recent years. On the periphery, crimes against persons, including murder, are frequent. Most of the people I interviewed there had not been victims of violent crime but had witnessed a great deal of violence in their neighborhoods or among people they knew. Statistics of crime analyzed in chapter 3 confirm this social distribution of crime.

In Jardim das Camélias, the increase in violence is something new, but it affects everybody. One of the women, whom I have known since 1978 and who is very active in social movements and local associations, told me that she thinks the neighborhood has improved in the last ten years, if one considers its infrastructure of commerce and services. Nevertheless, it has also become more violent, and a lot of people have died there. Although her evaluations parallel those of the woman whose interview is analyzed in chapter 1—there was progress but also regress—the quality of her experience is different.

2.15

Those who were killed were just kids, but they were heavy-duty bandits. They used to go around the favela. Some of them, the police killed. It has calmed down around here recently, but there was a time, I don't know if it was this year, I cannot say exactly if it was this year or last year, there was a bandit, he used to live in the street of the church. He killed two brothers here. Lord! It was something that revolted everybody here in the neighborhood. But some days later, someone killed him as well. After that, one of his associates who was with him was killed; then they killed, I think, another four. After that it stopped.
Housewife from Jardim das Camélias, age thirty-three, with
four children; her husband is a skilled worker in a small textile industry

Homicide rates are much higher in the working-class neighborhoods of the periphery than in the middle- and upper-class neighborhoods of the center. However, violence also occurs in other spaces where the working classes spend their everyday lives, such as the workplace and on public transportation. People who live on the periphery are also afraid of the police, for good reason: the police are responsible for a high number of killings there. Most people I interviewed on the periphery could tell me about homicides and physical assaults happening close by, and twice I arrived in Jardim das Camélias to hear reports of killings the night before. Residents are scared of what they see happening in their neighborhood, which was once calm and safe. A, one of the brothers I interviewed, commented:

2.16

> A: In the last ten years, a lot of our friends have died, even people who are in this book [my first book on Jardim das Camélias] have died, people who are in those pictures you took and which my mother has. Some were killed by the police; others by bandits, and others by disagreement [i.e., personal conflict]. Sometimes it is because of a fight on the street, then the other gets the idea of killing the person inside his house, in the way those two brothers were killed here.
>
> *How did this happen? It occurred in the street below here, didn't it?*
>
> A: It did. It played on Gil Gomes.[14] He [the killer] called one brother to kill him, then the other brother came out, and he killed both. Since that time they have killed other friends of ours down there. And then they killed another one here. Before they killed the two, they had killed one who used to like to fight with me in school—if he were alive, he would want to kill me. We used to fight all the time.

Everyday contact with violence may be new in Jardim das Camélias, but not on the periphery of São Paulo. Research by Cebrap's team in 1981 and 1982, in other neighborhoods of the periphery, indicated that everyday contact with death and crime was just another fact of life for the working classes. In various interviews for that research, as well as in those I undertook between 1989 and 1991, we heard many stories of violent crimes happening nearby. Many of them, like those in quotes 2.15 and 2.16 above, mentioned a series of murders, emphasizing their routine occurrence in the neighborhood. They also offered details, especially regarding the time they occurred, how they broke the flow of everyday life, and how they victimized innocent people, mostly workers either going to or returning from work.

The narrative in chapter 1 exemplifies the feelings of Moóca's residents and contrasts somewhat with those of residents on the periphery. Various residents of Moóca mentioned that their houses had been robbed, that their neighbors had been robbed, that their purses or wallets had been stolen on buses or in downtown areas. Each of these events was followed by new measures of security and, frequently, more concern with the *cortiços*. These residents did not, however, speak of murders.

In Morumbi, almost all the people I talked to have been victims of either burglary or robbery. The crimes they talked about occurred in restaurants, on the streets, at traffic lights, or in their own houses. It was quite common in Morumbi to listen to recollections of multiple burglaries. One woman told me that she had been burgled four times, another five, and several had been burgled at least once. Each of those episodes provoked new security measures, new alarm systems and electronic surveillance, many weekends without going out, reduced travel, and so on. The greatest fear people in Morumbi expressed, however, was that of being kidnapped.

2.17

We used to think that the lack of freedom and the censorship were bad. Today I think that the military regime should come back. For example, take the case of kidnapping. It's absurd the lack of security that one feels. I'm nobody, I don't have many assets, but I'm afraid that suddenly some guy gets my son in order to ask a ransom of five million. I'm scared to death. . . . Anyone may be kidnapped, because now kidnapping has become the fashion. Why? Because of impunity. We were talking about the military regime: when the AI-5 was introduced, do you remember?[15] Bank robbery ended. . . . It is impunity which makes us feel insecure.

Housewife married to a businessman;
late thirties, two children, lives in Morumbi

DILEMMAS OF CLASSIFICATION
AND DISCRIMINATION

Although the experiences of violence and the fears of people from different social groups are different, all are equally engaged in measures of protection and in what one might call symbolic labor to make sense of their experiences of violence. One of the main activities of this symbolic labor is to differentiate the image of the criminal as far as possible from oneself. When I refer to the category of the criminal, I am obviously not referring to a sociological analysis. Rather, I am talking about a category operating in everyday life whose main function is to make sense of experience. Thus, it is a category of thought embedded in everyday practice that symbolically organizes and shapes that practice. As with other categories in the talk of crime, the category of the criminal generalizes and simplifies. It poses clear-cut distinctions between that which belongs and that which does not. The basis for its distinctions is the opposition of evil and good; clearly, crime and the criminal are on the side of evil.

The categories of the talk of crime simultaneously carry a desire for knowledge and a misrecognition (cf. Balibar 1991:19). The category of criminal is a radical simplification to evil incarnate, and its construction fits exactly Mary Douglas's description (1966) of the treatment of matter out of place. As one who is dangerous and breaks society's rules, a criminal is conceived of as coming from marginal spaces and as polluting and contaminating. Although this type of categorization is a powerful way to think of the world, order narratives, and resignify experience, when more detailed and specific descriptions are needed, the function of misrecognition becomes obvious, and ambiguities necessarily arise.

Such ambiguities are especially present in the association of criminality and poverty. Discussions about crime that refer to poverty and the poor oscillate between two registers: the categorical level of stereotypes and general statements at which misrecognition is hidden or diverted, and the detailed and specific accounts that frequently contradict the categories and generate ambiguous discourses. Both levels produce knowledge, and there is no point in considering one as falsifying a reality that the other describes. The category of the criminal may be a misrepresentation of events, but, as a representation of evil it is crucial for ordering the world and making sense of experience. Moreover, the categorical discourse is important because it is the language of most political struggles over crime and thus shapes public policies. It also frames individual acts of protection and social interaction.

The tensions and ambiguities between the two levels of discourse can never be resolved because talk of crime never abandons its prejudicial categories: in fact, they constitute it. Categorical reasoning is always the basis on which people make sense of their experiences, even people against whom these categories discriminate. Not surprisingly, tension increases as the inadequacy of the categories becomes more evident, and relativizations are greater where there is closer proximity to those who are stereotyped. It is thus among the poor that discourses become more contradictory and elaborated.

Crime and criminals are associated with the spaces that supposedly engender them, namely favelas and cortiços. Both are liminal spaces: they house people, but they are not considered proper residences. Cortiços are subdivided houses that lack the spaces, installations, and separations that designate a home. Favelas are residences erected on land seized by squatters. Although individual wooden shacks might be similar to some residences on the periphery, the main difference between a favela and a poor neighborhood is that in the latter, people either bought the land on which they built their houses (however ramshackle) or pay rent. In a favela, although residents also build their own dwellings and sometimes pay rent, the residences are constructed on illegally obtained land, and their residents are considered to defy the classification of citizens: they live on usurped terrain, they do not pay city taxes, they do not have an official address, and they are not property owners. Moreover, in favelas houses are often made from discarded materials and are usually quite small (again lacking the separations and space allocations of a proper home). As somewhat anomalous residences, that is, ones that do not fit the classification of homes, favelas and *cortiços* are considered unclean and polluting. They coincide, then, with Douglas's formula by which "uncleanness or dirt is that which must not be included if a pattern is to be maintained" (1966:40). Excluded from the universe of the proper, they are symbolically constituted as spaces of crime, spaces of anomalous, polluting, and dangerous qualities.

Predictably, inhabitants of such spaces are also conceived of as marginal. The list of prejudices against them is endless. They are considered outsiders: *nordestinos*, newcomers, foreigners, people who are not really from the city. They are also considered socially marginal: they are said to have broken families, to be the children of single mothers or children who were not properly brought up. Their behavior is condemned: they are said to use bad words, to be immoral, to consume drugs, and so on. In a way, anything that breaks the patterns of propriety can be associated with criminals, crime, and its spaces.

These generic categories of crime and criminals result from a clear opposition of bad and good. To talk about specific favelas, *cortiços*, or *nordestinos* is more complex. The most ambiguous and most elaborated discourses occur when the speaker is a resident of a neighborhood in the periphery which has favelas inside its borders or a resident of a favela or *cortiço*.

In the periphery interviews, although many people talked carefully about the residents of favelas nearby and wanted to think of them as being similar to themselves, a certain suspicion was always expressed, in ambiguous ways. When the talk was of crime, chances were that the prejudicial categories would be used. The following is an interview from 1981, in Cidade Júlia, with an owner of a small grocery store who had been robbed a few times.[16]

2.18

Where do you think that the people who rob here come from?

It can only be from the favela! But I won't say that it *is* the favela, because there are a lot of good people there too. So I think that they come from other places, including those two who robbed me and, in a period of five to seven days, all those people around here. After some days, the mother of one of the kids who was robbed here told me that the police killed three guys down there [in the favela]. After that, nobody has seen anything and nobody was robbed anymore. . . .

So I believe that those who robbed me and the people around here—
we don't wish them harm—but . . . thank God nobody else has shown
up to rob here anymore. . . .

Do people who live in the favela come here to buy?

Of course they do. So many people come here that I don't know
where they come from.

But do you know people from the favela?

By their smell they ought to be from there; because of the smell I think
they are! . . . Maybe there are very nice people who come by here
and live in one of those shacks—I don't know if they are from the
shacks or not. There are people who live in a big house and don't
want to show off. There are people like that, who have all of the best
and think that they have to live like the others do. Sometimes there
are people who live in a shack and who would like to be a Madame
and dress up like a Madame. . . . So that's it: you don't know who
someone is.

Resident of Cidade Júlia, age thirty-seven,
married with two children; her husband is unemployed

It is hard to tell a person's true nature, the interviews suggest. Appearance is not everything, but sometimes it is all one has to rely on. Often people
rely on appearances and on generic categories to pass judgments, but they
do so reluctantly and doubtfully. On the one hand, people associate crime
with the favelas and denigrate the favelados, but, on the other, they try to
make allowances for the favelados' poverty and assert that the ones they
know personally are workers (i.e., good people). However, relativizations do
not exclude denigrations, which are always there in small comments, for example, the observation that one can identify favelados by their smell. The
stereotypes that explain crime and the criminal are derogatory, and even
people who live close to the favelados and the poorest people, and think of
them as honest workers, find no other modes of explanation. In fact, as I
have argued, they need such stereotypes more than others do because their
social proximity to the favelados makes it important for them to assert their
differences; hence they emphasize their own dignity, cleanliness, good citizenship, home ownership, and good family.

Narrative ambiguities and the struggle with stereotypes were expressed
in an especially compelling way in a series of 1981 interviews with a woman
who was a neighborhood leader in Jaguaré, in the west part of town. As the

resident of a legally acquired piece of land across the street from a famous favela, she needed to differentiate herself and her family from the favelados. However, as a neighborhood leader campaigning for improvements in her neighborhood and street, she also felt obligated to include the favelados in her petitions and speeches. She realized that her legitimacy as a neighborhood representative derived from the support of a broad constituency of residents. Her descriptions of her activities in the neighborhood and her interactions with the mayor and the city administration reveal how she oscillates between excluding and including the favela in her arguments and her activism.

When this woman was interviewed, she had been living in Jaguaré for thirteen years.[17] In keeping with the typical devices of the talk of crime, she divided the history of the neighborhood into the good time before the arrival of the favela and the bad time that followed. In the case of Jaguaré, it is appropriate to talk about the "arrival" of the favela because it was transferred by the city administration from another neighborhood, Vergueiro, which was undergoing intensive remodeling for the construction of a subway line. As she said: "After they brought the favela it turned into hell!" She decided to go to City Hall and complain.

2.19

> When I arrived there, I explained the situation. I said I was representing the neighborhood, and he [the mayor] asked me if it was a matter of holes on the street, if it was a matter of trash. . . .
>
> *Did you talk directly with the mayor?*
>
> Yes, with him. So I told him, "No sir, it is not a matter of holes, because if it were holes, we would not come to bother you, because there is a lot of dirt in all the house lots there, and we would fill them. And trash, we would burn it, incinerating the worst." I said, "It is worse than trash, because if we set fire to it we will be arrested and that is a calamity. Don't even think about that." And he said, "Well, what is it?" I said, "The favela that you're supporting." Then he wanted to give me a moral lesson. He looked at me and said, "My dear Madame, they're people *[gente]*!" And I said, "No sir, they're indigents *[indigente]*! People are my husband who works all day long to eat at night. That's people! But there, you're supporting a school of murder, of banditism and we, as poor people, I want to give some moral standards to my children, and it is impossible! It's impossible! At 9 P.M.

it's bang-bang, murder in front of your house. We don't need television at home: it's live! Ten in the morning on a Sunday when we get up and want to go to the front of the house, we cannot: it's swear words of a very high caliber out there; it's some black women doing striptease. It means there is no way that we, as poor people, can educate our children for a better life. . . . It is not a question of putting them down, because we know: you work, you are honest; you are a worker. But if you are a whore, without shame, provoking others, then no one is going to do anything for you." . . . Then he organized a search and seizure operation called a "fine-tooth comb." He sent a whole army.

Husband: A real fine-tooth comb, a yank-them-out-of-bed operation. One time, once was enough.

Six A.M.! That's what we wanted. He sent the whole army, with dogs, machine guns, and they even came to inspect my backyard. My mother thought it was a revolution going on. A whole army! They closed it off. They got so many bandits, marginal people!

Housewife and neighborhood organizer, Jaguaré, age thirty-five, with four children; her husband is a skilled worker in a textile factory

As a citizen, homeowner, and neighborhood leader, the interviewee did not hesitate to go directly to the mayor to demand an armed repression of the people living in the favela who she felt were disturbing her life and preventing her from enjoying the living standards she deserved. That she was received by the mayor was not unusual in São Paulo in the context of democratization and the organization of social movements. Neighborhood organizations knew that they had a chance of being received by politicians, who were starting to think of the shift from appointment to office by direct selection of the military to free elections. In fact, many associations and leaders took advantage of this situation and were in fact received.[18] What is especially revealing about the above narrative is the series of contradictions it reveals. The mayor appointed by the military regime democratically receives the neighborhood leader claiming to represent the neighborhood and initially tries to defend the residents of the favela. However, in the most traditional authoritarian way, he apparently ends up sending the military police to do a "cleaning operation" anyway—and gains the support of the interviewee, who says that things improved after that.

In spite of her action against her neighbors, this local leader realized that her relationship with the favela could not remain antagonistic. Her visit to the mayor took place in the mid-1970s, that is, at the beginning of the *abertura* (political opening) process. As this process developed, however, and as more and more social movements made their way to City Hall, individual actions lost their efficacy. The social movements created a pattern of interaction in which the legitimacy of the demands had to be demonstrated.[19] This leader changed her actions accordingly. A few years after the search and seizure operation, she realized she had no option but to ally with the residents of the favela to demand improvements for the neighborhood, including paving and lighting for the street she shares with the favela and improvements to the public school that both her children and children from the favela attend. She needed their signatures on her petition and recognition as their representative to legitimate her demands.

Her description of her efforts attempts to balance her negative views of the favela residents with her recognition that they are people facing similar problems. It is a complex exercise of simultaneously claiming commonality and maintaining differences. She told us, for example, how she would phrase a petition for paving:

> On the petition to the mayor, I would write: "We, your taxpayers— because I was a little late with the city tax and they already sent me a letter from the Judiciary—so, I would say, we, your taxpayers, residents of X street, and the non-taxpayers, who depend on you—the people from the favela—because as much we, who pay tax, and they [who don't] need this asphalt, these improvements here.

But the choice of words was not her only problem. She had trouble approaching the people from the favela she had campaigned against and convincing them to support her. She told us they were scared, wondering if their signatures would mean having to pay for things, or, even worse, that she would be interested in ferreting out "the bandits." She assured them that she was not out to get bandits, because she knew that this was not only their problem but one that was common everywhere in the city. She told them, "I just want improvements for us, for me and my children, and for your children." As she continued to describe her interactions with them, however, the differentiations started to appear:

> They have always been afraid, but this time I decided to be brave and to enter there; I think they thought I was a social worker. And as I was telling you, there are some little shacks there falling apart, an incredible bad smell, five children sleeping on the floor, the shack almost falling down.

One of her undertakings was to improve the local public school, which, according to her, had been affected by crime. She decided that the most important objective was to have police in front of the school, especially during the morning session attended by the youngest children, who might not know how to cross the streets.

> I teach my children to cross the street, I go with them, I show how, and I go after them to observe. But those children from the favela, usually the parents don't go with them to a place such as Lapa, downtown. They don't say to their children: look, this is the way you cross the street. They don't have time. So the children go like dizzy, directionlessly, and the drivers go like crazy!

Even when it is politically necessary for residents of the same street to work together, their differences are maintained. She felt it necessary to distinguish in her petition between the real citizens and the "non-taxpayers," although both would benefit from the paving and school improvements. This differentiation was a matter not only of citizenship status but also of belonging to the proper social space or to the improper space of crime, a place of criminals, inadequate homes, bad smells, children sleeping on the floor, mothers who do not teach their children to cross the street, black women doing a striptease by the window, bad words, scenes against moral standards, extreme poverty . . . an endless list indeed. At the end of the interview, perhaps feeling she had expressed too many prejudices, she contradicted them:

> So, I got to mix with them [the favelados]. . . . They *are* people [*gente*]! In the beginning they were afraid because they thought I wanted to do something about criminality. But I will never mess with banditism because no bandit—if there are bandits in this favela—none has ever disturbed us. . . . The problem is that favelado is a marginalized name. Unfortunately, for society the favelado is marginalized. And they are traumatized by this. Now, here in our favela it's different. The majority of them, I guarantee, I can pull together for anyone who wishes to see—they are people as much as we are *[são gente tanto quanto a gente]!*[20]

The recognition of the favelados' humanity, which made them equal with the interviewee, and of the fact that they are victims of negative stereotypes, does not preclude the speaker from using those same stereotypes to keep the non-taxpayers at a distance from herself, from her demonstrations of good citizenship, and from the standards she wants to guarantee for her own family. The ambiguities and contradictions of her discourse arise from the fact that the expression of distinction among the poor frequently relies on negative stereotypes, such as those of the favelado, which have to be simultaneously enforced and relativized. Because this kind of stereotype is made up of prejudices that especially affect the poor, and because these still shape poor people's own explanations and attempts at expressing distinction, their use always implies an effort of displacement: the stereotypes have to be directed toward a worse place, even if it is the other side of the street. The dramatic dimension of this effort, which ends up criminalizing and discriminating against people from the same social group, is that the dominated do not have an alternative repertoire for thinking of themselves but must usually make sense of their own world and experience with the language by which they are discriminated against.[21]

The same kinds of ambiguities and contradictions mark the talk of Moóca residents about the *cortiços* and their residents, the *nordestinos* (see, for example, quote 1.1). In both the talk of periphery residents about the favelas and the Mooquenses' discussions about the *cortiços*, we find similar derogations against the inhabitants of the improper spaces and similar relativizations, ambiguities, and contradictions.

2.20

I think that in the last couple of years there has been the entrance of too many foreign people, in quotation marks, who are from other states. So the neighborhood is different from that Moóca of former times when all were traditional people, I mean descendants from Italians, Spaniards, mainly, and also Portuguese. Today we have a lot of infiltration of Brazilians, our people, but who came from the northeast. Thus, their level of capacity, of education, is much lower. They are people who came, let's put it this way, from the countryside of the northeast, so in this sense Moóca changed a lot. The Moóca that I remember from former times was made of people who knew each other for twenty, thirty, forty years. And because of the advancement of progress, those avenues, the subway line, they also had their effects on Moóca. So, many traditional families had to move out to a region far away. . . . The area where I live is a place where the infiltration of foreigners hasn't happened yet. I say foreigners with real affection because they also deserve all respect. I never want to suggest that because someone has come from the north, the northeast, he is specifically a criminal. That is not it. We know many of them and know that they are honest. But the differentiation I want to make is the following: Moóca of twenty years ago was made of people whom we had known for twenty years, and now a person that we hardly know comes to live nearby, and until we can get to trust that person it takes time. That is what I wanted to say. I don't want to say that the person who came is a criminal. That is not it. But that it changed for the worse, it certainly did.

Wholesaler, Moóca, age forty-five,
married, lives with his wife and two children

Although it is impossible to say that all *nordestinos*—the "foreigners" who have infiltrated the neighborhood and occupy its *cortiços*—are criminals, to this speaker their presence certainly symbolizes the negative transformations in the neighborhood. Some of the changes relate less to crime itself than to the disruption of the old urban space and of patterns of sociability. People feel lost and insecure, and they blame their feelings on the increase in criminality and on "invaders" whose stereotypical image comes from the repertoire of bad social characters. To call them foreigners obviously distinguishes them from the local community. That this distinction is made by children of immigrants with reference to Brazilians from other states indicates once more the hegemony of the repertoire of derogation: people use against others the same stereotypes that are used against themselves.

The power of the category that equates *nordestinos* and criminals manifests itself even in the talk of people who want to question the association. One Moóca resident had already been robbed five times, according to him by very different types of people: a handsome blond, three white people, and two who looked like *nordestinos*. Although he insisted that it is impossible to generalize, that within each category of people there are good and bad, his category of the *nordestino* is made up of predominantly negative qualities.

2.21

In São Paulo there are good people and bad people, we cannot generalize. Now, what usually spoils the *nordestinos* is that they have hot blood. Sometimes they are neither robbers nor bandits, but if their blood begins to boil, they get a knife and kill. . . . But it does not make sense to say they are the criminals. If I were robbed by *nordestinos* every time, I would agree, but that is not true. In fact, those who are against the *nordestinos* are the descendants of Europeans, of Italians. My brother-in-law talks like this: the *nordestinos* arrive here and immediately buy Raybans [sunglasses], they buy a big knife, pull out their teeth and put in false ones or stay without the teeth. I think not all of them do this; you cannot generalize something like that. Just because half a dozen do that, all the others shouldn't have to pay. To the contrary, if São Paulo has grown so much, it was due to them. If they didn't come here, we would have to do the hard work. But our labor force would be more expensive. To build the subway, they [the employers] pay whatever they want; but we wouldn't accept that, we would demand higher salaries. My dream—so as not to say that I lack the desire to leave São Paulo—is one day go to the north to help to improve the north. For example: to create an irrigation system so that they would not suffer anymore what they suffer, to educate those people, to start from below instructing them, showing them what life is all about, giving them culture. . . . It's not that I am against their coming here. They come here, and they are labeled stupid, ignorant, killers, all of that. What they come to do here, to improve São Paulo, they should do in their own land to improve it.

Unemployed salesman, age thirty-two, single,
lives with a married sister in Moóca

Nordestinos may not all be criminals, but the list of their supposed weaknesses is long: they have "hot blood," they are a cheap labor force that does not know how to demand the right pay, and they are uneducated, without culture, ignorant of what life is all about. Moreover, the paternalism implicit in of volunteering to civilize them (so they would not have to come to São Paulo) is evident, as is the middle-class prejudice against their consumption patterns: they arrive in São Paulo, buy Rayban sunglasses, and go to the dentist and (maybe because they are not rational) substitute false teeth for their own. A couple of decades ago, having one's teeth removed or sometimes replaced was a mark of status for the rural population because it showed that one had access to an expensive service only available in the larger cities.

Obviously the prejudices against *nordestinos,* which frequently coincide with those against the favelados, are not exclusive to Moóca residents: they are part of the repertoire of residents from all around the city. In the interviews, for example, they were used by an executive descended from Lebanese immigrants, who lives in Morumbi. He thinks that Brazilian impoverishment started with the 1972–1973 oil crisis, but he maintains that the question is not only economic or social but also a matter of education.

2.22

I remember very well when São Paulo was a place where you would find many Europeans. When the people from the north started to come, the customs were modified. They brought other customs. We used to be better educated. I am not against the *nortistas,* but that is what happens, the custom has changed, the respect that we used to have for what belonged to someone else has changed, the respect for that which is yours and that we see so beautifully in the United States: when the light turns red, everybody stops, you can walk safely across the street, which is exactly the opposite of what happens here.

Real estate developer, mid-forties,
lives with his wife and three children in Morumbi

I have been interpreting the repeated affirmation and denial of prejudices as an oscillation between two registers of the talk of crime. There is, however, another, complementary interpretation. The quotes indicate how people try to distance themselves from prejudices and derogations in spite of the fact that they obviously share them. Such self-consciousness and ambiguity also mark other dimensions of Brazilian society, such as the attitude toward black people. Considering what was said against favelados and *nordestinos,* it is especially remarkable that on no occasion during the interviews did anyone make a direct statement against blacks or affirm that they are criminals. I heard phrases such as the one in quote 2.19, in which the women doing "striptease" in the favela are identified as black, but there is no elaboration.

In spite of its absence from the talk of crime, however, discrimination against blacks is pervasive in Brazil. Recent studies using census data for 1980 and 1991 show that by any indicator, black people are in the worst social situation (Goldani 1994; Hasenbalg 1996; Lopes 1993; Silva and Hasenbalg 1992; and Telles 1992, 1993, and 1995). These studies, along with a black movement reinvigorated by the new social movements, are helping to challenge Brazil's myth of racial democracy.[22] One of the main tactics that has helped maintain this myth is a sophisticated politeness code that considers it bad taste to name black people directly as black or to put into words anything offensive to them, as if it were possible to eliminate racism by not speaking the words. This is one of the reasons why several Brazilian censuses omitted questions about race and why people use euphemisms (*moreno* or *escurinho,* for example) to refer to a black person. This is also why the black movement finds it difficult to enlist activists who openly identify themselves as black and abandon "whiter" categories such as mulatto, and trials have been rare and frustrating after the 1988 constitution defined racism as a crime (see Guimarães 1997). The constant need to censor one's words, learned in the context of racial relations, may very well have influenced the expression of derogations referring to other social categories. Although people do pass negative judgments in relation to *nordestinos* and favelados (both of which are also possible euphemisms for black people), as they do toward poor people in general, they try to correct themselves, to attribute the opinion to others, or to relativize it. The art of discriminating while denying it ought to be full of ambiguities. But it is an art at which Brazilians excel (see Caldeira 1988).

In more or less elaborate forms, residents I interviewed in all neighborhoods employed some of these paradoxical modes of expression with regard to the poor, the favelados, the people who live in *cortiços,* and the *nordestinos.* However, some residents of Morumbi offered a somewhat different description of criminals. They associate the increase in crime with increasingly sophisticated drug trafficking and criminal operations. A housewife told me that none of the people she knew who had been assaulted had been robbed by a "beggar." Big robberies, she argued, are carried out by "well-dressed people, very well-dressed. People tell you that if someone wearing a zip-jacket approaches you, you should be very careful because a jacket always hides a gun." Another couple, who were robbed in a restaurant but decided to accept crime as the price of living in São Paulo, which they enjoy, elaborated on the discrepancy between the usual image of the criminal as poor and the greater likelihood of being robbed by someone who does not look poor.

2.23

Q (wife): These days, any person we see crossing the street [in our direction], we already get tense.

R (husband): It's true, but usually the fear is associated with the figure of a poorer guy. . . . Today we hear people talking about the theft of autos by two people who come on a motorcycle. Two guys come on a motorcycle, stop besides the car, point a gun at you, and say, "Get out." The one on the back takes the car and they both get away. The guys on the motorcycle, I have never seen it happen, but they should not be badly dressed.

General director and co-owner of a chemical factory, age
thirty-seven, and his wife, a housewife, age thirty-six, two children

In the rich neighborhoods, the image of the poor criminal is not very detailed, probably for the simple reason that residents do not think they could be mistaken for criminals. Their discourses about criminals rarely leave the realm of the generic, and this secure social distance even allows them a sort of symbolic proximity. Someone who is a criminal may not match the criminal stereotype: he may be well-dressed. It was only in Morumbi that people referred to the image of modern professional criminals with leather jackets, motorcycles, and weapons, interested in dollars, and with resources for sophisticated crimes, such as kidnapping.

Real proximity to the stereotype of the criminal, however, demands an elaborate discourse of distancing and separation. When I was interviewing people on the periphery or in Moóca, I wondered whether my interest in crime might automatically generate anxiety, doubts about whether I suspected them of being criminals, and the consequent urge to highlight differences. The poor people I interviewed always went to great lengths to differentiate themselves and other "honest, working people" from the image of the criminal. This anxiety about separation does not originate exclusively in a drive to display better social status or in a symbolic exercise. In fact, the confusion of poor people with criminals may have serious consequences, as the police operate with the same stereotypes, frequently mistaking poor people for criminals and sometimes killing them. The paradox of the working poor's attempts to separate themselves from the stereotype of the criminal is that this is achieved by using the same strategies against one's neighbors that have been used against oneself. As a consequence, the category of the criminal and its repertoire of prejudices and derogations are rarely contested. Rather, the category is continuously legitimated, and prejudices and stereotypes against poor people (favelados, nordestinos, residents of cortiços) are reenacted on a daily basis.

The symbolic universe of crime is not limited to socioeconomically based references or to the types of prejudices and denigration I have just analyzed. Crime is also a matter of evil, and its explanations are also a matter of authority and of cultural constructions intended to tame the forces of evil. It is important to investigate these conceptions about controlling the spread of evil because Paulistanos use them to attack human rights, to support abuses by the police, vigilant groups, and death squads, and to justify the death penalty.

EVIL AND AUTHORITY

Crime is a matter of authority. The people I interviewed in São Paulo think that the increase in crime is a sign of weak authority, be it of the school, family, mother, church, government, police, or justice system. These authorities are held responsible for controlling the spread of evil. In the talk of crime, evil is conceived of as something powerful and easily spread. Once evil corrupts someone in a weak position—for example, someone in one of the improper spaces or lacking the proper attributes of a member of society—it is likely to dominate this person and is hard to eradicate. People I interviewed felt that the authorities and institutions were clearly failing in their task of controlling places and behaviors: that is, they were leaving open spaces for evil to spread.

The verbs used to describe the increase in crime and the context in which it occurs were *infiltrate, infest,* and *contaminate.* Since evil is contagious, the danger of its spreading fast is immense. One significant outcome of this theory of contagion and the perceived failure of the authorities to control it is that people intensify their private measures of enclosure and control, of separating and building barriers, both symbolic (like prejudice and the stigmatization of some groups) and material (walls, fences, and electronic security devices). Moreover, they tend to support violent, illegal, and private measures of protection, such as vigilantism and police abuses.

The interviews suggest that people from all classes conceive of evil as a natural force that can be controlled only by the labors of culture and reason. The model that many of São Paulo's residents seem to have is quite similar to Hobbes's conception of the state of nature, which grounds the necessity of the social contract. In the absence of a common contract that ties people to restrictive rules, and in the absence of authorities who are able to enforce that contract, there exists a "war of all against all." When the social contract fails, people revert to the violence of the state of nature, that is, to feud, retaliation, and revenge. While evil spreads easily, order and peace are difficult to maintain. These conceptions are also similar to Girard's (1977; see also chapter 1).

Evil is also conceived as being in opposition to reason. It is that which does not make sense and that which takes advantage of people whose rationality is considered precarious. Children, women, teenagers, the poor, and people in a state of disturbed consciousness, such as drug users, are thought to be those most vulnerable and in the greatest need of control. Because little children and women are considered easier to control, the group most susceptible to evil is young men. They are too young to defend themselves from evil, and because they are not yet totally rational they still need to be controlled. Being male, however, they resist control and are drawn to environments where evil abounds, primarily the street. Here they encounter drugs, which render them easy targets for the forces of evil.

Although all human beings are vulnerable to evil, poor people are considered to be closer to nature and necessity and farther from reason and rational behavior than other people. In addition, they are physically closer to the spaces of crime. Consequently they are considered to be at greater risk for being infected with evil.

In what amounts to a pervasive conception of social order, authority, institutions, work, reason, and control are viewed as the weapons against evil. When people see crime increasing, they often blame the public institutions and diagnose a need for strong authority (as in quotes 2.4, 2.17). Alternatively, when the existing public institutions fail, people feel that they have to take matters into their own hands. When the environment is considered to have become too dangerous, the best response is building barriers everywhere and intensifying all types of private control. People intensify their prejudices, and for that the talk of crime is instrumental, but they also hire private guards, build walls, adopt electronic measures of surveillance, and support vigilante groups and private and illegal acts of police vengeance.

I asked residents of São Paulo both in 1981–1982 and in 1989–1991 what would transform a person into a criminal. The answers were strikingly similar. A couple of them packed together many elements associated with evil and the improper; others referred to a few elements at a time. One comprehensive answer is given by a resident of Jardim Peri-Peri, on the western periphery of the city, commenting on a murder close to her house that was apparently motivated by a dispute over a sweater.[23]

2.24

> I think that the city itself contributes to this. For example: probably he [the murderer] saw the other with a lot of clothes, sweater, jacket, and everything, and he was without a sweater, feeling incredibly cold, seeing the other dressed, he went there, stabbed him, I don't know how many times, and took his sweater and went away. . . . I think that the city itself contributes to this. You see, the majority of people here, where did they come from? They came from the northeast, from the south—although I think that people from the south are more civilized. I think that people from the north and the northeast, they live in such horrible conditions. Horrible! . . . There is this damned advertisement that they show on television in the northeast and which brings this image to them: "Look, people who go to São Paulo manage to become rich." Then what do they do? They gather up the family, sell the little they have there and come here. When they arrive here, they don't

have anywhere to stay. Sometimes they know someone and go to this person's house, and then you get that heap in a very small house of a living room, a bedroom, bathroom and kitchen, or even in a favela. Then it is like this: ten, twenty, thirty people inside a house—you can imagine what happens! The children see the parents going out to work and stay the whole day by themselves. Then those children get together with other people's children, plus other people's children, and plus the children of no one knows who. . . . And without eating, you know, because the parents make little money. Then what happens? That is already a violence, because he sees that one person has everything and he thinks, "That person has everything and I don't have anything. I'll take some of what he has and maybe that will be beneficial for me." The majority of the robbers, what do they think? That they are going to be able to take something and that the police will never discover that they had stolen it. Do you understand? So I think that the cause is the person's own condition of life. . . . Hunger is the worst thing. So these people who come from there to here, they are going hungry. So, they don't have how to struggle [lutar]. They don't. They don't have how to struggle. Thus, they go rob and kill in order to have something.

> *Computer operator in a large factory, age thirty-three, Jardim Peri-Peri,*
> *lives with her mother, who is a janitor, and an aunt*

This stereotypical view of the causes of crime includes a long list of elements. There is always the question of improper places. Even if the *nordestinos* do not all live in the favelas, they are said to live in promiscuous houses with too many people and a lack of adequate boundaries, where children mix with countless other unknown children, all without proper supervision by parents. In the background are the always present but never sufficient social conditions: hunger, poverty, and unequal distribution of wealth. Finally there is the perceived failure of the police and of the justice system to punish crime. The combination of all these elements creates conditions of life that leave people without the ability to struggle. *Lutar*, to struggle, is a verb commonly associated with persistence and hard work; it is what it takes for people to move up socially (see Caldeira 1984: chapter 4). (The verb *lutar* and the noun *luta* are also used on the periphery to refer to social movements.) People in a weakened position, who cannot struggle, are believed to run a high risk of being infected by evil.

The same elements were repeated in many interviews. When we asked a young man in Moóca if he agreed that crime was related to the *nordesti-*

nos, he answered that it might be, since migrations and robberies were both motivated by economics. However, when he was asked to describe the kind of person who might have taken his watch, his answer was very different.

2.25

I imagine that this person may even be unemployed but, look, for one to fall into these conditions [of committing a robbery] is very easy. It only takes, for example, a bad relationship in the family, it only takes a wife, I don't know, a bad relationship in general. A failure at work. It only takes little things. And there is another detail: it only takes a weak morale, and an insignificant education. It only takes having a mediocre culture. And what is this? Unfortunately, this is the majority of the population. It is from this majority that those things [robbery] come. The robber may even come from a middle-class family. Another may in fact come from a favela. So I think that what fosters [crime] are general things, social things, which are part of the culture, which affect everybody, which can catch anyone who is overwhelmingly affected by those things.

Unemployed college graduate, age twenty-three, Moóca, who has a degree in communications with a major in radio and lives with his parents

It takes more than economic and political conditions to produce a criminal, but it still takes very little: any small push in the direction of the improper can tip the balance. To resist the danger requires a strong mind, something the poor are believed to lack.

2.26

Everything [prices] went up 100 percent, and salaries have not gone up a single cent. That is, for someone who makes a little, the minimum wage or a little more, a person like that I think throws himself into the abyss. You think: a head of a household with three or four children, he goes to work, he works, works, and works, the work is boring, then he goes back home and sees no means, no way out, then I think that this throws many people who don't think well into the abyss. And then they start to want to rob, to steal, to kill, to take out their frustration on their family, a colleague at work, the boss.

Semiskilled factory worker, age thirty-nine, Jardim das Camélias

I asked the neighborhood activist quoted in extract 2.19 what she thought made boys into criminals.

I don't know. Sometimes I think it is because of the relationship of the father and the mother, a separation, or sometimes because the child was already born revolted with life, even with the father and the mother. Do you think it is only vice? A lot of them drink, and people say that they drink because it's a vice, they smoke—I don't know, it's all confusing. I think that it is also bad company, a person's own colleagues who lead them to crime. That is to say, it's all that: it comes from the home, it's the street, I don't know, they lose their heads. And once one loses his head, that's it.

Many of the interviewees think that people who have to face very stressful conditions or who grow up in adverse environments need a strong mind in order to avoid despair and to resist bad influences. But if they lose their heads (i.e., their reason and good judgment), they are lost. And there is no better way of losing their heads than to become involved with drugs. The correlation of drugs and crime was one of the most common in the interviews, and it has consistently been described as a cycle: people come from an improper environment, they are subjected to bad influences in the streets, they are given drugs for free, they become addicted, and finally they become criminals to support their addiction.

People from all social classes believe that a strong mind originates within a strong family, one that properly disciplines children and protects them from bad companions.

2.27

E (mother): I think that if all these young people here worked more, they would have less time for this [violence]. Take a look, those kids who grew up here, who are fifteen, sixteen, seventeen, they stay all day in the street. They are not thinking of anything else if they don't have anything to do. You [her daughter] at least study, it's different. They don't study, don't work, they want money, they don't have any place to get it, so what are they going to do?

D (daughter): And what about the unemployment?

E: There is unemployment, but if they looked for a job, they would find it—why is it that those who look for it find it?

D: There are a lot of people unemployed out there looking for a job without finding one!

E: I think that if they looked they would find, but they prefer to hang around hustling. . . . There are thirteen-year-old kids around here carrying a gun!

D: Why is that? Why are they carrying a gun? Because the majority of those kids grew up without the mother being at home. Why? Because the mothers had to work to put food on the table. What is this kid going to learn in the street? To rob! There will be things missing at home because the mother's salary is small, it's impossible to have everything, then he starts robbing. So, this means that they are not guilty; society is guilty!

E: I think that guilt is everybody's, not only society's.

D: Society is everybody.

[The discussion continues, and C argues that mothers should not go to work and leave their fifteen- and sixteen-year-old sons at home with nothing productive to do. She thinks that if the mothers had more authority, this would not happen. She also thinks that everything would be easier if there were more dialogue between parents and children, and if parents watched less television and talked more to their children. The interviewer asks her if her ten-year-old boy used to play in the street.]

E: No. He was working until last week.

This little boy?

E: He was working in the drugstore until last week. He left it because it is the end of the year and he is having trouble in school.

D: He went to work in the drugstore because we used to lock him inside the house. . . .

E: In order to avoid contact with the others.

D: The problem is that he used to escape. He would get the key, and if you were not paying attention, he was already in the street. So the contact that he would have with the kids would not be good for him. Therefore we put him in the drugstore. He doesn't earn practically anything, but the little change he gets is just for him, and that is enough to keep him off the street.

E: I think that the environment and friendships influence a great deal. Friendships influence a lot, and there are certain friendships that we must avoid, so this was a way to keep him away from the bad companions.

Housewife, Cidade Júlia, around forty, and her daughter, aged twenty.
The mother has another biological child and two adopted children.

Opinions about the necessity of controlling children and keeping them away from strangers are widespread and cross all social classes. They constitute a strong argument against living in apartment buildings: people in apartments and condominiums have more trouble controlling their children and keeping them away from acquaintances who might be considered unsuitable. When it is a question of proximity and friendships, people of all classes use exactly the same phrases. Here are the views of M, O, and P, the women from Morumbi quoted in excerpt 2.14:

2.28

Why do you prefer to live in a house instead of in one of the condominiums?

O: Freedom. To me, freedom first of all, and then the contact of too many children that I would be unable to prevent [in order to] control the friendships of my children.

P: That's right.

O: The famous fear of drugs. My sister-in-law lives in a condominium: all day long you have children from here, there, everywhere. You don't know who the children belong to . . .

M: Because the houses there are not enclosed, the house doesn't have walls. . . . Only the condominium's wall, but the house has only the grass, and in a while it is already another house. American-style.

O: All open, and you don't know the contact your child has. How are you going to keep them separate? You don't have a wall, how are you going to say, "No, my son, you receive the friends at home that I think are better, I am going to select these friends"? Because nowadays you must select, I think, you must at least select the friendships. And there it's impossible, so there is no way I would move there. . . . You know, children's ideas are transmitted to other children. The child may be very calm, tranquil, but with the influence of a tougher group . . . There are cases of a child robbing another child's house in order to steal dollars to buy marijuana. I won't name names, but there are cases . . . in a condominium. I wouldn't stand that, there is no way I would live there.

> It may happen to my children as well, but then, I've tried to do the best.
> Only at the moment when I feel that they have good little heads to face
> the world by themselves will I tranquilly open the doors so that they do
> whatever they want. But till then I want to have the control.

Whatever their social class, people seem to share the idea that bad influences spread easily and that a principal means of preventing their spread is to control one's children carefully. Two of the upper-class women just cited, and the working-class woman cited before them, are housewives who decided not to work in order to control their children. They feel uncomfortable about it. The working-class woman feels that the burden on her husband is heavy indeed; and the upper-class women (one of whom has a college degree) feel the pressures of their own social environment, in which a growing number of women work. They all think, however, that their sacrifice is necessary to the well-being of their children. They suggest that women who work outside the home are responsible for their children's deviance, an accusation expressed in many interviews. Thus working women in Brazil have to deal with strong feelings of guilt. Although men run a higher risk of becoming criminals, mothers are considered to be more responsible than fathers for the criminal behavior of their children. According to the stereotype shared by many people I interviewed, women who work abandon their children to the street and cannot keep them on the "right path" (see quotes 2.19, 2.24, 2.27). This view disregards the fact that most children whose mothers work do not stay home alone and abandoned but are cared for by grandmothers, aunts, neighbors, siblings, teachers, or maids. Many people insist, however, that the mother must be around, as if her presence alone could keep things right.

One could argue that evil is one of the most democratic elements in the universe of crime. It comes from everywhere, can affect anyone (although the weak are more vulnerable), and consequently implies that everybody requires controlling. However, the consequences of this concern with constant surveillance transcend the universe of crime. People used to exercising a high level of control have a hard time accepting any limits to their surveillance or recognizing other people's individual rights. They do not think of their children as having rights of privacy or choice, for example in selecting playmates. Children should do what their parents want them to do and play with the companions their parents select for them: lessons in separation and prejudice start early. One can only wonder when people's rights of choice are supposed to start, especially the rights of those "in need" of tighter control, such as young people and women. One can also wonder about the immense difficulties that an integrated public school system would have in Brazil.

Would upper-class parents consider working-class children appropriate play-mates for their kids? Would parents in Moóca let their children play with *nordestinos?* Certainly it is not only because public schools have deteriorated that middle- and upper-class children attend only expensive private schools.

Another element revealed in the discussions about controlling bad influences is the necessity of occupying people's minds and time. An old man from Jardim das Camélias once told me that "an empty mind is the devil's workshop."[24] In popular culture, the best protection from the devil's influence is believed to be work, as Alba Zaluar has also demonstrated in many of her studies of the universe of crime in Rio de Janeiro and of relationships between workers and bandits in working-class neighborhoods.[25] Even if people are not working, they should be occupied with something. The small boy mentioned in extract 2.27 was sent to work in a pharmacy to keep him occupied and off the streets. Unoccupied time is a risk for everybody. Men can lose their heads when unemployed, and women who do nothing are said to leave their minds open to bad influences.

People also think that prisoners are hard to resocialize both because it is difficult to eradicate evil once it has infected someone and because in prisons they are left unoccupied. Thus, many think that the only way to resocialize prisoners is to force them to acquire work skills while in jail. This is, for example, the opinion of an interviewee from Moóca. He thinks that one of the problems with prison is that people who are there for petty crimes, for example poor boys who stole out of necessity, are put together with dangerous criminals, and "by osmosis they absorb all that bad knowledge." They should instead be forced to select a craft to learn and to practice it.

2.29

> People should not leave a prisoner unoccupied, because it is like that story says—and here comes my macho side—it is like the woman who stays at home alone, without working, stays the whole day there and she keeps thinking of silly things: "Where would he be that he hasn't come home yet?" So, put the prisoner to work![26]
>
> *Bar owner, Moóca, has a law degree but does not*
> *work as a lawyer; single, lives with three roommates*

People believe that to rehabilitate someone who "gets into the wrong path" is often impossible. Many people who argue for the death penalty point out the peril represented by those dominated by evil. They say that death is the only effective way of extinguishing the evil. To control evil is always a difficult undertaking. Evil spreads easily by osmosis, through contact; it takes only an unguarded moment, a temporarily unoccupied mind, a situation of instability with its loose boundaries and uncertainties about mixture. As a consequence, people want barriers to prevent the spread of evil and to re-organize a world too easily taken over by chaos.

The elements I have analyzed so far do not constitute all the explanations of crime advanced by residents of São Paulo. Another set of views focuses on problems of the individual, either moral or psychological. These explanations are often invoked when references to environment and propriety are insufficient to explain a crime. When people come from the right places and have had proper supervision, when appearances contradict behavior, an understanding of violence can still be found in "nature"—or more exactly in "perverted nature"—and, in some cases, perverted consciousness. Residents of São Paulo say that rich people may rob "for meanness" *(por malvadeza)*. Violence can also be justified by a "psychological drama," or insanity, an extreme case of "losing one's head." Sometimes people become criminals simply because that is their "destiny."

These types of arguments are used especially in accounting for violence. Rape, for example, in general requires an explanation based on perversity. Moreover, references to deviance from human nature and reason appear to justify crimes in which violence is considered gratuitous, as in the case of a robber who, after getting everything he wants, kills the person he has robbed. According to one interviewee, an undergraduate who lives in Moóca with her parents, "Something like that has no explanation; it can only be that he was out of himself, under drugs." Only crimes against property can be explained by purely socioeconomic motives.

The explanations that refer to perversion, destiny, chance, and passion, are also used to explain crimes committed by those who do not fit any of the criminal stereotypes. Crimes committed by people from the upper classes, who, as people say, "have everything of the good and the best," can be explained only by some kind of perversity. Two undergraduate students interviewed in Moóca clearly separated economically motivated crimes (committed by someone who is, for example, unemployed and desperate) from crimes committed by people "who have such a nature." They think that drug use is widespread not only among working-class men but also among the middle-class men with whom they socialize in the upper middle-class neighborhood of Jardins. In fact, they think that it is more widespread in the richer group because these people have more money for indulging in drugs, and they rob for stupid reasons, stealing little things, such as sneakers.

The young working-class men from Jardim das Camélias also think that crimes committed by upper-class people are associated with drugs, as are crimes in general. However, drugs alone do not offer a sufficient explanation for crimes committed by the upper classes.

2.30

> A: There are people who rob and don't need to, they rob because they are shameless. Like the time when the sons of rich people were throwing bombs inside restaurants. Why did they do that? I think it is a distraction for them, they don't have anything to do and decide to abuse our patience.
>
> C: If they were poor, the police would get them and beat them . . .
>
> A: But since they are rich, they may even be the son of a general, a major, if the police get them, they have to release them.

For residents of Jardim das Camélias and Moóca, rich people are perceived as being outside the law and society; their social position assures that they will not be punished. Perception of this additional inequality, which perverts classifications and social contracts, is at the center of the total pessimism many residents of São Paulo feel about creating a more just society in Brazil. Since it is difficult to impose order through existing institutions, which are unable to control evil and therefore unable to build a better society, people feel that they are constantly exposed to the natural forces of evil and to the abuse of those who place themselves outside the law. To protect themselves, they have to rely on their own means of isolation, control, separation, and distancing. In order to feel safe, that is, they have to build walls.

PART 2

Violent Crime and the Failure of the Rule of Law

CHAPTER 3

The Increase in Violent Crime

As violent crime has increased in São Paulo in the last decade, so have the abuses and violence of the institutions in charge of preventing crime and protecting citizens. In this chapter, I discuss the problems of measuring and explaining these increases. Crime statistics produced by the police suffer from various distortions. Available explanations of crime, based on models that associate crime with socioeconomic and urbanization variables as well as variables in state expenditures on public security (including the number of police officers and their equipment), fail to account for what has grown the most in São Paulo in the last decade and what particularly concerns the population: the increase in violence, and not only in crime. To understand the growth of violence, it is necessary to look at the breakdown of both institutions of order and attempts to enforce the rule of law, and to examine the increasing adoption, both by state agents and by civilians, of extralegal and private measures to face crime. It is also necessary to look at city residents' experiences with and perceptions of the police, as well as their conceptions of individual rights, punishment, and the body. The increase of violence is the result of a complex cycle that involves such factors as the violent pattern of reaction of the police; disbelief in the justice system as a public and legitimate mediator of conflict and provider of just reprisal; private and violent responses to crime; resistance to democratization; and the population's feeble perception of individual rights and its support for violent forms of chastisement.

TAILORING THE STATISTICS

Concerns with producing population statistics have been central in modern societies since at least the beginning of the nineteenth century. The development of statistics is associated with the consolidation of the modern perception of society as a "sui generis object, with its own laws, its own science, and eventually its own arts of government, . . . the object to be understood and reformed" (Rabinow 1989:67). As Foucault (1977) has taught us, statistics are part of disciplinary power and a central element of the technology of power of modern states. Figures on crime—always official records—have been among the oldest and most carefully produced of statistics. They provide information not only about crime or abnormal behavior but also about how a society functions normally. As Chevalier puts it, crime is recorded as "a normal fact of urban life in order to acquire a more intimate knowledge of its [urban life] forms" (1973 [1958]: 8).[1] Statistics were supposed to be a neutral instrument for revealing social reality, a scientific tool that would reliably demonstrate society's most general trends. Instead, they produce peculiar and specific views of social reality.

Criminal statistics are no exception. They are constructions that generate particular views of some segments of social reality. They construct images of patterns of crime and criminal behavior. Today it is hard to argue that they are a representation of "real" crime—if one can still talk in those terms. At most, one can claim that the statistics indicate some tendencies of criminality. But if the information they give on crime is restricted, they may nevertheless reveal other facts about the society that produces them. São Paulo's criminal statistics may not represent "real" crime, but an analysis of their peculiarities contributes to an understanding of the institutions of order and the lack of respect for the rule of law.

Most of the statistics analyzed in this chapter are from police reports on crime (called BO, *boletins de ocorrência*), produced by the civil police. In other words, I deal mostly with officially reported crimes. These are only one indication of criminality: they refer to the first record made at police stations when an offense occurs, and they precede any investigation. As such, many of the reports may be inconclusive. Moreover, they are produced by a specific institution, the civil police of the state of São Paulo, whose particular practices and perception of criminality shape the production of the reports. It is impossible to measure all the consequent distortions in the statistics, but some of the most important problems must be discussed, as they severely limit what we can conclude from the numbers.

In general, studies of crime assume that the statistics register only a fraction of the total crime. People who commit illegal acts often succeed in concealing them. Moreover, surveys of victimization reveal that many victims of crime do not report the offense. The only victimization survey for Brazil dates from 1988; it was carried out by IBGE (Instituto Brasileiro de Geografia e Estatística), the Brazilian census bureau.[2] This survey identified people who had been victims of larceny *(furto)*, robbery *(roubo)*, or physical assault *(agressão física)*, between October 1987 and September 1988.[3]

In the metropolitan region of São Paulo, 5.67 percent of the population said they had been a victim of one of these crimes, while another 1.85 percent declared themselves victims of attempted robbery or larceny. Of the total number of people who were victims of either robbery or larceny, 61.72 percent did not report the incident to the police, which means that the majority of those crimes are not represented in the official statistics. Among the reasons people gave for not reporting crimes were that they "did not believe in the police" (34.33 percent) and that "it was not important" (22.33 percent). In addition, 14.40 percent said they "had no proof" and 9.10 percent declared they "did not want to involve the police." In brief, the majority of cases of nonreporting were associated with negative images of the police.

Among people who said they were victims of physical assault (1.08 percent of the population), 55.67 percent did not report it to the police.[4] The percentage of women (62.2 percent) who did not report is higher than the percentage of men (56.46 percent). The reasons for not doing so also varied according to gender. For men, the main reasons were distrust of the police (22.64 percent); the assertion that it was not important (20.75 percent); that they solved the conflicts by themselves (15.09 percent); that they did not want to involve the police (13.2 percent); and fear of revenge (also 13.2 percent). For women, the most common reason was fear of revenge (25.99 percent). Next was distrust in the police (24 percent); the fact that they did not want to involve the police (18 percent); that they had solved the conflict by themselves (16 percent); and finally, that it was not important (9.99 percent). Although the majority of both men and women who did not call the police said that the person who assaulted them was unknown, 17.99 percent of the women were assaulted by a relative, whereas only 0.76 percent of the men were. These figures thus offer some indication of the extent of domestic violence suffered by women.[5]

The majority of occurrences of larceny, robbery, and physical abuse, then, are not reported to the police. People either do not trust the police to deal with conflicts and crime, or they fear them because of their well-known brutality (see chapters 4 and 5). Similarly, the justice system is perceived as ineffective by the majority of the population. According to the same survey, of those involved in at least one conflict during the years 1983–1988 in the southeast region of Brazil, 50.71 percent did not use the justice system.[6] The main reasons given are that people solved the problem by themselves (41.70 percent); the incident was not important (11.09 percent); people did not want to involve the justice system (10.87 percent); people did not have proof (10.46 percent); and people thought that the justice system would not solve the conflict (6.31 percent). The distrust in both the police and the justice system—that is, in the public institutions in charge of keeping order—is probably associated with the fact that people prefer to solve their problems privately, even if the problem is crime. In fact, of all those who were part of criminal conflicts in southeast Brazil, only 27.44 percent entered the justice system. In contrast, 70.83 percent of labor conflicts detected by the survey entered the justice system.

The distortion of crime statistics is not only a quantitative issue but also a qualitative one. Since the police produce the statistics, their view of the potentially criminal population, their evaluation of different crimes, and their responses to different types of events all influence the results. Paixão (1982; 1983) has studied the classification methods of contemporary Brazilian police partially following the approach of ethnomethodology. He shows that police classification practices are not shaped by legal and formal classifications but rely on a special practical code that he calls "logic-in-practice" (lógica-em-uso, Paixão 1983), which transforms events and individuals in categories and articles of the penal code. As a consequence,

> official criminal statistics should be seen not as an indication of criminal behavior and its social distribution, but rather as organizational products which reflect operational, ideological, and political conditions of the police. Therefore, on the one hand, discontinuities and changes in the organization's routines of gathering and classifying data, variable sensibilities of the police authority towards certain types of crimes, or police responses to "moral crusades" and to political pressures, generate distortions in criminal accounting which are not to be neglected. (Paixão 1983:19)

Similar conclusions were reached by Lima (1986) and Mingardi (1992). Although Paixão's analysis develops an important theoretical distinction between formal and informal classifications that is absent from Mingardi's work, in what follows I refer primarily to the latter. Mingardi's research is specific to São Paulo, whereas Lima's was done in Rio de Janeiro and Paixão's in Belo Horizonte, where the police and the statistics are organized differently.

Before I discuss Mingardi's study, it is necessary to review the organization of the police in the state of São Paulo and in Brazil in general. The police are organized at the state level and are divided into two bodies: the civil police (Polícia Civil), and the military police (PM, Polícia Militar), both under the authority of the secretary of public security (Secretário de Segurança Pública) of the state.[7] The civil police is in charge of the administrative police (who issue identification cards, register guns, etc.) and of the judiciary police. The latter's duties include recording complaints and criminal events, investigating crimes, producing proof, and initiating (or not) judicial processes (*instalação de inquérito*). The civil police, in consequence, produces both the reports on which the statistics are based and the records and evidence from which the judiciary system will work. The current military police, created by the military regime in 1969, is in charge of uniformed street policing. It is subordinate to the army and has a separate organization and system of recruitment and instruction. Rivalry and conflict between the two police bodies are traditional and shape their everyday patterns of performance.

In each state there is also a branch of the federal police, in charge of frontiers and national security and also of controlling drug trafficking. Finally, some cities, such as São Paulo, have a local metropolitan guard (Guarda Metropolitana) with little power, whose task is more to keep order in public spaces (such as parks, public administration buildings, and theaters) than to deal with crime.

After completing a course at the Police Academy (Acadepol), Guaracy Mingardi worked during 1985 and 1986 as a civil policeman (investigator) in a neighborhood police station on the periphery of São Paulo. His work presents a detailed ethnography of everyday life in a police station and reveals its logic-in-practice and the kinds of distortions introduced into the production of statistics and the treatment of complaints. According to Mingardi (1992: part 1), illegal practices, such as corruption and torture, are not only the norm in the civil police but are interdependent and tend to occur together. They constitute what he calls the working method of the civil police. "We want to show that the bad treatment inflicted upon the arrested person is part of a process which starts with the selection of the suspect and ends either with handing him to the judiciary or with the *acerto* (settlement) which frees him" (Mingardi 1992:52).

Mingardi argues that as soon as the civil police catch someone with a criminal record, they start a well-known, three-step game. First, the suspect is tortured (most often using a technique known as *pau-de-arara*)[8] so that he or she will confess to one or more crimes. Second, the police call the suspect's lawyer. This lawyer, who is usually known as the "jail door lawyer" *(advogado de porta de cadeia)*, works only with certain police stations and is responsible for all the negotiations and payment of bribes there. The lawyer negotiates and arranges payment of an *acerto*. *Acerto* translates as "settlement," but in police slang it means the payment agreed on between the police and the suspect, through the mediation of the lawyer, to be divided among all the officers involved. According to Mingardi, the most common form of corruption is someone paying the police not to institute a legal suit *(instalar inquérito)* by sending the case to the judiciary. Once the *acerto* is paid, the suspect is released and the report "cleaned" to show crimes of a lesser degree (larceny instead of robbery, for example), or even to erase them.

According to Mingardi, the rules about who is tortured are clear. He claims that the instrumental logic of the civil police reveals a rationality that he cannot find among the military police who, he argues, "in general beat up [suspects] . . . for emotional reasons" (1992:58). Commentaries such as this reveal the extent to which rivalry between the two police bodies marks their everyday relationships, resisting even important efforts of description and criticism of their practices. Mingardi, an ex–civil policeman, is able to find rationality in the torture practiced by his own organization but not in the violence practiced by the PM!

The ethnographic analysis by Roberto Kant de Lima (1986) of the workings of the civil police in Rio de Janeiro corroborates the work of Mingardi. Lima also observes that torture is "deeply rooted in police routine" (1986:156). His explanation, however, is quite different. In Mingardi's view, the police torture because they are corrupt: money is their aim. Lima, however, does not connect the routine of torture to the routine of corruption, a marginal theme in his analysis of the police. He believes the police torture because their investigative proceedings rely heavily on confession. "The necessity of finding out the truth through confession becomes responsible for the socially legitimated use of torture as an investigation technique" (1986:154). Lima also says that torture is so deeply embedded in investigative practices by the civil police that "when they are prevented from using torture the failure of the investigation is said to be certainly expected" (1986:156).

The practice of torture and its tacit acceptance by the population is a complex issue that cannot be ascribed entirely to a single rationale, whether of corruption or of the role of confession in criminal proceedings. It is related to both these logics, as well as to other patterns of police brutality and to various conceptions of punishment and physical chastisement prevalent in Brazilian society. The fact remains that the use of torture introduces biases in the shaping of events that are classified as crimes and, consequently, in the statistics. According to Mingardi, three main rules govern torture among São Paulo's civil policemen: (1) The right way of torturing is the *pau-de-arara*, because other forms may leave marks. Mingardi declares that he learned this lesson in the Police Academy. (2) People of the upper classes and those without criminal records should not be tortured. (3) A person with a criminal record and money is not tortured if payment for release is offered at the outset (1992:55–57). People with money can always avoid legal charges. As a result, "Who is beaten up is poor; white-collar is not beaten up, makes *acerto*," as one of his informants put it (1992:57).[9] Moreover, those who cannot pay may end up facing legal charges. "In a crime involving people from different classes, the weight of *police justice* will generally fall on the poorer part," concludes Mingardi (1992:178, emphasis in the original).

In sum, the peculiar working methods of the civil police not only are based on illegal behavior but also enforce a clear class bias. Consequently the working classes have good reasons to distrust the police and avoid any involvement with them. White-collar crime, mainly corruption and fraud, is frequently reported in newspapers, but it rarely leads to jail sentences. Newspaper coverage of this crime is often more expansive than reports from the police. This situation is an indication of the level of impunity existing in contemporary Brazilian society and the lack of accountability of the judiciary institutions: the public may know about crimes that are ignored by the judiciary system, yet this knowledge generates little action, either officially or at the level of public opinion.

With all the *acertos* and cleaning of records, the statistics are inevitably distorted. Mingardi tries to be specific about the kind of distortion related to different crimes. According to him, theft and larceny are not taken seriously by the police: when the value of the property is small, they tend not to be recorded.[10] When the victim insists, the police issue a document acknowledging that a crime has been reported; but it has no legal value, and in police slang it is called *papel de bala* (candy wrapper) because it is not useful for anything (1992:42).[11] According to two ex-secretaries of public security whom I interviewed, this approach was also used before 1983 to lower the official recording of some crimes when the population was complaining about high criminality.

Burglaries are well investigated when upper-class residences are robbed. Upper-class people may pay the police for having stolen property returned; they may also ask the police to "be tough" (to torture) to get information. However, burglaries of poor people's homes tend to be ignored. Robberies and assault receive the same kind of treatment: the upper-class victims get attention, and the working class victims do not (1992:43, 45).

According to Mingardi, cases of violence against women are recorded very reluctantly *(com muita má vontade)* because policemen believe that the women will change their minds the next day and withdraw the complaint

(1992:46). He also adds that police stations located in neighborhoods on the periphery are more likely to ignore a crime (1992:47). Homicide investigations are handled by a special division of the police (DHPP, Departamento de Homicídio e Proteção à Pessoa, previously called DEIC, Departamento Estadual de Investigações Criminais).

Mingardi's ethnography thus indicates that the population's rationale for not reporting crimes and their distrust of the police have a solid basis. His data also indicate that the social distribution of crime is misrepresented. Lima's research also suggests that police reports are quite arbitrary (Lima 1986:chapter 4). According to him, the *registro de ocorrência* (recording of a fact as relevant for the police) "depends on the discretion of police authorities, often exercised in disobedience to the law" (Lima 1986:103). Police practice shows a clear bias toward criminalizing the poor and decriminalizing the upper class (1986:114–21). Lima's and Mingardi's analyses—whose conclusions also coincide with those of Paixão (1982; 1983) and of Coelho (1978)— lead us to conclude that the statistics overrepresent crimes in which the victim is upper-class and underrepresent those in which the victim is working-class. Moreover, they tend to underrepresent crimes committed by the upper class and overrepresent those committed by the poor, especially by nonprofessional criminals who cannot or do not know how to pay for the *acerto*. It is also probable that more serious crimes are underrepresented, as they may be classified as a less serious crime. It is difficult to estimate how extensive those distortions may be. What we know for sure is, first, that there are various possibilities for the manipulation of information and, second, that contemporary São Paulo exemplifies in a clear and perverse way how the working class is not only stigmatized as the dangerous class but is indeed constructed to be that way in the practice and statistical reports of the police.

Other researchers have reported other common distortions. Brant's analysis of the prison population of the state of São Paulo (1986) shows clear distortions in relation to the black population. While people classified as white constituted 75 percent of the population of the state of São Paulo in 1980 (census), they made up only 47.6 percent of the prison population. The black and mulatto population constituted 22.5 percent of the general population and 52 percent of the prison population. As Brant argues, this does not necessarily mean that blacks are more involved in crime; it does mean that they are more frequently assumed to be criminals. As some of the policemen interviewed by Brant put it, "A Black man running is a suspect" (1986:43). This is probably associated with the finding of Pinheiro et al. (1991:110) that blacks are also overrepresented in the number of people killed in confrontations with the police. Finally, a recent study by Adorno (1995) on São Paulo's criminal justice system shows that although whites and blacks commit violent crimes in identical proportion, blacks tend to be harassed more by the police, to face greater obstacles in their access to the justice system, and to have more difficulties in securing their rights to an adequate defense. As a result, blacks are more likely to be found guilty than white defendants.

Distortions also occur in the recording of crimes in which the victim is a woman, such as rape and assault. The 1988 PNAD indicated that more women than men fail to report physical abuses to the police, and Mingardi has confirmed that policemen receive their cases without sympathy. Rape is commonly considered to be a type of crime that is underrecorded. In Brazil, it is common knowledge that women who do report rape are treated as though they were responsible for the aggression and are subject to humiliating physical examinations. Even if the case goes to trial, a woman is unlikely to see her male attacker found guilty.[12] Aware of those problems, during the administration of André Franco Montoro the government of São Paulo established the first women's police station (Delegacias de Defesa da Mulher) in 1985. (The same administration created the first council in charge of women's questions—Conselho da Condição Feminina—at the state level.) All the officers working in those stations are women, and a campaign in the mass media encouraged women to report crimes to those special stations. In 1996 there were 9 such stations in the city of São Paulo, 11 in the other municipalities of the metropolitan region, and 104 more in the state's interior.[13] In the year following the establishment of the first women's police station, the number of rapes reported in the metropolitan region of São Paulo increased by 25 percent. This increase is probably a good indication of how reports reflect conditions other than the actual incidence of crimes.

In cases of vehicle theft or break-ins, many insurance policies require owners to provide a copy of the police report in order to process claims. This rule probably makes for more accurate statistics for vehicle larceny than for other types of larceny.

Finally, it is usually accepted in studies of crime that statistics of homicide are the most accurate and the best for comparison, because they are relatively immune to problems of definition or to variations in policy. This is also probably true in Brazil, where homicides are reported in various ways: not only by the families of the victims but also by other institutions, such as hospitals that have to complete death reports and the IML (Instituto Médico Legal, or Legal Medicine Institute), which is in charge of verifying deaths. Even so, not all homicides are reported; anyone who reads Brazilian newspapers knows about unidentified bodies found in empty lots with gun-shot wounds. Moreover, the fact that mortality statistics may be less dis-torted does not mean that they are problem-free. The circumstances of a death determine who reports it and to which institution, thus affecting the elaboration of different statistics. In particular, not all unnatural deaths are classified as homicides. The large numbers of deaths provoked by the mili-tary police are registered by the civil police not as homicides but as a spe-cial type of occurrence called "resistance followed by death" *(resistência seguida de morte)*, later classified as "other occurrences" in the final tabu-lations of crime.[14] As a consequence, these deaths (1,470 in 1992, compared to a total of 2,838 registered homicides) are not represented in the statistics I analyze here. They are discussed separately in chapter 5.

There are also different forms of records for violent deaths. In most coun-tries, at least two records are kept: one from the criminal or judiciary sys-tem and one from the health authorities. In Brazil, things are complicated even further by the existence of two branches of the police. For example, for deaths in car accidents, at least three official records are made in São Paulo: one by the civil police, which records cases brought to police stations, often by relatives considering a legal suit; one by the military police, the branch that is called to the scene of the accident and receives reports from the IML; and one by the civil registry (Registro Civil), which registers births and deaths and produces vital statistics.[15] From 1981 to 1986, the civil po-lice registered less than half of the cases reported by the military police (3,017 compared to 1,141 in 1983, for example). Moreover, the civil registry records do not coincide with either of the police sources and since 1987 have been significantly higher than both. In 1996, the military police registered 1,113 deaths, the civil police 1,436, and the civil registry 2,368. In some years the civil registry numbers were lower than the military police data, perhaps be-cause it classifies victims according to their place of residence (which may be outside the municipality of São Paulo), whereas the data from the mili-tary police are categorized according to where the accident occurred. Fur-ther, in 1986 the military police changed its methodology: instead of rely-ing on reports from the IML, it started to count the victims at the accident site. Thus, in later years, accident victims who died in hospitals were not in-cluded in the military police records. In addition, neither of the two police sources accounts for deaths on federal roads, which are registered by the federal road police (Polícia Rodoviária Federal). This is only one example of the problematic nature of the available numbers.

Given these distortions, one might wonder if it is even worth looking at the statistics. The affirmative answer relies on two facts. First, police reports are the only source of quantitative data available. Second, we can probably assume that distortions are relatively constant over time, and thus we can identify temporal trends. Even this possibility is limited, however, because changes in reporting methods preclude the construction of long historical series. In 1980, the department of public security of the state of São Paulo changed the way crimes were grouped, introducing problems of comparison. After that date, however, the statistics started to be shown in more detailed categories, allowing a more sophisticated analysis for the period 1981–1996. For this reason, my analysis focuses on these years. Only two categories could be compared for previous years. They are the broad categories "crimes against persons" and "crimes against property," for which I was able to construct a series for the period 1973–1996 for the metropolitan region of São Paulo—more exactly, for the Police Region of Greater São Paulo (Região Policial da Grande São Paulo), which does not coincide exactly with the administrative division of the metropolitan region.[16]

CRIME TRENDS, 1973–1996

Table 2 presents the most important categories of crime used by the civil police to produce statistics. These are based on definitions established by the Brazilian penal code. It also presents the English translation I have adopted. These classifications have some peculiarities. One of them is to consider a death that occurs during a robbery (latrocínio) as a crime against property and not, like murder, as a crime against persons. Another is to consider rape as a crime against custom and not against persons. In the same category are crimes such as unusual sexual acts, seduction, prostitution, and oral sex (penal code, title IV). Moreover, the code maintains a distinction between "honest" and "dishonest" women. According to the penal code—which dates from 1940 and contains articles that contradict the 1988 constitution—in the case of rape the judicial object to be protected is custom, not the woman's body. Because rape does not appear as an isolated classification in the statistics that I am considering before 1981, it is impossible to analyze its previous evolution, and its incidence is not reflected in the following analysis, which is based only on the categories of crimes against persons and against property. These classifications of crime are a good indication of the Brazilian conception of individual rights and its embedded disregard for the individual and his or her rights, which can be extreme in the case of women and children. They also reveal a great deal about Brazilian

TABLE 2 Brazilian Categories of Crime Statistics and English Translations

Crimes contra a pessoa	Crimes against persons
Homicídio	Homicide
Homicídio doloso	Murder
Homicídio culposo	Manslaughter
Lesão corporal dolosa	Aggravated assault
Acidentes de trânsito	Traffic accidents
Homicído culposo	Manslaughter
Lesão corporal	Assault
Outros (infanticídio, aborto, omissão de socorro, etc.)	Others (infanticide, abortion, failure to render aid, etc.)

Crimes contra o patrimônio	Crimes against property
Furto	Larceny
Furto qualificado	Aggravated larceny
Roubo	Robbery
Latrocínio	Robbery followed by death
Estelionato	Fraud
Outros	Others

Crimes contra os costumes	Crimes against custom
Estupro	Rape
Sedução	Seduction
Prostituição	Prostitution
Outros	Others

Crimes contra a incolumidade pública	Crimes against public safety
Tráfico de entorpecentes	Drug trafficking
Uso de entorpecentes	Drug use
Outros	Others

conceptions of sexual roles and of women's sexuality. Although Brazilian feminists have been active in making suggestions and trying to approve changes in the ordinary legislation, and although they were able to introduce important provisions regarding gender equality in the 1988 constitution and considerably change laws regarding the family (for example, eliminating the notions that the husband is the chief of the family and that the wife owes him obedience), the existing legislation and statistics are still shaped by traditional male-oriented notions.[17]

Deaths and physical injury resulting from car accidents are high.[18] In spite of their importance, I did not include these data in the general calculations of crimes against persons for the period 1973 to 1996 because, being accidents, they are very different events from murder and aggravated assault.

The trends in crimes against persons and against property in the metropolitan region of São Paulo (MRSP) between 1973 and 1996 are shown in figure 1.[19] Property crimes have been responsible for more than 50 percent of the reports since the early 1980s.[20] On average, they grew 6.09 percent annually during the period considered, while crimes against persons increased by an average of 2.18 percent. As a result, the proportion of crimes against property jumped from around 30 percent of total crime in the mid-1970s to more than 60 percent from the mid-1980s to the present, reaching 69.36 percent in 1996. At the same time, the proportion of crimes against persons in total crime remained relatively stable, oscillating between 15 and 23 percent of the total. Because the number of crimes against persons in 1980 was underestimated, due to the change in the methodology of aggregation of crimes, I disregard the decrease of 1980 and the increase of 1981. Total crime is more than the sum of crimes against persons and property crimes.

Property crime reached its highest level in 1994 (2,339 crimes per 100,000 population). However, the years that marked a change in the level of property crimes were 1983 and 1984, when rates increased 26.78 percent and 33.34 percent and stabilized at a new plateau. Property crimes had already increased considerably during 1978 (22.14 percent) and 1979 (16.99 percent), but at that time the rate per 100,000 population (1,187) was half of what it became after the mid-1980s (around 2,000 from 1984 on).

Growth of crimes against persons is not as high if one considers all types of occurrences in this category together. The worst years were the most recent, especially 1993 and 1994 (with 817 and 819 crimes per 100,000 population). Although during the late 1970s the rates of crimes against persons were quite elevated (656 crimes per 100,000 population in 1978, for example), it is clear that since the middle 1980s these crimes have also increased considerably. Their rate in 1994 was double what it was twenty years before (412 per 100,000).

The pattern of criminality in the municipality of São Paulo (hereafter MSP) shows some important differences from the other municipalities of

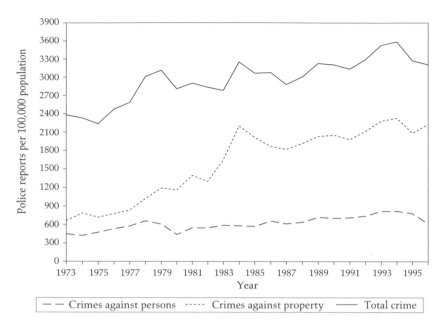

FIGURE 1.   Rates of crime, Metropolitan Region of São Paulo, 1973–1996.

the metropolitan region (hereafter OM). Figure 2 shows that the rates of total crime per 100,000 population are considerably higher in the city of São Paulo than in the other municipalities. Moreover, in some years criminality in the capital and in the other municipalities had opposite patterns, the clearest example being 1986. The data also indicate that whereas crimes against persons increased an average of 0.39 percent per year in the city of São Paulo between 1976 and 1996, they increased an average of 4.89 percent annually in the other municipalities. As a result, the OM have more than doubled their share of the total number of crimes against persons in the metropolitan region during the period considered (from 20.92 percent to 46.35 percent). The average rate of increase of the crimes against property was also higher in the OM (7.66 percent per year) than in the MSP (6.35 percent) in the period 1976–1996. In sum, as the interviews in chapter 2 also indicate, increases in violence have been lower in the center, where the wealthier population lives, than in the outskirts, where the majority of the population is poor. A recent study by the Núcleo de Estudos de Seguridade e Assistência Social indicates that in the municipality of São Paulo, the rates of crimes against property are highest in the upper- and middle-class neighborhoods, whereas the rates of homicide are highest in the poorest districts of the city (1995:tables 42A and 43A of the annex).

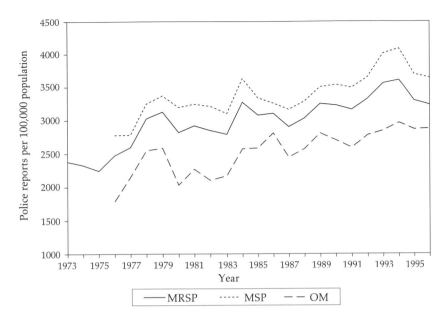

FIGURE 2.   Rates of total crime, MRSP, MSP, and OM, 1973–1996.

Statistics are constructions, and, depending on how they are designed and how the numbers are aggregated or separated, they can give different pictures of "social reality." Such shifts become clear when, instead of looking at the larger categories, we examine specific types of crime. This kind of analysis is possible for the period 1981–1996. It is important to keep in mind that although in 1981 the level of crime had already decreased after the peak of 1978–1979, it had increased considerably in the late 1970s.

Violent Crime

That more violent forms of crime increased more than less violent forms can be seen by aggregating the totals of homicide and attempted homicide, aggravated assault, rape and attempted rape, robbery, and felony murder into a single category of "violent crime." At the beginning of the 1980s they represented around 20 percent of the total of reported crimes; after 1984 they represented around 30 percent of the total, reaching 36.28 percent in 1996. This striking change indicates that in the early 1980s it was not only the quantity of crime that increased but also, and maybe more important, its *quality*.

In addition to showing a growth in violence, data indicate that violent

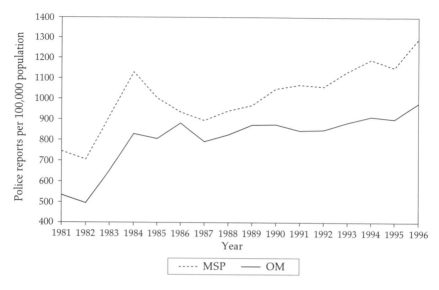

FIGURE 3.   Rates of violent crime, MSP and OM, 1981–1996.

crimes grew more in the OM (average of 5.0 percent per year) than in the MSP (4.22 percent). Nevertheless, rates per capita are still higher in the city of São Paulo. Figure 3 also indicates that the peak of violent crime both in the MSP and in the OM in the period considered occurred in 1996, after significant increases in 1983 and 1984 (1986 in the OM). Rates of violent crime have been increasing consistently since 1988, especially in the MSP. Since 1990, rates of violent crime have exceeded 1,000 occurrences per 100,000 population in the MSP and 850 in the OM.

Crimes against Persons

I consider separately three main types of crimes against persons: homicide (murder and manslaughter), aggravated assault, and rape. They do not correspond to the category of crimes against persons I have considered before because of the inclusion of rape and the exclusion of the category "others," and they do not correspond to the category of violent crimes because they exclude violent property crimes. Frequently in the official statistics, the number of reports for one category of crime includes "attempted" crimes: for example, homicide and attempted homicide. In the following analysis I specify when I am considering attempted crimes as well. In most cases, I do not take into consideration the numbers of attempted homicides but include only homicides, as is usually the practice in crime analysis. However, I do con-

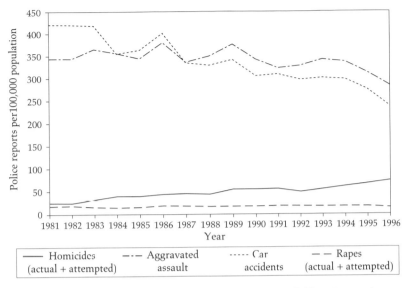

FIGURE 4.   Rates of selected crimes against persons, MRSP, 1981–1996.

sider the attempted rapes, because in Brazil the reports of rape are unreliable, and probably many rapes are classified only as attempted rape. Figure 4 compares the rates of homicide and attempted homicide, aggravated assault, rape and attempted rape, and victims of car accidents (both fatalities and injuries) in the whole metropolitan region. As expected, the rates of aggravated assault are significantly higher than the others. In fact, aggravated assault represents on average 10 percent of total reported crime, whereas homicide represents less than 1 percent and rape around 0.5 percent. As a consequence, aggravated assault influences the shape of the curve of crimes against persons more than the other types of crime. Because aggravated assault either decreased (in the MSP) or increased only a little (in the OM), the increase in rates of crimes against persons was moderate. If we look at each category separately, however, the picture is quite different.

As I mentioned before, differences between the MSP and the OM are important, with crimes against persons increasing more in the OM. In the case of aggravated assault, there was a decrease in the MSP (−2.50 percent annual average) and an increase in the OM (1.96 percent annual average), which surpassed the rates per 100,000 population of the MSP in 1985. In 1996, the rates of aggravated assault per 100,000 population were 371.70 in the OM and 234.15 in the MSP, the lowest levels since 1981. In the case of rape , the variations were similar until the 1990s, when the city's rates began to de-

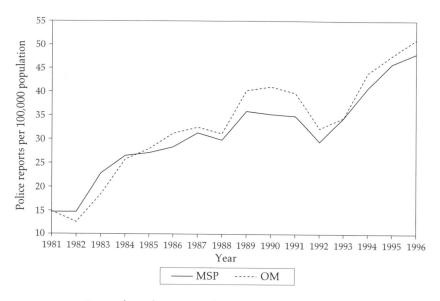

FIGURE 5.   Rates of murder, MSP and OM, 1981–1996.

cline. Rates in the OM have been higher than those in the MSP for the whole period (around 19 per 100,000 population, compared to 14 in the MSP). However, both assaults and rapes are probably underestimated because of people's failure to report them. The highest number of reports of rape occurred in 1986, following the opening of the first women's police station.

Murder was the crime with the highest rates of average increase between 1981 and 1996. The average annual variations were similar in the city of São Paulo (9.28 percent) and in the OM (10.05 percent). As figure 5 shows, both in the center and on the periphery of the metropolitan region, the rate of murder increased constantly in the 1980s. It reached 47.29 murders per 100,000 population in 1996, a figure significantly higher than the 14.62 of 1981. These rates were determined according to police reports and differ from those determined on the basis of compulsory death registration and classified according to the ICD categories.[21] As table 3 demonstrates, the differentials are high during the whole period considered. However, the discrepancy seems to represent a problem of volume but not of tendency of growth, as figure 6 makes evident: the annual rates of growth of murder registration by the civil police and the civil registry have been quite similar, especially in the municipality of São Paulo. In other words, although the data from death registration consistently indicate more murders than data from the civil police, both show a similar pattern of growth between 1981 and 1996.

TABLE 3 Murders by Source, MSP, MRSP, and OM, 1981–1996

Year	MRSP Civil Police	MRSP Civil Registry	% Difference	MSP Civil Police	MSP Civil Registry	% Difference	OM Civil Police	OM Civil Registry	% Difference
1981	1,875	2,758	47.09	1,251	1,754	40.21	624	1,004	60.90
1982	1,820	2,645	45.33	1,275	1,737	36.24	545	908	66.61
1983	2,837	3,964	39.73	2,009	2,613	30.06	828	1,351	63.16
1984	3,559	4,907	37.88	2,369	3,248	37.10	1,190	1,659	39.41
1985	3,766	4,914	30.48	2,436	3,186	30.79	1,330	1,728	29.92
1986	4,110	5,117	24.50	2,576	3,209	24.57	1,534	1,908	24.38
1987	4,462	5,734	28.51	2,868	3,573	24.58	1,594	2,161	35.57
1988	4,402	5,419	23.10	2,772	3,258	17.53	1,630	2,161	32.58
1989	5,546	6,492	17.06	3,370	3,819	13.32	2,176	2,673	22.84
1990	5,639	6,911	22.56	3,345	4,025	20.33	2,294	2,886	25.81
1991	5,634	6,973	23.77	3,342	4,305	28.82	2,292	2,668	16.40
1992	4,749	6,307	32.81	2,838	3,895	37.24	1,911	2,412	26.22
1993	5,434	6,459	18.86	3,324	3,894	17.15	2,110	2,565	21.56
1994	6,652	7,419	11.53	3,959	4,432	11.95	2,693	2,987	10.92
1995	7,410	8,802	18.79	4,485	5,379	19.93	2,925	3,423	17.03
1996	7,842	n.a.[a]	n.a.	4,710	5,465	16.03	3,132	n.a.	n.a.

SOURCE: Seade, *Anuário Estatístico do Estado de São Paulo*, various years.

NOTE: Data from the civil registry correspond to the ICD categories E960–E969, frequently referred to as homicide. Since this classification excludes unlawful deaths of undetermined intentionality, I name it murder, making it comparable to the civil police category of *homicídio doloso* (murder), which excludes manslaughter (*homicídio culposo*). Civil registry data refer to people whose residence was in the municipality of São Paulo.

[a]n.a. = not available

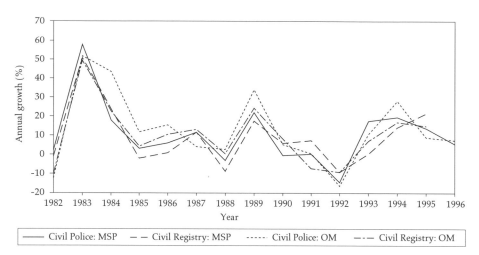

FIGURE 6.   Evolution of murder registration, MSP and OM, 1981–1996.

Feiguin and Lima suggest that the large discrepancy in homicide records may be explained by the fact that police reports refer to incidents instead of to individual deaths, as is the case in death registration. One incident of murder may involve several deaths. As a result, when analyzing data from 1988 to 1993, they suggest that the discrepancy may be associated with an increase of multiple deaths (called *chacinas*) in recent years, a phenomenon whose existence is asserted by the press (Feiguin and Lima 1995:77). Nevertheless, since the difference in the beginning of the 1980s is higher than or comparable to discrepancies of more recent years (see table 3) it is difficult to demonstrate a trend toward multiple murders in recent years.[22]

Feiguin and Lima also suggest two other hypotheses to explain the discrepancies. The first is that they have different geographic references, the police reports referring to the place of the event and the death certificates to the place of the death, which could be a hospital away from the site of the crime.[23] However, this does not seem to be the case. If it were, the differentials in the city of São Paulo, which has a higher concentration of hospitals, should be higher than the differences in the OM, where one could argue that more events would happen.[24] However, in some years exactly the opposite happens, with the differences in the OM being higher. The second additional hypothesis Feiguin and Lima advance is that the differences are deliberately introduced to "avoid the dissemination of panic among the population" (1995:78). For this to be correct, however, would require the existence of an explicit policy to hide information, which seems improbable given the public authorities' insistence that there has been an increase in violence. Moreover, it seems unlikely that such a policy would affect the civil registry.

My alternative explanation takes into consideration the deaths caused by the military police. According to the department of public security, these deaths are recorded as "resistance followed by death" in the category "other crimes" and are not therefore registered as either murder or manslaughter by the civil police, though they may be registered as such by the civil registry. Since in some years the number of these deaths is elevated (more than 1,000—see below), they could help to explain the differences. Another explanation is the exclusion from police murder statistics of deaths that occurred during a robbery (latrocínio); these are probably classified as murder by the civil registry, and in recent years there have been around four hundred per year in the MRSP. If we add the number of killings by police not classified as murder, the number of felony murders (latrocínio) also not included in the civil police totals for murder, and the number of multiple murders registered as one event of murder, we can account for a significant portion of the total difference between the two sources. For example, in 1993 the difference was 1,025. In that year, there were 333 felony murders and 243 killings by the police in the MRSP, or a total of 576, which account for 56 percent of the difference. In 1994, felony murders and police killings can account for 87.2 percent of the difference and in 1995 for 46.7 percent.

In addition to indicating that police reports underestimate the number of murders, the data based on compulsory death registration allow for a more complex analysis of the recent increase in violence. In the last fifteen years, the proportion of violent deaths (accidents, homicides, and suicide) among total deaths has almost doubled in the metropolitan region of São Paulo: they accounted for 8.95 percent of deaths in 1978, 15.82 percent in 1991, and 14.11 percent in 1993. Since 1989, violent deaths have been the second leading cause of death in Brazil, whereas in 1980 they were the fourth (Souza and Minayo 1995:90). In São Paulo, they have been the second leading cause in recent years (after respiratory diseases).

Murder is responsible for the significant increase in this group of causes, since the proportion of the other "external causes" in the total number of deaths has remained relatively constant. Whereas in 1978 murder caused 1.44 percent of the deaths in the city of São Paulo, in 1994 it caused 6.57 percent, an increase of 356 percent. In 1994, murders accounted for 19.15 percent of the deaths of people between twenty and forty-nine years of age in the MSP, becoming the main cause of death in this age group. This rate is dramatically different from that of 1976, when murder accounted for only

4.9 percent of the deaths in the same age group. The rate has been especially elevated among youths. In 1994, 44.40 percent of the deaths of people aged fifteen to twenty-four were caused by murder. During the 1980s, murders increased 80 percent among ten- to fourteen-year-olds (Souza 1994:49). In 1994, 61.6 percent of the victims of murder in the MRSP were between fifteen and twenty-nine years old. Adolescent criminality has also increased, but in a proportion significantly lower than that of adolescent victimization (see Feiguin and Lima 1995:78–80). Moreover, violent deaths affect five times more young men than young women (Souza and Minayo 1995:94). In 1994 in the MRSP, 93.0 percent of all murder victims were men.

In addition to increasingly affecting the young, and more males than females, there are indications that murder also disproportionately affects poor people. A recent study by the Núcleo de Estudos de Seguridade e Assistência Social, comparing homicide rates and socioeconomic indicators in the ninety-six districts of the city of São Paulo, showed that the districts with the highest incidence of homicide had a bad quality of life and a predominance of low-income families (1995: especially tables 40A, 42A, and 43A). According to Pro-Aim (Programa de Aprimoramento de Informações de Mortalidade no Município de São Paulo) data for 1995, the districts of the city of São Paulo with the highest murder rates were mostly very poor (96.87 per 100,000 population in Jardim Ângela, 88.44 in Grajaú, 83.20 in Parelheiros, 76.86 in Jardim São Luís, and 75.28 in Capão Redondo). Others with high rates were deteriorating central districts of town (87.93 in Sé and 79.51 in Brás). The lowest rates were among middle- or upper-class districts in central areas (2.87 in Perdizes, 11.50 in Moema, 12.54 in Vila Mariana, 13.52 in Bela Vista, and 13.78 in Pinheiros).

Contrary to pre-1979 trends, as well as to the pattern in the United States, where deaths in motor vehicle accidents are on average double those from homicide, in the city of São Paulo homicides have caused more deaths than motor vehicles since 1983, and in 1992 this proportion was doubled (6.18, compared to 2.98). These are data from death registration. According to both the civil police and the military police, the number of injuries and deaths in car accidents decreased in the MSP (an average of −4.31 percent per year) and in the OM −0.45 percent). However, according to health authority data analyzed by Mello Jorge and Latorre (1994:30), the rates of deaths by car accidents per 100,000 population have remained relatively stable since 1970 (around 25), after having increased 151 percent between 1960 and 1970. Although deaths and injuries have not increased much in recent years, the number of car accidents in the MSP has more than doubled in the last two decades, according to the military police. In 1996, there were 195,378 car accidents in the MSP, an average of 535 accidents per day. Of these, 13.16 percent resulted in fatalities or injuries.

The increase of violent deaths is not restricted to São Paulo. Homicide rates increased in most Brazilian metropolitan regions during the 1980s (Souza 1994:53–55). As a consequence, the homicide rates for Brazil, which were similar to those of the United States in the early 1980s (around 10 per 100,000), were more than twice the American rates by the late 1980s. The U.S. homicide rate has historically been high compared to Western European and Japanese rates.[25] In other words, the contemporary Brazilian homicide rates, above 20, are very high indeed compared to those of the United States, European countries, and Japan in recent decades. However, national rates hide local disparities, and many urban areas have homicide rates considerably higher than the national average. In Brazil during the late 1980s and 1990s, Rio de Janeiro, Recife, and São Paulo were the three most violent metropolitan regions, with homicide rates higher than 40 per 100,000 people, according to data of death registration (Souza 1994). In the United States in 1993, some cities had much higher rates, such as New Orleans (80.34), Washington, D.C. (78.54), Detroit (56.76), and Atlanta (50.38). In other large cities, the rates are comparable to those of São Paulo, but still lower. In 1993, Miami's was 34.09, Los Angeles's 30.52, and New York's 26.48. However, homicide rates in the United States have oscillated less than in Brazil, and they have decreased significantly since the early 1990s. It is hard to obtain comparable information for other third world cities and countries. National data on causes of death compiled by the United Nations are not available for most African and Asian countries. Latin American countries in the 1990s have had relatively high homicide rates (on average, more than 5 per 100,000), and the Caribbean has had even higher rates (more than 10). Colombia has one of the highest rates in the world: 74.4 in 1990. Brazil (20.2 in 1989), Mexico (17.2 in 1991), and Venezuela (12.1 in 1989) have the next highest rates in Latin America.[26]

Crimes against Property and Other Crimes

Crimes against property in São Paulo represent the majority of reported crimes: larceny accounts for around 37 percent of the reports and robbery for around 17 percent. Robbery has seen the second highest increase (8.95 percent average annual growth), just behind murder. The worst years for crimes against property were 1984, 1985, and the early 1990s, as can be seen

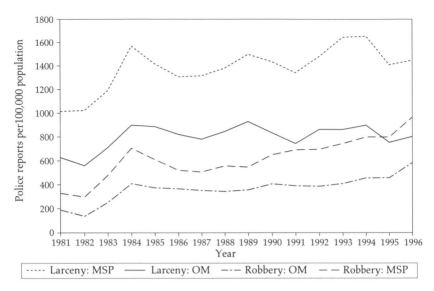

FIGURE 7.   Rates of larceny and robbery, MSP and OM, 1981–1996.

in figure 7. Robbery increased more than larceny (an average of 8.95 percent and of 2.44 percent, respectively), and the average growth of robbery
in the OM (10.57 percent) was a little higher than in the MSP (9.18 percent). This trend repeats the pattern of increase in crimes against persons:
more violent forms of crime increase at a higher rate, and rates of growth
are higher on the periphery than in the center of the metropolitan region.
However, we should be careful with these conclusions, because in general
violent crimes are better reported because of their severity. Moreover, rates
of property crimes per 100,000 population remain higher in the MSP than
in the OM. Larceny and robbery of motor vehicles constitute an average of
20 percent of all larceny and robbery. These crimes have grown at similar
rates in the MSP and in the OM (5.44 percent and 5.78 percent, respectively), but the rate per capita is twice as high in the center (854 compared
to 443 crimes per 100,000 population in 1996). According to the study of
the Núcleo de Estudos de Seguridade e Assistência Social for the city of São
Paulo, the wealthy and central districts have the highest robbery rates (1995:
table 43A).

Another way of evaluating the increase in violence is to look at the registration of guns and reports of illegal possession of weapons. The annual
number of registered guns purchased in the metropolitan region jumped
from 9,832 in 1983 to 66,870 in 1994, an increase of 580 percent. These num-

bers, however, are far from accurate in portraying the increase of weapons among the population, since the apprehension of nonregistered guns has also increased considerably. Police reports of illegal possession of guns grew an average of 8.62 percent a year between 1981 and 1996 in the MSP and 10.51 percent in the OM. In 1996, the police registered 5,563 cases of illegal possession of guns in the MRSP. As reported in the media, many of these guns are smuggled into the country, and some (especially those used by drug dealers) are more powerful than those used by the police. As gun possession has increased, a higher proportion of homicides have been committed with guns. According to death registration data, in 1980 homicides by firearms accounted for 14.8 percent of all homicides in São Paulo; in 1989 they accounted for 31.2 percent (Souza 1994:55), and in 1992 29.26 percent. The increase in the possession of guns not only indicates an increase in crime and violence but also shows how São Paulo's residents are increasingly taking the task of defense into their own hands.

Drug trafficking and police violence have played a role in the changes in crime trends. The latter is a significant component of the increase in violence in Brazil, and I analyze it separately in chapter 5. Reports of drug trafficking range between 18 and 30 incidents per 100,000 population in the MRSP for the period 1981–1986. However, it is hard to detect a pattern, for rates fluctuate sharply. Nevertheless, both public authorities and the media assert that drug trafficking—especially the crack trade in São Paulo—has led to an increase in violence. However, such claims are difficult to confirm because of the lack of concrete information.

LOOKING FOR EXPLANATIONS

Social scientists usually offer three main types of explanations for criminality and its variations. First, crime is related to factors such as urbanization, migration, poverty, industrialization, and illiteracy. Second, it is connected to the performance and characteristics of the institutions in charge of order: primarily the police, but also courts, prisons, and legislation. Third, psychological explanations focus on the personality of individual criminals. I consider the first two types of explanations, which are usually combined, but I do not address psychological factors, since I focus not on individual but on social phenomena. Moreover, to understand the present picture of criminality in São Paulo, it is necessary to consider three additional factors that cannot be quantified. Among these are, first, cultural elements such as dominant conceptions about the spread of evil and the role of authority, and conceptions of the manipulable body. In Brazil, these concepts are associated with the support of violent practices and with the delegitimation of individual rights. Second is the widespread adoption of illegal and private measures to combat criminality, whose effects undermine the mediating and regulating role of the justice system and feed a cycle of private revenge. This cycle can only increase violence. Third are policies concerning public security and traditional patterns of police performance: the violent action of the state in dealing with crime can only enhance violence, not control it. I start to present those arguments in this chapter and develop them in chapters 4, 5, and 9.

Any attempt at explaining crime in São Paulo is severely limited by the quality of the data. Criminality in São Paulo and in Brazil has not been studied in depth, especially in recent years. The more detailed studies available, both for Brazil and for Latin America, examine criminality at the beginning of the twentieth century, and almost all of them focus on the question of crime in early industrialization, following an international approach emphasizing the effects of the imposition of an urban social order.[27] More recent studies of violence in Latin America usually refer to exceptional situations, such as the dirty wars in Chile, Argentina, and Uruguay, the war in Central America, the drug-traffic conflicts in Colombia, and the guerrilla movement in Peru.[28]

Only after criminality became an issue at the beginning of the last decade did some researchers look at the statistics for the metropolitan region of São Paulo. Most studies, however, either focus on even shorter historical series than I have been able to put together (Batich 1988; Feiguin 1985; Feiguin and Lima 1995; Mingardi 1992; Nepp 1990) or analyze specific types of crime separately (Minayo 1994; Souza 1994; Souza and Minayo 1995). In general, these studies are descriptive and do not advance detailed explanations but only suggest in generic terms that the increase in crime might be associated with the economic crisis of the early 1980s and with high rates of unemployment. The only exception is the study by Pezzin (1987). There are studies for other cities, such as those of Paixão (1983; 1986; 1988; 1990) for Belo Horizonte and Coelho (1978; 1980; 1988) for Rio de Janeiro. Their main contributions were methodological critiques indicating the limitations and biases of official statistics and undermining traditional views that associate crime with poverty and marginality. More recently, there have been a series of studies of the spatial distribution of crime that try to access the risk of violence in Brazilian cities.[29] Although these maps show a strong correlation between poor areas and violence, they do not advance explanations for the increase in violence. For Rio de Janeiro, Zaluar has conducted important ethnographic studies in working-class areas, and Velho (1987; 1991) among the middle classes. Zaluar has analyzed the interrelationships of workers and "bandits" and their views of crime and life (1983; 1985; 1987; 1990; 1994), but she does not develop any quantitative analyses.

Recent studies on criminal patterns in the United States and Europe seriously question the association of poverty and criminality that is considered commonsense in everyday talk about crime (Chesnais 1981; Gurr 1979; Lane 1980, 1986; Tittle, Villemez, and Smith 1978). These studies reconsider the conventional association of rising crime with the rapid growth of cities and urban poverty that marked the beginning of industrialization—an argument advanced, for example, by Chevalier (1973 [1958]). Moreover, these studies dispute the commonsense notion that violence increases with urbanization and industrialization. In a broad study comparing crime statistics for European countries and the United States from the mid-nineteenth century through the late 1970s, Jean-Claude Chesnais argues that, although the feeling of insecurity may have increased, "there was during the last centuries and the last decades a considerable regression of violent criminality" (1981:14). According to him, looking at this long period, "globally, *direct violence against persons* . . . is in a clear decline by comparison to the past and it is exactly for the most serious crimes that the decline is the most evident. The trend is indisputable, perhaps even more accentuated than the numbers suggest, because the records have rather improved and in any case they are more certain the more serious the crime" (1981:441, emphasis in the original).

For Chesnais, the *longue-durée* pattern of decrease in violence against persons was driven by processes such as the diminution of scarcity and poverty; the demographic revolution, with decreasing mortality and the valorization of life; and, especially, the growth of the state with its repressive institutions (the police and the justice system) and disciplinary institutions such as schools and the army. These processes were accompanied by a deep transformation of mores and mentalities that are described by Norbert Elias (1994 [1939]) as a taming of instincts. Chesnais's hypothesis is that this process had different effects in various regions in Europe and the United States but that it ultimately spread everywhere, reducing interpersonal violence. Chesnais even argues that "according to a classic law of criminology, the *movement of global criminality increases with economic development, while serious criminality regresses*" (1981:443, emphasis in the original). According to Chesnais, violent crime decreased consistently from the Middle Ages until the late 1970s, and to understand this transformation it is necessary to look at institutional and cultural transformations instead of focusing only on socioeconomic variables.

Roger Lane also disputes the simple association of rising crime with the growth of cities and industrialization, arguing that the famous "offenses against the order" of early urbanization "fluctuated more often in response to changing public policies than to changing behavior" (1986:2). Moreover, both violent crimes—especially homicide, the most serious and best recorded of all crimes—and some property crimes seem to have decreased continuously during urbanization.

> Although crimes against property usually tended to increase in times of hardship and decrease in times of prosperity, while crimes of violence reacted to the economic cycle in precisely the opposite way, these short-term fluctuations only masked the fact that both types of crime were decreasing over the long term, often sharply so. The downward trend began typically sometime toward the middle of the nineteenth century. It continued for a long time, in most places until the middle of the twentieth century. Only recently has the incidence of crime begun to increase again, most clearly from about 1960. The typical pattern, then, has been a long U-curve rather than a simple line running parallel to urban growth and development. . . . This U-curve in criminality has proved a nearly universal pattern. (Lane 1986:2)

Probably because he focuses on more recent periods, Lane describes a U-curve instead of the linear decline indicated by Chesnais, who tends to disregard short-term variations in order to emphasize broader tendencies. But such variations are important for understanding contemporary issues. Explanations for the U-curve, and especially for the increase in violence after the 1960s, are still vague. For the preceding period, the role of the consolidation of the state and institutions of order seems incontestable, as does that of the "civilizing process" and the consequent internal pacification of European societies described by Elias. It also seems clear that the bottom of the U-curve coincides with the maturity of capitalism (what some would call its Fordist phase) and the optimism of the postwar period.

Current patterns of crime, however, differ from those of early industrialization. For example, violence in association with property crime is growing, as indicated by the fact that armed robbery has increased faster than any other crime in the United States (Lane 1986:173) and in São Paulo. Moreover, the general shape of the curve cannot reflect specific experiences. For the African-American population, for example, the experience of crime has followed not a U shape but a linear upward trend. For Lane (1986), culture and historical experience, more than poverty or income, account for this reality. If data were available, we would probably find a similar pattern for Brazilian blacks, who constitute the majority of those killed by the police in São Paulo (Pinheiro et al. 1991) and a disproportionate number of those inside the penitentiaries (Brant 1986).

Such analysis of criminal patterns in the United States and Europe may help us formulate some explanations for contemporary São Paulo's violent criminality. This perspective suggests that trends in violent criminality can be explained in part by the history of institutions of order and by long-term cultural patterns molding individual behavior and interpersonal relationships. Because the statistics are precarious—we cannot prove or disprove the existence of a long-term U-curve in São Paulo—the hypotheses we can formulate are restricted. However, contrary to Pezzin's analysis, the recent pattern of increase in violent crime cannot be explained by economic and urbanization variables alone.[30]

Although the studies by Pezzin and by Coelho remain attached to socioeconomic explanations for the increase in crime, their analyses help to qualify the alternative hypothesis I present at the end of the chapter. Liliana Pezzin's (1987) study is based on temporal and cross-section models in which she correlates the rates of crimes against persons and crimes against property with variables such as levels of urbanization, demographic density, population growth, residential distance from downtown, poverty rate, unemployment rate, industrial activity, migration, and state per capita expenditures on security. The design of her variables was directly inspired by the long tradition of studies of crime in the contexts of industrialization and urbanization. However, for the period that she studied (1970–1984), she might well be viewing the other side of the U-curve, which demands new explanations. Moreover, to explain the increase in violence as well as in property crimes, which is in fact the most important change in the criminality pattern in the 1980s, she might have to look at other processes.

Pezzin was unable to find significant statistical correlation between her variables and crimes against persons. She concluded that crimes against persons (what she calls crimes of "psychological strength") are not much affected either by socioeconomic variables and levels of urbanization or by state expenditures on public security (Pezzin 1987:108–9). This finding contradicts other studies of criminality that show that violent crime, in the long run, decreased with the cultural and institutional changes that accompanied urbanization, industrialization, the demographic transition, the consolidation of nation-states, and the institutionalization of the police forces (for example, Chesnais 1981: introduction and chapter 1, and Gurr 1979:356–58). Moreover, in the short run, one would expect violent crime to diminish with an economic crisis (Lane 1986:2), exactly the opposite of what happened in

São Paulo in the period analyzed by Pezzin. Because the socioeconomic variables used by Pezzin probably cannot account for the increase in violent crime, she is left without explanations, and disregards some findings by associating them with, for example, psychological factors.

Pezzin found that, in contrast to what happened to crimes against persons, crimes against property were positively and significantly correlated with urbanization, poverty, migration, and unemployment (1987:108–9). State expenditures on security were also significantly correlated with property crime, and their values were clearly bigger than those associated with the urbanization and poverty variables. However, Pezzin based her conclusions exclusively on the correlation of property crimes with urban poverty variables, insisting that the increase in crime was related to the economic recession of the early 1980s and the level of poverty it produced.

Nevertheless, not all of Pezzin's socioeconomic indicators behaved as expected in relation to property crimes. Illiteracy, though significantly related to both crimes against persons and against property, demonstrated a negative correlation. Unable to explain this finding, Pezzin attributed it to problems of collinearity (1987:109). However, research conducted by Brant (1986) among the prison population of the state of São Paulo showed that the level of formal education of the prisoners (only 3 percent illiterate, 54.9 percent with four years of primary education, and 36.1 percent with high school education) "is above [the] national average and, in some cases, even above the average of the state of São Paulo" (Brant 1986:50). Moreover, he showed that 54.3 percent of the prisoners were employed when they were arrested (1986:81) and that 37.2 percent of the unemployed had been unemployed for less than six months (1986:82). A large number of the prisoners had a continuous occupational history and had held various regular jobs (1986:50). These findings indicate not problems of collinearity but rather aspects of a social reality not addressed by old theories and stereotypes. In addition, Brant's conclusions contradict the only hypothesis Pezzin could present to address that which any other variable could explain, the increase in violence: "The increasing intensification of violence in property offenses seems to be . . . a symptom of new streams of contingents (of criminals) without the necessary *skill* or *experience*, and who compensate for this deficiency through the use of weapons" (Pezzin 1987:111, emphasis in original).

Besides not being supported by the data, this hypothesis presupposes that professional criminals are nonviolent, and that it is novices, perhaps those pushed into criminality by the economic crisis, who turn to violence. Moreover, it assumes that the majority of violent crime is committed by non-professionals. This assumption is in direct opposition to assertions by

Coelho (1988), Paixão (1983), Mingardi (1992), Zaluar (1994), and other crime analysts (such as newspaper reporters who cover the police and public security authorities on a daily basis) who insist that in the last decade crime has become increasingly organized and professional, and that this trend is exemplified in the use of guns, drug trafficking, and large-scale undertakings such as the robbing of whole buildings and the kidnapping of businessmen. As the newspapers have reported in detail, the networks associated with some kidnappings involve drug dealers, illegal lotteries such as *jogo do bicho*, politicians, lawyers, organized gangs inside prisons, and even the police. We are seeing the increase of organized and armed crime, not a wave of offenses committed by inexperienced individuals who turn to crime in a crisis.

But if Pezzin's hypothesis seems to have no merit, it is nevertheless coherent with the universe in which it was formulated, one that conceives of crime and violence in relation to indicators of urban poverty and marginality. When reality resists this model, these explanations weaken. In fact, socioeconomic explanations seem to weaken even more when the question is not just crime but *violent* crime. It is primarily violence we are trying to explain because, as indicated above, it was violence that radically changed the pattern of crime in 1983–1984.

Pezzin focuses almost exclusively on socioeconomic variables and does not pay much attention to the correlation between levels of criminality and state expenditures on public security. Coelho (1988), in contrast, seems to be willing to disregard socioeconomic variables and focus mainly on those associated with the repression of crime.

> First, until contrary empirical proofs appear, it would be advisable to forget the theories according to which poverty, illiteracy, unemployment, income inequality or economic crisis constitute cause or determinant factors of criminality. . . . Second, there is nothing surprising in the verification that the dissuasion variables have a deeper effect on criminality levels than socio-economic variables: the number of policemen in the streets has a direct relationship with options available to the potential offender, and what does not occur, for example, with the number of unemployed people at a certain moment. (Coelho 1988:153)

We should be careful with those conclusions. A greater investment in public security after 1984 did not in fact decrease the level of violent crime. Moreover, Coelho's assumptions seem to be based on an image of the police that does not coincide with Brazilian reality: in recent years, the police have become increasingly violent and involved with criminality. The ability of the police to control crime is thus called into question, and the police role in aggravating violence might be significant. Nevertheless, the majority of the population seems to think like Coelho, asking for more police on the streets and, worse, for a more violent police force. The case of the police can give us some important hints on how to consider violence in relation to other questions besides variables of economic performance and urban growth.

It is also important to consider state investment in public security. Rates of expenditures on public security presented by both Pezzin (1987:150) and Coelho (1988:180), although not coincident, show the same tendency: a sharp decrease in investment from 1979 on, reaching its lowest level in 1984. In other words, the years of greatest increase in crime rates coincide with both the lowest levels of investment in public security and the worst years of the economic crisis. It is therefore difficult to determine which factor had a stronger influence. Pezzin's data show that the highest level of investment occurred during the economically prosperous years of 1974 to 1978, when crimes against property also grew (1987:150). Moreover, intensive investment after 1984 was unable to drop rates of violent crime at the end of the decade.

A study by Nepp of the expenditures on public security for 1983 to 1989 shows that they increased continuously after 1984 (Nepp 1990:157). Expenditures refer to the increase of personnel and equipment. The total number of people (officers as well as administrative staff) in the military police in the state of São Paulo jumped from 53,829 in 1980 to 69,281 in 1989 and to 73,000 in 1995; in the civil police there were 15,874 staff in 1980; 26,383 in 1989; and 31,987 in 1995 (Nepp 1990:64, and department of public security). Considered together, these data show a personnel increase of 50.62 percent in the two police bodies, while the state population increased 31.38 percent. As a result, population to police ratio changed from 359:1 in 1980 to 308:1 in 1989 and to 313:1 in 1995. The number of police vehicles also increased. Between 1979 and 1982—the administration of Paulo Maluf, the last governor elected indirectly during military rule—only 391 new vehicles were bought. Between 1983 and 1986, during Franco Montoro's administration, 1181 new vehicles were purchased, and in 1987 and 1988, the first two years of Orestes Quércia's administration, 1136 were added (Nepp 1990:52). Moreover, the later administrations invested heavily in upgrading the police telecommunications system and electronic equipment, creating new police stations, and adding new services, such as stations specializing in women's issues and consumer questions (both of which were first created during Montoro's administration). All variables indicate an expansion of investment in public security and related services from 1984 to the present; yet violence continued to grow. One might argue that the effects of these investments will be seen only in the long run. If that is true, however, annual expenditure rates should not be related to rates of crime in the same year.

In the following chapters, I suggest that the increase in violence cannot be explained either by socioeconomic and urbanization variables or by state expenditures on public security alone, but arises from a combination of factors that culminate by delegitimating the judiciary system as a mediator of conflicts and privatizing the process of vengeance, trends that can only make violence proliferate. In order to explain the increase in violence, we should understand the sociocultural context that frames the population's support for the use of violence, conceptions of the body that legitimate violent interventions, the status of individual rights, the disbelief in the judiciary and its ability to mediate conflicts, the violent pattern of police performance, and reactions to the consolidation of democratic rule.

The deep inequality that permeates Brazilian society certainly frames everyday violence and crime. The association of poverty and crime is always the first to come to people's minds in discussions about violence. Moreover, all data indicate that violent crime is unevenly distributed and affects the poor especially. However, inequality and poverty have always marked Brazilian society, and it is hard to argue that they alone explain recent increases in violent criminality. Further, this argument often misrepresents violent criminality by allowing the view that poverty and inequality lead to poor people's criminality. In reality, if inequality is an important factor, it is so not because poverty correlates directly with criminality, but rather because it reproduces the victimization and criminalization of the poor, the disregard of their rights, and their lack of access to justice. Similarly, if police performance is important in explaining levels of violence, it has less to do with the number of officers and their equipment and more with their patterns of behavior, patterns that seem to have become increasingly illegal and violent in the past few years. The police, far from guaranteeing rights and preventing violence, are in fact contributing to the erosion of people's rights and the increase of violence.

CHAPTER 4

The Police

A Long History of Abuses

One of the most disturbing aspects of the increase in violence in contemporary São Paulo is not that violent crime is increasing—which is happening in various Western cities at similar rates—but rather that the institutions of order seem to contribute to this increase instead of controlling it. Studies of patterns of crime in modern societies have shown that the institutions of order (criminal law, police, courts, and prisons) "can only restrain common crime if they reinforce underlying social forces that are moving in the same direction" (Gurr 1979:370). Contemporary São Paulo seems to represent a case in which the institutions of order are indeed reinforcing underlying social forces: those of violence, illegality, and a tendency to bypass the justice system in the resolution of conflicts. Even explicit attempts to enforce a rule of law in recent years in São Paulo, such as that of Governor Franco Montoro (1983–1987), have been opposed by the population, who prefer violent, extralegal, and private methods of dealing with criminality to the recognition and respect of rights. As a result, violence is high, and the number of people who die every day, either at the hands of vigilantes and private guards or at the hands of the police, is growing. In 1991, the military police alone killed 1,140 people in the state of São Paulo during "confrontations with criminals"; in 1992, that number was 1,470. This includes 111 prisoners massacred inside the Casa de Detenção, São Paulo's largest prison, on October 2. The majority of police killings (87.5 percent in 1992) have occurred in the city of São Paulo and its metropolitan region. A comparison reveals the significance of these numbers: in 1992, the Los Angeles police killed 25 civilians in confrontations, and in New York City, police killed 24 civilians (Chevigny 1995:46, 67). In 1992, police killings represented 20.63 percent of all homicides in the metropolitan region of São Paulo, but only 1.2 percent of the total in New York and 2.1 percent in Los Angeles.[1]

In São Paulo, as in other Brazilian cities, the police are part of the problem of violence. Police use of violent, illegal, or extralegal methods is documented from Brazil's independence in 1822 to the present. During this whole period, the state has found ways both to legalize forms of abuse and violation of rights and to conduct extralegal activities without punishment. The repression of crime has targeted the working classes in particular and frequently has been intertwined with political repression: what the elite once called the "social question" has always been "a matter of the police." Consequently, the population, and especially its poorer sectors, have continuously suffered various forms of police violence and legal injustice and have learned not only to distrust the justice system but also to fear the police. Nevertheless, the persistence of police violence and its contemporary increase have been possible at least in part because of popular support. Paradoxically, even the working classes who are the main victims of such violence support some of its forms. Police behavior seems to accord with the conceptions of the majority, who not only believe that good police are tough (i.e., violent) police and that their illegal acts are acceptable but also have been unwilling to support some governors' attempts to enforce the rule of law and respect for individual rights. Therefore, the popular support of police abuse suggests the existence not of a simple institutional dysfunction but of a pervasive and unchallenged cultural pattern that identifies order and authority with the use of violence. The delegitimation of civil rights is inherent to this pattern.

The history of the decrease in violent crime in Western European cities over the last two centuries reflects the consolidation of the authority of the state and its institutions of order—the police and the justice system—and its monopoly on the use of force. This process coincides with deep cultural changes concerning the control of instincts and of the body, the disciplining of populations, and the expansion and legitimation of the notion of individual rights (Elias 1994 [1939]; Foucault 1977; Marshall 1965 [1949]; Chesnais 1981). Brazilian society, although connected in complex ways to European liberalism and its institutions, has a different and specific history. Although we can talk of a progressive monopoly on the use of force by the state since independence, the Brazilian police forces have never refrained from using violence and have never framed their work of controlling the civil population in terms of respect for citizens' rights. Violent police action intertwines in complex ways with the rule of law and with patterns of domination and legitimation.

In this chapter, I analyze the history of the Brazilian and Paulista police and their pattern of violent and illegal means of controlling the population.

I start by establishing a theoretical framework for the analysis of the institutions of order in Brazil. I criticize interpretations of the Brazilian case as an example of "incomplete modernity," interpretations that take as their reference European and American patterns of consolidation of the police and the justice system. My intention is not to excuse the Brazilian pattern of abuse and injustice by referring to its (colonial) past but rather to demonstrate that violence and abuse are constitutive of Brazilian institutions of order and class domination, of its pattern of expansion of citizenship rights, and, therefore, of its present-day democracy. By so doing, I establish a background for the development of arguments I pursue in Chapters 5 and 9.

A CRITIQUE OF THE INCOMPLETE MODERNITY MODEL

Violence and disrespect of rights by the police have a long history in Brazil. A constant pattern of abuse of the population by police forces, particularly harassment of the working classes, has repeated itself during both liberal and conservative governments, dictatorships and democratic periods. However, because the number of serious abuses by the police in the late 1980s and early 1990s is especially high, and because they took place during a democratic consolidation in which the respect of citizenship rights extended to various other arenas (especially political rights), they present a puzzle. These seemingly contradictory developments are not an unusual kind of paradox in Brazil's history. In fact, historians tend to think of Brazilian society as being marked by deep faultlines. Frequently, these are articulated in dualistic arguments that oppose the modern and the retrograde aspects of the society.[2] I address some of the most influential versions of this idea, especially as they deal with the question of violence and the institutions of order, to contrast them with my own perspective on contemporary Brazilian democracy and its pattern of state violence.

In its most general formulation, the dualist interpretation of Brazilian paradoxical developments suggests that Brazil has never become a fully modern society (a model identified with either Western Europe or the United States). Instead, Brazil is marked by a split between a hierarchical order (private, informal, personal) and an egalitarian order (public, formal, legal), and the two relate in complex ways to produce the peculiarly Brazilian culture. The main contemporary proponent of this interpretation is Roberto DaMatta (1979, 1982, 1985).[3] For him, the hierarchical order is the legacy of colonial (i.e., slave-based) relationships and institutions. It represents the organization of social life on the basis of personal and unequal ties, the most important of which are clientelism and favor. The egalitarian order is the model of Western (in DaMatta's view mostly American) liberalism, its procedures, and its institutions, especially rational public administration, the justice system, and the rule of law, which—I would add—is the paradigm of a complete modernity.

> Everything suggests that there is a complex, circular interplay in what can be called Brazilian "modernity." This interplay is constituted by a complex dialogue between an explicit written constitutional code, founded on the principles of equality and individualism, and an implicit, unwritten, hierarchical, complementary, and "holistic" moral code. When the egalitarian pole grows stronger, the hierarchical structure does not automatically fade or disappear; it finds new ways to react and reinforce itself. (DaMatta [1979] 1991:154–55)

Violence is a crucial element in DaMatta's framework: it is an instrument of inequality, and it works as a kind of operator between the two opposed social codes or universes. "Violence is prone to be used in the Brazilian world when other means to establish hierarchy prove to be a total failure" ([1979] 1991:165). Described in these terms, violence is extraordinary, the last resort. In a later work focusing directly on violence (1982), DaMatta makes his argument more complex. He still posits two opposing universes, but adds another, "the other world" of religious beliefs. Moreover, he suggests that violence may be used not only by the powerful but also by "the weak." Nevertheless, he maintains that violence has a mediating role: it is always a force that brings about a change in positions and a transference between one universe (hierarchical) and the other (egalitarian). It is also the last means to which people have recourse when they lose patience with what they consider to be wrong (among the powerful, being treated without due deference; among the weak, being subjected to excessive injustice). When used by the powerful, DaMatta suggests, violence asserts hierarchy and disqualifies equality; when used by the weak, it may assert equality (by exposing the excessive character of inequality), and in this sense it "individualizes" (1982:35–38). This interpretation, which conceives of violence as a mediator and an operator of reversion, fails to reveal, however, how violence is *constitutive* of various dimensions of social life, including some of the most legalistic and individualistic.[4]

Indeed, the history of the Brazilian police clearly indicates that violence is the institutional norm, not a mediator between universes. The same is true of domestic violence—the beating of children and women—a type of violence DaMatta tends to downplay, relying as he does on a notion of the house as a universe characterized by protection (see below). Brazilian police have used violence as their regular and everyday pattern of controlling the population, and frequently they have done so under the protection of the law. It is certainly true that the elites have been able to use their personal ties and status to avoid such mistreatment—and in this sense their behavior conforms to DaMatta's description—but for the working classes violent treatment has been the norm. Moreover, for the working classes the code of inequality may be unwritten, but it is explicit. (Sometimes it is also written: Brazilian legislation guarantees preferential treatment by the police and the prison system to anyone with a college degree.) Violence is the regular language of authority, whether of the state or the head of the household; it cannot, therefore, be seen as an operator between universes or a force used only as a last resort. Thus to understand Brazilian social relations and the role of violence within them, it is necessary to abandon both the view of violence as extraordinary and the interpretation of the social order as split into a universe of hierarchy and personal ties and one of equality and law. Violence is constitutive of the social order.

Thomas Holloway (1993) wrote a history of the police in Rio de Janeiro from 1808 to 1889. He demonstrates how the constitution and progressive institutionalization of the police forces have been intrinsically associated with the use of violence and arbitrariness, something to be expected in the context of slavery. He presents the history of the formation of the police forces in imperial Rio de Janeiro as an incomplete transition from private to public forms of control. "This study examines the process by which modern police institutions buttressed and ensured the continuity of traditional hierarchical social relations, extending them into impersonal public space. The apparent contradiction is an example of the incomplete or discontinuous historical processes that help account for many of the characteristics of contemporary Brazil, including the divergence between formal law and the institutions ostensibly charged with enforcing it and sociocultural norms guiding individual behavior" (Holloway 1993:6).

The citation, which echoes DaMatta's views, implies that hierarchical social relations (by principle unequal) are meant to exist in contradiction to impersonal public space (ideally egalitarian). However, an ideally egalitarian public space, not marked by domination and hierarchy, arguably has never existed anywhere. Even the allegedly impersonal public space of modern Western Europe and the United States is, in fact, structured on the basis of unequal relationships of class, ethnicity, and gender. In this sense, Brazil is not even peculiar. The combination of egalitarian principles with structures of domination and various sorts of inequalities is deeply rooted in Western modernity and does not constitute any special case of incompleteness. This is, for example, the conclusion of Michel Foucault's *Discipline and Punish*, in which he shows that the reproduction of domination and inequalities through the disciplines is the complement to the legitimization of the juridical apparatus of the contract society (Foucault 1977:218–28). Dumm (1987) arrives at the same conclusion for the United States. Moreover, an important feminist critique of contract theories has demonstrated that the free contract among equals is in reality a contract among males which has by principle assumed the exclusion and subordination of women (for example, Pateman 1988). Brazil is, moreover, not the only country to have incorporated liberal principles of equality into its constitution before abolishing slavery. The same happened in the United States. Until the late nineteenth century, however, the Brazilian national elite was not deeply divided over slavery, and it was never involved in a civil war over this issue. This unity allowed various institutions inherited from slavery—including physical chastisement—to persist largely unchallenged.

The central question is not whether there are social formations with contradictory principles and practices, something we could probably find in any society, but rather how we should interpret these contradictions. Dualistic interpretations of "the character of Brazilian society" may be criticized on two grounds. One critique, which does not apply directly to DaMatta, was formulated by Roberto Schwarz (1977: chapter 1). It shows that to assign liberal principles and slavery to two opposite social universes is to insist on the artificiality of (inappropriately imported) Western principles as related to existing social practices. Consequently this reality is interpreted in terms of incompleteness, deviance, and discontinuity. Further, Schwarz suggests that the "misplaced ideas" of liberalism have been instrumental in organizing social practices and relationships—were, indeed, constitutive of them—and therefore cannot be dealt with in social analysis by being labeled as contradictory to them.

> Liberal ideas could not be put into practice, and yet they could not
> be discarded. They became a part of a special practical situation, which
> would reproduce itself and not leave them unchanged. Therefore, it
> does not help to insist on their obvious falsehood. We should rather
> observe their dynamics, of which this falsehood was a true component.
> Faced with these ideas, Brazil, the outpost of slavery, was ashamed—
> for these were taken to be the ideas of the time—and resentful, for
> they served no purpose. But they were also adopted with pride, in
> an ornamental vein, as a proof of modernity and distinction. And, of
> course, they were revolutionary when put in the service of Abolitionism. Subordinate to the demands of place, and not losing their original

claims, they circled, governed by a peculiar rule whose merits and faults, ambiguities and deceptions were peculiar as well. To know Brazil was to know these displacements, experienced and practiced by everyone as a sort of fate, for which, however, there was no proper name, since the improper use of names was part of its nature. (Schwarz 1992:28)

Another criticism is that dualistic explanations of Brazilian social relations and institutions—and this critique does apply to DaMatta's analysis—tend to assume or propose separate, clear-cut, and dichotomous distinctions in social life such as personal and impersonal, private and public, hierarchical and egalitarian, house and street, principles and practice, legal and illegal, formal law and applied law, and so forth. [5] These dichotomous categories force distinctions that do not exist in social life, where categories routinely coincide and collapse into each other. In other words, these dichotomies fail to capture the dynamic character of social practices. For example, the misleading opposition between the stereotyped universes of the house and the street has become a commonplace in Brazilian anthropological analyses; it serves as a title for one of DaMatta's books (1985). By associating the house with what is private, personal, and protected, and identifying the street with the public, impersonal, and violent, it transforms violence into a problem of public relationships, and frequently of interclass or intergroup relationships, obscuring its pervasive presence in interpersonal and domestic relationships in all social groups. If we want to understand the popular support of a police force that kills, of the death penalty, and of the opposition to human rights, we must address the widespread practice and support of violent interventions against the body (which includes the beating of women and children inside the home). In other words, private violent practices and public violent practices cannot be set in opposition to each other, and, more important, they cannot be set apart from notions of individual rights and the rule of law.

Another example of misleading oppositions refers directly to the police and the justice system and is suggested by Holloway (1993), who contrasts formal law and institutional framework on the one hand and police abuses and application of law on the other. These oppositions similarly prevent us from understanding Brazilian institutions of order and their role in the reproduction of violence. In fact, ambiguities, unequal treatment, exceptional rules and legislation, privileges, impunity, and the legitimization of abuses are intrinsic to the institutions of order and not external to them (that is, manifestations of malpractice). The problem is neither one of liberal principles versus a personal and violent practice nor one of a constitutional framework versus an illegal practice, but rather a problem of institutions of order that are constituted to work on the basis of exceptions and abuses. As the history of the police and recent policies of public security clearly indicate, the boundaries between legal and illegal are unstable and ill-defined, and they change continuously in order to legalize previous abuses and legitimate new ones. Holston concurs (1991b) on the basis of an analysis of land conflicts. In Brazil, law and abuses are simultaneously constitutive of the institutions of order. To try to crystallize these dimensions as belonging to opposed universes is to miss the intrinsically flexible character of Brazilian patterns of domination and the fact that in Brazil the state has never been formal and impersonal and frequently does not abide by the laws it creates.

The practices of violence and arbitrariness have been constitutive of the Brazilian police, to varying degrees, since its creation in the early nineteenth century. Similarly, police abuses of the discretionary power, usurpation of functions of the judiciary system, and the torture and battering of suspects, prisoners, and workers are deeply rooted in Brazilian history. Such practices have not always been illegal, and frequently they have been exercised with support of the citizenry. At various times, the police have had wide discretion in their actions. At other times, legislation was changed to accommodate existing delinquent practices or to cover them up. Usually laws of exception were passed during dictatorships, but not uncommonly they survived under democratic rule, becoming part of the constitutional framework. The legal parameters of police work have shifted frequently, creating the conditions for a routine of abuses that is now the police modus operandi. In this whole history, the only element consistently lacking is a strong will on the part of state authorities and the citizenry to check the abusive behavior of the police.

ORGANIZATION OF THE POLICE FORCES

The constitution of the police forces in nineteenth-century Rio de Janeiro (Brazil's capital until 1960) can be seen as a series of experiments in institution-building, crystallized in legislation enacted between 1809 and the proclamation of the republic, including a criminal code created in 1830 and revised in 1832. These experiments continued during the First Republic (1889–1930) and the Vargas era (1930–1945). The search for an institutional framework for police work, associated with the need to adapt police institutions to changing political regimes, accounts for the constant redesigning and renaming of those institutions from the early nineteenth century until 1969, when the military regime restructured the police forces into their current form. The continual changes in the name and character of the police force make its history confusing.[6] Nevertheless, some traits of the institutions have persisted. The most important of these are the division of the police since 1831 into a civil and a military force—which have usually competed amid considerable hostility—and, since the mid-nineteenth century, the progressive dominance of the militarized force in patrolling the streets. There has always been a civil police in charge of judiciary and administrative tasks and, at times, responsible for overseeing the patrolling corps. This force has been organized under the authority of a police chief and various district *delegados*. Street patrolling has in general had a separate and different structure of authority, usually militarized, although at times it has been under the authority of the police chief (as during the Estado Novo). During some periods (for example, between 1926 and 1969 in the state of São Paulo), patrolling has been divided between a military corps (Força Pública) and a civil corps (Guarda Civil).

The arguments supporting the militarization of the police are well known: a militarized and hierarchical police would be more disciplined, isolated from the population, and have a stronger esprit de corps, all characteristics seen as necessary to avoid corruption and to bring an urban population perceived as disorderly and dangerous under control by people of their own class. Duque de Caxias, the hero of the Brazilian army, organized the first military police in the 1830s. However, although it has been organized in military terms, the military police has never been a direct part of the army but rather is a parallel organization, frequently under civilian authority. It has therefore been characterized by some police historians as a hybrid institution (see Fernandes 1974).

During the Empire (1822–1889), not only were the new police institutions ill-defined, but the boundaries between patrolling and judicial tasks (including punishment) were also vague.[7] In general, as Holloway shows (1993), the police exercised wide discretion not only in making arrests but also in determining "correctional" punishments, such as battering and incarceration, without consulting judges. At certain times, these practices were legal, and for a long period in the nineteenth century, police officials had local judicial powers (Holloway 1993:168; see also Flory 1981).

The police exercised violence in various ways. They were legally empowered to punish slaves. Holloway argues that the physical punishment of slaves was more violent in Brazil than in other countries, such as the United States (Holloway 1993:54). Toward the poor in general, the police used beatings and arbitrary arrest as forms of both intimidation and immediate punishment (correction). Even after judicial authority was taken from the police in 1871, correctional detention continued to be the norm (Holloway 1993:284). Through successive reforms during the century, the amount of violence, especially court-ordered whipping and public whipping, diminished somewhat (Holloway 1993:230). However, it is quite obvious that the relationship of the police (and also of the courts and the law) with the population has been one of violent repression rather than of safeguarding civil rights.[8]

The main work of the police, indeed, was control of the poor. Holloway argues that "the overwhelming majority of police activity was devoted to the arrest and summary punishment of people who, by their victimless public behavior, violated norms or order and hierarchy as defined by those who created and maintained the increasingly elaborate and efficient police response"(1993:271). Slaves, foreigners, and indigents were the main targets. Violations of public order included everyday forms of social gathering among the urban poor, such as meetings in the streets and taverns, and especially backyard *batuques* (reunions with music and dance). Noise, music, loud talking, public displays of affection, and confrontations were considered to "violate patterns of decorum dear to those in charge" (Holloway 1993:275). Among the most heavily persecuted practices was *capoeira*, a form of performative fight practiced by the black population, slave and free, that is frequently interpreted as a form of resistance to domination. Although it does not appear in the 1830 and 1832 criminal codes and was made illegal only in 1890 (in the Republican Code), *capoeira* served to justify not only large numbers of arrests but also summary physical punishments (Holloway 1993:223–28). The same is true for prostitution, which became a crime only in 1940 but has always been persecuted.

Not only in Brazil but in rapidly growing cities all over the world, the main mandate of the police was to control a poor population considered to be dangerous.[9] In the case of Rio de Janeiro under the First Republic (1889–1930), Bretas (1995: chapter 2) shows that until the 1920s police were mainly concerned with public-order offenses. Arrests for vagrancy peaked in the first decade of the 1900s. As during the Empire, a vaguely defined offense of this kind offers a convenient means for exercising arbitrary power over a population broadly perceived as dangerous. In the 1920s, according to Bretas, traffic offenses and accidents joined the list of the police's main concerns, along with censorship of entertainment.

Fausto indicates similar concerns with keeping order by targeting groups in São Paulo. On average, between 1892 and 1916, misdemeanors (vagrancy, disorder, and drunkenness) accounted for 79.9 percent of all arrests, while crimes against property accounted for 11.7 percent and crimes against persons for 8.4 percent (Fausto 1984:46). In other words, in São Paulo imprisonment was used as an instrument for controlling the population. Blacks, who constituted 10 percent of the population between 1904 and 1916, constituted 28.5 percent of all those arrested (1984:52). Foreigners accounted for the majority of arrests (an average of 55.5 percent for 1894 to 1916), but they also made up the majority of São Paulo's population at that time. Fausto's analysis demonstrates that although prejudices against immigrants were well-rooted among public-order authorities at the time of high immigration, the pattern of criminalization of foreigners was more complex than that of blacks and poor nationals (1984:59–69). On the one hand, foreigners were targeted less often for public-order offenses such as vagrancy (28.7 percent compared to 71.3 percent for 1904–1906) but were more frequently indicted for felonies (61.3 percent of all homicides and 60.3 percent of the larceny and robbery cases from 1880 to 1924) (1984: 44, 62). On the other hand, they were able to defend themselves better by denouncing the discrimination they suffered in various working-class newspapers they ran and by organizing support networks to help pay for their legal defense.

There are also indications that during the Old Republic, the Paulista elite's concerns about the police did not focus exclusively on the control of a potentially disorderly population. If the civil police continued its tasks of dealing with crime and disorderly public behavior, the Paulista elite seems to have had other plans for the military police. That period was marked by a realignment of political forces and by a consolidation of some regional oligarchies. São Paulo's was one of the main oligarchies disputing national power, and one of the important achievements of the Paulista elite was to structure the provincial police as a counter both to the national force (represented by the army and controlled by the federal government) and to the local forces controlled by local *coronéis*. Starting in 1868, alongside its judiciary civil police São Paulo had a provincial police (the Corpo Policial Permanente). In the late nineteenth century, it also established separate police forces for the interior and the capital.

In 1901 the state reorganized its police forces, unifying all patrolling under the Força Pública. The judiciary civil police existed all along. As Heloísa Fernandes shows (1974), during the following three decades provincial authorities acted to equip, train, institutionalize, and professionalize this "hybrid" police force, which was organized in military terms but controlled by the civil authorities. As part of this effort, the province brought a French mission to São Paulo in 1906, which shaped the Força Pública thereafter. In addition to controlling "public disorder," especially the growing trade-union movements of the 1910s and 1920s, the Paulista Força Pública proved to be important in opposing the central government: in the Revolution of 1932, the Força Pública was the crucial force behind the Paulista uprising. In 1926, the province also created the Guarda Civil, in charge of street patrolling. Although during the Estado Novo the federal government acted to control the provincial police forces, the dual structure of the patrolling forces (Força Pública and Guarda Civil) existing side by side with the civil police lasted until 1969, when the military government unified the two patrolling forces under the auspices of the military police (Polícia Militar).

The Vargas era (1930–1945), and especially the dictatorship years of the Estado Novo (1937–1945), were marked by the attempt to put state forces under the control of the federal government. Moreover, the police assumed a strategic role in enforcing the wishes of the federal administration and silencing its political opponents. The civil police became central to these efforts and as a consequence grew powerful. It was organized as a separate entity and frequently ranked above the judiciary system. Many important supporters of the regime, such as Francisco Campos, Vargas's minister of justice, publicly defended the use of violence as a means of maintaining order (Cancelli 1993:20). Others, writing in the officially sponsored journal *Cultura e Política*, clearly stated the opposition between police and justice and argued that it was better for the state to rely on a "more mobile" and arbitrary institution such as the police (Cancelli 1993:23). The police and their "flexibility" were crucial for Vargas's dictatorship.

Underscoring its strategic role for the regime, Vargas completely restructured the police at the national level. The police department of the federal district (the civil police of Rio de Janeiro) was put under the direct jurisdiction of the president and of the Ministry of Justice and Internal Affairs (1933). On July 2, 1934, the government issued a five-hundred-page decree (Decree 24,531) that detailed the functions of the police at all levels and provided a model for patrolling the main cities. This decree laid the foundations for the federalization and centralization of the police, which was completed after 1937 (Cancelli 1993:60–64). In practice (although not necessarily in law), all state policies were subordinated directly to the federal district police (instead to the state governments). According to Cancelli, Filinto Müller, the powerful police chief of the federal district between 1933 and 1942, had more power than any judge or any of the ministers of justice, and he organized all work of repression, both political and criminal. Directly under the jurisdiction of the police chief of the federal district was the Delegacia Especial de Segurança Pública e Social (Special Police Station of Public and Social Security) which after 1941 coordinated all information, intelligence, and censorship services (1993:54–5).

The repressive action of the police apparatus during the Estado Novo targeted especially foreigners and alleged Communists, who were frequently lumped into a single category (Cancelli 1993:79–82). To control the foreign residents, the Brazilian state made various expatriation agreements with other nations and relied on denunciations *(delação)* by individual citizens and institutions, such as the various trade unions controlled by the Ministry of Labor (1993:82–92; 92–97; 140–58). Moreover, the Estado Novo issued a series of resolutions aimed at controlling immigration (which was widespread and sponsored by the state in the late nineteenth and early twentieth centuries), promoting nationalization, and monitoring foreigners living in the country (1993:121–59). During World War II, German and Japanese residents, as well as Jewish residents, were the focus of special repression.

The next major change in police structure came during the military regime that came to power in 1964.[10] Facing internal political opposition, the new regime reorganized the police forces. All preexisting state uniformed police (in São Paulo, the Força Pública and Guarda Civil) were unified into a state military police (PM—Polícia Militar), subordinate to the army, by Decree 667 of 1969.[11] This reform was considered necessary to face a strong opposition partially organized in guerrilla movements. The same tactics were applied to the task of controlling crime, regarded as the "internal enemy." During the military years, the institutions in charge of repression were the state military police and various organizations within the army. However, the civil police had a complementary role and was also involved in fighting political opponents. Both the civil police and the military police practiced abuses of various sorts, from disregarding existing laws to torture and killing.[12]

In 1983, after the first direct elections for state governors, each state military police was subordinated to the area's commander in chief of the army, and it was up to this figure to remove the military police from the governor's control (Pinheiro 1983). This structure has been largely preserved since the end of military rule. The democratic constitution of 1988 maintains a civil police (in charge of judiciary and administrative tasks) and a military police (in charge of "ostensive and uniformed patrolling") but subordinates them to the state governors and their secretaries of public security instead of to the army. The military police was also defined as a reserve auxiliary force to the army *(força auxiliar e de reserva do exército)*, which is in charge of national security. Although the 1988 constitution defines public security as a responsibility of the states, it also establishes a federal police in charge of defending the nation's interests, serving as its judiciary police, controlling drug traffic, and guarding the frontiers. The 1988 constitution also defines the tasks of the road and railroad federal police forces.

A TRADITION OF TRANSGRESSIONS

The practice of violence and arbitrariness by the police forces has shown remarkable continuity in Brazilian history, from imperial times to this day.[13] Yet resorting to violence as a form of social control is hardly a Brazilian peculiarity. The physical punishment of slaves, criminals, and suspects in general was common until the end of the ancien régime and the creation of penitentiaries in the United States and Europe. Even after that time, controlling the extralegal use of physical punishment by the police, that is, the use of physical punishment at their own discretion, was possible only through serious efforts by the state, the justice system, and the citizenry. This control is always precarious, and outbursts of police violence continue to occur even among vigilant societies. However, Brazilian efforts to control police violence have been feeble, and the state has been unable to curb the routine physical abuse of free citizens even since it became illegal. Moreover, in some circumstances no such efforts have been made.

The Brazilian legal apparatus authorizing the police use of force is extensive and has not been completely eliminated by democratic governments. In the colonial period, physical punishment was legally regulated. Judicial torture and various sorts of physical punishment were an important part of the Philippine Code that governed criminal law in Portugal and its colonies (Holloway 1993:29). Intense debates about the nature and intensity of physical punishment, its connection to production and authority, and its just or excessive character, marked the colonial period both in Portugal and in Brazil (Lara 1988).

Physical punishment is also inherent to the institution of slavery, which was abolished in Brazil only in 1888. Physical punishment of slaves could be carried out not only by the state but also by slave owners. After independence and during the nineteenth century, there was a tendency for state agents to replace private owners in the administration of physical chastisement to slaves (Holloway 1993). Because physical punishment was legally regulated, its practice is documented. There are, for example, reasonable records of the legal processes in which slaves complained about their masters and asked either to be sold to other masters or to buy their own liberty on the basis of claims of excessive and unjustified physical punishment (Lara 1988; Chalhoub 1990).

After the abolition of slavery in 1888 and the end of the Empire in 1889, many other legal measures perpetuated the use of violence by police forces. In 1925, following the popular revolt of 1924 in São Paulo, the Delegacia de Ordem Política e Social (DOPS: Police Station for Political and Social Order) was created, to keep a "more serious and permanent surveillance on activities which disintegrate the traditional principles of Religion, the Country, and the Family" (cited by Pinheiro and Sader 1985:80). This station served as the model for others in all the states, and it survived for more than sixty years, playing a central role in the repression of political opposition during the military government (1964–1985).

Not surprisingly, the Vargas era (1930–1945) was particularly active in the enactment and enforcement of exception laws, as many were needed to legally create and sustain his dictatorship after 1937. The laws of exception approved by Congress in 1936, after the alleged Communist rebellion of 1935, established that Congress could empower the president to declare the existence of a state of "grave internal commotion" that would suspend all constitutional guarantees. These laws offered a legal way to give Vargas the powers of a dictator. The most important piece of legislation of the period, however, is probably the constitution of 1937, which inaugurates the Estado Novo by abolishing Congress and all forms of political representation and organization.

One of the institutions created in 1936 and later made permanent by the 1937 Constitution was the Tribunal de Segurança Nacional (Court of National Security). Functioning on the basis of exception rules, it can be described as a parallel justice system controlled directly by the executive; it therefore operated above the judiciary. This court specialized in the summary and fast trial of actions classified as "against national security," a vague category including mostly political activities but also so-called crimes against popular economy or any other act interpreted by members of the government as being against the ruling order. According to Elizabeth Cancelli, the trials lasted no longer than sixty hours, and the physical presence of the defendant, witnesses, and lawyers was not mandatory (1993:103). This court did not accept appeals, nor did the military tribunal have the power to overrule its decisions (1993:104). The Court of National Security "tried 6,988 processes involving ten thousand people, condemning 4,099 of them with penalties varying from a simple fine to up to a 27-year term" (1993:104).

The military regime that took power in 1964 also created various exception laws (called institutional acts) and promulgated a new constitution in 1967. Rules governing the military police include some exception laws that put them above the civil justice system. Decree-law 1,001 of 1969—still in force—establishes that all crimes committed by military bodies should be considered military crimes and judged by a special military justice, even if they were committed in peacetime and in the performance of civilian functions. In other words, since 1969 there has been a special justice for the military police. This exception became the norm with the constitution of 1988. Written under a democratic rule by a freely elected Congress, the 1988 constitution maintained the military police as the institution in charge of "the ostensive policing and the preservation of the public order" (article 144, paragraph 5) and the military justice as the authority for dealing with crimes committed by military policemen. In May 1996, after a massacre by the military police (in Pará, north Brazil), President Fernando Henrique Cardoso supported a bill in Congress proposing that military policemen be tried by civil courts. That it was not immediately approved indicates the support that the military police still enjoys, despite its violent nature. The bill was finally approved in August (Law 9299 of August 7, 1997) but in a milder form. The new law shifts to ordinary courts jurisdiction over murders involving military policemen and soldiers. However, all other crimes, including manslaughter and physical assault, remain under military jurisdiction. Moreover, the determination of whether a killing should be regarded as murder or as manslaughter remains with the military police investigators.

Centro Santos Dias, a human rights defense group associated with the Archdiocese of São Paulo, analyzed 380 trials under the military justice from 1977 to 1983. It intended to cover all trials of policemen but was prohibited further access to the documents. For the period analyzed, it found that of eighty-two policemen accused of murder, only fourteen were found guilty (15.9 percent). Of forty-four policemen accused of crimes against property, fourteen were found guilty (31.8 percent). Finally, of fifty-three policemen who faced trials for matters of discipline, twenty-eight were found guilty (52.8 percent). These data indicate that the military justice is rigorous as far as internal discipline is concerned, but is not as tough if the question is the murder of civilians.

Impunity is intrinsically associated with the excessive use of force. As Chevigny demonstrates in his analysis of police abuses in six cities in the Americas (1995), the reduction of abuse is directly related to the enforcement of systems of accountability. When police officers are not held accountable for extralegal or illegal behavior, violence and abuses escalate. Analyzing the civil police in the Old Republic, Bretas suggests that their abuses might be explained by the public authorities' lack of interest in controlling the police, which has allowed for the creation of a "very independent police system, virtually without control or accountability" (1995:246). He adds that although there were some attempts at control during the Old Republic, they have never been effective. Some qualifications should be made here, for Bretas analyzes only Rio de Janeiro's civil police, and his conclusions do not seem to apply to the general case. Fernandes, for example, shows (1974) that during the same period the militarized Força Pública of São Paulo was under tougher scrutiny and control from the local oligarchy and the French mission in charge of training them. We can speculate, therefore, that a unified policy of public security did not exist at that time and that control over the police forces was in large measure shaped by political concerns. Moreover, tougher control over the police forces does not mean less abuse but rather the contrary. Dictatorships, such as those of Vargas and the military in Brazil, brought the police under tighter control. However, these regimes put in place laws of exception and guarantees of impunity to protect those who perpetrated abuses on behalf of the regime. Accountability might still exist, but it certainly means different things under dictatorships and under democratic rule.

In a democratic context, laws of exception exist in open contradiction with other constitutional principles. The legal exception that takes the current military policemen out of the civil system of accountability, in addition to weakening the rule of law, extends the impunity and violence of the military police in dealing with the civilian population and indirectly assures them wide latitude for arbitrary behavior. Thus current police institutions, although under democratic rule, allow arbitrariness and violence to continue. Moreover, they create a space in which rights may be directly contested, as in the identification of human rights as "privileges for bandits."

The legal measures of exception that legitimated the practice of violence and arbitrariness by the police and the state also functioned as a cover for many everyday abuses that constituted the modus operandi of the police during the Republic. Such abuses have been documented since the first years of this century in working-class newspapers, especially those of anarchist orientation, but also in the most conservative newspapers, such as *O Estado de S. Paulo*. As Pinheiro shows in detail (1981) , since the late nineteenth century the press (along with foreign diplomats) has complained frequently about the excessive use of force of by police against suspects and especially against organized workers on strike (see also Pinheiro 1981; 1991a; Pinheiro and Sader 1985). Excessive force has been used to control all popular revolts. The repression of the working classes included not only torture and battering but also illegal imprisonment, denial of trial, mass deportation of foreign workers (who constituted the majority of the working classes in Brazil at the beginning of the twentieth century), and banishment *(desterro)* of Brazilians after they became a significant force in revolts at the turn of the century.[14]

Pinheiro emphasizes (1981; 1991a; Pinheiro and Sader 1985) that the repression of crime has always been intertwined with the repression of popular revolts, strikes, and political opposition. In this sense, the Brazilian state and the police have never made a distinction between the working classes, the political opposition, and the dangerous classes. Moreover, this long history of illegality constitutes a long tradition of acquiescence and impunity.

> In spite of the profusion of inquisitions and investigations by the state itself, those cases—rough treatment, torture, disrespect of the defendant—recur monotonously, and the searches never lead to any concrete results. Investigation—sometimes conducted by the same organs under accusation—has become in Brazil a ritual of dissimulation which in the short run is used to stop a revolt provoked by some excess, but which never has any reason to stop a practice which is mixed with power itself. It would be an illusion to expect that the state, without deep alterations in the basis of its political organization, would interrupt the practice of illegitimate violence that efficiently collaborates for its sustenance. (Pinheiro 1981:54)

Abuses that occurred during the dictatorships (both Vargas's and the military regime) against political prisoners therefore constitute no novelty. In fact, they show how those abuses could be taken as routine. Maybe the only difference was that during those periods the violence also affected middle-class people.

Among the best-known records of the Vargas police abuses are the books and memoirs of former political prisoners, many of them Communists, such as the famous *Memórias do Cárcere* by the novelist Graciliano Ramos. However, because illegal practices were not always perceived as serious irregularities, another source of documentation is the judiciary system itself. In its records there are many petitions by prisoners disclosing their physical abuse, pleading for their lives, and denouncing the irregular procedures through which they were frequently detained. Many prisoners had been under no formal investigation or formal process, and others were kept beyond the limits of their sentences. According to Cancelli, most prisoners suffering illegal abuses during the Estado Novo were under the authority of the police chief, who could decide their destinies regardless of the judiciary's decisions (1993:206–15).

The same illegal practices continued under democratic rule for people accused of being criminals. During the military years (1964–1985), various judiciary processes against political prisoners contained descriptions of torture, physical abuses, and illegal procedures. Because records were well kept by the military justice, the team that produced the book *Brasil Nunca Mais* was able to use them to document human rights violations in Brazil. From these records the team secretly obtained and analyzed descriptions of tortures, the places in which they occurred, and the names of 441 torturers, as well as indications of illegal judiciary procedures related to arrest, imprisonment, and trial. From a total of 7,367 defendants in political trials during the military regime, 1,918 declared in court that they had been tortured, 81 percent between 1969 and 1974. Many others who were tortured did not declare so in court (Arquidiocese de São Paulo 1985:87–88). Moreover, *Brasil Nunca Mais* was able to show that in the years 1964 to 1979, at least 144 people were killed for political reasons in Brazil, and another 125 disappeared.[15] The reports on how those records were obtained during testimonies only give the impression that the judges were dealing with business as usual (Weschler 1990: chapter 1). There is no contradiction here between a judicial system operating according to certain rules and a malfunctioning repressive apparatus operating according to others. Together they constituted an order in which respect for citizens' rights had no place.

Another type of abuse during the military regime was practiced by the Esquadrão da Morte (Death Squad) and reported by Bicudo (1976; see also 1988), the solicitor general in charge of investigating its activities. Members of the civil police, under pressure from members of the recently created and powerful military police, decided to improve their image in the fight against crime. They chose "to simply eliminate criminals, enjoying the support of the top of the institution and even of the state governor" (Bicudo 1976:24–25). One of the leaders of the squad was the civil police chief Sérgio Fernando Paranhos Fleury, who was also in charge of political arrests, torture, and executions (Arquidiocese de São Paulo 1985:74). Fleury, police chief for more than a decade, and the members of the Esquadrão da Morte were also involved in drug trafficking (Bicudo 1976; 1988).

The activities of the Esquadrão da Morte escalated in 1970 after a military policeman was killed: its members had promised, according to Bicudo (1976:27), to kill ten suspects for each dead policeman, and they did not hesitate to take prisoners out of prisons for this purpose. It is not known how many people were killed by the Esquadrão da Morte; media estimates range from a few hundred to two thousand. However, because its members were from the civil police, some were brought to trial by the state solicitor general. Although the judges faced all sorts of threats and intimidation, and although some of them, such as Hélio Bicudo, were forced off the case, the judiciary was able to contain the activities of the Esquadrão.

Various practices of abuse continue. The 1988 constitution carries provisions meant to prevent some of the worst arbitrariness and abuses practiced by the police. It establishes that torture is a crime not subject to bail or executive clemency and sets forth procedures to prevent arbitrary and unsubstantiated arrest. In 1992, Brazil ratified the United Nations Convention against Torture and Other Cruel, Inhuman or Degrading Treatment or Punishment. However, these provisions are not only disregarded but, more important, are largely opposed by the population and by right-wing politicians—not to mention by the police themselves. They argue that the new procedures foster crime because they hinder police work and ultimately serve only to protect bandits. The police pattern of abuse still constitutes a model of good police work in the view of a considerable part of the population.

It is only occasionally that police arbitrariness is criticized by the public. One of these instances came at the end of the military regime, when the unlawful behavior of the police and the state led to an important social movement against it. The middle classes—whose members had been victims of torture and illegal imprisonment—organized a movement demanding political amnesty and defending human rights. But popular support for the defense of human rights disappeared when the victims of abuse were no longer either middle-class or political prisoners.

Going back to the question of "incomplete modernity," I would like to add two observations. First, the history of Brazilian institutions of order suggests that nations around the world can engage with the same crucial elements of what we might label modernity and yet produce very different versions of it. Instead of looking at Western Europe and America as the models for modern institution-building, therefore, it is more interesting to conceive of the rule of law, liberalism, and citizenship as part of a broad repertoire from which, in the course of the last centuries, various nations borrowed elements and engaged them in terms of their own social practices. There is no single model of modernity by which countries may be measured and completeness determined. There are, however, various versions of modernity, and Brazil certainly embodies one of them.

Second, Brazil's specific pattern of arbitrariness and injustice has had consequences for its institutions of order. Because the boundaries between the legal and the illegal are unstable and because police abuses are committed with impunity, not only are the police forces feared, but the justice system is also delegitimated and perceived as unreliable for the just settlement of disputes. This pattern of abuse and delegitimation is deeply rooted in Brazilian society and has not immediately been modified by the adoption of a democratic political system. As I show in the next chapter, the combination of a violent police and a delegitimated justice system is fatal for the control of civil violence in any situation, even in a democracy.

CHAPTER 5
Police Violence under Democracy

Although violence and disrespect of rights by the police have a long history in Brazil, the abuses of the 1980s and especially 1990s in São Paulo are especially egregious, for two reasons: first, because of their elevated numbers and the incorporation of abuse almost as "business as usual" into the everyday life of the city; and second, because they have continued during the consolidation of democratic rule, and as the respect for other rights of citizenship, especially political rights, has expanded. Past experience and tradition alone do not explain the present picture of routine violations. Rather, the recent history of police abuses demonstrates that although brutality is constant and enjoys significant popular support, it is also responsive to policies of public security and to systems of accountability. If abuses have grown during the democratic period, they have done so because of administrative decisions and political options rather than because of an intractable pattern inherited from the past. Therefore, it is important to investigate how the policies fostering abuses (or the ones trying to control them) were formulated, how they have played on—and been influenced by —the population's fears and expectations, and why they were formulated when they were. These investigations indicate the disjunctive character of Brazilian democratization and show how civil rights are not only the most delegitimated aspect of Brazilian citizenship but also an arena in which democracy is openly resisted and discredited.[1] Exploitation of the fear of crime becomes at certain moments a political weapon.

The issue of police violence has been central to politics in the state of São Paulo over the past decade. Crime control became a point of political disagreement after the end of the dictatorship. Franco Montoro, the first elected governor after the military rule, took office with a program of police reform and a commitment to human rights. He was in office between

1983 and 1987, that is, exactly when crime was dramatically increasing. His administration faced strong opposition not only inside the police and among politicians but also from the public. In spite of suffering all kinds of opposition and accomplishing little, Montoro's administration took important measures toward controlling police violence. However, his successors Orestes Quércia (1987–1991) and Luís Antonio Fleury (1991–1995), responding to popular support for a tough and violent police, returned to the old scheme. Montoro was able to start controlling the most violent branches of the police (such as Rota); his successors brought them back. They not only reversed Montoro's policies but also helped manipulate the fear of crime to disqualify the question of human rights and give the police more license to act illegally. The number of people killed by the police increased year after year, reaching the astonishing number of almost 1,500 in 1992, the year in which 111 prisoners were massacred at the Casa de Detenção. After that, Fleury himself had to adopt measures to curb the police. Mário Covas, who took office in 1995 and was reelected in 1998, is once again adopting policies meant to control police violence and has had to face strong resistance from the police, which provoked strikes and riots in 1997.

ESCALATING POLICE VIOLENCE

Because Brazil today is a democracy in which political rights, as well as freedom of organization and expression, are largely assured, the main targets of police violence are not political opponents.[2] Rather, they are "suspects" (alleged criminals), mostly poor and disproportionately black. Human rights violations are a public affair, reported daily in an uncensored mass media, which either fail to provoke any organized form of protest or reaction or are supported by a population that classifies human rights as "privileges for bandits."

Recently, torture and summary executions by the police, as well as deteriorating conditions in the prisons and problems in the judiciary system, have been well documented by institutions defending human rights. These include Amnesty International (1988; 1990), the Americas Watch Committee (1987; 1989; 1991a; 1991b; 1993) Human Rights Watch/Americas (1994; 1997), the Justice and Peace Commission of the Archdiocese of São Paulo, Centro Santos Dias, Comissão Teotônio Vilela (1986), Núcleo de Estudos da Violência, the OAB (Ordem dos Advogados do Brasil, the Brazilian bar association), and Brazilian social scientists. The media has already broadcast scenes of torture; the summary execution of 19 rural workers of the Movimento dos Sem Terra by the military police of Pará (April 17, 1996);

and scenes of extortion and abuse in the Favela Naval in Diadema, in the metropolitan region of São Paulo (including one execution), and in Cidade de Deus in Rio de Janeiro (March 1997).

As one of the Americas Watch reports on police violence in São Paulo and Rio summarized, "The military police, a uniformed patrol force, is responsible for summary executions, and the civil police, charged with investigation, is responsible for torture" (1987:6). As far as torture is concerned, this finding is confirmed by various studies, including those by Lima (1986) and Mingardi (1992), which present torture as almost routine for the civil police in dealing with suspects and a method connected with corruption. According to the Americas Watch: "Torture of ordinary suspects, not only by beatings, but also by relatively sophisticated methods, is endemic in the precincts of São Paulo and Rio de Janeiro. There is persuasive evidence that it is prevalent in other places in Brazil as well" (1987:9).

Although documentation exists, the prosecution of policemen involved in torture and other crimes has not been common. Moreover, information about such prosecutions in the state of São Paulo is available only for the period after 1983. Data from the *juiz corregedor* (disciplinary officer) of the civil police of the state of São Paulo indicate that between 1983 and July 1987, there were investigations of 259 cases of torture (these do not represent the total number of cases, only those for which documents are available); 362 policemen were acquitted, and 218 were convicted (Americas Watch 1987:36). According to Pinheiro (1991a: 53), from 1981 to 1989, there were 580 policemen involved in trials and 362 acquitted. Members of the human rights group Centro Santo Dias declared in an interview that many cases never reach the judiciary system, either because the victim and family are afraid or because proof is hard to obtain.

Since 1988 the incidence of torture in São Paulo station houses has apparently dropped (Chevigny 1995:171–72;Americas Watch 1993:21) because of efforts by some disciplinary judges *(juízes corregedores)* in the state of São Paulo and by the attorney general, who decided to enforce the new principles expressed in the 1988 constitution. A staff of prosecutors now investigates claims and brings charges. The civil police have therefore probably reduced their use of torture because they are afraid of being caught. This diminution indicates the importance of a civil system of accountability and punishment, as well as of the political will of public authorities to enforce existing rules.

As regards summary executions, table 4 presents the number of civilians and military policemen who died or were injured in confrontations in São Paulo after 1981. Some facts are clear: that a high number of civilians die in confrontations with the police every year; that the number of civilians is much higher than the number of military policemen who died; and that the number of civilian deaths reported greatly exceeds the number of injuries. Comparing police violence in six regions in the Americas (including Los Angeles, New York, Buenos Aires, Mexico City, and Jamaica), Chevigny (1995) found many types of abuse (especially torture, corruption, and excessive use of deadly force), but could not find any other situation that came close to that of São Paulo in the 1980s and 1990s. In South Africa, which carries out half of all the judicial executions in the world, in 1987—the year that registered the highest number of executions since 1910—172 people were executed (Amnesty International 1989:204). In other words, São Paulo's police in 1992 summarily killed 8.5 times more than South Africa's apartheid regime in its worst year.

Deaths of civilians in confrontations with São Paulo's military police can hardly be regarded as accidental or resulting from the criminals' use of violence, as the PM claims. If this were the case, the number of policemen killed should also have increased. In São Paulo the ratio between civilian and police casualties is disproportionately high. In New York City between 1978 and 1985, the ratio of civilians to policemen dead was 7.8 to 1. In Chicago the ratio was 8.7 to 1; and in Australia between 1974 and 1988 it was 2.3 to 1 (Pinheiro et al. 1991:99). In São Paulo, the ratio was 7.3 to 1 in 1983, 17.2 to 1 in 1985, and 18.8 to 1 in 1992. Moreover, in the countries mentioned above, total casualties are much lower. In Australia, with a population similar to that of the metropolitan region of São Paulo, from 1974 to 1988 only 49 civilians and 21 policemen died. In Canada, 119 civilians died between 1970 and 1981 (Pinheiro et al. 1991:99). Chevigny demonstrates that in New York City the number of deaths has consistently declined since 1971 (Chevigny 1995:66–7).

The number of policemen killed in São Paulo includes those who died off duty, mostly while working as private guards. Data from the secretary of public security show that in 1994 and 1995 the number of policemen who died either working as private guards or commuting to work was four times higher than the number who died in the line of duty.[3]

Moreover, in São Paulo the proportion of civilians killed in relation to those wounded deviates significantly from the ratio elsewhere. In New York, for each civilian who dies in a police confrontation, on average three are wounded; in Los Angeles, the ratio is one dead to two injured. In São Paulo, in 1992, for each civilian wounded by the military police there were 4.6 who died; in 1991, the ratio was 1:3.6 in the metropolitan region; and for the other years, there was an average of more than two deaths for each person injured.[4]

TABLE 4 Deaths and Injuries in Military Police Actions, State of São Paulo, 1981–1997

Year	Civilians Deaths	Injuries	Policemen[a] Deaths	Injuries
State of São Paulo				
1981[b]	300	n.a.	n.a.	n.a.
1982[c]	286	74	26	897
1983[d]	328	109	45	819
1984[e]	481	190	47	654
1985[f]	585	291	34	605
1986	399	197	45	599
1987	305	147	40	559
1988	294	69	30	360
1989	532	n.a.	32	n.a.
1990	585	251	13	256
1991[g]	1,140	n.a.	78	250
1992	1,470[h]	317	59	320
1993	409	n.a.	47	n.a.
1994	453	331	25[i]	216[i]
1995	500	312	23[j]	224[j]
1996	249	n.a.	32	n.a.
1997	253	n.a.	26	n.a.
Metropolitan Region of São Paulo				
1986	359	152	29	254
1987	268	125	19	223
1988	411	159	22	223
1989	532	n.a.	32	n.a.
1990	585	n.a.	13	n.a.
1991	898	251	21	n.a.
1992	1,301[h]	165	3[k]	63
1993	243	194	3[k]	66
1994	333	194	72[l]	194
1995	331	220	51[l]	205
1996	183	n.a.	n.a.	n.a.

SOURCES: For the state of São Paulo: 1981–1989: Pinheiro et al. 1991:97. 1990–1993: Núcleo de Estudos da Violência da USP, based on information from the Coordenadoria de Comunicação Social of the military police. 1994–1997: Department of Public Security of the state of São Paulo, press office.

For the metropolitan region of São Paulo: 1986–1988: Nepp 1989:11 and 1990:81. 1989–

TABLE 4 *(continued)*

1990: Data from the military police published by *Folha de S. Paulo,* 7 August 1991. Data from the same source for 1988 coincide with those of Nepp, and for 1986 and 1987 are very similar to those of Nepp. 1991: Núcleo de Estudos da Violência da USP, based on information from the Coordenadoria de Análise e Planejamento of the Department of Public Security of the state of São Paulo. 1992–1996: Department of Public Security of the state of São Paulo, Press Assessory.

NOTE: n.a. = information not available.

[a]Although the sources do not specify, there are indications that the totals for deaths and injuries of officers in various years probably include off-duty incidents. The majority of police deaths and injuries seems to occur when officers are either commuting or working as private guards. Information available for 1993 and 1994 demonstrates this trend (see notes i to l). *Folha de S. Paulo* (10 December 1991), citing data from the military police, indicates that only 30 percent of the deaths of military policemen occur during confrontations. The Department of public security of the state of São Paulo acknowledged in a report (*Relatório Trimestral da Ouvidoria da Polícia do Estado de São Paulo,* December 1995–February 1996, 44) that the majority of deaths probably occur when policemen are working as private guards. Deaths of civilians shown in the table refer exclusively to those occurring in confrontations with the military police.

[b]Estimate of *Folha de S. Paulo.*

[c]Americas Watch 1987:25 reports 425 deaths of civilians and 20 police deaths in 1982.

[d]Americas Watch reports the same number of civilian deaths but only 30 police deaths.

[e]Americas Watch reports the same number of civilian deaths but only 35 police deaths.

[f]Americas Watch reports 564 civilian deaths and 27 police deaths.

[g]Americas Watch 1993:4 reports 1,074 civilian deaths in 1991.

[h]Includes 111 prisoners killed in the Casa de Detenção on 2 October.

[i]Totals refer only to on-duty events. Data from the Department of Public Security of the state of São Paulo, press office, indicate that in 1994, while 25 policemen died in the line of duty, another 104 died in off-duty periods, many probably working as private guards. In 1994, 297 officers were injured off-duty.

[j]Totals refer only to on-duty events. Data from the Department of Public Security of the state of São Paulo, press office, indicate that, in 1995, while 23 policemen died in the line of duty, another 90 died off-duty. The number of policemen injured off-duty was 289.

[k]Data for police deaths in the metropolitan region in 1992 and 1993 probably include only those who died in the line of duty. The source does not specify the context of the deaths.

[l]The total of police deaths in the metropolitan region is greater than the figures shown for the state, probably because the off-duty deaths are included. The information for the metropolitan region and for the state comes from different sources.

In other words, the police in São Paulo, and in other Brazilian cities such as Rio de Janeiro and Recife, kill more people than they wound. These data indicate that the police are probably using their weapons more than is necessary to subdue suspects. The massacre at the Casa de Detenção is an extreme example of this tendency.

According to the military police, the majority of deaths (63.6 percent) occurred in situations of "resistance/reaction to the police." Only 8.1 percent occurred in cases of escape and 5.8 percent in cases of people "caught in the act." However, the team that studied the reports concluded that, more than indicating a tendency of ordinary criminality, these reports indicate the existence of a "prefabricated pattern" used by the police when a death occurs (Pinheiro et al. 1991:107, 106). Whatever the circumstances, reports are filed as cases of "resistance to the police followed by death" and classified and processed separately from occurrences of homicide. Barcellos (1992) describes the same pattern.

An additional indication of police abuse is the relationship between the number of people killed by police and the total number of murders. From 1986 to 1990, police killings represented an average of 8 percent of the total number of homicides in the metropolitan region of São Paulo; in 1991, this percentage jumped to 12.9 percent, and in 1992 to 20.63 percent.[5] In New York City in the 1990s, the average percentage has been 1.2 percent, and in Los Angeles, 2.1 percent.

Table 4 also shows sharp variations in the annual number of killings: it decreases from 1986 to 1988 and then increases, especially in 1991 and 1992, when the number reaches an astonishing level. After 1992, the numbers again decrease substantially. These variations can be understood if we consider the policies of public security in place since the beginning of democratic rule. The high level of summary executions in 1991 and 1992 may have resulted from a "tough" policy of public security adopted by Luís Antonio Fleury, first as secretary of public security during Orestes Quércia's administration (1987–1990) and then as governor (1991–1995). Moreover, the decreases after 1986 and 1992 may also have resulted from efforts to curb abuses undertaken first by Montoro's administration, then by Fleury given the repercussions of the prison massacre, and after 1995 by Mário Covas. Public policies do not offer the only explanation for these changes. In fact, the tradition of abuses—supported in public opinion and the mass media, and inherent in the autonomy of the police—plays a crucial role and interposes strong barriers to policies aimed at controlling abuse. Nevertheless, where there is political will, partial control, at least, can be exercised. And if this will coincides with popular perceptions (as after the massacre) instead of having to struggle against them (as during Montoro's administration), control comes more easily and faster. To substantiate these claims, I analyze the policies of public security of the state of São Paulo, their context, and the interference of public opinion since the end of the military rule.

PROMOTING A "TOUGH" POLICE

André Franco Montoro was the first elected governor after military rule. A longtime opponent of the military regime, Montoro symbolized the expectations for change and for democratization in the early 1980s. The last years of the military regime were marked by a sharp increase in political opposition, an intensive organization of social movements and institutions among civil society, denunciations of the illegal acts committed during the military years, and support for a movement demanding amnesty for political prisoners. The opposition to the military was expressed by the slogan *retorno ao estado de direito* (literally "return to the state of right or law," which I translate as "return to the rule of law"). This meant not only a return to constitutional rule and democratic elections, but also the control of all sorts of abuses of power. In São Paulo, PMDB (Partido do Movimento Democrático Brasileiro) represented a broad political coalition opposing the militaries under the idea of "rule of law." Montoro, PMDB's candidate for state government in the first direct elections to be held in twenty-one years, was elected with 49.4 percent of the votes in the state of São Paulo in 1982, when the military were still in the federal government.[6] He took office in March 1983 and was governor until 1987.

Montoro took seriously the task of building a rule of law and a democratic government, and in his view this task included controlling the police. His plan of government, summarized in a document called *Proposta Montoro* (Montoro Proposal, hereafter *Proposta*), included police reform. Regarding the civil police (*Proposta* 1982:33), the document recognized its "internal authoritarian and inefficient structure, susceptible to cases of corruption and abuse of power," which would bring "more fear than tranquility to the citizens." It proposed, among other things, reforming the Corregedoria da Polícia Civil (disciplinary office) to assure "the efficient control of the cases of corruption and violence" and reforming the top of the police hierarchy by having some of its directors elected by police chiefs.

The military police was a more difficult subject because it remained subject to the army, which was still in command of the federal government. Despite this, the proposal carefully stated the need to bring the PM within the parameters of the law, making its "repressive action more efficient, less supportive of violent reactions and actions, and more in accordance with the law which, ultimately, aims at the citizen's security" (*Proposta* 1982:34).

Montoro's commitment to these ideas was affirmed by his choice of state secretaries. For secretary of justice he nominated José Carlos Dias. Dias was a well-known lawyer for political prisoners during the military years and ex-president of the Justice and Peace Commission of the Archdiocese of São Paulo, the main institution defending human rights during the dictatorship. As secretary of justice Dias headed the judiciary system, including the prisons, where disrespect for human rights was high. It became clear, however, that to defend human rights under democracy was almost as difficult and controversial as during military rule.[7]

As secretary of public security (to whom both police branches report), Montoro chose Manoel Pedro Pimentel. He was a former secretary of justice, unconnected to corruption, and someone who, given his ties to previous governments, could facilitate the transition period. He took office with the task of creating a "new police" according to the *Proposta*'s guidelines. However, the obstacles to this project were such that Montoro had to change secretaries three times in one year, replacing Pimentel with Miguel Reale Jr. and then with Michel Temer. Temer left in 1986 and was replaced by Eduardo Augusto Muylaert Antunes, who remained in office until the end of Montoro's government. Within a few months it was clear that reforming the police was much more difficult than had been thought and that the defense of humanitarian and democratic principles was not enough to bring about reform.

Mingardi gives two explanations for Montoro's failure to reform the civil police (1992: part 2) . First, it was an institution more independent than it was supposed to be, and its illegal "habits and costumes" had deep roots in police practice and enjoyed widespread popular support.[8] According to Mingardi, to change those habits in a situation of increasing criminality became impossible. Second, he claims that the project of the "New Police" was betrayed by the secretaries who came after Pimentel: they made decisions that not only prevented reform but also returned to power those who were supposed to be removed.

Mingardi's description of the history of the policies of public security is biased by the fact that he presents only the view of those involved with Pimentel. Moreover, although he mentions the opposition of the population and some resistance (1992: part 3), he does not really explore those questions. I argue, instead, that Montoro's failure to reestablish the rule of law was due to a lack of substantial support for this idea from either the population or the police, with the latter sticking to their long tradition of abuses and arbitrariness.

As expected, attempts to reform the police faced strong internal resistance, including protests and strikes, some of which were registered by the press. In the municipal campaign of 1986, for example, several *delegados* (heads of police stations) signed a manifesto openly criticizing Montoro's policy. I interviewed two secretaries of public security from this period, Miguel Reale Jr. and Eduardo Augusto Muylaert Antunes, and the secretary of justice, José Carlos Dias. They described the task of imposing a new modus operandi on the police as slow and difficult, and they told me about various episodes of opposition and resistance. Reale Jr. and Muylaert acknowledge that they achieved far less than they wanted to, but they indicate what they thought were important achievements. First, the attitude of the police toward labor actions and public protests was transformed. Whereas the previous regime had considered such actions a threat, they were now to be accepted, and the police had to learn to help in the organization of demonstrations, not their repression. They also mentioned, and data cited in chapter 3 confirm, that Montoro's government started with a police force armed with small amounts of old-fashioned equipment, and that the government invested heavily in equipment, personnel, and salaries. They also said that their government was concerned both with producing good statistics—which was not the case before—and with giving more power to the Corregedoria do Estado (disciplinary office) in order to investigate abuses by police.

As regards the enforcement of discipline within the police forces, most statistics are available only for the period after 1983. As Mingardi confirms (1992:69–70), the Corregedoria became more active. Although the numbers in tables 5 and 6 are still low considering the routine of abuse, both tables show higher numbers of policemen punished during Montoro's administration, especially among the PM: in 1984 the number of policemen punished corresponded to 1.0 percent of the total number of military policemen (56,072). Most of the punishment was related to the control of Rota, which was a focus of government attention. During Fleury's administration (1991–1995), however, the numbers for the civil police are especially low.

Montoro's administration tried to also establish more effective forms of control over the use of weapons. It determined, for example, that technical data on any death caused by police should be sent directly to the secretary, and it established new rules for keeping track of guns used by the military police. Before that, each PM team was assigned their guns daily as a lot, signing a single receipt. When the guns were returned, the receipt was destroyed. This made it impossible to connect any one gun to a particular officer or shooting.[9] Although even these fundamental rules of control faced opposition, they seem to have had some effect. The number of policemen punished increased, and the number of people killed by the police decreased, although the level was still high. In 1986, there was a decrease of 32 percent in civilian deaths. Muylaert, secretary in 1986, says that although the numbers "were not glorious," they indicated the results of the controls imposed on the military police.[10]

Moreover, the secretaries of public security during Montoro's administration seem to agree that their commitment to establishing a rule of law

TABLE 5   Punishment of Civil Policemen, Department of Public Security,
State of São Paulo, 1981–1988, 1991–1993

| Year | Punishment | | | |
	Dismissal	Suspension	Reprimand	Admonition
1981	12	n.a.	n.a.	n.a.
1982	13	n.a.	n.a.	n.a.
1983	39	481	202	13
1984	66	600	173	15
1985	37	640	173	4
1986	45	590	123	10
1987	68	724	235	30
1988	60	478[a]	133[a]	49[a]
1991[b]	29	128	17	6
1992[b]	28	138	23	8
1993[b]	105	155	22	0

SOURCES: For dismissals in 1981–1982 and 1988: Mingardi 1992:69. For 1981–1988: Corregedoria da Polícia Civil, Corregepol, cited by Nepp (1990:83). For 1991–1993: Secretaria da Justiça e da Cidadania, Report prepared for the Fiftieth Session of the Commission on Human Rights of the United Nations, Geneva, 1994, Appendix D-3 (Data from the Corregedoria da Polícia Civil).

n.a. = information not available

[a]Until July.

[b]Data for 1991–1993 refer only to cases of violence (assault, torture, abuse of power, etc.) and corruption (extortion, smuggling, etc.).

and their discourse had some effect on controlling police violence and abuse, although real change is a long-term project. In an interview on July 25, 1990, Muylaert commented:

> What I said to Fleury when I handed him the department was the following: "Fleury, be careful with your language!" In the police, when you say, "I don't want any violence; the policy of the government does not tolerate it, whoever practices violence will be punished," even saying that, when you turn your back they exceed the limits. If you say that it is necessary to respect the human rights only of the good citizens and that it is necessary to act boldly with the bandits, they go out and kill whoever they want. You don't have any means to control this, because of what they understand from your language. When the secretary says, "There will be no violence," they say, "OK, only a little bit"; when you say, "Act boldly," they will go out killing.

TABLE 6 Military Policemen Dismissed and Expelled, Department of Public Security, State of São Paulo, 1981–1993

Year	Number punished	Year	Number punished
1981	179	1988	589
1982	181	1989	379
1983	435	1990	n.a.
1984	587	1991	404
1985	448	1992	384
1986	406	1993	391
1987	436		

SOURCES: For 1981–1989: Secretaria da Segurança Pública, Estado Maior da PM, 1989, cited by Nepp (1990:85). For 1991–1993: Secretaria da Justiça e da Cidadania, report prepared for the Fiftieth Session of the Commission on Human Rights of the United Nations, Geneva, 1994, Appendix E-2 (Data from the Corregedoria da PM).

n.a. = information not available.

Reale Jr. observed:

> Our task was to transmit values. You had to transmit the idea that any person, even the criminal, had rights. It is not because he committed an offense that the death penalty can exist, having the officer as both judge and executioner. To transmit those values is something that takes a long time, something that you have to face resistance to. It is easier for the policeman who lives in tension because he is fighting violence straight, face to face; it is much easier for him to have a simple answer, to react with violence and kill the person. Why is he going to care about arresting someone if he can kill, if impunity is assured? How to transmit values to those policemen who came from a long authoritarian habit? . . . All of this was very difficult, it involved a complete change of mentality, a deep change of values. This only happens slowly. However, while this is done step by step, any word to the contrary dismantles the work. That was what Quércia did. Quércia dismantled the work that Montoro and his security secretaries did in order to change the mentality. Everything went back. It became really easy. Because it is easier to have impunity assured and violence legitimated, especially by the hierarchical superior. One word of a superior saying, "Be violent," and this goes from top to bottom incredibly fast. The colonel said, the next day the soldier knows. If the colonel says something towards restraint, prudence, common sense, equilibrium, it takes time to get to the soldier. But one word authorizing the practice of violence runs like a fuse. So, it is a very slow process. (Interview, 8 August 1990)

These observations closely echo the conceptions of the spread of evil articulated by private citizens in chapter 2. For Reale Jr., violence spreads easily and fast; its control, however, is a long-term project of cultural elaboration, with fragile results subject to rapid reversal. But if the change of values is a long-term project, Montoro's administration nevertheless has demonstrated that a political determination to control violence and impose the rule of law can have some effect in the short run.

The absence of political will to control police violence in the two administrations following Montoro's not only reversed the small gains but helped violence to proliferate. Both as secretary of public security in Quércia's administration and as governor, Luís Antonio Fleury supported a police "acting boldly." His attitude resulted in a huge increase in the number of deaths caused by the police, a state of affairs that both Fleury and his first secretary, Pedro Franco de Campos, were ready to defend. However, the responsibility does not lie only in the executive's choices. Montoro's decision to try to reestablish the rule of law and control police violence enjoyed little popular support. What he and his team could do was limited both by popular opposition and by police resistance. Among São Paulo's residents, violence is still seen as a good way of dealing with criminality, and it was by promising more "energy" and violent methods of patrolling that Fleury built his reputation and was elected.

The history of Rota offers a good example of both the support for a violent police and the possibilities of controlling them through public policies. Rota—Rondas Ostensivas Tobias de Aguiar—is a special division of the military police, and it is known to be responsible for most of the killings of civilians in the metropolitan region of São Paulo shown in table 4. It was organized in 1969, during the military regime, to fight terrorist attacks, especially bank robberies. Its approximately seven hundred officers are organized in groups of "four armed men with high gun power, mobility and communication" (Pinheiro 1982:59). After the end of the repression of political opponents to the government, Rota was directed to fight criminality. According to Pinheiro, citing Rota statistics, from January to September 1981 Rota shot 136 civilians, killing 129 of them and wounding 7, while one officer died and 18 were injured.[11] Moreover, it arrested 5,327 people, only 71 of whom had been previously convicted. In a pattern common since the Empire, all the others were "detained for investigations," which means there were no formal charges against them, merely a "suspicion." The journalist Caco Barcellos has followed many of Rota's cases and published the results in the best-selling book *Rota 66* (1992). He demonstrates that Rota policemen frequently act on the basis of suspicion, and their common reaction is to shoot.

To cover up, they claim there was a threat to their lives, when often there was none. As Barcellos puts it, "The dead person is always guilty of his own death" (1992:74). Because the majority of people killed by Rota had no criminal records, legal investigation into their deaths is difficult. Barcellos shows that a minority of Rota policemen are responsible for most of the killings, and he supplies the names of those who have killed most frequently.

Although in 1983, when Montoro took office, there was less information about Rota available than there is today, the force was already famous for its use of violence, and it became a symbolic target for Montoro's government. Even before Montoro took office, the control of Rota was a hot topic, not only because of the corps's resistance but also because of the population's support of it. During the electoral campaign, newspapers announced that Montoro intended to abolish Rota. Protests came from everywhere, and Rota was defended by its leaders. On 10 October 1982, in an interview with the paper *Folha de S. Paulo,* the chief of Rota, Niomar Cirne Bezerra, presented an argument that was to become famous in the following years: "Rota is adored in the periphery and hated by middle-class intellectuals who live in the center of town."[12] In other words, violence was favored by the masses and opposed only by intellectuals, who were known to support Montoro. Rota's chief concluded his interview, which took place a month before the elections, by saying: "We—Rota—are the only thing that the criminals fear. And as the old saying goes, fear leads to respect, which is transformed into admiration and leads to love."

Of course, Bezerra disregarded the population's fear of Rota, but his philosophy seemed to be popular. In December 1982, a poll by *Folha de S. Paulo* revealed that 85.1 percent of the people interviewed were against eliminating Rota.[13] In February 1983, before taking office, the secretary of public security announced that Rota was not going to be eliminated but would instead be transformed into a special group to assist in emergencies (*Folha de S. Paulo,* 8 February 1983). The task of policing the periphery was taken away from Rota. In June, Manoel Pedro Pimentel acknowledged in an interview that the pressure to put Rota back on the streets was strong and that people preferred its violent methods. He also revealed how torn he was between enforcing human rights, as the state administration and some groups desired, and bringing back Rota, to make the population happy. In an article in *Folha de S. Paulo,* titled "Pimentel Admite Pressões para a Rota Voltar, mesmo Matando," (2 June 1983), he remarked:

> When we allow the military police to kill, there is a violent reaction
> from those who find human rights disrespected and even pray a mass
> for the soul of the criminals. On the other hand, the population clamors

for security and wants Rota in the street to kill criminals. That is what people ask here in my office daily. They come in groups asking for Rota, knowing that it is going to kill. . . . Isn't that ironic? The same people who today accuse us of inertia, if we act, tomorrow will accuse us for killing. Because if a heavy force such as Rota goes out, it is clear that it will kill.

What is especially striking in this statement is the way in which the secretary's doubt was expressed: he sees a clear choice between yielding to the human rights groups (the allusion to the Catholic Church and its defense of "criminals" is clear) and an increase in deaths, with both presented as undesirable options. Pimentel, unlike other secretaries, seems not to have envisioned ways of controlling Rota: if the force existed, obviously it would kill. Also striking is how this possibility is matter-of-factly discussed by the secretary of public security with the press.

In August 1983, one day before Pimentel was succeeded by Reale Jr., *Folha de S. Paulo* published another poll evaluating Montoro's policy on public security. Of the respondents, 40.7 percent classified it as "regular" and 39.1 percent as "bad." Moreover, 71.8 percent of the respondents declared that the policy of public security should be "tougher" (*mais dura*, more violent) in fighting criminality.

It was thus against the opinion of the majority of the population—as well as against the habits and interests of the police—that Montoro's government continued its efforts to control abuses and police violence and to establish a rule of law. In 1985, just before the mayoral elections, another *Folha de S. Paulo* poll revealed that 47.6 percent of the population thought that the main problem of the city was security.[14] During this political campaign the question of human rights was crucial, and the opposition to Montoro's government became explicit when the Association of Police Chiefs published a manifesto against Montoro's party and his policy of defending human rights. This theme was also central in the 1986 gubernatorial campaign. On both occasions, right-wing politicians in particular dedicated themselves to attacking human rights (see chapter 9).

Montoro's successor, Orestes Quércia, was elected in this context, and from 1988 until 1992, the policy of public security in the state of São Paulo explicitly supported a "tougher" police.[15] This policy included empowering policemen of the so-called "hard line," such as the new PM chief, Colonel Celso Feliciano de Oliveira, who took office declaring "an open hunting season on bandits" ("Linha-Dura na PM Aumenta Repressão ao Crime," *Folha de S. Paulo*, 21 November 1989). He believed that the only way to fight criminality was to increase the number of policemen on the streets—and of course to use violence. In the same article, he stated: "The goal of the state government is to give tranquility to the population. If this results in deaths, you can be sure that there was reaction from the bandits. We are not here to kill people. If it were like that, we would kill everybody we arrest."

In the week that followed this statement, the PM killed four people who had no criminal records. Interviewed about the deaths, the secretary of public security, Luís Antonio Fleury, enacted the discourse of "boldness" that both Muylaert and Reale Jr. identify as tacit permission to increase violence. In an article in *Folha de S. Paulo* on 28 November 1989 ("Fleury Diz que a PM Vai Matar mais este Ano"), Fleury declared that "the fact that this year there were more deaths caused by the PM means that it is more active. The more police in the streets, the more chances of confrontations between criminals and policemen." He added:

> We continue to respect the law. But it is necessary to consider that we live in a society with problems of violence. . . . If the military policeman needs to use rigor, he will have support from the top of the police. But if he commits an abuse, he will be punished. . . . It is necessary to keep in mind that the clash between policemen and criminals tends to increase. From my point of view, what the population wants is that the police act boldly.

The message is clear: killings by the police are a result of its effectiveness in carrying out its duties as desired by the public. When the secretary of public security speaks of the law and people's lives in such a casual tone, dreams of the rule of law clearly have become irrelevant. This "tougher" policy persisted, along with support for Fleury, who was elected governor a year after this interview. The same indifference to police killings and their association with efficiency were evident in statements by Fleury's first secretary of public security, Pedro Franco de Campos. Asked to comment on the 1,140 civilian deaths that occurred 1991, he said: "It is necessary to compare that number to the number of heads of households murdered" (*O Estado de S. Paulo*, 23 December 1991). A few days earlier he had said: "The numbers increased because the police are more present on the streets. However, the police only strike back. They always react to the violence of the criminal" ("Polícia Militar Mata mais de Mil em 91 e Bate Recorde," *Folha de S. Paulo*, 10 December 1991).

One indication of the support for police violence is the rate of punishment for abuses. Table 5 shows a considerably lower number of civil policemen punished during the first years of Fleury's administration. This figure may be partially accounted for by the fact that these data refer only to cases of violence and corruption, whereas for previous years there was no indication of the cause of proceedings. But some observations should be made. First, the number of policemen expelled increased substantially in 1993, that is, after Pedro Campos was replaced with Michel Temer and a new policy was adopted. Moreover, because cases of violence and corruption are presented separately, we can see that, as among the military police, violent abuses are not frequently punished. In fact, 86.85 percent of the cases of dismissal were brought for corruption. The majority (64.2 percent) of the 1,154 cases of violence investigated by the Corregedoria da Polícia Civil between 1991 and 1993 were shelved *(arquivados)*; 9.27 percent resulted in acquittal and 25.65 percent in some form of punishment. Among the 989 cases of corruption, 36.5 percent were shelved; 21.74 percent resulted in acquittal and 39.33 percent in punishment.[16]

The increase in killings by the police in the early 1990s relates to changes in Rota. It had been demobilized and restricted by Montoro's government but was given new cars and new equipment under Fleury, and in 1991 many former members were recalled. After Montoro's intervention, the number of people killed by Rota had diminished (Pinheiro et al. 1991). After a ceremony to incorporate more cars and old members back into the corps in early December 1991, Rota killed twenty people in one week.

To legitimate their actions, the military police continuously elaborates the "danger of bandits" and constructs the image of Rota as a protector of the poor, who support its violent methods in the periphery. In these constructions, the PM is frequently assisted by the media, such as the newspapers *O Estado de S. Paulo* and *Jornal da Tarde*. The latter reported on a Rota ceremony attended by the governor, who declared that he was honoring an electoral promise by giving Rota more equipment. On the same page, another article focused on the return of former officers under the heading "The Captain Returns to the Headquarters—As if Coming back from Exile" (2 December 1991). Reporter Marinês Campos tells the reader, in the sentimental language of romance novels, about the happy ending for the military policemen who had been expelled from Rota.

> The captain, one day in 1984, unloaded the gun, took off the holster, and went out to Tiradentes Avenue looking like someone who had left his heart behind inside a Rota vehicle. And it hurt like a bandit's shot. Afterward came almost three thousand days of exile. Thousands of hours, counted on the fingers like a prisoner who marks on the wall the time until liberty. The captain never left aside the *hand-talkie*, the radio of the PM, always tuned to Rota's frequency , and even from afar he used to listen the sounds of bullets and sirens. And it used to hurt.

But now Captain Antonio Bezerra da Silva has returned to his headquarters—seven years and nine months after governor Franco Montoro decided to disperse the men of Rota in an attempt to extinguish the police body which had become a myth. An excessive, violent myth, Justice Secretary José Carlos Dias used to say in the name of human rights.

But the calls for the governor to maintain Rota on the streets were very strong. He maintained it, but dispersed the men into other parts of the Military Police—the same men who now are going back to their headquarters like people returning from a long exile. Captain Bezerra is back there now. . . . Back to the place where he lived for ten years. From a window, he points to the garden and repeats: "When I die, I want to be cremated and have my ashes spread out just here."

There are a lot of people, says the captain, who cannot understand a man who has the Rota injected into his veins, who lives with machine guns, rifles, and a way of doing police work like a man who is happy beside a woman. . . .

"It is impossible to explain what we feel for Rota," says Captain Bezerra. He tries. "Maybe it is like jumping with a parachute for the first time," he compares. "A mixture of fear, happiness, something unknown, of challenge . . . " And three thousand days after his last round inside a vehicle of the Rondas Ostensivas Tobias de Aguiar, the captain goes to the streets to remember old times. With eyes shining, his heart jumping like a child on a roller coaster.

Violence, abuses, and illegalities have been forgotten—or transformed, along with respect for the law and human rights, into a kind of eccentric obsession of José Carlos Dias and Franco Montoro. In any case, such considerations must give way to the romantic return of the "heroes" whose lives are completely entwined with the violent police and for whom the pleasure of "criminal hunting" is equated with the pleasure of being with a woman and compared by the reporter, a woman, to riding a roller coaster. In fact, the reporter prefers to help enforce Rota's "heroic mythology" and forget their abuses. In her text, the return of the bandit-killers is unmistakably a good thing. With this type of public support from a press free from censorship, and with politicians' willingness to ignore the law, of course the PM felt free to kill in 1991 and 1992.

THE MASSACRE AT THE CASA DE DETENÇÃO

The massacre of 111 prisoners in São Paulo's largest prison, the Casa de Detenção (House of Detention), on October 2, 1992, symbolizes the culmination of Fleury and Pedro Franco de Campos's policy tolerating police abuses.[17] In fact, this event reveals a great deal about the paradoxical character of a society in which democratic institutions and abusive repressive practices coexist. The massacre was exhaustively documented by a free media which, as during the impeachment of President Collor, which had occurred just a few days earlier, took on itself the task of uncovering what public authorities were trying to hide. The coverage reveals not only the horrendous details of the massacre but also the views of public authorities, defenders of human rights, prisoners and their families, and the public in general, split between supporters and critics of the police action. Obviously, it also expresses the press perspective, which represents abuses in Brazilian society as business as usual.[18]

In an action apparently aimed at controlling gang fights inside the penitentiary complex of Carandiru, the military killed 111 prisoners in Pavilhão (pavilion) 9.[19] Not a single policeman died. Machine guns were used inside a closed space, and, as the Amnesty International report puts it:

> There is overwhelming evidence to suggest that the majority of prisoners, including the wounded, were extrajudicially executed by the military police after having surrendered, while defenseless in their cells. Forensic evidence indicates that shots were fired from the doorways into the backs and sides of cells, and no shots were returned. The high proportion of bullets (60.4 percent) fired at the head and thorax of prisoners indicates no use of minimum force restraint, but a clear intention to cause fatalities. (Amnesty International 1993:28).

The massacre had Dantesque overtones, as prisoners were not only shot randomly but were also beaten, attacked by dogs specially trained to bite the genitals, and stabbed with knives. Naked, many of the survivors were forced to watch executions, to carry the bodies of dead inmates, and to clean away the blood that flowed everywhere, because the police were terrified at the prospect of contracting AIDS. In fact, one reason the police gave to justify their actions was that the prisoners had attacked them with darts dipped in HIV-contaminated blood. Although the police and the government tried to hide the massacre (local elections were to be held on October 3, and the news would damage the governor's candidate), shocking pictures appeared in the press everywhere two days later: naked and mutilated bodies, with big black numbers written on their legs, arranged side by side in open coffins in the corridors of the Institute of Legal Medicine—a concentration camp–type vision. A few days later, images from inside the Casa de Detenção were published, showing piles of bodies, close-ups of shot prisoners, naked prisoners carrying corpses, and the destruction inside the cells. These were complemented by images of desperate relatives being attacked by dogs and by the police at the door of Carandiru as they tried to find out what had happened to the prisoners inside, and of people crying outside the Institute of Legal Medicine, where they had to view all the corpses in order to identify their relatives.

The images unmistakably revealed the abuse of force. Unconvincing attempts by the governor, his secretary of public security, and police commanders to downplay the events and to blame the prisoners for the killings outraged a good part of the population. Similarly, when the press was shown the injured policemen and the weapons apprehended by the military police, people became indignant: there was not one single serious injury, just bruises; not one single powerful weapon, just old knives, pieces of wood, and a few old guns. (This was no doubt why the police had to claim the fear of AIDS as their main justification for shooting.) All the magazines and newspapers wrote strong editorials against the massacre and opened their columns to the general public, intellectuals, human rights organizations, and public authorities to express their indignation.[20]

However, indignation was not universal. In fact, in a telephone survey by *Folha de S. Paulo,* one-third of the population of São Paulo endorsed the police action. According to a poll by *O Estado de S. Paulo,* 44 percent of the population supported it. Many people took to the streets to demonstrate in favor of the police and against defenders of human rights. Many right-wing politicians and state representatives publicly defended the police and helped organize demonstrations supporting them.

In general, state and police authorities not only avoided criticizing the massacre but tried to diminish its significance and evade responsibility for it, although the press insisted that both the governor and the secretary of public security had been consulted beforehand. During the first hours after the news became public, Campos's declarations to the press, as well as Fleury's support of him, demonstrated open disrespect of rights and lives. They also suggest that the massacre was not totally alien to their policy of public security. Campos repeatedly denied that what happened at Carandiru could be called a massacre, claiming instead that it was a necessary intervention "to prevent a mass escape" (*Folha de S. Paulo,* 7 October 1992). He also said that the delay of almost two days (days of local elections) in informing the population was due to the need for a good evaluation of the facts and "protecting the population."[21] Fleury declared that he found that the actions of the police had been "adequate" considering that the prison was populated by "a confrontation of well-armed gangs" (*Jornal da Tarde,* 5 October 1992). Trying to sell the massacre as acceptable and playing on the belief that the working classes favor a violent police, the governor also declared that "Brazil is only going to have a First World police when it becomes a First World country. The police is a reflection of society, and society is violent. My maid, who is working class, approved [of the massacre]."

Colonel Eduardo Assumpção, commander of the PM, offered one of the most striking defenses. Here are excerpts from his interview with *Folha da Tarde* ("Os Policiais Matam dentro da Lei, Afirma Comandante da PM," 6 October 1992) :

COLONEL: If the PM is received with bullets, they are not going to respond by throwing roses. When the PM kills someone, it is doing it according to the law, as legitimate defense. . . . Society trusts the PM . . .

REPORTER: Was there a massacre of prisoners in Pavilion 9 of the Casa de Detenção? Was there an order to kill the prisoners?

COLONEL: As far as I know, there was no order to kill anybody. It is not possible to state that it was a massacre, because that would be a prejudgment. . . .

REPORTER: The pictures of the rebellion show naked prisoners killed with gunshots. In general, prisoners take off their clothes following police orders after the rebellion is controlled. How do you see the accusation that various prisoners were killed after they had surrendered?

COLONEL: I don't know how to answer, because I did not see them surrender and I did not see the scene. All I know is that there were 2,000 prisoners there and 111 died. If there was a predetermination to kill, all would have died.

This interview reveals in a nutshell not only how the use of violence is naturalized and accepted as legitimate inside the military police but also how the commanders of the institution find ways of escaping responsibility for it. They are not afraid of using bizarre arguments, such as that if the police had intended to kill, all the prisoners would have been killed. That interviews such as this appeared in the press without any further consequence also indicates that such abuses are publicly accepted. Moreover, the fact that the detailed press coverage did not help to generate a single conviction reveals the limits of democratic institutions in Brazil.

In March 1993, a civilian criminal justice prosecutor brought charges against one of the commanders, and the military justice prosecutor presented charges against 120 military police officers and soldiers "for the 'military crimes' of homicide, attempted homicide and grievous bodily harm, while on active duty" (Amnesty International 1993:27). On March 8, 1993, the judge of the First São Paulo Military Tribunal accepted the charges brought by the prosecutor. As of December 1999, there has still been no trial. However, in May 1996, the Eighth House of Public Law of the Court of Justice (8ª Câmara de Direito Público do Tribunal de Justiça) found that the state of São Paulo was not responsible for the massacre. The superior judge hearing the case, Raphael Salvador, also vice president of the Paulista Association of Judges, ruled that the prisoners were responsible: "They initiated the rebellion, destroyed a pavilion, and forced society, through its police, to defend itself" (*O Estado de S. Paulo*, 4 May 1996). So far, the only concrete action generated by this episode has been taken by the executive branch. Under pressure from the media and the population, Fleury demoted the six main commanders of the massacre. Moreover, although he at first supported the secretary of public security, Fleury had to replace him and change his policy of tolerating police violence. Michel Temer, who had been secretary under the Montoro administration, was called in. He immediately adopted a discourse of legality and tried to enforce new rules: policemen responsible for shootings were taken off the street patrol and sent to counseling sessions and a course on human rights given by Amnesty International. He reduced the number of killings significantly (see table 4), demonstrating that the public authorities do in fact have means of restraining police brutality.[22]

The administration of Mário Covas, who took office in 1995 and was reelected in 1998, is once again committed to controlling police abuses. As table 4 shows, the killings of civilians have dropped since then.[23] The secretary of public security, José Afonso da Silva, attributes this drop to two initiatives. The first is the PROAR, the program to retrain police involved in high-risk situations (Programa de Reciclagem de Policiais Envolvidos em Situações de Alto Risco), created in 1995. Through this program, all policemen involved in fatal shootings—not only the officers who fired shots but all those on the team—are removed from patrol duties for three months and sent to a retraining program where they also receive counseling. They are reevaluated before returning to their previous duties. The second is the creation of a police ombudsman for civilian complaints, a post assumed by Benedito Domingos Mariano from the Centro Santos Dias, a well-known human rights group. In the first six months of the program (December 95 to May 96), the ombudsman received 1,241 complaints, 246 of which dealt with police violence committed by both forces (abuse of authority, beatings and torture, and homicides). In its 1997 evaluation of human rights practices worldwide, the U.S. State Department credited the ombudsman with "increasing the number of internal criminal investigations opened by the São Paulo police from an annual average of some forty to more than one hundred between November 1995 and June 1996" (Human Rights Watch/Americas 1997:53).

Since 1995, the São Paulo state policy to control police violence has been supplemented with a federal effort, of which the main symbol is the National Plan for Human Rights (Plano Nacional dos Direitos Humanos) adopted by Fernando Henrique Cardoso's administration in May 1996. His administration has also created a National Human Rights Prize to honor people defending human rights and has started to offer reparation to victims of abuses during the military regime. For the first time in several decades, human rights are being publicly defended by the federal government. The Cardoso administration has also promoted the transference of murder trials involving military policemen from the military justice to the civil courts. At the state level, the Covas administration adopted a State Program of Human Rights (Programa Estadual de Direitos Humanos) in 1997.

Although such policies are successful in controlling human rights abuses, they are not easy to implement. In June and July 1997 Congress was debating the law that would make military policemen accountable to the civil courts. At the same time the federal government, through its National Secretariat of Human Rights, was elaborating a police reform proposal to be sent to Congress, and Governor Covas presented a proposal for transferring all patrolling activities to the civil police and eliminating the division between the two police forces. On the pretext of demanding salary increases, the police responded with strikes and riots in all the major capitals, and in some cases the two forces exchanged shots and aggression. These incidents were broadly documented by the media.

Resistance to reform comes not only from the police but also from the population and the media. Despite the public outrage after the 1992 massacre, and new public policies and their positive results, significant support for a "tough" police persists. In the week following the 1992 massacre, for example, policemen and some politicians, such as the deputy Conte Lopes, organized demonstrations in favor of the PM. These drew considerable crowds and caused extensive traffic jams. Events from the electoral campaign of 1994 reveal further perversities and ambiguities. The commander of the PM during the massacre, Colonel Ubiratan Guimarães, presented himself as a candidate for the state assembly. He was part of a group of right-wing state politicians who support a violent police. This group calls itself *bancada da segurança* (security bloc).[24] Legislative candidates in Brazil are identified by numbers composed of two parts: the first two digits represent the number of the candidate's party, and the last three identify the candidate. Both Guimarães and Afanasio Jazadji (who belonged to different parties) arranged to be identified by the number 111, the number of deaths at Casa de Detenção. They thus made clear not only what kind of police they support but also how much latitude exists to endorse publicly and directly the practice of violence. The number of votes the *bancada da segurança* candidates received was not impressive compared to the votes some of them had received in previous elections, but it was sufficient to elect three of them.[25] Together, they had 191,231 votes, or 1.76 percent of the total. This result is encouraging if one considers that in 1986 Jazadji had been elected with more than half a million votes in a campaign based on the attack of human rights.

The episode of the Casa de Detenção and its coverage by the press bring together some of the most important topics of public debate during the consolidation of democracy in Brazil. In the debates that appeared in the press after the massacre, the subject of the judiciary system was almost totally ignored. There was little discussion about the parameters of legality versus illegality or about the role the judiciary should play in investigating the actions (for example, the issue that the military justice, not the civil system, was going to be in charge of the investigations). Instead, the press called for executive and legislative investigation and punishment. It pressed the governor to replace the secretary of public security and staged a discussion about the opening of an investigation inside the state assembly. This outcome reveals not only the limits of awareness about the role of the judiciary and civil rights in Brazil but also some biases about how to resolve conflict. The judiciary—largely perceived as ineffective—was not considered as the appropriate institution for conducting an investigation, reparation, and punishment; either the executive or the legislative was expected to perform these tasks. By failing to bring the issues of legality, justice, and the judiciary to the front of the debate, the press helped to reproduce discussions of violence at the level of popular sentiment: they tacitly acknowledged that autonomous decisions by the police were not subject to a system of accountability, and that private and illegal revenges routinely bypassed the judiciary system. One could argue that the press was only truthfully reporting on a social issue, a view confirmed by the fact that so far the only punishment arising from this case has been an executive act (the suspension of six police commanders by Governor Fleury and the dismissal of the secretary of public security). However, because the same press took such pride in having instigated change, that is, forcing an investigation of executive corruption and the impeachment of a president a few days before the massacre, it was reasonable to expect that it would perform a similar role after the massacre. That it did not reveals the challenges that the issue of violence and justice present to the democratization process.

The recent history of policies of public security shows that two governors have preferred the more popular approach of guaranteeing impunity to the police and closing their eyes to violations and to the escalating violence that comes with them. To enforce the rule of law in the field of civil and individual rights is an unpopular policy, although it was adopted by Franco Montoro and Mário Covas. We can conclude that because the tradition is one of abuse, it is simpler to acquiesce in it than to attempt to consolidate the rule of law. It is also clear that a strong democratic will is necessary but not sufficient to create a society respectful of human rights and to reverse a traditional pattern of abuses if part of the citizenry opposes it.

This history of abuses that culminates with the episode of the Casa de Detenção also indicates the importance of public opinion and of conceptions of violence as a remedy for violence. It is important, then, to investigate the popular view of the police and the justice system and the logic behind its support of violence. This inquiry also helps explain the weakened role of the judiciary and the preference for solving conflicts either through an executive act or through a private process.

THE POLICE FROM THE CITIZENS' POINT OF VIEW

The Brazilian working classes experience violence on a daily basis, at the hands of family members, criminals, and the police who make the working classes their main target. As a consequence, members of the working classes do not trust or respect the police; mostly they fear them, and with reason.

5.1

> Look, if someone approaches me and says, "I'm a bandit, I'm going to take you home," I would accept it more than if a guy in an uniform approaches me saying "I'm a policeman, and I'm going to take you home." No, I don't trust the police. I'm afraid of the police.
>
> *Airport janitor, Cidade Júlia, thirty-four, married,*
> *with three daughters; her husband is unemployed*

5.2

> You know that the police get confused, or that many times in order to show off, they mindlessly kill an innocent guy accusing him of being

a bandit. They put a gun in some poor guy's hands. Look, if you don't
have important friends, if you don't have wisdom, your son dies as a
bandit without his being a bandit because the police killed him by mistake and said he was a bandit. . . . I know of a student who, because
he was not carrying his identity papers, ran away afraid from the
police, and he was shot and declared to be a bandit, even though
he wasn't.

Housewife and neighborhood organizer in Jaguaré, thirty-five,
with four children; her husband is a skilled worker in a textile factory

5.3

The police only arrest those guys who work, workers, heads of
households. Those they arrest, beat, do whatever they want. Now,
those bandits, they don't [arrest]. . . . If a worker, if a head of a
household, forgets his papers at home, even if he is carrying his lunch
box *[marmita]*, if the police get him, he goes to jail. But if it is a bandit,
no. . . . The guy steals in the afternoon, they arrest him, divide the
money. . . . The world is completely turned upside down.

Office assistant, eighteen, Jardim das Camélias,
lives with his parents, a sister, and two nephews

Most members of the working classes see the actions of the police as arbitrary. Their descriptions of mistaken killings and police cover-ups coincide
with the reports of human rights organizations and with Barcellos's accounts
(1992): the pattern is well-known. The police mistake workers for criminals,
use violence against them, and try to cover up their errors. For the police, as
for many people, the boundary between the image of the poor worker and
that of the criminal is very thin indeed. As a consequence, members of the
working classes can be harassed by the police. Their natural reactions (like
running away) may be interpreted as the behavior of criminals. The narratives of working-class people are often punctuated by references to signs
that should prove their identities as workers. Central among those signs is
the *carteira profissional,* or professional identification, a document that registers a worker's occupational history: profession, labor contracts, the names
of employers, salaries, vacations, social security entitlements, etc. The
carteira profissional is the workers' most important proof of citizenship.
Other signs are the *marmita*—the lunch container—and calluses on their
hands as proof of manual labor.

Nevertheless, even the clearest signs may be ignored by a police force that, in popular opinion, may be violent with workers but is soft on criminals. The reasons workers give for thinking that criminals receive "better treatment" fall into two categories. On the one hand, they believe the police have monetary interests in crime and criminals: they are corrupt and may be directly involved in crime themselves. On the other, they are convinced that the police are not well prepared to perform their duties. In both circumstances, the imagery used to describe the criminal may also be used to describe the police.

5.4

Yesterday I was listening to the radio, and the reporter said that three policemen and a police chief were arrested because they're stealing. It means that policemen themselves are bandits as well. . . . The worst is that Rota, they sometimes kill innocent people. They kill the innocent while the bandits are free on the streets. Now, why don't they arrest the bandits? Because they give them money. I think it is because of that. Because they rob, then they divide up the money with them [the policemen], and everything is OK.

Housewife from Jardim das Camélias, thirty-three, four children; has participated in various social movements and local associations; her husband is a skilled worker in a small textile factory

5.5

I don't think of the policemen as state functionaries, I think of them more as people who are out there to defend their own interests related to drug traffic, to prostitution, to networks of those hotels you rent per hour. And inside the police there are many personal interests among them, agglomeration of males, I have always thought of that as something tending to deviance. . . . In sum, for me the police is also corrupt. Gun licenses, guns, drugs, those things involve a lot of money. The police are in charge of apprehending those things; so they apprehend and use the money to create capital to buy hotels.

College graduate, twenty-three, Moóca, unemployed, has a degree in communications with a major in radio, lives with his parents

Even when the police are not considered corrupt, they are thought to be underprepared for the job. In general, the police are said to be close to the evil elements of the environment of crime: perversion, sickness, prostitution, and bad influences are only a few elements on a long list.

5.6

What do I think of the police? Look, I think the following: they're lamentable—in relation to workers like us. It's lamentable that the police today are very unprepared. It's not the policeman's fault, but once more it is the general structure which is very unprepared.

[The speaker argues that the men who become policemen are very young and lack the necessary training. Because of that, they feel insecure and are afraid of confronting criminals. As a consequence, they use their guns more than necessary to overcome their fear or sometimes just "to show that they are men." Moreover, because they lack training, they do not have the notion that they are out there to serve society, that they are paid with tax money, and that they should not harass ordinary citizens.]

These days, for the policemen, everybody is a bandit, everybody is marginal, everybody deserves to be arrested, and everybody should respect them. It's lamentable, it's lack of training. The police have always been unprepared and are getting worse. They have never been good.

Bar owner, Moóca, has a law degree but does not work as a lawyer; single, lives with three roommates

5.7

The police are a public disaster! I think this is because the lack of ability of the policemen. I think that they get anyone to become a policeman, they get anyone who comes there from Paraíba, from Maranhão, from the middle of nowhere, doesn't even know how to read and is already a policeman, a PM! What does a person like that know about things and principally about the law? It must be that. You don't see in the police force people born in São Paulo; all you see are *nortistas*. . . . Any ten cruzeiros buy a policeman. They are just to get money. They want money, especially the PM.

Retired skilled worker, Jardim Marieta, late fifties, married with two children

5.8

The police? The police are afraid of facing armed criminals! Only the Rota doesn't hesitate—the Rota is like the Esquadrão da Morte. You know that if you needed to depend on a policeman to defend

you, you might as well forget it. Among one thousand you're going
to find one, because the rest only think of their families. . . . The
police don't have training, they don't have education. Now they
are starting to be a little polite with the public, but the majority of
them are like horses, animals, and illiterate! . . . If I had to depend
on the help of the police, it would be easier to ask the help of a
bandit to protect me from another bandit. Because they [policemen]
say: "I have a child to raise, I have a household to support, I'm not
going to die here, because I don't make enough money for that."
That is, we criticize, but we shouldn't criticize the policeman, but
their foundation. And what is that? The government. The government should give them more support, both moral and financial,
because they are exposed to danger, and we should see this.

> *Housewife and neighborhood organizer in Jaguaré, thirty-five,*
> *with four children; her husband is a skilled worker in a textile factory.*

Even when people may understand the poor and dangerous working conditions of the policemen—many of whom live in their own neighborhoods—
and find some justification for their inefficiency, they still criticize them.
The police are associated with the stereotypes and elements that compose
the image of the criminal: they are considered to be from the northeast, uneducated, animalistic, ignorant of their public role, and so on. In fact, when
people talk of crime, the two main characters of the universe of crime—the
criminal and the policeman—are not opposed but compared.

Many times, and especially in narratives of the upper classes, the police
are described by the same stereotypes used to denigrate the poor. For example, in quote 5.6 above, the arrogance of the policeman (portrayed as someone without an education) with a weapon in his hands is described in the
same way that an upper-class woman describes the arrogance of a working-
class person who buys a new car (quote 2.14). This tendency is also revealed
in the following comment about the risks involved in the expansion of private security services.

5.9

Logically, if you let those guys from firms [of private security] go
armed around the city, this is an additional risk. With the police
it is already something horrible, imagine if you expand the number
of armed people! . . . You can even argue that it does not matter

if it is public or private, since the guys who are armed are all from
the same mentality, from the same social class, and equally unprepared, and equally ready to use the guns for any stupid reason.

Freelance journalist, forty-three, Morumbi, divorced, with two children

The merging of the images of criminals and policemen, and of both with images of the poor, is frequent in discussions of crime. In all circumstances the confusion can led to death—of working-class people. As a consequence, not only are people always afraid and uncertain, but they also find it difficult to figure out the right reaction—to run or not to run—when encountering either the police or criminals. In facing criminals, to pretend ignorance is one of the best bets.

5.10

Many times, when there is a robbery, the neighbors say, "It was that
one, that one." But the police say, "We haven't caught him in the act,
so we don't arrest him," and they go away. And what happens? The
guy wants vengeance and goes around killing a lot of people, as it
happens today. When a crime happens on the street, the population
doesn't collaborate with the police because of that. . . . It's fear of
vengeance, they don't say anything, say they haven't seen anything.
If I see a robber killing someone, I won't want to know anything about
it. I'll pretend I haven't seen anything. If the police ask me, I'll say,
"I haven't seen anything."

If by any chance you're robbed, do you think it is worth reporting it?

I don't think it is worth it. We go to the police to file a claim, we do
everything and still go out of there mad, because we know that [when]
we turn our backs on them, they throw the paper away.

*Eldest of three brothers who live in Jardim das
Camélias, twenty-two, an auto mechanic, married*

In situations of crime and violence, workers feel powerless. They are paralyzed between fear of the police, fear of a criminal's vengeance and, as we shall see, a belief that the justice system is unable to provide justice. Without protection, their modus vivendi is to adopt silence as a way of maintaining good relations with criminals they might know personally.

Ironically or not, those views were confirmed by a policeman, a PM who lives in Jardim das Camélias, describes himself as a worker and member of the working classes, and shares many of his neighbors' opinions about crime, including the view that silence is a good tactic for dealing with threats of vengeance.

5.11

Long weekends are a disaster. People go traveling, and when they come back on Monday or on Sunday night, we get a lot of calls that the house was burglarized, people have taken everything. And the worst is that the neighbors don't see anything. In fact, they see, but they are afraid of calling the police.

Why are they afraid?

Because of the fragility of the laws. People know that if they call the police, either the PM or the civil police, they are not going to have any protection. We cannot provide individual protection if we don't have a superior order. If we're simply passing by and someone says, "There are two bandits inside that house," we go there and arrest the guys, but that person stays at the bandit's mercy. We cannot pass by his house every hour to check if everything is all right. . . .

What do you think should change to help your work?

If there were only justice! It's discouraging to take someone to the police station. There is corruption everywhere. I'm not trying to exempt the PM from this, for there are some corrupt policemen. However, in the civil police here in São Paulo it is worse. It's discouraging to take an individual to the station, and the commander—I have already seen that—takes money from the guy and says to him, "Let the PM leave [the building] so that it doesn't look bad, and I'll release you." I have already seen this happening, I left and saw the guy leaving through the back door. . . . The other day I was talking with another PM, saying that Brazil has become a Paraguay. Here, everything works on the basis of money. If you want to get something, you pay. Understand? There are a lot of people out on the street who should be in prison and are free because of corruption. There should also be efficient legislation in relation to corruption. . . . If there were justice, and some legal reform, it wouldn't take much. . . .

The PM is ridiculed. I was saying that some time ago it made you proud to go around in uniform. Nowadays, it's a source of shame. If a PM is in uniform, he walks looking to the side, checking if everything is OK.

People keep looking at him, and he thinks they are laughing at him. This happens sometimes because of lack of respect, and sometimes because of the brutality of the policemen themselves. Let's not attribute all wrong to society. I think that today the police are not prepared to exercise their duties. Wherever they go, they pull out their badges and say, "I'm police," and so forth. This should not happen. It's an abuse. He likes to take advantage of the uniform, and the fact that he is a policeman, to get what he wants. . . . The people say as much, they don't like the police. I don't know whether it is because of the laws. I don't know, but I know that in a way the people don't like the police. People even are afraid of the police these days.
Military policeman, Jardim das Camélias, early thirties, married to a woman who works as a secretary in a factory, one child, works off-duty as a private guard

In their descriptions of criminals, the people I interviewed always reminded me that it is necessary to be careful with generalizations, that in any category there are both good and bad elements. The same is true of discussions about the police. Even when an officer performs the way he should, popular distrust is so widespread that people prefer to hold on to their negative evaluations and see the instance as an exception. This was the attitude of a woman from Moóca who told me that a policeman had returned three gold chains stolen from her at a traffic light. When the officer called to her, she assumed that he wanted money or was going to harass her. When she realized he was returning the chains, she was so amazed that she wrote a letter to the reader's column of *Folha de São Paulo*. In spite of that incident, however, her general view of the police is unchanged: "This case hasn't convinced me, but even today I admire him."

If one takes into consideration the arbitrariness and violence of the police, the constant confusion (workers mistaken for criminals, policemen mistaken for criminals), the identification of criminals with policemen (both symbolic and material) and of both with poor people—in sum, the context of uncertainty, confusion, and fear of both policemen and criminals—one can only conclude that the police are far from being able to offer a feeling of security to the working and lower middle classes. The population often feels pressed against the wall, without alternatives.

5.12

How are you going to look for an alternative? There is no solution. What kind of solution are you going to look for? If you're going to put in a complaint about a policeman, he is going to harass you afterwards.

And we are afraid of dying, because those people are all armed!
So you cannot do anything. You're in bad shape, you want to do
things but you cannot. If you're going to do anything, you're arrested,
and are sentenced to die!

Retired skilled worker, Jardim Marieta, late fifties, married with two children

The justice system is so far from being seen as a reliable resource that in
many interviews it was not even mentioned as an element in the control of
crime: the universe of crime seems to include only criminals, policemen, and
powerless citizens, who have to negotiate their security. The justice system
is widely seen as extremely biased against workers. In the interviews with
people from all social classes, the most common reaction to mention of the
justice system was "It's a joke!" *(É uma brincadeira, uma piada)*. Frequently
people did not want to elaborate: it was too obvious. Some people, however,
did elaborate their views.

5.13

The justice in this country does not work. The justice, the law in this
country does not exist. The judiciary sector does not exist. A lawyer's
life is a kind of farce in this country. Unfortunately, the majority (of
lawyers) have to become corrupt in order to survive, they have to
favor people with power. I adore the image of the lawyer, but the
universal image of the lawyer; the image of the lawyer in Brazil is
insulting. In order for you to remedy something you have suffered and
that you have to depend on the law to do, in addition to the fact that
you are going to get old with the loss and to the fact that the thing is
not resolved in the short run, you spend a lot of money. Today people
who use a lawyer have to have money.

College graduate, Moóca, twenty-three, unemployed, has a
degree in communications with major in radio, lives with his parents

5.14

He [Doca Street] should stay in prison, get a life term, because he
killed the woman coldly, I saw that, he shouldn't be free in any
circumstances.[26]

And why do you think that they let him go free?

I think it was a lot of money, a lot, because someone who kills another
person in cold blood as he killed her should be imprisoned for the rest

of his life. He was acquitted. You see, we cannot say if the justice is just or not. . . . I can assure you that if he were a poor person, who did not have money, he would still be in jail. . . . A very rich guy may hire the best lawyers and with this he is free; a poor person, he does not have money for anything, how is he going to pay for a lawyer? . . . I don't know, the justice, you see the case of this other man: he was innocent because he killed in order to defend [his family], inside his house, he shouldn't be in prison!

> *Housewife, former maid and industrial worker, Jardim das Camélias,*
> *twenty-eight, married with three children; her husband is a hospital attendant*

5.15

I always say when I get revolted with something: there is no law here in Brazil. The country is without law, isn't it? If something, a disaster happens with the guy who is poor, nothing happens. I even have proof of a case which happened . . .

[He tells of a nineteen—year-old man who worked as an assistant to a truck driver in a moving company. He was killed by another truck making a wrong turn in a gas station. People saw the truck, had its license plate number, and went to the company, but the owner refused to give the name of the driver, and the police did nothing.]

When something happens, for example, a businessman is kidnapped, then it makes the news for a whole year. The police go after, investigate thoroughly.

> *Unemployed salesman, thirty-two, single, lives with a married sister in Moóca*

These views are clearly confirmed by available indicators. Of all the crimes reported to the civil police in the municipality of São Paulo in 1993 (389,178 *boletins de ocorrência*), only 20.4 percent resulted in police fact-finding proceedings *(inquéritos instaurados),* which are necessary for judicial action of any sort. In the last decade, that rate has varied between 17 and 21 percent. In 1993, for crimes of murder, it was a low 73.8 percent, although for drug dealing, it reached 94.4 percent (Seade, unpublished data).

In dealing with the feelings of fear and vulnerability engendered by a corrupt, biased, and ineffective police and judiciary, some people simply accept the status quo. Others look for alternatives. These are usually extralegal and may take one of two forms. On the one hand, people consider reacting privately and taking justice into their own hands. This is more often an alternative of discourse than of practice: people may express their frustration by defending personal vengeance, but they do not necessarily act on their words. On the other hand, people support the use of deadly force against alleged criminals. These are paradoxical reactions, for people are usually asking the police, whose violence they fear , to take violent action "against the side that deserves it." Their rationale is clear: once dead, criminals no longer pose a threat. However, the paradox remains: by supporting the violent action of the police, workers are only helping violence to spread and greatly increasing their own chances of victimization. One interviewee told of his problems with the company he had worked for until a couple of days before, which did not pay him what he was owed according to labor legislation (the company had failed to deposit his *fundo de garantia,* a type of unemployment insurance). He filed a suit against the company in the labor court but has had trouble pursuing it.[27]

5.16

Tell me where the law is!? Where is the law? Is there any law?

The law exists, in my opinion, it exists.

I'm someone revolted because of injustice! I cannot accept one thing: why does the government screw the worker so much? . . . The law only works to one side. To which side? Which? To the one they are making money from! To the side of money! It's logical! Man, you don't think that a guy has to be revolted? But if I get revolted by myself, is that going to make any good? . . .

Only money rules. And does justice exist in this world? Because of that I said to my boss today when I went to get what was coming to me: I'm going to shoot you, I know where you live! Man, I'm going to die in jail.

Don't talk like that, man!

The other partners, they are bastards too. There is no law in this world. So law is something you have to take into your own hands.

And what does this get you?

It's worth something because you get justice. Since there is no law, at least you make justice with your own hands. I think that this is great.
        Skilled metalworker just dismissed from his job, aged twenty-seven, Cidade Júlia

The strong feeling of continually being a victim of injustices, no matter how much or how well one works (the interviewee had been working since the age of eleven), is dramatically expressed. Private, individual vengeance is defended as the speaker's only recourse—although it would probably destroy his life. Sometimes, however, people imagine alternative, less risky forms of vengeance. They believe that the administration of summary justice should be a task of the police. This is the type of reasoning that supports the police's summary executions and by which the violence and illegality of the police may be seen as positive. In this context the Esquadrão da Morte and Rota, instead of being feared, are admired by the public—an admiration that military policemen are always ready to use to justify their killings. Exactly the same kind of perception leads to vigilantism and to support for the idea of lynching.

5.17

I wish the Esquadrão da Morte still existed. The Esquadrão da Morte is the police that only kills; the Esquadrão da Morte is justice done by one's own hands. I think this should still exist. It's necessary to take justice in one's own hands, but the people who should do this should be the police, the authorities themselves, not us. Why should we get a guy and kill him? What do we pay taxes for? For this, to be protected. . . . It is not worth it for us to lynch, they [the police] should have the right, they have the duty, because we pay taxes for this. . . . The law must be this one: if you kill, you die.

Office assistant, Jardim das Camélias, eighteen;
lives with his parents, a sister, and two nephews

5.18

Esquadrão da Morte was cool; it was the best police that existed. São Paulo stayed until 1972 without as many crimes as it used to have before. It was wonderful. Then they started to condemn the guys from Esquadrão da Morte. [The Esquadrão da Morte] was good, but [you have] to kill the right guy, you know, the right one. Because the guy who is no good has to die.

But who decides who is the right guy and the wrong guy?

Has to be by catching the guy in the act. If they know that the guy is dangerous, then go get him. If they get him, kill him, no one to arrest. To arrest is out!

Driver, Jardim das Camélias, thirty-two, used to be a taxi driver and now
works as a driver for a public institution; married with four children

For some people, then, asking the police for justice means asking them to exact immediate vengeance—as they frequently do—without the mediation of the justice system and without giving the criminals the opportunity to offer bribes. In these views, the police have nothing to do with law and the judiciary—each considered to be biased and unjust—but are not acting privately, either (like vigilantes). They are still seen as public agents, paid with tax money, but they are paid for exacting immediate revenge, for carrying out violence that may be illegal but is considered just and efficient. This view implies the implosion of the legal models of the roles of the police and of justice. The perversion of these models finds its logic in the everyday experience of abuses and injustices practiced by the institutions of order, in the absence of a notion of individual rights, and in people's desire for justice and vengeance. If the law were effective, if the constitution were respected, maybe none of this would be necessary. But since the institutions of order have failed, private vengeance is necessary, and people may go as far as to defend lynching, which has also increased in contemporary Brazil.[28]

One of the most paradoxical effects of the continuous arbitrariness and injustice suffered by the working classes is that the law may be perceived as an additional form of injustice. The application of legal principles or the recognition of some rights may be seen as only another form of harassment and disregard for the rights of the working classes. One such indication is the campaign against human rights that I analyze in chapter 9. Another is the often-repeated assertion (for example, in quote 5.14) that it is unfair to condemn a man who kills to defend his family.

5.19

I think that the police give too much space for the criminals. Something which revolts me is that a bandit may kill a head of household, but the head of a household cannot kill a bandit. If he enters inside my house, it means that I cannot do anything, but he can do whatever he wants. I get revolted. I say firmly, I'm in favor of the death penalty, God forgives me. . . . I know someone, he owned a little grocery store, the bandits entered for the third time, they stole, and he thought it was too much. He shot them. One died, and the other was arrested. He, poor man, he had to escape. He closed the grocery store, abandoned everything, went to the interior of the state. The other one was freed; he was arrested, and the day after, he was already on the street. Now he said that when he encounters him, he is going to kill. They enter, they steal, and they still threaten the head of a household who had to abandon his house, his home, everything. He closed it, he hasn't touched anything, he has never gone back there because he was afraid. I don't agree with that in any sense.

Housewife from Jardim das Camélias, thirty-three, four children;
she has participated in various social movements and local associations;
her husband is a skilled worker in a small textile factory

The example of the poor worker who is punished for defending his family or livelihood reveals people's perplexities over the application of the law. Why should people be punished for the "defense of honor"? This argument brings us dangerously close to the justification for acquitting men who kill their wives. The working classes, however, ask another question: why should the law, which never works anyway, punish in this case? We have come full circle: even when justice works properly, it looks unjust because it does not take into consideration the context in which things happen, a context defined by the inefficiency of public forms of reparation and protection. The dangers of this view are immense, for they are articulated outside the legal system and a public system of restitution. Two interviewees saw quite clearly the dangers of privatizing such a system:

5.20

Today's problem is this: impunity. I wouldn't know how to solve this. I'm not the savior of the country. I'm seeing the problems and I don't know how to solve them. This is the authorities' job.

Close to where I live, people knowing about the government's inefficiency and about impunity have decided to hire guards, to keep guns at home. . . .

I think that this would be the extreme option, would be the end of the nation, the end of the government. If the government were unable to contain the spread of criminality, it would be the end, would be chaos.

Wholesaler, Moóca, forty-five, married, lives with his wife and two children[29]

5.21

This is a vicious circle. The population is extremely revolted because of the barbarities that the robbers, the criminals do. And they really do. Talking personally, I think that if someone killed somebody in my family, and I saw that the guy wasn't sent to a trial, wasn't condemned, I would order someone to kill him, or I would do it myself. This at the personal level, considering all the emotions. But at theoretical level, the way in which the rule of law works, how justice works, then I think that things should work in another way. Human rights are the basis of civilization.

Real estate agent, fifty-six, divorced; started working in 1990, lives in Alto de Pinheiros with one daughter

The distinction between private sentiments of revenge, the law, and the defense of a rule of law was made by several people, especially those from the middle and upper classes. Although these people represent a minority among those I interviewed, it is clear that questions of the police and the law are experienced and thought about in a different way by the upper classes. They are often quite aware of the violent and arbitrary pattern of police behavior and may criticize Rota for its excessive use of force. Unlike the working classes, the upper classes are rarely victims of police confusion and violence or of the justice system. Moreover, they are not worried about the lack of police protection because they can buy sophisticated security systems and pay for private guards; in fact, everyone I interviewed in middle- and upper-class neighborhoods had some form of private security. As far as the law is concerned, the upper classes have the luxury of choosing to disregard it.

During my interviews in Morumbi, I explored this question by asking the residents' opinions about giving permission to their under-age children to drive without a license, a practice relatively common among the upper classes. Some people told me that they would not allow it, arguing that laws exist to be respected and that children should know about limits. These responses most often came from people who classified themselves as conservatives and were in favor of disciplining children. Others, however, openly defended the practice.

5.22

I raised three daughters, and this is my conception: I don't permit two things, to drive a motorcycle and drugs; the rest, you can do whatever you want. . . . I'm a person who likes to follow the rules, I've never liked to have attention called to me because I have made a mistake. I used to see a fourteen-, fifteen-year-old kid with a car and think that that was absurd. Life is dynamic, not static. If you ask me if I'm going to give a car to my son when he is fifteen, I'll say yes. Do you know it is against the law? I know it is against the law. Why would I give it to him? I don't feel safe letting a fourteen-, fifteen-, sixteen-year-old kid use public transportation: he is going be robbed, he is going to have things stolen. Or else he is going to go in a car with a friend whom I don't know and don't trust. So I'll give him a car when he is fifteen in order to avoid what? So that he doesn't suffer aggression. So I think this is fine.

Engineer, high-ranking technician working for the police,
fifties, married, five children, Morumbi

What follows is a discussion among people holding differing opinions. Two women say that they would not let their children drive before they are eighteen (the legal limit). P thinks that "each thing has its own phase"; the other, O says that there is a rule, and she likes to follow rules. However, their friend M says she would certainly give a car to her children because she raises them to be trustworthy, and because if something were to happen to them, she would prefer that it happen because of something they did and not "because he was in a taxi and the driver attacked him, or he was robbed inside a bus." In addition to expressing different perspectives, the discussion among these three friends makes it clear that defending the principles of the law is a relative matter.

5.23

What about the legal aspect of the thing, the fact that there is a law?

M: We know about many cases of taxi drivers who rape, or accidents, buses, a series of things. Maybe it wouldn't work to raise them like that, but my husband has convinced me that the legal aspect at this point is the least important. What is going to happen? Are you going to be arrested? No, you are not. Only if he kills someone on purpose. Maybe they're going to take my driver's license, or the father's, but we know about that.

O: I think that if there are laws, we have to follow them.

M: I don't worry about the legal aspect. I worry much more about my son as an individual . . .

And what about this thing she is mentioning: what do the laws exist for?

M: Is there law here in Brazil? [She laughs.] If I were living in Switzerland, I would be the first one to agree.

O: But you're living here, you have to respect the laws that exist here.

M: What laws? This is a mess which starts up there . . .

O: But you cannot educate your son like that . . .

M: You have to follow where you're living: while they don't change, why am I going to change by myself? . . . It is not that I am against the law, but that I think that above the law there are more important things.

What kind of laws do you think are respected in Brazil, and what kind are not?

M: It's difficult to say.

O: Normally, laws are enforced against the lower classes, the classes of small purchasing power. For them the laws are well "respected." They make them follow the law, obey the law. We from the middle class, from the upper class, we don't need to respect the law because we pay for it with money. I don't think this is just.

[Later in the interview these conceptions of the law proved to be more complex. When the discussion turned to the effects of the Plano Collor, it became clear that O's husband had a *caixa 2* in his business (a parallel and unregistered set of accounts), something she felt was necessary. The friends did not miss the opportunity to point out this contradiction.]

M: Law is good when it is on the other side of the wall, not on this side. That's why I say we have to get used to things.

O: It's right, we should follow the laws, we changed, but if we don't see any results, I can guarantee that I'll steal again, I certainly will.

M: But where is the law? You are being contradictory.

O: No. This type of law, no, it's too obvious . . .

M: But laws, that is what she asked, don't you have to respect them? You have to respect everything.

O: The laws were established, but you cannot respect them so easily. You know, her husband knows, my husband knows, they are owners of enterprises, they know . . .

> *Neighbors in Morumbi, all in their late thirties; each has two children.*
> *O and P are housewives and married to businessmen; M works as a*
> *sports instructor in an elite club and is married to an upper-echelon public*
> *servant who also has a personal business.*

These women are privileged in being able to choose to not respect the law: most likely nothing will happen to them, and they have the money to buy their way out of any difficulty. When the law serves their interests, people defend it; when it does not, they disregard it. As one of the women acknowledges, however, working-class people do not have that choice.

Despite the immense gap separating the experiences of different classes in Brazil and marking their relationship to law and the justice system,[30] they share some common features. Reactions from all social groups to everyday experiences with violence and failing institutions of order seem to be leading to a delegitimation of the rule of law. People who are victims of arbitrariness, violence, and injustices practiced by the institutions of order feel that they are left without alternatives within that order. People who take advantage of the weaknesses of the institutions of order can choose to ignore them and do what they think appropriate. In both cases, however, reactions are framed in private and frequently illegal terms. In both cases, the rule of law is delegitimated. These tendencies are also manifested by the spread of private security services (legal and illegal), which encourage a private reaction to crime.

SECURITY AS A PRIVATE MATTER

The expansion of private security services in São Paulo in the past few years cannot be associated exclusively with either an increase in crime and fear or the dysfunctions of the police and the justice system. The growth of the industry (including both equipment and services) is a characteristic of Western societies in general and not specific to São Paulo. Security equipment is becoming increasingly complex, and private services are growing considerably both in quantity and in scope.[31] In the United States, the number of people employed in the private security industry jumped from 300,000 in 1969 to 1 million in 1980 and 1.5 million in 1990. Moreover, private guards already outnumber policemen in the United States by almost three to one, and in Britain and Canada by two to one (U.S. House 1993:28, 97, 135; Bayley and Shearing 1996:587). Private services are purchased not only by businesses and institutions but also by middle- and upper-class citizens and even branches of the government. In all cases, consumers depend on private services for the identification, screening, and isolation of undesired people, as well as surveillance and protection of their property. Private security has become a central element of the new and already widespread pattern of urban segregation based on fortified enclaves.

But although the growth of private security services and technology is an international tendency, in Brazil it takes on some distinctive characteristics.[32] In a context of police disrespect of rights and of immense social inequality, private security services make matters worse.

Private security in Brazil started as a product of the military state. The most repressive phase of the Brazilian military dictatorship was inaugurated in 1969 by the so-called law of national security (Lei de Segurança Nacional). One month after it was issued, Federal Decree 1,034 (21 October 1969) required the use of private security services in financial institutions, mainly banks. This decree, which was contemporary with the creation of both the military police and Rota, constituted part of the military government's effort to fight bank robbery. The decree generated a considerable market for security services overnight.

Initially, the demand came only from banks and was frequently met by enterprises already providing them with other services. In São Paulo, Banco do Brasil asked the company providing its cleaning services to offer security as well. Pires Serviços de Segurança Ltda., the enterprise created in response to this request, is now the largest private security company in the state of São Paulo, employing ten thousand guards in 1996. Other large banks, however, decided to create their own services along the lines of what is called "organic security." Banespa, the bank of the state of São Paulo, is one of these. Organic security is the expression used to designate the services of security provided internally by employees of a company—whether a factory, bank, apartment building, closed condominium, or even an individual household—instead of by an outside company.

Since 1969, there have been three phases of state regulation of private security services: from 1969 to 1983, from 1983 to 1995, and from 1995 to the present. The first phase, regulated by Decree 1,034 , offered only vague guidelines. It did, however, reveal concerns with controlling the guards and with their political backgrounds. Their names had to be submitted to the National Service of Information (SNI—Serviço Nacional de Informação). The 1969 decree also established that the state secretary of public security and the civil police chief were in charge of controlling local private security services, and that the civil police should provide instruction and testing. Finally, the decree established that private guards on duty would have "the status of policemen."

This scenario changed with the enactment of Law 7,102 on 4 July 1983 (revised by Decree 89,056 of 24 November 1983). This law is much more specific than its predecessor, but the increase in regulations and responsibilities did not necessarily result in more control over the services. Law 7,102 shifted the training of guards from the police to the private sector and the control of private security enterprises from the state secretaries of public security and the civil police to the Ministry of Justice and the federal police.[33] A five-member commission in the Ministry of Justice was to work with commissions at state branches of the federal police to oversee the industry. In the state of São Paulo, the Comissão de Vistoria had four members in 1991 to control 108 enterprises throughout the state. In my interviews in the early 1990s with private security businessmen, there was a consensus that control was looser than before, although the number of requirements had increased, especially training and labor requirements.

The training courses, for example, had to be provided by private enterprises specifically for this purpose. Although these are usually associated with one or more private security enterprises, they have to be legally and physically independent of them, thus requiring new investment by existing companies. The courses were supposed to offer 120 hours of instruction and provide certification for guards, who were no longer subjected to a test at the Police Academy. It was widely acknowledged that most courses in the state of São Paulo (twenty-seven in 1991 and thirty-five in 1996) do not provide guards with the skills necessary for the job.

Once they complete the courses offered by their future bosses, aspiring guards register with the secretary of public security, and their names are sent to the Ministry of Labor. Finally, under Law 7,102 , private guards can carry .32- or .38-caliber guns, but only while at their posts. The guns are owned by the companies and not the guards. Under the new law guards no longer had the status of policemen.

In 1994, the federal government introduced changes to Law 7,102 that considerably modified its scope. Law 8,863 of 28 March 1994 changed the definition of private security to include organic services, which until then had been unregulated. Law 9,017 of 30 March 1995 established that anyone hired to perform private security services must have a diploma and be registered as a private guard with the secretary of public security.[34] People buying the services have to fulfill many additional obligations related to uniforms, installations, and registration of guns, to the point that people in the sector I interviewed in 1996 considered the legislation impossible to comply with. The legislation also mandated tighter control over security services in financial institutions. Finally, it shifted the control of the private security sector from the Ministry of Justice to the federal police alone.

The new law also expanded the Comissão Consultiva, or Consulting Commission.[35] This comprises representatives of the federal police, army, bankers, insurance companies, and enterprises and employees in public security. It is in charge of suggesting policies, authorizing new enterprises, and adjudicating complaints brought against existing enterprises. In practical terms, however, one of its main functions is to convey to the federal authorities the interests of private enterprises, whose representatives make up the majority of the commission's members. In 1996, businessmen I interviewed considered the commission to be the best thing created by the new legislation. Obviously it favors them: the registered enterprises were the only ones legally able to offer services. For the existing organic services to conform to the new legislation, they would have to pay for courses for private guards offered by only a few enterprises (represented in the commission). In spite of the good relationship with the federal government, the private sector still has many complaints: excessive regulation, restrictions on more powerful weapons, and the lack of authority of the guards, who still do not have the status of policemen.

The different laws reveal a change in the way security services have been framed in Brazil. They were initially subordinated to a policy of national security and strict control by the police. With the second law, this control became looser, while the labor regulations increased. What used to be a tool to fight political opposition was adapted to fight criminality. The third law, signed during democratic rule and following rapid expansion of security services in response to the population's growing concerns, attempts to extend state control to encompass the entire security services market. Ironically, though, the new law immediately increased the illegal field of these services, as unregulated organic security still accounts for a significant portion of the industry. Nevertheless, the state is clearly trying to control a profitable sector that has grown rapidly, that is still largely irregular, whose regulated sector is effective in lobbying for its own interests, and that obviously poses significant challenges to the state's own authority.[36]

Indeed, the expansion of the private security sector presents challenges for the organization of policing anywhere, to the point that its analysts in developed countries argue that it "has profound implications for public life, . . . the vitality of civil rights, and the character of democratic government" (Bayley and Shearing 1996:586). If this is true in well-consolidated democracies, one can only imagine the consequences in the Brazilian context, with the delegitimation of its institutions of order and its police abuses. In such a context, the breaking of the state monopoly of policing and the change of the "nature of governance," which seem to be general tendencies (Bayley and Shearing 1996:598), have especially troublesome characteristics.

According to the Ministry of Justice, in 1986 there were fifty-one officially registered private security enterprises (including those for transportation of valuables) in the state of São Paulo.[37] In June 1991 there were 111 enterprises and 27 training courses registered: that is, the number of enterprises had more than doubled in five years. These 111 companies employed 55,700 registered guards. Considering that the total number of policemen in the state of São Paulo in 1991 was approximately 95,000 (22,000 civil police and 69,000 military police), there were 1.6 policemen for each registered private guard, and one private guard per 549 inhabitants. By 1996, there were 281 legally registered enterprises in the state, 35 courses, and 7 armored-car enterprises. These employed around 100,000 guards, a number almost equal to the 105,000 policemen of the state (31,987 civil police and 73,000 military police).[38]

However, this figure does not constitute the whole market. There are two other components: organic security and clandestine services, which may be as large as the legal sector. Each segment of the market has serious problems. I start by examining the still-small legal market and the initiatives of its powerful lobby. I then discuss organic security, which became largely irregular with the new legislation; and last, I address the clandestine segment. One of the main problems common to all sectors lies in the relationships between private security and the police, which tend to exacerbate the already immense social inequality by differentiating the type of security that each social group has access to and is subjected to.

The legal segment of the private security market is small and well-organized.[39] The owners of private enterprises realize the increasing desirability of their services and the potential for expansion in a deeply unequal society afraid of high crime rates and unable to count on its police forces. Owners of private security enterprises are in favor of state regulation of the sector if it means expansion of their business, but at the same time they resist regulation of their activities. To protect their market, they pressure the Ministry of Justice to maintain the law that makes private security obligatory for banks; and they want to establish, through decree, a minimum number of guards per bank branch. They have profited from the added regulation of organic security, and they campaign against the clandestine market.[40] At the same time, they oppose supervision of their services by state secretaries of public security because they fear stricter control, and they complain bitterly about their labor obligations.[41]

To avoid state control, the owners of private security enterprises are developing a discourse emphasizing the private nature of their services and contrasting private efficiency with public inefficiency. They insist on the separation of private and public and on the specificity of their services: some of their arguments seem to eliminate any reason for them to continue to submit to state controls. The most ambitious of those enterprises, such as the Pires Serviços de Segurança Ltda., envision creating model private prisons and selling their services to the state, as well as establishing a training center so sophisticated that they would be able to sell training services to the police.[42] They understand that their services constitute a luxury commodity that confers distinction, and they are not ashamed of expressing class discrimination. "Leave the civil and the military police for the less favored, according to the law—which does not work!" José Luiz Fernandes, president of the owner's association Abrevis, has said.[43] The accentuation of social inequality and the splitting of security between a public sector, for the poor, and a private sector, for the better-off, is not simply a negative consequence of the expansion of private security, as is usually the case in developed countries, but part of the active policy of the companies selling those services in Brazil.

In spite of the enterprises' attempts at opposing themselves to public policing, the relationship between the two sectors is complex. The situation is exemplified by Colonel Erasmo Dias. He was a two-term São Paulo state secretary of public security during the military regime, then a federal deputy, and he is currently a state representative (his third term began in 1995). From this position he has campaigned against human rights and in support of private prisons.[44] He faces various accusations of torture by former political prisoners and is responsible for, among other violently repressive acts against social movements, an invasion of the Catholic University of São Paulo in 1978 in which several students were severely burned. Since 1986, he has also been one of the directors of Pires Serviços de Segurança Ltda. and an instructor in the guards' training course. He has written a book (Dias 1990) in which he defends the necessity of a private security service, separate from the police, for those who can afford it. His position as a director of Pires indicates the intricate connections between public and private security in São Paulo, between the police and private enterprise, and between legal and illegal behavior.

Although organic security is still largely unregulated according to the terms of the new laws, it is not an illegal market: the guards in this sector usually have formal labor contracts. However, particularly in large companies, they may be registered under other occupational categories, not as guards, even when they have some formal security training. Many shopping centers, office complexes, and apartment buildings and closed condominiums rely on organic security. According to the presidents of both the employees' and the employers' trade unions for private security, approximately 50 percent of private security services in the state of São Paulo are provided by organic security. The federal police estimates that in 1996 there were around ten thousand enterprises with some kind of organic security.

In addition to organic security, there is a clandestine market that disregards both labor laws and those of private security. Because it is an illegal activity, it is difficult to obtain a reliable estimate of its dimension, and guesses vary wildly. According to Erivan Dias, president of the security employees' trade union, there were approximately seventy illegal enterprises in the state of São Paulo in 1990, employing fifty thousand people.[45] The president of Abrevis declared in 1991 that this estimate was exaggerated and that the number of illegal companies was small. In 1996, however, after the new legislation, José Luiz Fernandes declared that São Paulo had around three hundred clandestine enterprises employing around twelve thousand people (*Gazeta Mercantil*, 30 July 1996). The federal police, which closes at least two of them each month, has said that there were around four hundred clandestine companies in 1996, mostly small ones.

Most of the people involved in the marginal market of private security are either ex-policemen or policemen, who cannot be registered as private guards. In general, they use police weapons and work on days they are not on police duty, taking advantage of their schedules (forty-eight hours on duty followed by forty-eight hours off). According to data from the secretary of public security, they die more frequently at security jobs than working as policemen. In 1994, for 25 policemen who died in the line of duty, another 104 died in off-duty periods; for 1995 the numbers were 23 and 90. Of course, this illegal market does not adhere to labor legislation. It also uses illicit weapons, often many times more powerful than those permitted to the registered guards or even the police. Some of the enterprises closed by the federal police were run by ex-policemen involved with the Esquadrão da Morte or well-known *justiceiros* (vigilante groups) like Esquerdinha.

Although exact figures are not available, most of the people I interviewed agree that the illegal market is quite large. I observed for myself that many of the closed condominiums in which I did research utilize the services of this illegal market. Prices charged by the regular enterprises are much higher than those of the illegal firms, whose costs are lower: for example, they do not pay insurance and benefits to their employees. Moreover, it is complicated for a condominium to hire private guards directly and fulfill all the requirements, particularly regarding the acquisition and registration of guns. In this context, it seems easier to use the illegal market and employ ex-policemen or policemen, who have their own guns as well as good relationships inside the police "to clean up any major problem" (i.e., murders), as the person in charge of security in a large condominium put it.

One of the most ominous dimensions of the clandestine security market is its connection to the death squads and *justiceiros* acting in the metropolitan region of São Paulo. *Justiceiros*, literally "justice makers," are groups of men who kill people they consider to be criminals, especially on the periphery. Many times they are policemen, ex-policemen, or others associated with policemen (Bicudo 1988:109–24). Frequently they operate behind the façade of a private security enterprise. Moreover, *justiceiros* may be the only type of private security available to the poor. Feeling that the regular police does not protect them, and unable to afford other private security services, many people, especially merchants on the periphery, turn to the *justiceiros*. Sometimes local merchants will pay to keep order in the neighborhood; sometimes groups formed by residents of a neighborhood take the task of keeping order into their own hands. Frequently *justiceiros* are involved with gangs and drug dealers. As a category, *justiceiros* are notorious among São Paulo's population, and their crimes regularly appear in the newspapers. According to press reports, they were responsible for at least three hundred deaths in the city of São Paulo between January and August 1990 (Pinheiro 1991a: 53). Some of the well-known *justiceiros*, such as Cabo Bruno (who has confessed to more than fifty murders), Esquerdinha, or Juca Pé-de-Pato, become popular heroes.[46] Sometimes, when they are arrested, working-class people of the neighborhoods they "protect" try forcefully to liberate them, and crowds fill the courtrooms when they are brought to trial. They are also lionized in radio programs that specialize in retelling crimes.

The intertwining of private and public security, of legal and illegal activities, defies one of the main arguments of the regulated private sector, which is that the private can serve as an alternative and corrective to the police. Although we do not have data on abuses and corruption by private guards, the simple fact that the personnel of the two sectors may be the same, and the connections of private security enterprises either with *justiceiros* or with officials involved in violations of rights by the military, invalidates any clear-cut differentiation. In fact, although private and public policing may from some perspectives (especially the consumer's) look like opposites, they share a matrix of relationships and structures. In Brazil, the matrix is of unstable relationships between legal and illegal, of abuses and violence; in other cases, the matrix is of the respect for the rule of law, as in North America and Western Europe.

In Brazil this complex interpenetration of legal and illegal activities, of the police and private enterprises, poses more serious questions than how to regulate legal enterprises eager to expand their field of activities or how to limit the use of force and the discretion of private guards. The central issue is respect for the rule of law and consolidation of democratic rule. The state should be able to control the arena in which illegal private security firms merge with the *esquadrões da morte* and *justiceiros* and with the illegal actions of the violent police itself. The illegal market cannot be separated from the abuses of the police force, already difficult to contain. It will be hard to control a sector that prefers to be left alone to serve the elite, knows how to organize to defend its own rules, dynamics, and profits, and enjoys the support of a significant portion of the population for vigilante actions.

There is also the question of social inequality. The privatization of security leads to the deepening of inequality (Bayley and Shearing 1996). In Brazil, where the gap between classes is wide, where the working classes have always been the targets and the main victims of a violent police, this problem is especially acute. With the spread of private security, the discrimination against the poor by "security" forces becomes twofold. On the one hand, the poor continue to suffer the abuses of the police. On the other, as the wealthy opt to live, work, and shop in fortified enclaves, using private security services to keep the poor and all "undesirables" away, the poor will be victims of new forms of surveillance, control, disrespect, and humiliation.[47]

THE CYCLE OF VIOLENCE

Although there has been a long tradition of abuse by the institutions of order and distrust of the justice system in Brazil, under democratic rule these trends have reached unprecedented levels. While democratic procedures have been consolidated in some fields—with free elections, a legitimate Congress, free party organization, trade unions, social movements, and a free press—other fields like crime, the police forces, and the justice system have resisted democratization, and abuses continue to be committed with impunity and, frequently, popular support. Public authorities, private enterprises, and citizens all contribute to the problem of violence in contemporary São Paulo. As violent crime increases, as the abuses persist, and as people look for private and frequently illegal means of protection, we enter into a vicious cycle that will only result in the increase of violence.

As people turn to illegal and private ways of dealing with crime, crime and violence are removed from the sphere in which there may be a legitimate, comprehensive mediation of conflicts: that is, the judiciary system. Analyzing the spread of violence and its control in nonmodern societies, René Girard formulates a hypothesis about the privileged role of the justice system in stopping cycles of violence. He assumes that both aggressiveness and revenge are innate to human beings and that "because they detest violence ... men make a duty of vengeance" (1977:15). Vengeance is, then, a vicious circle with devastating consequences, and it is crucial for societies to come up with mechanisms to break these circles. Even if we do not agree with Girard's assumptions about innate aggressiveness and instead root the origins of violence in specific social processes, it is interesting to explore his hypothesis about the control of these events.

Girard groups into three categories the methods employed by different societies for avoiding an interminable cycle of revenge. First, there are preventive measures put in place by sacrificial rites, in which the spirit of revenge is diverted into surrogate channels. Second, there are compensatory measures, such as feuds and trials by combat, whose curative effects are precarious. Third, there is the judicial system, "the most efficient of all curative procedures" (1977:20–21). The reason why the last institution is the most effective in restraining a cycle of vengeance is that it transforms vengeance from a private into a public matter. "Our judicial system ... serves to deflect the menace of vengeance. The system does not suppress vengeance; rather, it effectively limits it to a single act of reprisal, enacted by a sovereign specializing in this particular function. The decisions of the judiciary are invariably presented as the final word on vengeance" (Girard 1977:15).

The principle according to which both private and public vengeance operate is the same: revenge. The crucial difference, however, and one that has enormous social consequences, is that "under the public system, an act of vengeance is no longer avenged; the process is terminated, the danger of escalation averted" (Girard 1977:16). For the judiciary system to interrupt a cycle of vengeance, it must maintain its authority and legitimacy. It must be able to stop parallel forms of private vengeance and have a monopoly on the exercise of revenge. This is exactly what does not occur in contemporary São Paulo. Although the judiciary has never enjoyed much legitimacy, recently it has lost even more credibility because of its inability to contain the extralegal summary executions by the police and the private revenge of *justiceiros* and death squads, and because people tend to bypass it to solve conflicts personally or by private arrangement.

If the justice system is in fact crucial to preventing the spread of violence, then the consolidation of democracy in contemporary Brazilian society and the interruption of the current cycle of violence depend on the reform of this system according to principles of the rule of law, accountability, and respect for civil rights. Because these principles have never really been upheld in Brazil and run contrary to a long history of abuse, privatization of justice, and unstable boundaries between the legal and the illegal, the dimensions of the task are considerable.[48]

Controlling police abuses and the creation of new policies of public security are crucial dimensions both of democratic consolidation and of stopping the cycle of violence. In contemporary São Paulo, not only have the police had the latitude to act illegally and with impunity, but, more important, they have maintained it with violence. In other words, these forces have themselves entered into a cycle of private revenge instead of acting to avert it, and they have done so with at least some support from public authorities and the citizenry. In such a situation, there is no legitimate institutional or public space from which the cycle of violence can be controlled.

When the institutions of order fail to provide proper arbitration of conflict, legitimate forms of revenge, and security, private citizens are likely to act on their own. In fact, the organization of private, frequently illegal, and violent means of protection has increased in São Paulo in the last decade. These acts only serve to intensify the cycle of violence. Citizens could have an effect by forcing public authorities to control abuses and reform the justice system. Such initiatives have, however, been passionately opposed by at least part of São Paulo's population. As a result, violence has continued to escalate and the democratic rule of law has been undermined.

In spite of everything, in recent years there have been some encouraging signs: human rights plans, policies to curb police violence in the state of São Paulo, and diminishing support for the "security bloc." These policies may encounter resistance from the population and especially the police, but they are the only ones that can broaden Brazilian democracy and control the current cycle of violence.

Most of the elements that have generated the current cycle of violence have a socioeconomic basis. Poverty and social inequality—to mention only the most obvious—are crucial to explaining some of the inequalities and injustices associated with distrust for the institutions of order and with the spread of violence. However, socioeconomic variables and the explanations they generate are insufficient to account for the growth of private and illegal forms of revenge and consequently for the increase in violence. It is not indicators of economic crisis, unemployment rates, urbanization, or even state expenditures on public security at which we must look in order to understand contemporary violence. Rather, we have to consider the everyday functioning of the institutions of order, the continuous pattern of abuses by the police forces, their disrespect for rights, and routine practices of injustice and discrimination. We must consider everyday rituals of segregation and how citizens resort to private revenge as the judicial authorities fail, and the unwillingness of many public authorities to bring police activities within the parameters of the rule of law or to develop democratically based policies of public security.

Violent crime and its control are not the only contexts in which we can observe tendencies toward privatization, delegitimation of public mediation, and increasing inequality. These tendencies are shaping urban space, its patterns of segregation, new forms of residence, work, and circulation, public interactions and, consequently, public life. I analyze these aspects in the next three chapters. In chapter 9, I return to the disjunction between the escalation of violence, privatization, and illegal practices of vengeance and the process of democratic consolidation in the political system. The paradoxical character of this configuration derives from the obvious fact that the logic of a cycle of violence is the opposite of the logic of a democratic order based on the respect of citizenship rights and institutions. I suggest that there is widespread association of exercise of authority with infliction of violence. This association is at the root of the cycle of violence I have described and of the delegitimation of individual rights in Brazilian society.

PART 3

Urban Segregation,
Fortified Enclaves, and Public Space

CHAPTER 6
São Paulo
Three Patterns of Spatial Segregation

Segregation—both social and spatial—is an important feature of cities. Rules organizing urban space are patterns of social differentiation and separation. These rules vary culturally and historically, reveal the principles that structure public life, and indicate how social groups relate to each other in the space of the city. Throughout this century, social segregation has had at least three different forms of expression in São Paulo's urban space. The first lasted from the late nineteenth century to the 1940s and produced a condensed city in which different social groups were packed into a small urban area and segregated by type of housing. The second urban form, the center-periphery, dominated the city's development from the 1940s to the 1980s. It has different social groups separated by great distances: the middle and upper classes concentrated in central and well-equipped neighborhoods and the poor exiled into the hinterland. Although residents and social scientists still conceive of and discuss the city in terms of the second pattern, a third form has been taking shape since the 1980s, one that has already exerted considerable influence on São Paulo and its metropolitan region. Superimposed on the center-periphery pattern, the recent transformations are generating spaces in which different social groups are again closer to one another but are separated by walls and technologies of security, and they tend not to circulate or interact in common areas. The main instrument for this new pattern of spatial segregation is what I call "fortified enclaves." These are privatized, enclosed, and monitored spaces for residence, consumption, leisure, and work. Their central justification is the fear of violent crime. They appeal to those who are abandoning the traditional public sphere of the streets to the poor, the marginalized, and the homeless.

My interest in describing and analyzing these changes, especially those of the last fifteen years, is twofold. First, I want to demonstrate the need to remake the cognitive map of social segregation in the city, updating the references through which everyday life and social relationships are understood. Unless the opposition of center and periphery is revised, and the way in which we conceive of the embodiment of social inequality in urban form is modified, we cannot understand the city's present predicaments. Second, these spatial changes and their instruments are transforming public life and public space. In cities fragmented by fortified enclaves, it is difficult to maintain the principles of openness and free circulation that have been among the most significant values of modern cities. With the construction of fortified enclaves the character of public space changes, as does citizen participation in public life. The transformations in the public sphere in São Paulo are similar to changes occurring in other cities around the world, and therefore they express a particular version of a more widespread pattern of spatial segregation and transformation in the public sphere.

The art historian T. J. Clark analyzes the organization of urban life and class interaction in late nineteenth-century Paris and shows how it is expressed in contemporary painting. Writing of Degas's painting "Place de la Concorde" and the characters depicted in it, he argues that

> the typical scene—this the new painting certainly suggested—was likely to be one in which the classes coexisted but did not touch; where each was absorbed in a kind of dream, cryptic, turned in on itself or out to some spectacle, giving off equivocal signs. . . . Class exists, but Haussmann's spaces allow it to be overlooked. . . . History exists, but Haussmann's spaces have room for it to be hidden. . . . Their inattention is *provided for* by the empty spaces and the stream of sights. (Clark 1984:73, 75)

This insight into the relationship between urban forms, class interactions, and artistic expression suggests ways to consider São Paulo's patterns of spatial segregation, especially the recent transformations. Clark identifies the main characteristics of the new type of public space (and its representation) that were exemplified in the late nineteenth century by the redevelopment of Paris. Haussmann's boulevards embodied conditions of anonymity and individualism, allowing both free circulation and inattention to differences and therefore helping to consolidate the image of an open and egalitarian public space. These are exactly the values that are under fire in contemporary São Paulo and in many other cities, where public space no longer relates to the modern ideals of commonality and universality. Instead, it promotes separateness and the idea that social groups should live in homogeneous enclaves, isolated from those who are perceived as different. Consequently, the new pattern of spatial segregation grounds a new type of public sphere that accentuates class differences and strategies of separation.

In what follows, I outline the general characteristics of the São Paulo's three patterns of segregation and use geographic, demographic, and socioeconomic indicators to characterize each and describe the processes of change. In chapter 7, I focus on the most revealing aspects of the new model of segregation: the creation of the walled and private spaces occupied by the upper and middle classes. In chapter 8, I discuss the resulting transformations in public life and public interactions and use the case of Los Angeles for comparison.

THE CONCENTRATED CITY
OF EARLY INDUSTRIALIZATION

From the 1890s to about 1940, urban space and social life in São Paulo were characterized by concentration and heterogeneity.[1] In the 1890s, the population of São Paulo grew 13.96 percent per year (see table 7), but the urban area did not expand proportionally; by 1914, the city's population density was 110 inhabitants per hectare, compared to 83 inh/ha in 1881 (F. Villaça, cited in Rolnik 1997:165). With the advent of industrialization, the once-calm city devoted to services and the financial business associated with the export of coffee—the dominant economic activity in the state of São Paulo until the 1930s—was transformed into a chaotic urban space. At the turn of the century, construction was intensive: new factories were built one after the other, and residences had to be built quickly for the waves of workers arriving every year.[2] Functions were not spatially separated: factories were built close to houses, and commerce and services were mixed with residences.

Although the elite and workers lived relatively close to each other, the elite tended to occupy the highest part of town—toward the *espigão central,* where Avenida Paulista was to be located—and workers to live in the lower-lying areas along the margins of the Tamanduateí and Tietê rivers and the railroads. In the beginning of the century, social segregation was also expressed through housing arrangements: while the elite (of industry and coffee production) and a small middle class lived in their own mansions or houses, more than 80 percent of São Paulo's dwellings were rented (Bonduki 1983:146). Home ownership was definitely not an option for workers, most of whom lived in *cortiços* or *casas de cômodo.* These precarious constructions constituted a good investment for landlords, and they proliferated throughout the city. Like those existing today in central neighborhoods such as Moóca, they were houses with a warren of rooms in each of which a whole

TABLE 7 Evolution of the Population, City of São Paulo and Metropolitan Region, 1872–1996

Year	São Paulo	Annual Growth Rate (%)	Other Municipalities	Annual Growth Rate (%)	Metropolitan Region Total	Annual Growth Rate (%)
1872	31,385					
1890	64,934	4.12				
1900	239,820	13.96				
1920	579,033	4.51				
1940	1,326,261	4.23	241,784		1,568,045	
1950	2,198,096	5.18	464,690	6.75	2,662,786	5.44
1960	3,781,446	5.58	957,960	7.50	4,739,406	5.93
1970	5,924,615	4.59	2,215,115	8.74	8,139,730	5.56
1980	8,493,217	3.67	4,095,508	6.34	12,588,725	4.46
1991	9,646,185	1.16	5,798,756	3.21	15,444,941	1.88
1996	9,839,436	0.40	6,743,798	3.07	16,583,234	1.43

SOURCES: For 1872–1991 IBGE, Brazilian census; for 1996, IBGE *Contagem* 1996.

The metropolitan region of São Paulo is formed by the municipality (city) of São Paulo and thirty-eight other municipalities around it.

family slept, cooked and entertained, and shared external or corridor bathrooms and water sources with other families.[3] There were no apartment buildings. A minority of skilled workers rented single-family homes, which were generally constructed in rows *(casas geminadas)*. Sometimes factories built these row houses for their skilled workers as a means of both attracting them with better housing and disciplining them with the threat of eviction.

In such a concentrated city, which had grown and changed so fast, concerns with discriminating, classifying, and controlling the population were strong. As was typical in European cities during early industrialization, these concerns were often expressed in terms of health and sanitation, which were always associated with morality. Questions of how to house the poor and how to organize urban space in a society undergoing industrialization were tied to sanitation. Together, they became the central motif of the elite's concerns and of the government's policies during the first decades of the twentieth century.

The Paulista elite diagnosed the city's social disorders in terms of disease, filth, and promiscuity, all ideas soon associated with crime. In 1890, the state of São Paulo created the Sanitary Service, which was followed by the Sanitary Code of 1894. Immediately thereafter, state agents started visiting poor residences, especially *cortiços*, looking for the sick and keeping statistics and records. These visits generated negative reactions: sanitary services were associated with social control by the working classes. [4] In addition to controlling the poor, the elite started to separate themselves. Fearing epidemics—as they fear crime today—and identifying the poor and their living conditions with disease, they started to move out of the densely populated city center and into exclusive developments. One of these areas was a new neighborhood in an isolated area of town that they hoped to keep only for themselves: Higienópolis—literally, hygiene city. They also moved to two other new exclusive areas: Campos Elísios and Avenida Paulista. At the same time, elite leaders in the city administration and in institutions such as the Federation of Industries were planning to organize, clean, and open the city center as Haussmann had done in Paris, and to move the workers out, settling them in single-family houses to improve their moral standards. They identified the concentration of workers and the unsanitary conditions associated with them as an evil to be eliminated from city life. They imagined dispersion, isolation, openness, and cleanliness as solutions for the chaotic urban environment and its social tensions.

During the 1920s and 1930s—years that can be considered a transition period between different patterns of organization of social differences in the city and between different modes of intervention by the public authorities—concerns with sanitation and social control are evident in the municipal government, the association of industrialists, the trade union and popular movements, and the federal government. At the municipal level, mayors and officials sought to open avenues, widen streets, embellish, and organize the downtown area. However, the city was ill-equipped to deal with the urban transformations resulting from the huge influx of new residents at the turn of the century. Ideas of urban planning and of state intervention in the space were quite undeveloped until the second decade of the twentieth century. (Morse 1970: chapters19 and 21; Leme 1991). The only early urban legislation—the Código de Posturas of 1875, revised and consolidated in 1886—showed a preoccupation with sanitation, natural resources, and the ordering of public space and public behavior. It established the width of streets and avenues, the height of buildings and the number of floors, and the dimensions of doors and windows, and it prohibited most types of private use of the streets, which were meant to be kept open for circulation (see Rolnik 1997:32–35). The first laws on construction and zoning were passed in the mid-1910s, and the most important pieces of urban legislation and intervention came in the late 1920s.[5]

The main effect of this early urban legislation was to establish a disjunction between a central territory for the elite (the urban perimeter), ruled by special laws, and the suburban and rural areas inhabited by the poor and relatively unlegislated, where laws were not enforced. The mechanism that produced this disjunction is equivalent to what I described in chapter 4 in the case of the police: legal ambivalence. This mechanism is constitutive of Brazilian land occupation and legislation since the beginning of colonization (Holston 1991b). Because the boundaries of the legal and illegal are ill-defined, the executive has the de facto authority to give the final word on land disputes and to determine legality on a case-by-case basis. The urban laws of the 1910s established a division of the city into four zones: central, urban, suburban, and rural. Most of the laws created during that period applied only to the central and urban zones, leaving the other areas (to which the poor were moving) unregulated. When legislation was extended to these areas, such as requirements for registering developments and rules for opening streets, exceptions were soon formulated. The requirements that new streets have infrastructure and minimum dimensions, for example, could be legally bypassed after 1923, when a new law offered the possibility of creating "private streets" in suburban and rural areas. The legal rules for the urban perimeter would not apply to these "private streets." But probably the best example of this mechanism relates to the installation of urban infrastructure by the city which, starting at the beginning of the century, depended on the legal status of a street. Most of the new streets, especially in the suburban and rural areas, were by principle either irregular or illegal and therefore lacked urban infrastructure. And although they were progressively assimilated into the urban legality through various amnesties (1936, 1950, 1962, and 1968), the decrees were each sufficiently ambiguous as to leave to executive discretion the determination of which streets met the criteria for legalization, and therefore for urban improvement, and which did not.[6]

The most famous urban undertaking of the municipal government in the beginning of the century led to a transformation of the pattern of segregation and represented a shift in the conception of state intervention in urban planning. It was the so-called Plano de Avenidas (plan of avenues), elaborated by Francisco Prestes Maia during the administration of José Pires do Rio, the last mayor of the Old Republic.[7] The plan proposed opening a series of large avenues radiating from the center to the outskirts. It required considerable demolition and remodeling of the downtown area, whose commercial zone was renewed and enlarged, stimulating real estate speculation. Consequently, the working classes, who could not afford the increased rents, were driven out. The Plano de Avenidas also chose to enhance roads instead of expanding public trolley transportation in the city. One of the causes of the city's concentration was its dependence on the trolley system, which required expensive installations and so expanded slowly. Because the system covered only a small area, it was difficult to move poor residents away from the center, where they worked. The launching of a bus system, associated with the progressive opening of new avenues, made possible the expansion of the city toward the periphery.

The second major influence on urban transformations was the group of industrialists congregated at the Federation of Industries and headed by Roberto Simonsen. They were interested in studying the patterns of working-class consumption and housing in order to change them. They promoted the creation of institutions that specialized in the study and documentation of working-class living conditions, especially housing, considered to be the "the preeminent social problem" (Bonduki 1983:147). Convinced that employers could not bear the responsibility of solving this problem, they favored home ownership for workers, which could reduce their housing expenses and increase their disposable income. They were also, obviously, interested in organizing the city space for industrial expansion.

The third influence was the trade union movement, which became quite strong under anarchist influence. It promoted a series of important strikes in São Paulo during the 1910s (Fausto 1977), and in the 1920s it joined forces with other opposition movements. This coalition led to the overthrow of the Old Republic, ruled by rural oligarchies (among them the Paulista coffee producers), in 1930. Housing was an important theme in the working-class movements, expressed primarily in discussions about rent and rent control. After the 1910s, the anarchist unions proposed the formation of "renters' leagues" *(ligas de inquilinos)* to go on rent strikes. Despite this mobilization, and in spite of its contribution to change the political regime, no collective action was taken on the "housing question."

The fourth influence on urban change was the federal government, especially after the revolution of 1930, which initiated what would become the populist dictatorship of Getúlio Vargas. Vargas created a totally new structure of labor management in Brazil, which remains largely in place to this day and which was partially inspired by the Italian Fascist corporatist model. The newly created labor ministry defended the creation of opportunities for the urban classes to become homeowners. In the same way as the industrialists, labor officials were interested in cutting housing expenses, and in disseminating the value of home ownership, which they considered to be one of the bases of social stability. To increase home ownership the federal government took several initiatives, not all of them equally successful.[8] The change that was to have the greatest effect on the city—and on housing arrangements for workers in modern Brazil—occurred in 1942, in the context of a housing crisis marked by high rents provoked by the economic crisis associated with World War II and the remodeling of downtown areas in various Brazilian cities. This factor was the *Lei do Inquilinato* (renter's law), which froze all rents at December 1941 levels. It was supposed to last for two years but was successively renewed for residential properties until 1964, with only a few minor increases in response to high inflation. In São Paulo, the immediate consequence was a tightening of the rental market, as fewer rental units were built. This trend accelerated the departure of the working classes to the periphery, where they could find cheap (and irregular) land on which to build their own houses.[9]

The interaction of these various initiatives and policies, along with a sharp increase in internal migration to the city after the early 1930s, led to a pattern of urban segregation that was to characterize São Paulo for the next fifty years.[10] In the new arrangement, poor and rich lived apart: distance, economic growth, and political repression allowed a peculiar inattention to one another.

CENTER-PERIPHERY: THE DISPERSED CITY

The new pattern of urbanization is usually called the center-periphery model, and it has dominated São Paulo's development since the 1940s. It has four principal characteristics. (1) It is dispersed instead of concentrated: population density dropped from 110 inhabitants per hectare in 1914 to 53 in 1963 (F. Villaça, cited by Rolnik 1997:165). (2) The social classes live far apart in the city space: the middle and upper classes live in central, legalized, and well-equipped neighborhoods, the poor on the precarious and mostly illegal periphery. (3) Home ownership became the general rule for both rich and poor. (4) Transportation depends on roads, with buses for the working classes and automobiles for the middle and upper classes.[11] This pattern of urbanization was consolidated at the same time that the city became the industrial center of the country, as modern heavy industries replaced the traditional textile and food manufacturers (a change associated with automobile production), and as the city received a flood of migrants from the northeast of Brazil.[12] During this period, urban expansion and industrial dynamics surpassed the limits of the municipality of São Paulo, stimulating rapid transformations of its surrounding areas, formally named the Metropolitan Region of São Paulo.

Roads, Illegality, and Autoconstruction:
The Expansion of the Periphery

The launching of a public bus system was a driving force in the new pattern of urbanization. Although the price of land on the periphery was relatively low, and there had been subdivisions of land *(loteamentos)* for sale since the 1910s,[13] the outskirts of the city remained unoccupied mainly because of the lack of transportation. Until the end of the 1930s, the only occupied *loteamentos* away from the city were those close to railroad stations. However, these were few and the possibility of expansion limited, for people had to walk to the station.[14] At the end of the 1930s, the opening of the new avenues made possible the widespread use of buses. The first buses started running in 1924, and by the end of the decade they were already challenging the monopoly of the trolley system owned by the São Paulo Tramway Light & Power Co., popularly known as Light.[15] Requiring less infrastructure and thus being more flexible, buses were brought through unpaved streets to neighborhoods far from the city center. Whereas in 1948 commuting trips by trolley accounted for 52.2 percent of all commutes on public transportation, in 1966 they were down to 2.4 percent of the total. At the same time, commutes by bus jumped from 43.6 percent in 1948 to 91.2 percent in 1966 (R. Velze, cited by Kowarick and Bonduki 1994:153). Trolley transportation was ended in 1968.

The main agent of the expansion of bus services was not the government, but private entrepreneurs, most of them also real estate speculators.[16] As a consequence, the system was irregular and aleatory: it was designed to serve real estate interests rather than residents. It made possible the sale of lots in remoter areas, but it helped create as a counterpart a peculiar type of urban space in which occupied and vacant areas are distributed randomly through a large region. There was no plan of development: the areas that were occupied were those in which speculators decided to invest. Their strategy was to leave vacant areas in between those that were occupied so that the former could be put onto the market later, at higher prices.

In fact, the urbanization of the periphery was left mostly to private initiative, with little control or assistance from government authorities until the 1970s. In spite of elite and government discourses promoting home ownership for the poor and the rational planning of the city's expansion, the process of opening and selling lots in the periphery, which expanded the city dramatically from the 1940s on, was chaotic. The law itself guaranteed the exceptional status of the periphery: while it carefully regulated the defined urban perimeter, it left suburban and rural areas largely unregulated and therefore open to exploration and exploitation. Speculators developed a multitude of illegal and irregular practices aimed at maximizing profits, from outright fraud to failure to provide the basic urban services or minimum lot dimensions required by law. As a result, the majority of workers who bought land on the periphery to build their own houses discovered eventually that their deeds were jeopardized by some form of illegality. They might have bought a fraudulently sold lot or one that could not be registered either because its dimensions were below the legal limits or because it was located in a development without the infrastructure required by municipal codes. In addition, workers usually built their houses without registering them, an extra cost they could not afford. Consequently, even when the lots were legal, frequently the construction was not.[17]

São Paulo's Planning Bureau has recently estimated that 65 percent of the entire population of the city lives in residences that are illegal in some respect (Rolnik et al. n.d.: 95). Nevertheless, workers have always understood that it is exactly the illegality of the lots and the construction, and the precarious legal character of the periphery as a whole, that enables them to become homeowners and solve their housing problems (see Caldeira 1984: chapters 1–3; Holston 1991b). The lots were affordable both because of their illegality and because they were in the middle of nowhere: a long bus ride from the center in neighborhoods without paving, electricity, water, sewage services, telephones, schools, or hospitals.[18] Such urban infrastructures and services were installed or improved only during democratic periods and under pressure from political action by the residents. In the 1950s, populist politicians, especially Jânio Quadros, established a policy of exchanging urban infrastructure for votes; this practice resulted in the urbanization of the first ring of the periphery, which in turn became his political base. The most important mobilization of residents of the periphery, however, started in the late 1970s and was marked by the organization of autonomous social movements on the outskirts of the city.

The workers on the periphery were further neglected in that they never received any kind of financing to build their own houses. The few lending programs created for them either had requirements they could not fulfill or were quickly redirected to the middle classes, as was the case with the National Housing Bank (Banco Nacional de Habitação, hereafter BNH). Therefore, workers ended up building their own houses by a process called *autoconstrução*, or autoconstruction. This is a lifetime process in which the workers buy a lot and build either a room or shack at the back of it, move in, and then spend decades expanding and improving the construction, furnishing, and decorating the house. This process radically changed the resi-

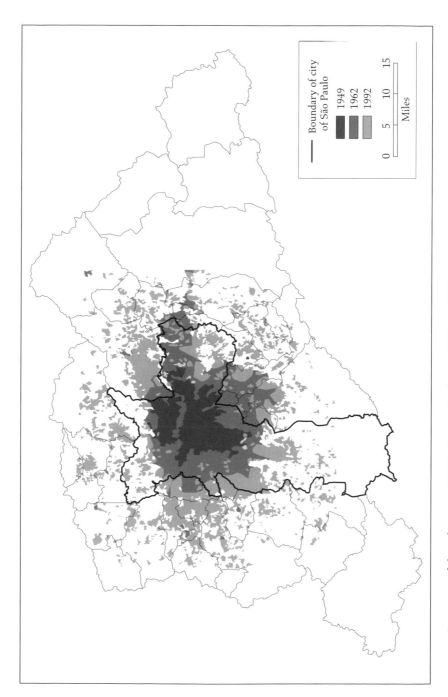

MAP 1.   Expansion of the urban area, MRSP. *Source:* Emplasa and Cebrap, LED.

dential status of the majority of the population. Beginning in the 1940s, home ownership in São Paulo expanded considerably, and the number of renters decreased. Whereas in 1920 only 19.1 percent of domiciles were owned by their residents, in 1960 41 percent were owned, and in 1991 63.2 percent were in this category.[19] Today, the proportion of dwellings owned by their occupants in peripheral neighborhoods (68.51 percent) is higher than the city average (63.57 percent), confirming that autoconstruction is the main form of working-class housing (see table 8 below).

The expansion of the urban area, resulting primarily from the movement of the working classes toward the periphery and from the installation of industries in some of these areas, is shown in map 1.[20] The greatest expansion occurred during the 1950s. From the 1940s to the 1980s, peripheral expansion affected not only the city of São Paulo but also the thirty-eight surrounding municipalities that formed a conurbation to constitute the metropolitan area of São Paulo. In fact, many of these municipalities demonstrate the same precarious urban character and same high rates of demographic growth as the districts in the capital's periphery, and they function as an extension of the periphery. These municipalities also accommodated many of the new industries established in the 1950s and 1960s. The main area of industrial development was the ABCD region southeast of the city.

As the metropolis expanded, the concerns of public authorities with regulating the built environment, taming expansion, and remedying its most perverse effects also grew: regulations and urban plans multiplied geometrically after the 1950s. Nevertheless, as had happened since the early 1900s, the effects of these urban public policies were felt mostly in upper- and middle-class areas, while the peripheries were almost completely neglected until the mid to late 1970s.

Housing the Rich and Improving the Center

The pattern of housing for São Paulo's middle classes also changed, especially after the late 1960s. They too became property owners, but through a completely different process. In contrast to what was happening to the working classes, the middle and upper classes received financing and did not have to build their own residences. They were moving to apartment buildings, the first type of housing to be produced by large enterprises. The apartment housing market expanded significantly in the 1970s, transforming the central neighborhoods. High-rises also became the main form of office building, not only downtown but also in new areas in the southern and western parts of town.

An analysis of the history of São Paulo's intense vertical build-up can provide insights into how public authorities, both local and federal, tried to regulate urban expansion and shape the richer areas of town. Municipal zoning and construction regulations determined where high-rises could be built and what dimensions they could have, and they created barriers to the construction of apartments for the working classes. Federal policies dictated the conditions for financing apartments for the middle classes and for the proliferation of the big real-estate development enterprises that have dominated the collective housing market since the 1970s. Together, those policies helped make apartment buildings the main type of residence for the middle and upper classes.

The construction of high-rises in São Paulo began in the first decade of the twentieth century and, according to the urban pattern of that period, was concentrated in the downtown area. As Nádia Somekh Martins Ferreira shows, until 1940, 70 percent of all high-rises were in central neighborhoods and 65 percent were nonresidential. In 1940, only 4.6 percent of the population of the city of São Paulo lived in apartment buildings, and only 2.1 percent of the domiciles were apartments (Ferreira 1987:54,75).[21] During the 1940s, the construction of high-rises remained limited to the downtown area and to a few surrounding neighborhoods, but the percentage of residential buildings started to increase. It was already possible to sell units in apartment buildings, but the majority of residential high-rises were rented.[22] According to Carlos Lemos, a historian of Paulista architecture (1978:54), when construction of residential apartment buildings began in the 1940s, they were stigmatized by their association with *cortiços*, poverty, and a lack of privacy and freedom. The apartment building was thus the choice only for that part of the bourgeoisie that could not afford to live in a detached house in the center of the city. This interpretation is confirmed by a survey carried out by Ibope (Instituto Brasileiro de Opinião Pública e Estatística) in December 1945 among upper- and middle-class residents of the city of São Paulo, in which 90.8 percent of the those surveyed declared that they preferred houses to apartments, and 83.3 percent were in fact living in houses.[23] At that time, the majority of those interviewed were paying rent. Only 17.2 percent of the men interviewed owned their homes; 53.2 percent intended to buy a house, but only 1.6 percent intended to buy an apartment.

Until the late 1950s, the construction of high-rises was relatively uncontrolled by the city. From 1957 on, however, municipal laws aimed at controlling the expansion of construction in the city affected, in particular, the building of high-rises. The laws had two main effects. On the one hand, they excluded the low-income population from buying apartments; on the other, they directed the high-rises out of downtown. Both of these effects accompanied the remodeling of the downtown area that expelled the poor to the new peripheries. These tendencies have persisted from the 1950s to the present.

In 1957, Municipal Law 5,261 limited for the first time the *coeficiente de aproveitamento*, or the terrain's utilization rate: it could not exceed six in commercial buildings or four in residential buildings (that is, the total built area could not exceed four or six times the size of the lot).[24] Moreover, it determined that the *cota mínima de terreno* per apartment should be 35 square meters; that is, each individual unit should correspond to at least 35 square meters of the terrain area. Although this law has never been fully enforced—developers have always submitted their plans for residential buildings to City Hall as if they were commercial, thus managing to raise the real utilization rate—it ended up increasing the size of apartments and directing the construction of residential high-rises to areas away from the city center, where lots were cheaper. From this time on, apartments became almost exclusively a middle-class form of residence.

If the municipal laws explain why the construction of lower-income apartments was interrupted and why high-rise construction started to move out of the downtown area, they do not explain why, a few years later, the middle classes were moving into apartments. This phenomenon can be better understood in relation to the next important intervention in the apartment market, this time on the federal level: the creation in 1964 of the BNH and the Sistema Financeiro de Habitação (the housing financing system, SFH). This system, which started to operate on a large scale in 1967, was created specifically to promote the construction and financing of homes for low- and very low-income families. However, by the 1970s the BNH had instead become the most important source of financing for the middle classes, and it financed mostly apartment units in newly constructed buildings. Of the total funds provided by the SFH between 1965 and 1985, only 6.4 percent went to families with an income lower than 3.5 minimum salaries (MS) (Brant et al. 1989:98).[25]

The SFH provoked a deep transformation in a real estate market that had been dominated by relatively small entrepreneurs and by families building their own houses. It stimulated the formation of big real estate development companies, which borrowed money from the SFH to build high-rises or complexes of houses to be sold with BNH financing. Although data for São Paulo are not available, Ribeiro and Lago show that in Rio de Janeiro, from the total number of real estate developers registered in the city in the late 1980s, 60 percent entered into business during the 1970s (1995:375).

These developers had much more capital than previous entrepreneurs and completely dominated the real estate market from the 1970s on, first in the central areas of the metropolitan regions and later on the peripheries as well. These developers build primarily high-rises but also some horizontal closed condominiums.

Especially during the 1970s, the military years of the so-called economic miracle, the BNH (associated with big developers) played a central role in the real estate market. In São Paulo, 80.8 percent of the residential apartment buildings put on the market between 1977 and 1982 received financing from BNH (Salgado 1987:58). The SFH's entrance into the real estate market more than doubled the number of apartment buildings registered per year in the municipality of São Paulo.[26] Since 63 percent of the units financed by the SFH between 1970 and 1974 were for the so-called middle market (i.e., for the middle classes), 25 percent for the economic market, and only 12 percent for the lowest-income market (Rolnik et al. n.d.: 111), it is not difficult to conclude that apartment buildings were middle-class housing. In other words, the middle classes were getting cheap mortgages subsidized by the government, and the working classes, who could not afford to buy on the formal market and who only rarely met the BNH requirements for a loan application, were building their houses by themselves on the periphery without any public financial help. Moreover, the massive financing of apartment buildings by the SFH is probably one of the main reasons that the middle classes in São Paulo have abandoned the dream of the single-family house.

As would be expected, during the 1970s the distribution of apartments in the city expanded considerably, mostly in the southwest part of town. The type of buildings and their spatial distribution were again influenced by a new municipal regulation: the São Paulo Zoning Code, approved in 1972, which divided the city into eight zones with different utilization rates and land uses (residence, commerce, industry, services, etc.). The maximum utilization rate in the city was fixed at four and was allowed in an area corresponding to only 10 percent of the total urban area. Most of the elite neighborhoods fell in zones classified as exclusively residential and with low utilization rates. Since it had become more difficult to approve fraudulent plans once the BNH started to finance construction (it only financed residences), the new code caused an increase in land prices and reinforced the trend to locate apartment buildings away from central areas.

Middle-class apartment buildings continued to be built mostly toward the southwest, farther and farther from the center. At the same time, the first big developments of closed condominiums were built, on the pattern of quasi-clubs, some of them on the outskirts of the city. This type of development was stimulated by the new zoning codes, which allowed buildings to exceed the utilization rates in some zones if they lowered the occupant rate and provided common green areas and facilities for collective use. The construction of commercial and office high-rises during the 1970s followed the same trend. Downtown São Paulo was no longer the only center of commerce and services. Offices had spread to Avenida Paulista, the neighborhoods called Jardins, and Avenida Faria Lima, all in the southwestern part of town. High-rises for both commerce and residence were being built one after another in an ever-expanding area.

Large Distances, Large Disparities

By the 1970s, São Paulo had become a city in which people from different social classes were not only separated by large distances but also had radically different housing arrangements and quality of life. Since the late 1960s, the city had been undertaking studies that indicated these disparities. In 1968 the Plano Urbanístico Básico (PUB—basic urban plan) showed that 52.4 percent of all domiciles lacked water, 41.3 percent lacked sewage services, and 15.9 percent lacked garbage collection (cited in Camargo et al. 1976:28).[27] Moreover, it indicated that 60 percent of the streets were unpaved and 76 percent had no street lighting (São Paulo—Sempla 1995:19). The distribution of infrastructure and public services was uneven. Whereas in the central district (Centro) 1.3 percent of the domiciles lacked water, 4.5 percent lacked sewage treatment, 1.7 percent lacked paving, and 0.8 percent lacked garbage collection, in Itaquera, a new district in the eastern periphery, 89.3 percent of the domiciles lacked water, 96.9 percent lacked sewage services, 87.5 percent lacked paving, and 71.9 percent lacked garbage collection.[28]

The expansion of the periphery under these circumstances created serious sanitation and health problems. As a consequence, mortality rates, and especially infant mortality rates, which had decreased between 1940 and 1960, increased between 1960 and the mid-70s. Life expectancy dropped from 62.3 years in the period 1959–1967 to 60.8 years in the period 1969–1971. At the same time, infant mortality rose from 62 per 1,000 live births in 1960 to 80 in 1975. Infant mortality rates were much higher in the periphery than in the central districts. In 1975, for example, the rate in São Miguel Paulista, in the eastern periphery, was 134, whereas in the wealthy district of Jardim Paulista it was 44.6. (São Paulo—Emplasa 1982:419).

In sum, in the 1970s the poor lived on the periphery, in precarious neighborhoods, and in autoconstructed houses; the middle and upper classes lived in centrally located and well-equipped neighborhoods, a significant portion of them in apartment buildings (see photos 1 and 2). The dream of the Old Republic's elite was fulfilled: the majority owned and lived in single-family houses, with the poor out of their way. This pattern of residential segregation depended on roads, cars, and buses,[29] and its consolidation occurred at the same time that São Paulo and its metropolitan region were becoming the main industrial center of the country and its more important economic pole. The new heavy industries were located on the city's periphery and in surrounding municipalities. Commerce and services remained in the central areas, not only in the traditional downtown but also close to new middle- and upper-class areas toward the southern zone of the city.

The censuses of 1970 and 1980 demonstrated the extent of the center-periphery split. A 1977 study produced by Seplan (Secretariat of Economy and Planning of the State of São Paulo), based on data from the 1970 census, illustrated the segregation. It did a factorial analysis using the following variables for each district of the city: family income, domiciles connected to the sewage system, demographic density, population growth, and residential use of urban land. This study found that the districts of the city were distributed into eight homogeneous areas, that is, groups of districts with similar urban and social characteristics. Area I was central, the richest, and best equipped; area VIII was the poorest, with the least urban infrastructure, and the most distant from the center (São Paulo—Seplan 1977). Of the others, the richer districts lay closer to the center. Data from the 1980 census confirmed this pattern. In Area I, which had only 6.9 percent of the domiciles and 6.3 percent of the population, 99.1 percent of the domiciles had electricity, 97.6 percent had sewage services, and 73.2 percent had telephones. In area VIII, which had 22.0 percent of the domiciles and 24.1 percent of the population, 98.8 percent of the domiciles had electricity, but only 19.1 percent had sewage services, and only 4.9 percent had telephones. With respect to household income, in area I those receiving less than five minimum salaries accounted for 18.4 percent of the total; in area VIII they were 64.6 percent of the total (Caldeira 1984:26–28).

This separation of social groups in the city was associated with a period of relative inattention to class differences. At least three factors account for this inattention and helped to create a silence and a separation between the classes that many saw as a sign of social tranquility. First, the spatial separation of classes made their encounters infrequent, restricting them mainly to circulation in a few central areas. Second, the economic growth from the 1950s on, and especially during the 1970s—the "miracle years"—generated optimism and helped strengthen the belief in progress and social mobility.

PHOTO 1.   Consolação, a central district of São Paulo that combines residential and commercial buildings, 1980. Photo by Teresa Caldeira.

Third, the repression of the military regime (1964–1985) banished political organization and public dissent.

The calm did not last long, however. In the last years of the military regime, the trade union movement was reorganized in the metropolitan region of São Paulo, and social movements demanding urban services and equipment were organized throughout the periphery. The elite had not foreseen that home ownership, instead of ensuring social stability and working-class docility, would, to the contrary, politicize the working classes and make them claim their rights to the city. As soon as the military regime decided to start the so-called political opening in the mid-70s, social movements based in poor neighborhoods emerged throughout the periphery. The poor residents of São Paulo, who had been forgotten on the outskirts of the city, learned quickly that if they could organize, they could probably improve the quality of life in their neighborhoods.[30]

The political mobilization of those previously excluded from the political arena made the population of São Paulo conscious of its pattern of social segregation and spatial organization. The center-periphery model was invoked in political negotiations between government officials and representatives of the social movements. It was also the model used by the mass media in their frequent reporting of demonstrations, and by social scientists

PHOTO 2.   Jardim das Camélias, a neighborhood on the eastern periphery of the city of São Paulo, 1980. Photo by Teresa Caldeira.

who observed with fascination a politicization they had not foreseen. It quickly became a common reference for residents, political organizations, government planners, and social theorists. However, as the periphery was finding its way into the political and intellectual life of the city, other processes were already changing the configuration of the city so that, in a short time, the center-periphery model no longer accurately represented the social and spatial dynamics of the city.

PROXIMITY AND WALLS IN THE 1980S AND 1990S

São Paulo in the late 1990s is more diverse and fragmented than it was in the 1970s. A combination of processes, some of them similar to those affecting other cities, transformed the pattern of distribution of social groups and activities throughout the metropolitan region. São Paulo continues to be highly segregated, but social inequalities are now produced and inscribed in different ways. New forces are already generating other types of spaces and a different distribution of social classes and economic activities. São Paulo today is a more complex metropolitan region that cannot be mapped out by the simple opposition of center-rich versus periphery-poor. It is no longer a city providing conditions for inattention to class differences, but rather a city of walls, with a population obsessed by security and social discrimination.

In the 1980s and 1990s the rate of population growth in the region dropped significantly as a result of a sharp decrease in fertility rates (see chapter 1) combined with emigration: that is, population trends that had characterized the city for the last hundred years were reversed. This demographic shift intersected with a transformation in residential patterns, especially for the richest and the poorest residents. For the first time in the history of modern São Paulo, rich residents are leaving the central and well-equipped areas of the capital to inhabit distant areas. Although wealth continues to be geographically concentrated, most upper- and middle-class central neighborhoods lost population between 1980 and 1996, while the proportion of wealthier residents increased substantially in some municipalities in the northwest of the metropolitan region and the south of the city, where previously only poor people lived. In these new areas, the main type of housing is the fortified enclave. At the same time, home ownership through autoconstruction on the periphery has become a less viable alternative for the working poor because of the impoverishment caused by the economic crisis of the 1980s, the improvements in the urban infrastructure in the periphery, and the legalization of land resulting from the pressure of social movements and action by local governments. In other words, while incomes went down, the periphery improved and became more expensive. As a result, many poor residents had to put aside the dream of home ownership and increasingly opted for living either in favelas or in *cortiços*, numbers of which increased substantially.

The economic dynamic and the distribution of economic activities changed as well. The industrial sector, especially in the city of São Paulo, lost its main economic role to new tertiary activities. Former industrial areas decayed, while new sites of office and commercial development attracted both wealthy residents and high investment. Finally, the increase in violent crime and fear since the mid-80s provoked the rapid walling of the city, as residents from all social classes sought to protect their living and working spaces. Moreover, as fear and crime increased, prejudices related to the talk of crime not only exacerbated the separation of different social groups but also increased the tensions and suspicions among them.

To analyze these processes and their effects on the pattern of segregation in São Paulo and its metropolitan region, I use demographic and socioeconomic indicators from the censuses of 1980 and 1991, the population count of 1996 *(Contagem da População)*, and the PNADs (Pesquisa Nacional por Amostra de Domicílio, the national survey of households), all produced by IBGE, the census bureau. For analyzing recent transformations in the urban space, all these sources present limitations. The PNADs, which are biennial, are available only for the metropolitan region as a whole. For a more detailed analysis, it is necessary to break down the information by municipalities or by districts. However, the subdivision of the city into districts was completely revised between the two censuses, making direct comparisons impossible.[31] Since there are no other appropriate data available for the 1980s, I have had to rely on an analysis that looks at each year and tries to compare the main trends.[32] The same problem does not exist for the other municipalities of the metropolitan region, whose boundaries remained practically unchanged and which are smaller and more homogeneous.

Reversing the Pattern of Growth

In the 1980s and 1990s the images of uninterrupted and rapid growth that have described the city since the nineteenth century lost their referents. From some perspectives, the city that "cannot stop" almost did. Its urban area still expanded and its population still increased, but at rates that pale compared to previous ones (see map 1). São Paulo's urban area expanded by 12.68 percent between 1980 and 1994 (from 733.4 square kilometers to 826.4 square kilometers [São Paulo—Sempla 1995:30]), compared to an expansion of 37.5 percent between 1965 and 1980. In the metropolitan region, urban expansion was still significant, 24 percent (from 1,423 square kilometers in 1980 to 1,765 square kilometers in 1990), but much lower than the 91.2 percent increase in the period 1965–1980 [Marcondes 1995, cited by Leme and Meyer 1996:9]).[33] However, one of the most significant reversals of the 1980s and especially the 1990s was the sharp decline in population growth. As table 7 shows, the annual growth rate of the population in the city was 1.16 percent between 1980 and 1991 and 0.4 percent between 1991 and 1996, compared to 3.67 percent in the 1970s. For the other municipalities of the metropolitan region, the rates were still high, at 3.21 percent and 3.07 percent in the two periods, but half the 6.34 percent rate of the 1970s. Between 1980 and 1991, almost 760,000 people left the city of São Paulo.[34] The central and more urbanized part of the city in particular lost population, as is shown by the census data, while the western and northern parts of the metropolitan region gained.

In fact, 40.6 percent of the districts of the city (in which 33.5 percent of its population lived in 1991) had a population decline between 1980 and

1991;[35] and from 1991 to 1996, 59.4 percent of the districts lost population. These numbers include the whole of the expanded city center, the area with the richest population and best urban infrastructure. The tendency for the center to grow less than the periphery has been clear since the 1950s, when some of the city's oldest industrial areas (Pari, Brás, Moóca, Bom Retiro) and the old downtown (Sé, Santa Ifigênia) started to lose population,[36] although most of the central areas continued to grow. In the 1980s, however, the depopulation affected traditional middle-class neighborhoods such as Santo Amaro, Pinheiros, Consolação, Perdizes, Vila Mariana, and Itaim Bibi, which had grown a great deal in the previous decades. These districts continued to lose population at even higher rates during the 1990s.[37] The same process affected the first ring of the city's periphery, developed mostly in the 1940s and 1950s (Vila Maria, Ipiranga, Vila Guilherme, Vila Prudente, Santana). Moreover, more distant areas of the periphery, which had grown more than 10 percent a year in the 1960s, hardly grew at all (less than 1 percent a year) during the 1980s and lost population during the early 1990s. These areas include Freguesia do Ó, Limão, Campo Belo, São Miguel, Socorro, Jaçanã, Artur Alvim, and Jaguaré, neighborhoods located throughout the periphery that saw significant infrastructure improvements during the 1980s. The only areas that continued to have high rates of growth were those on the edges of the city that had not been urbanized before.[38]

In the other municipalities of the metropolitan region, the average population growth has been significantly higher than in the capital (table 7). The lowest rates of growth were either in rural municipalities on the fringes of the region or in important industrial centers such as the ABCD area and Osasco, which are again some of the most urbanized municipalities, with better urban infrastructure. Some of the latter also had emigration, whereas all the others received new migrants.[39] The highest rates of growth were in the west and north, and in the 1980s in a few eastern municipalities. In general, the western areas reveal a new economic and social dynamic. The increase in population there may be partially due to the relocation of residents from the city of São Paulo, especially richer ones, as well as to economic transformations. The city with the highest migration rate in the metropolitan region was Santana do Parnaíba. This was the site of intensive real estate investment in upper-class residences as well as new office and commerce complexes. Meanwhile, the growth on the east side seems largely to stem from autoconstruction. Nevertheless, I am talking about general tendencies; the west also has autoconstruction, and the east has several new tertiary developments.

Improvement and Impoverishment in the Periphery

The urbanization of the city's outskirts, caused by the settlement of the poorest residents, continued, although at a much lower pace than in the preceding decades. In 1991, the twenty districts with the highest percentage of heads of households making less than 3 MS per month were districts at the limits of the city, especially the eastern region.[40] In eleven of these districts, more than 50 percent of the heads of households earned less than 3 MS. As could be expected, the poorest districts tend also to be very homogeneously poor, including only a very small proportion of residents with higher incomes. In the poorest districts, the ratio of residents making less than 3 MS to those making more than 20 is around 350:1.

The poorest residents of São Paulo settling in the limits of the city continued to rely on autoconstruction and illegality, as a comparison of census data and the city registry of urban properties indicates. The areas in the periphery that had the highest increase in population and number of domiciles are those in which there is the largest discrepancy between the number of domiciles counted by the 1991 census and the number of residential units officially recorded at TPCL in 1990. TPCL (Cadastro de Propriedades Urbanas) is the municipality's register of urban construction. It includes only legal constructions, whereas the census records all types of domiciles.[41] Therefore, the discrepancy between the two sources indicates the extent of illegal construction. The most dramatic discrepancy is from the district of Guaianazes at the eastern limits of the city, where it was 433.12 percent![42] Guaianazes had a population growth of 145 percent between 1980 and 1991 (the highest in the city), and an increase of 230 percent in the number of domiciles, but an increase in registered residential constructed area of only 65.8 percent between 1977 and 1987.[43] By contrast, in central residential neighborhoods, where the rich live, where there is a predominance of apartment buildings and which have always constituted the legal city, the difference between the census data on domiciles and TPCL is less than 5 percent.[44]

Other data indicate that the autoconstruction and peripheral expansion model has seen some important transformations during the 1980s and early 1990s. These years presented paradoxical conditions for the poor. At the same time that the working classes became important political actors, organizing social movements and demanding their rights and better living conditions, and at the same time that the infrastructure of the periphery indeed improved significantly, their incomes dropped, and their capacity to become property owners through autoconstruction was reduced.

All indicators of urban infrastructure improved both in the capital and in the metropolitan region from 1980 to 1991. The changes were especially important on the periphery and consequently diminished the degree of inequality in access to urban infrastructure and public services. Because of the change in district boundaries used by the 1980 and 1991 censuses, it is difficult to analyze in detail what happened in different areas of the city during the 1980s. To address this problem and to describe what was going on at the periphery, I aggregated various districts and created one large area comparable to the poorest periphery of the 1980s. I used as a reference a study by Seplan that established eight socioeconomically homogeneous areas of the city (São Paulo—Seplan 1977; see above). I considered the twelve districts that Seplan's study classified as belonging to area VIII, the poorest area of the city in the 1980s. I studied these districts on the map and identified the corresponding twenty-eight districts for 1991. Their limits do not correspond exactly, but they are very close. The comparative data indicate broad changes between 1980 and 1991.[45] Table 8 summarizes the indicators for this area and for the city in 1980 and 1991.

While the city's central districts lost population, the poorest periphery grew an average of 3.26 percent a year in the 1980s. In 1991, the area housed approximately one-third of São Paulo's residents. Its urban infrastructure improved: in 1991, 74.0 percent of the domiciles were connected to the sewage system (compared to 19.1 percent in 1980), 96.03 percent had piped water, and 96.5 percent had garbage collection. Paved roads and public illumination increased, too, and a subway line was constructed in the eastern region that improved public transportation. Moreover, many childcare centers, health clinics, and schools were built by the local and by the state administration in those districts. As a consequence, although incomes remained low (48.78 percent of heads of households made less than 3 MS in 1991), the quality of life on the periphery improved (see photos 3 and 4). A good indicator is the rate of infant mortality. In the city, it dropped from 50.62 per 1,000 live births in 1980 to 26.03 in 1991. In the poorest area of the periphery, the decrease was even more radical. In São Miguel Paulista, one of its poorest districts, where Jardim das Camélias is located, the infant mortality rate dropped from 134 in 1975 to 80.46 in 1980 and to 27.29 in 1994. Another indicator of the change in quality of life is the construction of a series of modern shopping and leisure centers in the periphery, such as large supermarkets.

The significant improvement on the periphery is to a large extent the result of the political action of its residents who, since the late 1970s, have organized social movements to claim their rights as city residents. These social movements are a central element both in the democratization of

TABLE 8 Socioeconomic Indicators, 1980 and 1991,
City of São Paulo and its Poorest Periphery

Indicators	Periphery 1980	Periphery 1991	São Paulo 1980	São Paulo 1991
Population	2,044,689	3,062,538	8,493,226	9,646,185
Households	453,140	732,491	2,062,196	2,539,953
households with sewage services (%)	19.12	74.00	57.73	86.31
households with piped water (%)	79.31	96.03	92.16	98.41
owned residences (%)	54.42	68.51	51.40	63.57
rented residences (%)	34.62	22.56	40.02	28.75
difference households/registered residences (%)[a]		164.23		69.51
vertical residences (%)[b]		5.71		33.62

SOURCES: For population and households: 1980 and 1991 censuses. For officially registered residences: TPCL in São Paulo—Sempla (1992:148–50).

[a]Refers to the proportional difference between the number of households observed by the census in 1991 and the number of residential units registered by the city (TPCL) in 1990.

[b]Refers to vertical residential units registered by the city (TPCL).

PHOTOS 3 AND 4.   A street in Jardim das Camélias in 1980 and in 1989. In
the early 1980s, only one street of Jardim das Camélias had asphalt and sidewalks;
none was illuminated or had sewers. By the 1990s, all streets had asphalt, sidewalks, lighting, and sewers, although many houses were still under construction.
Photo 3 by Teresa Caldeira and 4 by Teresa Caldeira and James Holston.

Brazilian society and in the change in the quality of life in many large cities.
São Paulo is probably the best example of these processes. The social movements and political democratization forced transformations in the action of
the state, especially the local administration, which reoriented its policies
to meet the demands of the residents on the periphery.[46] Even right-wing
politicians learned that their political future in a free electoral system depended on their paying attention to the periphery. In fact, in the late 1970s
and early 1980s, the municipal and state administrations of São Paulo (as
well as of various other Brazilian states) sponsored intensive infrastructure
development projects, especially in sanitation, which transformed Brazil into
the World Bank's largest borrower in the area of urban development (Melo
1995:343).

The social movements influenced the action of the local administration
not only in creating public services and urban infrastructure but also in
transforming the legal status of the periphery. One of the main demands of
the social movements was the legalization of properties on the periphery.
Social movements forced the municipal governments to offer amnesties to
illegal developers, making it possible to regularize their lots and bring them

into the formal property market. The approval of the Lehman Law (Federal Law 6,766) in 1979 made it easier to prosecute real estate developers selling land without the infrastructure required by law and therefore discouraged this common practice.[47] However, it also diminished the stock of irregular and cheap lots available, since land value increased as a result of both the construction of infrastructure and urban equipment and the regularization of lot subdivisions. Because legal developments and lots in areas with a better infrastructure are obviously more expensive than illegal lots in marginally developed areas, the neighborhoods that received these improvements became too expensive for the already impoverished population.[48]

The phenomenon of improvement plus legalization associated with a drop in population growth is most apparent not on the fringes of the city, where expansion through illegal autoconstruction continues, but in a ring inside it, which constituted the newest periphery in the 1970s. This includes an area on the eastern periphery, along the new subway line and around the old district centers. The new district of São Miguel Paulista, for example, which corresponds to the oldest part of the previous larger district, had an annual population growth of 2.66 percent from 1980 to 1991, while most of the districts in the eastern border of the city grew between 35 percent and 85 percent. Nevertheless, in various areas of the eastern periphery, including São Miguel, the rate of officially registered construction increased considerably from 1977 to 1987 (123 percent in São Miguel, 110 percent in Ermelino, and 84 percent in Itaquera), indicating their improvement and their legalization. Although this development has been limited, it seems that some of these areas are starting to enter the legal land market and to undergo a process of capitalization in housing development, as bigger entrepreneurs start to invest and build legal housing, especially apartment buildings.[49] This type of housing remains less accessible to the poorest population.

People who cannot afford to build their houses but still live on the periphery may become squatters. Residents in favelas represented 1.1 percent of the city's population in 1973, 4.4 percent in 1980, 8.9 percent in 1987, and 19.1 percent in 1993—that is, more than 1.9 million people. The majority of the favelas in 1993 were located on the periphery, especially on the southern and northern borders (Freguesia do Ó, Campo Limpo, Capela do Socorro, and Pirituba-Jaraguá) (Seade 1990:63 and São Paulo—Sempla 1995:77).

Estimates of the numbers of people living in cortiços in the city of São Paulo vary widely. Sempla estimates that in 1991, 15.8 percent (1,506,709) of the population of the municipality lived in cortiços (São Paulo—Sempla 1995:79–80). This is a much higher number than the estimate of Fipe (Fundação Instituto de Pesquisas Econômicas, Universidade de São Paulo) for 1993, which is 595,110, or 6 percent of the population, distributed among almost 24,000 cortiços.[50] All cortiços are rentals, the majority (55.6 percent) of the residents are younger than twenty-five, and the majority of the heads of households (54.3 percent) are between fifteen and thirty-five years old (Fipe 1994:13, 14). These data support the hypothesis that the cortiços are an alternative for a new generation of urban poor who cannot afford autoconstruction.

All sources agree, however, on the localities of the cortiços. Although there are cortiços on the periphery, the majority are either in the old downtown (Sé) or in old industrial areas and decaying lower middle-class neighborhoods, where many large houses and factories are transformed into cortiços (Moóca, Brás, Belém, and Liberdade). Some of these areas have shown a persistent decrease in population since at least the early 1960s. In fact, the highest rates of population loss are in industrial districts and working-class neighborhoods formed at the turn of the century. In the last decade, however, parts of these neighborhoods have shown signs of renewal and gentrification. Moóca is one such case. Although its residents consider the increase in cortiços to be one of its main problems, other processes are also affecting the neighborhood. These include the opening of the east-west subway line, which has been accompanied by the construction of new apartment buildings for the middle classes, some of which are closed condominiums. A few factories have also been turned into leisure and shopping centers. These transformations in urban, residential, and social patterns in those areas contribute to the sense of uncertainty and loss felt by the older residents.

Transformations in the Center and Displacement of the Rich

Wealth continues to be highly concentrated in a very small part of the city of São Paulo, as map 2 demonstrates. Therefore, the center-periphery model constituted in the previous decades still shapes the urban space. However, various indicators strongly suggest recent changes in this pattern. Although the concentration of wealth is still significant, an unprecedented displacement of rich residents and the construction of new areas of commerce and services are reshaping the spatial pattern of social segregation.

In the 1980s and 1990s, the middle and upper classes changed their lifestyles and their use of the city in various ways. As a consequence, the districts in which they used to live and the ones to which they were moving underwent various changes. In 1991, only 11.4 percent of the city's districts had a population in which more than 25 percent of heads of households made more than 20 MS. These districts contain 10 percent of the population but 41 percent of the heads of households who make more than 20 MS.[51] The majority of these districts lost population, or grew very little between 1980 and 1991. Only two had increased population growth: Morumbi (2.33 percent) and Vila Andrade (5.93 percent). Between 1991 and 1996, all but Vila Andrade lost population. The highest decreases were in traditional middle-class neighborhoods that had had higher rates of growth in the 1970s, which were associated with the boom of apartment buildings and financing for the middle classes. In fact, most of them have the highest rates of vertical construction and population density in the city. Two of these districts (Jardim Paulista and Moema) are the most homogeneously rich in the city.[52]

Because a significant proportion of the middle and upper classes live in apartment buildings, either in the neighborhoods that grew in the 1970s or the new neighborhoods to which they started to move in the 1980s, to look at the real estate market for apartments can help us to understand their displacement.[53] In the 1980s and 1990s, São Paulo's apartment market was much different from that of the 1970s. The change was caused not only by the economic crisis of the early 1980s but also by the reduction of BNH financing, which in 1987 was reduced to 10 percent of what it had been in 1980 (Nepp 1989:492). The single exception for the real estate market was 1986, the year of the Plano Cruzado, in which a short-lived economic re-

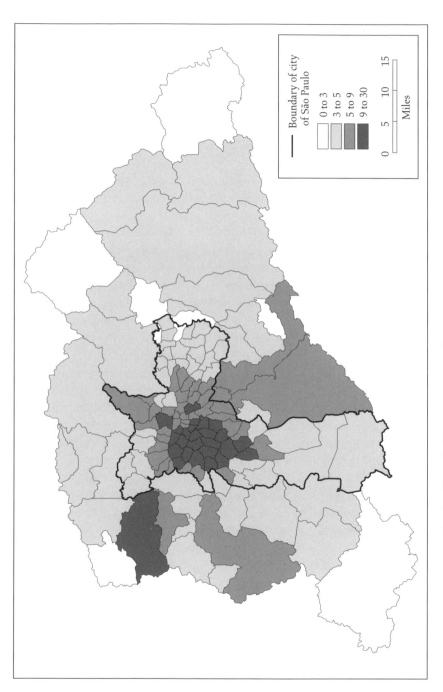

MAP 2. Average income of heads of households (in minimum salaries), MRSP, 1991. *Source: 1991* Census.

covery reduced inflation, increased the profits of many financial ventures, and increased both the number of developments launched (677) and the price per square meter.[54] Thereafter, however, the market dropped even lower, especially after the extinction of BNH at the end of 1986 and the return of inflation with the failure of the Plano Cruzado. In 1991 and 1992 the number of registered new developments was the lowest since the mid-70s (around 150). With high inflation and virtually no financing, it was much more difficult for the middle classes to buy their own apartments. As a result, there are indications of what some analysts call an "elitization" in the production of apartments, that is, the development of larger, more sophisticated residences for the upper classes (Ferraz Filho 1992:29).[55] After 1993, the number of developments started to increase again, and the annual average for the period 1993–1996 (365) is higher than that for the ten years preceding the end of the BNH (280, according to Embraesp 1997:7). One of the factors in this increase is the emergence of cooperatives of future homeowners and systems of autofinancing, which in 1996 were responsible for 10 percent of the new developments. Their introduction caused a decrease in the average price of apartments in 1996 (Embraesp 1997:32). The end of high inflation as a result of the success of the Plano Real, as well as new opportunities for long-term financing, made possible the increase in the real estate market after 1993.

Despite the real estate crisis, more apartments continued to be built. In 1957, apartment buildings were found in twenty central districts; in 1979, they were found in forty-seven districts (Ferreira 1987:77, 141).[56] In 1991, there was a significant number of apartment buildings in all but twelve of the ninety-six districts of the city. Apartments not only spread but were also being constructed according to different patterns, from popular complexes built by government housing companies to luxury developments. One of the most interesting phenomena in this regard, and the one producing the most important changes in the way the upper and middle classes live, is the growth of closed condominiums (condomínio fechado). This is a development of multiple residences, mostly high-rises, invariably walled and with security-controlled entrances, usually occupying a large area with landscaping, and including all sorts of amenities for collective use. In the last decade, they have become the preferred residence for the rich.

Closed condominiums are not constructed in the traditional central neighborhoods, as they require large lots that are affordable only in undeveloped areas. The change in the predominant style of apartment building is indicated by a change in the relationship between the total area of terrain and constructed areas. According to the TPCL, from 1980 to 1990 the total

constructed area of residential high-rises in the city increased 59.27 percent, while the total area used by residential high-rises increased 75.34 percent. As a result, the utilization rate of residential apartment buildings in
São Paulo dropped from 4.36 to 3.95.[57] The fact that construction shifted
from central to more peripheral areas is attested to by the unprecedented
development of two districts in the southwest part of the city, Morumbi and
Vila Andrade.

These two noncentral and adjacent districts are emblematic of the most
dramatic changes occurring in the city. (Similarly radical changes are happening in some municipalities in the northwest of the metropolitan region.)
They have been affected by the intensive real estate investment not only in
the new type of residences for the rich but also in new complexes of similarly enclosed office and commercial buildings. That the new developments
were located in these areas is partially due to favorable zoning codes that
allowed both mixed-use construction (instead of exclusively residential as
in parts of the central districts) and utilization rates as high as four. Some
of these areas were either rural or already inhabited by poor people. As a
result, as the new developments spread, they presented a new pattern of spatial organization: one that mixes rich and poor residents on the one hand,
and residence and work on the other, thus creating a new pattern of both
social inequality and of functional heterogeneity.

Morumbi and Vila Andrade had significant population growth in the
1980s.[58] Although Morumbi had been an upper-class neighborhood for at
least twenty-five years, after the early 1980s it changed radically. What used
to be a neighborhood of immense mansions, vacant lots, and green areas is
being transformed, after a decade of frenetic construction, into a forest of
high-rises. In the late 1970s, it was "discovered" by developers, who decided
to take advantage of its cheap land and favorable zoning code and transformed it into the fastest-growing neighborhood in the city during the 1980s
and 1990s. More than 400 new residential developments, with more than
14,000 new units, were built between 1980 and 1996.[59] In spite of that, it
still has only 0.6 percent of the city's apartments, compared to 5.75 percent
in Jardim Paulista. Whereas in Jardim Paulista 88 percent of the domiciles
are apartments, in Morumbi the figure is 33.6 percent. Vila Andrade, adjacent to Morumbi, is a extension of the same process in a place that used to
be poorer but has continued to expand as Morumbi has seemed to lose its
dynamism in the last few years.

The construction of closed condominiums began in the 1970s, during the
boom in the real estate market and state financing. The project that launched
the area's frenetic development was Portal do Morumbi. This complex of

sixteen twenty-five-story blocks was inaugurated in 1976. It has eight hundred apartments, half with four bedrooms, the other half with three bedrooms, and it houses 3,500 residents, one-third of whom are under fourteen years old. The total area of the development is 160,000 square meters, of which 120,000 are common areas, including parks, sports facilities, and entertainment facilities. This complex was literally put up in the middle of nowhere. All of the required urban infrastructure (including electricity, water, and street construction) was provided by the developer, Construtora Alfredo Mathias. To this day the back streets of the complex remain nonurbanized and without paving or sidewalks (see photos 5 and 6).

This type of development, with its low utilization rate, along with the fact that the transformation is recent and there are still many mansions and unoccupied spaces, explains why Morumbi and Vila Andrade still have a population density considerably lower than that of Jardim Paulista (3,500 and 4,200 inhabitants per square kilometer in comparison to 16,900). There are also important social differences between the two areas. Although they are all wealthy, Morumbi and Vila Andrade are not as homogeneously rich as the old central neighborhoods. In Morumbi today, 43.9 percent of heads of household make more than 20 MS (the highest percentage in the city), while in Vila Andrade, the proportion is 26.2 percent. The average income in Morumbi is 28.82 MS (the highest average in the city); in Vila Andrade it is 17.94. However, in both areas the ratio of heads of households making more than 20 MS in relation to those making less than 3 is significantly lower than in Jardim Paulista (2.55 in Morumbi and 0.87 in Vila Andrade, compared to 4.59 in Jardim Paulista and 3.98 in Moema).[60] While in Jardim Paulista only 8.36 percent of the residents make less than 3 MS, in Morumbi 17.22 percent do, and in Vila Andrade 30.02 percent do (whereas 26.19 percent make more than 20 MS). This greater heterogeneity in income distribution is a characteristic of the new areas of expansion of the city and the metropolitan region, where developments for people with higher incomes are located in previously poorer or uninhabited areas and apartments for the rich are constructed alongside huge favelas.

The neighbors of the closed condominiums around Real Parque and Giovanni Gronchi Avenue in the heart of Morumbi are residents of two of the most famous favelas in São Paulo. In 1987, there were 233,429 people living in favelas in the western and southwestern districts of the city, corresponding to 28.62 percent of São Paulo's residents in favelas.[61] By 1993, favelas residents in these districts had increased to 482,304, representing 25.36 percent of São Paulo's squatters (São Paulo—Sempla 1995:76).

After fifteen years of intensive real estate development for the upper

PHOTOS 5 AND 6.   Closed condominium "Portal do Morumbi," entrance and unpaved side street, 1994. Photos by Teresa Caldeira.

classes in areas with precarious infrastructure, combined with the proliferation of favelas, Morumbi exemplifies the new face of social segregation in the city (see photos 7 and 8). If one looks at the area around its main street, Avenue Giovanni Gronchi, and at the advertisements for its high-rises, one is struck by the imagination of the developers in endowing each apartment complex with "distinguishable" characteristics: in addition to monumental architecture and foreign, vaguely aristocratic names, the buildings display exotic features: one swimming pool per individual apartment, three maids' rooms, waiting rooms for drivers in the basement, and special rooms for storing crystal, china, silver, and so on. All this luxury contrasts with the views from the apartment windows: the more than five thousand shacks of the favela Paraisópolis, one of the biggest in São Paulo, which supplies the domestic servants for the condominiums nearby. For the people interested in living exclusively among their peers the walls have to be high indeed, and the rich residences do not conceal their electric fences, video cameras, and private guards.

Intense construction according to developers' interests and with little planning or state control has, in addition to completely transforming the landscape, created a chaotic space. Immense buildings were built one after

the other in narrow streets with inadequate infrastructure. In Vila Andrade, for example, only 57.6 percent of households are connected to the sewage system, a percentage much lower than in various districts on the poor periphery (for the whole periphery, the percentage is 74 percent). The buildings are immense, and many of the new streets do not have sidewalks— probably a feature intended to exclude people without cars. Traffic is very heavy, and traffic jams are routine.[62] In spite of heavy investment by the city and the construction of bridges, tunnels, and expressways connecting Morumbi to the city center across the Pinheiros river, the roads are insufficient, and public transportation is simply bad. This congestion increases the burden on the poor, but it is also inconvenient for the middle classes, as the neighborhood still lacks basic services and commerce. Although two big shopping centers and a couple of so-called hypermarkets are now operating in the area, buying groceries requires a car, a necessity unknown in most central neighborhoods in São Paulo, where, as people say, at least bread has to be available within walking distance. The transportation of children also depends on cars, even to the private schools in the neighborhood, one of its chief attractions.[63]

Unlike the old central neighborhoods and the poor areas in the periphery, then, Morumbi and Vila Andrade are not places where residents routinely walk on the streets. Ironically, these neighborhoods, with their nar-

PHOTO 7.   Morumbi, unequal neighbors,
1992: the individual swimming pools of these
apartments overlook the favela below. Photo
by Celio Jr., Agência Estado.

row streets, bad infrastructure, and poor connections to the rest of the city,
depend on cars for almost everything. As a consequence, moving to one of
the area's luxury apartments means enduring heavy traffic and poor urban
services. Nevertheless, for the residents of the new enclosures, the incon-
veniences seem to be more than compensated for by the feeling of security
they gain behind the walls, living exclusively among their equals and far
from what they consider to be the city's dangers.

Recession, Deindustrialization, and New Spaces for Tertiary Activities

It is not only the pattern of residence and distribution of poor and rich residents that is changing in the city and the metropolitan region. In the last
two decades, São Paulo has gone through a significant economic recession

PHOTO 8.   Morumbi, aerial view, 1992: luxury
apartment buildings and favela shacks are side
by side. Photo by Celio Jr., Agência Estado.

and a shift in the structure of its economic activities. Between 1980 and 1990,
the total value added decreased by 3.75 percent in São Paulo.[64] In 1990, the
total value added per capita was only 61.6 percent of what it had been in
1985 (Araújo 1993:35, 36). The crisis especially affected the industrial sector, which had been the most dynamic of the city and the metropolitan region since the 1950s. Although industrial production in São Paulo's metropolitan region continued to represent 30.7 percent of the national total in
1987, this proportion is significantly lower than the 43.5 percent it represented in 1970 (Araújo 1992:56).

   While in 1970 the city of São Paulo had almost half of the industrial
labor force of the state, in 1991 it had less than one-third (Gonçalves and Semeghini 1992; Leme and Meyer 1997:71). This decrease occurred throughout the state of São Paulo but was most pronounced in the capital.[65] While
in the interior of the state the industrial sector in 1991 (38.4 percent) was

practically the same proportion of the labor force as in 1970 (39.7 percent) after having increased in 1980 (45.1 percent), in the capital the participation of the industrial sector in the labor force diminished significantly to 32.1 percent in 1991, after increasing consistently since the 1950s and reaching 42 percent in 1980 (Gonçalves and Semeghini 1992; Leme and Meyer 1997:64).[66] In the metropolitan region as a whole, the percentage of the industrial sector as a total of the labor force has dropped continuously in recent years, from 36.5 percent in 1988 to 29.6 percent in 1993 (Leme and Meyer 1997:77).

As the industrial sector shrank, the role of tertiary activities in the urban economy increased.[67] There is a great debate among social scientists regarding whether this expansion is due to an increase in "modern" or "traditional" activities. Some (for example, Gonçalves and Semeghini 1992; Araújo 1992) argue that the extension of the tertiary sector is a consequence of the development of a more flexible type of production, in which many activities previously recorded as industrial production started to be bought as services and the role of modern technology and financing activities expanded. Others, however, try to relativize these assertions, showing that expansion occurred in sectors of tertiary activity that are very precarious, for example the informal commerce of street vendors (comércio ambulante) and unskilled and low-paid activities performed without formal labor contracts (see, for example, Leme and Meyer 1997:63–79). Although it would be beyond the scope of this work to develop this hypothesis, I suggest that both processes are probably happening at the same time, and in this sense what is going on in São Paulo is no different from the industrial restructuring occurring in Los Angeles and other so-called global cities (Scott and Soja 1996; Sassen 1991). It is a characteristic of these processes that the most dynamic and the most precarious poles of the economy expand simultaneously, provoking sharper patterns of social inequality.

These economic changes have all sorts of implications for the built environment, from the abandonment or conversion of factories to the creation of new urban spaces and new installations for commerce and offices. After moving from downtown to Avenida Paulista and Avenida Faria Lima in the 1960s, the main office complexes are now moving southwest, along the Pinheiros river and in the same direction as the new residential complexes, shopping malls, and hypermarkets.[68] Therefore, the new urban spaces for tertiary activities are developing through a process well known in the United States: the relocation of jobs and residences from central and urbanized areas to more distant ones. The new buildings are the result of large investments, frequently by real estate developers who abandoned the residential market when it became more difficult (Ferraz Filho 1992:29). They follow the same kind of architectural and planning model as the closed condominiums. If they are not necessarily walled like the residential complexes, they are certainly fortified and use extensive security services to keep out all undesirable people—and to control their own workers. As self-sufficient worlds, these arrangements can be placed anywhere land is cheap enough to make their investment profitable. As with the residential complexes, they are being installed in previously poor areas. The avenue that symbolizes the new expansion, Eng. Luís Carlos Berrini, has been quickly displacing an old favela under a program paid for by the new occupants of the area. By 1998, most of the slum-like dwellings had been removed, but many poor residences and commerce were still visible. It can be expected, however, that the avenue will soon be completely transformed by the new buildings, following a local version of postmodern architectural style, and will be purged of poor inhabitants. Until then, the avenue offers a spectacle of social inequality on a par with the Morumbi condominiums overlooking the favelas.

Finally, the displacement of the new tertiary activities to the west recreates an opposition between eastern and western parts of the city that the center-periphery model had eclipsed. While the new investments in office complexes and closed condominiums for the upper classes are concentrated in the city's southwest side, the eastern region, traditionally more industrial, has lost dynamism with the decrease of its industrial activities. Some of the old factories have been transformed into shopping centers, department stores, or leisure centers, but many have simply been abandoned. While the eastern and the southeastern zones remain the poorest, more industrial zones, expanding mainly through illegal construction and lacking a significant number of developments for the upper classes, the southwestern border houses the rich, their residential developments, and the new white-collar tertiary activities. This opposition adds complexity to a city landscape already transformed by the improvement of the periphery and the relative depopulation of the wealthy center. To complete the picture, however, it is necessary to look at the metropolitan region as a whole.

The Metropolitan Region

The other municipalities of the metropolitan region have frequently been treated as peripheral to the capital. This may have been true in the 1960s and 1970s, but in the last fifteen years the processes affecting these cities have been more complex. Urban infrastructure has improved significantly. From a demographic point of view, the other municipalities continue to demonstrate typical peripheral behavior, as they are still growing much more than the center (table 7). From an economic point of view, however, the crisis of the 1980s had different effects on the municipalities that were heavily industrialized and those that were not, changing the simple relationship of complementarity with the capital. While the more industrial areas suffered drastically, large investments in real estate and tertiary activities in formerly rural locations generated good economic performance with continuous rates of growth in the west and northwest (Araújo 1993:37). The dynamism of these areas is such that for the first time some of the other municipalities became receivers of rich migrants from the center.

Although São Paulo was hit worst by the economic crisis of the 1980s, the cities of Osasco and the ABCD region in the southeast region were also affected.[69] The latter can be seen as a symbol of the previous era of industrial development, housing most of the heavy metal and machine factories that supported the auto industry boom in the 1950s and 1960s. To this day it has the highest concentration of industrial jobs in the metropolitan region and has been the center of a strong trade union movement, from which the PT and its most important leaders emerged. It still has better urban infrastructure than most and an impressive concentration of wealth. Only five municipalities in the metropolitan region have more than 5 percent of the heads of the households making more than 20 MS on average, and two of these are in the ABCD region: São Bernardo (5.8 percent) and São Caetano (6.3 percent).[70] Nevertheless, the recent economic performance of these municipalities has been poor, and their population is growing very little (São Caetano has lost population in the last fifteen years).

Various industrial municipalities on the eastern and northern sides of the metropolitan region also suffered during the economic recession.[71] These are among the poorest municipalities of the metropolitan region.[72] In none of the eastern municipalities is the proportion of heads of households making more than 20 MS higher than 3 percent; and in all the municipalities in this region, between 30 and 50 percent of the heads of households make less than 2 MS a month.

In contrast, the western and northwestern municipalities of Santana do Parnaíba, Barueri, and Cajamar reveal a picture of great dynamism and represent a new type of development. These areas had the most impressive rates of population growth from 1980 to 1996. They also demonstrated strong economic performance in a decade marked by economic stagnation and decrease.[73] This performance is associated with high investment in real estate developments (mostly closed condominiums), office complexes, business centers, and shopping centers much on the model of American new suburbs. Because of that, many of the migrants to these areas are from the middle and upper classes (probably those abandoning the central part of the capital) instead of the working classes, as has been traditional on the periphery. Santana do Parnaíba, the city with the highest average income of the whole metropolitan region (9.8 MS), has a level of wealth that used to exist only in some of the central districts of São Paulo.

Santana do Parnaíba exemplifies what one might call a new suburbanization of São Paulo. Its growth has been neither the traditional expansion of poor and industrial areas nor the American suburban outgrowth of the 1950s and 1960s, but a new type of suburbanization of the 1980s and 1990s that brings together residence and tertiary activities. Santana do Parnaíba has not had the same economic performance as its adjacent municipalities, Barueri and Cajamar, but it shows more clearly how the area is becoming a new middle- and upper-class enclave. It was the municipality with the highest annual rate of population growth in the 1980s (12.76 percent) and the highest income.[74] Ninety percent of the population increase during the 1980s was due to migration, and it had the highest percentage of growth due to migration in the metropolitan region: 245 percent (São Paulo—Emplasa 1994:137). The immigrants were mainly wealthy residents. As the rich settle into areas that have been rural and extremely poor,[75] they create situations of dramatic social inequality, attested to by the fact that the GINI coefficient in Santana do Parnaíba is 0.7102, the highest of the metropolitan region.[76]

One of the differences between Morumbi and the new rich areas in the western metropolitan region is that their closed condominiums are mostly horizontal instead of vertical: that is, they consist of walled areas with detached houses instead of apartment buildings. Horizontal closed condominiums expanded at the same time that Morumbi was constructing its high-rises, and they share the same imagery as the apartment complexes. Today these condominiums are common around the metropolitan region of São Paulo and even in the interior of the state, especially in its richer and more industrialized areas. One of the most impressive, and one of the oldest, is Alphaville—named after Godard's movie about a fantasy city in a technologically dominated future. It includes not only enclosed residences but also shopping malls and offices. Together with the neighboring developments of Aldeia da Serra and Tamboré in the municipalities of Barueri and Santana do Parnaíba, the whole region has been aggressively marketed in Brazil as a true "edge city," or a new type of American suburb.

The New Segregation

Contemporary São Paulo is a more diversified and complex metropolitan region than it was fifteen years ago, when the center-periphery model sufficiently described its pattern of segregation and social inequality. These transformations have arisen from a combination of processes: the reversal in demographic growth; the economic recession, deindustrialization, and expansion of tertiary activities; the improvement of the periphery, combined with the impoverishment of the working classes; the displacement of part of the middle and upper classes from the center; and the widespread fear of crime that has made people from all social classes seek more secure forms of residence. In consequence, not only is São Paulo more unequal than it used to be—the GINI coefficient of the metropolitan region increased from 0.516 in 1981 to 0.586 in 1991—but this inequality has also become more explicit and visible as rich and poor residents live in closer proximity in the newly expanded areas of the city and of the metropolitan region. These new areas in fact have the highest GINI coefficients and the most shocking landscapes of adjacent wealth and poverty. Moreover, in the context of increased suspicion and fear of crime, and preoccupation with social decay, residents show no tolerance for people from different social groups or interest in finding common solutions to their urban problems. Rather, they engage in increasingly sophisticated techniques of social separation and the creation of distance. Thus, the fortified enclaves—apartment high-rises, closed condominiums, peripheral office complexes, and shopping centers—constitute the core of a new way of organizing segregation, social discrimination, and economic restructuring in São Paulo. Different social classes live closer to each other in some areas but are kept apart by physical barriers and systems of identification and control.

Contemporary São Paulo is a metropolis in which there are more favelas and *cortiços,* but in which many working-class neighborhoods in the periphery have improved considerably; in which old inner-city areas have been transformed by both gentrification and decay; in which rich people live in the central and well-equipped areas but also in new enclosed enclaves in precarious and distant regions, close to the very poor, either in the capital or outside it; in which the tertiary jobs are moving to nonurbanized areas; and in which an opposition between west (richer) and east (poorer) is becoming more visible. It is also a metropolitan area in which the physical distances that used to separate different social groups may have shrunk, but the walls around properties are higher and the systems of surveillance more obvious. It is a city of walls in which the quality of public space is changing immensely, and in ways opposite from what would be expected in a society that was able to consolidate a political democracy. In fact, the segregation and the model of obvious separation put in place in recent decades may be seen as a reaction to the expansion of this very process of democratization, since it functions to stigmatize, control, and exclude those who had just forced their recognition as citizens, with full rights to engage in shaping the city's future and its environment.

CHAPTER 7

Fortified Enclaves

*Building Up Walls and
Creating a New Private Order*

The guard in the fortified pillbox is new on the job and so is obligated to stop me in the condominium. He asks my name and desti-
nation, observing my shoes. He calls house 16 on the intercom and
says that there is a gentleman saying he is the brother of the house's
mistress. House 16 answers something the guard does not like, and
he says, "Hum." The gate of green iron bars and big golden rings
opens in a shuttered motion, as if reluctant to let me pass. The guard
watches me going up the hill, notices the soles of my shoes, and
believes that I am the first pedestrian authorized to cross that gate.
House 16, at the end of the condominium, has another intercom,
another electronic gate, and two armed guards. The dogs bark in a
chorus and then stop barking suddenly. A young man with a flannel in his hands opens a little lateral door and makes me enter the
garden with a gesture of the flannel. . . .

   The servant does not know which door I deserve, because I am
neither delivering something nor have the aspect of a visitor. He
stops, twists the flannel to drain the doubt, and opts for the garage
door, which is neither here nor there. Obeying convulsive flannel
signs, I skirt the automobiles in the transparent garage, climb a circular staircase, and get to a kind of living room with an uncommonly high ceiling, granite floor, inclined glass wall, other walls
white and nude, a lot of echo, a living room where I have never
seen someone sitting. On the left of this room runs a big staircase
that comes from the second floor. At the bottom of the big staircase
there is a small room that they call a winter garden, attached to
the patio where the ficus used to live. There is my sister in a robe
having her breakfast on an oval table.

Chico Buarque, Estorvo

Estorvo means hindrance, obstruction, inconvenience. In his 1991 novel,
Chico Buarque—the poet and singer of urban passions and everyday life,
of the 1970s resistance to the military, and of the early 1980s hopes for
political change—captures the feelings of the new life amid barriers in contemporary Brazilian cities.[1] The novel is set in Rio but could equally well

be set in São Paulo or any other city of walls. In these cities and especially for their elite, an everyday act such as a visit to a sister involves dealing with private guards, identification, classification, iron gates, intercoms, domestic servants, electronic gates, dogs—and a lot of suspicion. The man approaching the gate of the closed condominium warrants suspicion because he gives the wrong signs: he walks instead of driving a car and thus reveals himself as someone who uses urban public space in a way that the residents of the condominiums reject. Closed condominiums, the new type of fortified elite housing, are not places people walk to or even simply pass by. They are meant to be distant, to be approached only by car and then only by their residents, a few visitors, and of course the servants, who must be kept under control and are usually directed to a special entrance. As a consequence, a marginal member of the elite who insists on walking can only elicit doubts and ambiguous interactions with the condominium's employees. Unable to classify the pedestrian, the house servant decides to bring him in through an entrance that is neither the "social" nor the "service" door—the traditional division in middle- and upper-class houses and apartments.

Closed condominiums constitute the most desirable type of housing for the upper classes in contemporary São Paulo. In this chapter, I analyze this new residential type from a series of interconnected perspectives. I first define the closed condominiums and their relationship both with previous housing arrangements and with other enclaves producing the same segregational effects. Closed condominiums are not an isolated phenomenon but the residential version of a new urban form that creates segregation in contemporary cities. Second, I analyze the elements that transform São Paulo's residential high-rises, and especially the closed condominiums, into prestigious residences: security, facilities, services, and location. Third, I discuss problematic aspects of life inside the condominium walls: the difficulty of arriving at consensual regulations and of enforcing rules, the most dramatic expression of which is the rate of adolescent crime, especially vandalism and car accidents caused by teenagers driving without a license. Fourth, I analyze the ambiguities, contradictions, and rejections that this new model generates as residents of the city contrast it to other spaces, housing options, and lifestyles in the city. Although the new model has not eliminated all other possibilities, it provides the main paradigm of distinction for São Paulo's residents. In the city today, a widespread aesthetic of security shaped by the new model simultaneously guides transformations of all types of housing and determines what confers the most prestige.

PRIVATE WORLDS FOR THE ELITE

Closed condominiums are the residential version of a broader category of new urban developments that I call fortified enclaves. The latter are changing considerably the way in which middle- and upper-class people live, consume, work, and spend their leisure time. They are changing the city's landscape, its pattern of spatial segregation, and the character of public space and of public interclass interactions. Fortified enclaves include office complexes shopping centers, and, increasingly, other spaces that have been adapted to conform to this model: schools, hospitals, entertainment centers, and theme parks. All fortified enclaves share some basic characteristics. They are private property for collective use, and they emphasize the value of what is private and restricted at the same time that they devalue what is public and open in the city. They are physically demarcated and isolated by walls, fences, empty spaces, and design devices. They are turned inward, away from the street, whose public life they explicitly reject. They are controlled by armed guards and security systems, which enforce rules of inclusion and exclusion. They are flexible: because of their size, the new technologies of communication, the new organization of work, and security systems, they constitute autonomous spaces, independent of their surroundings, that can be situated almost anywhere. In other words, in contrast to previous forms of commercial and residential developments, they belong not to their immediate surroundings but to largely invisible networks (Cenzatti and Crawford 1998).[2] As a consequence, although they tend to be spaces for the upper classes, they may be sited in rural areas or on the old periphery, beside favelas or autoconstructed houses. Finally, the enclaves tend to be socially homogeneous environments. People who choose to inhabit these spaces value living among selected people (considered to be of the same social group) and away from the undesired interactions, movement, heterogeneity, danger, and the unpredictability of open streets. The fortified and private enclaves cultivate a relationship of rupture and denial with the rest of the city and with what can be called a modern style of public space open to free circulation. They are transforming the nature of the public space and the quality of public interactions in the city, which are becoming increasingly marked by suspicion and restriction.

Fortified enclaves confer status. The construction of status symbols is a process that elaborates social differences and creates means for the assertion of social distance and inequality. Fortified enclaves are quite literal in their creation of separation. They are well demarcated by all kinds of physical barriers and distancing devices, and their presence in the city space presents a clear statement of social differentiation. They offer a new way of establishing boundaries between social groups and establishing new hierarchies among them, and therefore of explicitly organizing difference as inequality. The use of literal means of separation is complemented by a symbolic elaboration that transforms enclosure, isolation, restriction, and surveillance into status symbols. This elaboration is evident from the real estate advertisements.

The transformation of fortified enclaves into prestigious spaces has required changes in the values held by the elite. First, collective residences have come to be preferred to individual houses. Collective housing, including apartment high-rises, has for a long time been devalued in São Paulo because of its association with *cortiços*. Until recently, detached, single-family houses were the paradigm of dignified residence and evidence of moral and social status. The values of privacy, individual freedom, and the nuclear family embedded in the detached house have supported both the war on *cortiços* and the promotion of home ownership among the working classes. Second, isolated, nonurbanized, and distant areas have been transformed into more valuable spaces than the traditional central and well-equipped neighborhoods. This shift has required a reversal of the values that prevailed from the 1940s to the 1980s, when the city center was unequivocally associated with the rich and the periphery with the poor. For the first time, something like the American suburb became popular among the elite, and distance from the center was resignified in order to confer status instead of stigma.

FROM *CORTIÇOS* TO LUXURY ENCLAVES

To live in multifamily residences, sharing both the use and the ownership of common areas, is not a new experience for the Brazilian middle classes. Condominiums have existed in São Paulo since 1928. Although it took a long time for them to lose the *cortiço* stigma and become popular among the middle classes, they became more common from the 1970s on because of changes in financing and the resulting construction boom. Several elements, however, differentiate the 1970s apartments from the closed condominiums of the 1980s and 1990s. Although the old type of apartment continues to be built and has expanded its market even to the working classes, the most sophisticated and expensive developments are of the new type. One difference is location: whereas in the 1970s apartment buildings were still concentrated in central neighborhoods, the closed condominiums of the 1990s tend to be in distant areas. Whereas earlier apartments were integrated into the urban network, recent condominiums tend to ignore it. Second, closed condominiums are by definition walled, whereas the high-rises of the 1970s tended to be open to the streets, although most of them have been recently fenced in. Third, the new type of closed condominium tends to have large (sometimes very large) areas and facilities for common use, whereas in the previous generation, common spaces were generally limited to garages, corridors and lobbies, small playgrounds, and maybe a room for parties.[3]

Whereas in the 1970s condominiums were basically apartment buildings, in the 1990s they may be of two types, vertical or horizontal. The former is frequently a series of high-rises in large areas with common amenities, and this is the predominant type in São Paulo. The latter consists of detached single-family houses, as in Chico Buarque's novel, and sometimes townhouses; this type predominates in the other municipalities of the metropolitan region. The detached houses are usually built by the individual owners, not by the developers, as is the case in the United States. As a consequence, they are not uniformly designed, although some developers include in the property deeds regulations regarding setbacks, open areas, walls and fences, house size, and use (residential only). They are still condominiums, since the property and use of common areas and amenities is shared and residents have to conform to collective rules and regulations.

Brazilian closed condominiums are obviously not an original invention but share various characteristics with American common-interest developments (CIDs) and suburbs. However, they demonstrate some revealing differences.[4] First, Brazilian closed condominiums are invariably walled and gated, whereas in the United States, gated communities constitute only about 20 percent of all CIDs.[5] Second, the most common types of closed condominiums in São Paulo are still apartment buildings, and although they may be marketed as an escape from the city and its dangers, they are still more urban than suburban. The first developments built according to the enclosed model are a good example. Ilha do Sul (Island of the South), built in 1973, is a middle-class complex of six high-rises, each with eighty three-bedroom apartments, located in the western zone of the city (Alto de Pinheiros). Its main innovations were its club-like amenities, occupying over 10,000 square meters and including sports facilities, a restaurant, and a theater, and its security: it is walled and access is controlled by security employees. At that time crime was not a central concern in the city, and the practice of controlling circulation was in fact feared by various groups: at the peak of the military dictatorship, many people regarded any investigation of identity as threatening. This fact indicates that enclosure was a marketing strategy, one that became dominant in the next decades: today, security procedures are a required feature in any building intended as prestigious. During the late 1970s and the 1980s, most closed condominiums constructed in São Paulo were vertical and were built in Morumbi, following the example of Portal do Morumbi.

Horizontal condominiums started to be built in the late 1970s, especially in the adjacent western municipalities of the metropolitan region. They feature some interesting differences from their American counterparts. Although social homogeneity is obviously valued, uniformity of design is not: houses with the same plan and façade are devalued and almost nonexistent. Traditionally in São Paulo, patterned houses were built for the working classes, and they are devalued not only by the population in general but also by the people who have no option but to live in them. Residents make strenuous efforts to transform their houses and to give them what they call "personality," that is, an individualized appearance.[6]

The high value attached to house "personality," shared by all social classes, probably explains why patterned houses are not common among the elite. It is also probably responsible for the fact that apartment buildings also have to show "personality"; Morumbi's buildings display a considerable amount of variation and attempts at individual distinction. Most important, however, this rejection of homogeneity, even among people who are social peers, may be related to the fact that in the ideological justification of closed condominiums in São Paulo, there is no positive reference to idea of a community, a feature always invoked in American developments. Condominiums are never called "communities," and they are never advertised as a type of housing that could enhance the value of doing things together. In fact, residents seem to resent deeply this idea of community. Another interesting point of comparison with the United States is the use of restrictive deeds and covenants. Although Brazilian condominiums necessarily have covenants, and although they are also segregative, historically they have not been considered an instrument of the real estate industry, as is the case in the United States, according to McKenzie (1994, especially chapter 2). It is only with the last generation of very large condominiums that developers have begun to include their own restrictions. In the old apartment buildings, these were confined to preservation of the architecture and façade, which is a different matter in high-rises. For working-class patterned houses, restrictions have never existed, or have never been enforced, and constant modifications are the rule.

The horizontal condominiums of the 1980s and 1990s represent São Paulo's process of suburbanization. This process is still in its incipient stages compared to the United States.[7] Before the 1980s, if real estate developers acted as private urban planners, their efforts have been more evident in the expansion of the poorer periphery than in the creation of wealthy suburbs. Until very recently, the most famous cases of planned neighborhoods for the elite were those designed at the beginning of the twentieth century, including Higienópolis, Avenida Paulista, and the famous Garden Cities of the 1920s.[8] These areas, however, have always been central. No property was held in common, and the houses were individually built. Moreover, although these developments had restrictions regarding design, some of their regulations were incorporated into the city construction code of 1929. Today they are regulated by the city's zoning codes, not by the determinations of the original deeds.

Developments for the elite away from the city center became significant only in the late 1970s. At that time, a few developers also began building something akin to American new towns or edge cities, that is, suburban areas that combine residential developments with office space and commercial centers. Some of the most famous and most aggressively advertised of these developments were Alphaville, Aldeia da Serra, and Tamboré, in the municipalities of Santana do Parnaíba and Barueri, the new area of middle- and upper-class development. Alphaville started in the 1970s, constructed by the same developers who had built Ilha do Sul and who are now building other horizontal condominiums nearby. Built on an area of 26 square kilometers that extends over two municipalities (Barueri and Santana do Parnaíba), Alphaville is divided into various walled residential areas (Residenciais), each enclosed by 3.5-meter-high walls and accessible by one controlled entrance; an office-building complex (Centro Empresarial); and a commercial center encompassing a shopping center (Centro Comercial). The first parts to be built, in the mid-70s, were the office center and two of the residential areas. In the early 1990s, Alphaville covered an urbanized area of 13 square kilometers and had a fixed population of around twenty thousand inhabitants. Its office center housed 360 enterprises, and the commercial area had 600 enterprises. On average, 75,000 nonresidents passed through it daily.[9] In 1989, 55.4 percent of the tax revenues of the city of Barueri came from Alphaville (Leme and Meyer 1997:20). Security is one of the main elements in its advertising and an obsession of all involved with it. Its private security forces have more than eight hundred guards and eighty vehicles. Each residential area, office center, and commercial center hires its own security force to maintain internal order, and there is a common security force to take care of the public spaces (the avenues and even the highway connecting to São Paulo).

Closed condominiums and new suburban quasi-towns are an invention of the real estate industry. Their transformation into elite housing is obviously associated with the construction of their image in advertising over the last two decades. It is interesting to follow this construction, the ways it is reproduced, and the ways it helps to shape people's fear of crime and sense of insecurity.

A TOTAL WAY OF LIFE: ADVERTISING RESIDENTIAL ENCLAVES FOR THE RICH

Advertisements aim to seduce. They rely on a repertoire of images and values that speak to different people's sensibilities and fantasies and thereby address their desires. As Augé tells us in his analysis of advertisements of French châteaus and domaines, their effect lies "in the unveiling or sudden revelation to a very precise individual of a place where, he imagines, life will be possible for him" (1989:28–29).[10] To achieve this effect, advertisements and the people to whom they appeal must share a common repertoire. If the ads fail to articulate images people can understand and recognize as their own, they fail to seduce. Therefore, real estate advertisements constitute a good source of information about the lifestyles and values of the people whose desires they elaborate and help to shape. I analyze advertisements of high-rises and closed condominiums published in the newspaper *O Estado de S. Paulo* from 1975 to 1996.[11] During this period, the collective and enclosed residence was elaborated as the most prestigious and desirable housing for São Paulo's upper and middle classes. The analysis reveals the elements of current patterns of social differentiation and distinction, and shows how the upper classes construct their own place in society and their vision of the kind of home where "life would be possible."

Across the most disparate cultures and in various social classes, the home crystallizes important symbolic systems and shapes individual sensibilities.[12] Residence and social status are obviously associated, and the home is a means by which people publicly signify themselves. As a consequence, the construction or acquisition of a home is one of the most important projects people undertake. The home makes both public and personal statements as it relates the public and the domestic. In creating a home, people both discover and create their own social position and shape their intimate world.

For the Paulista working classes, their autoconstructed houses are clearly their most important projects and may consume most of their energies and resources for many years. These houses embody statements about belonging to society and being modern, and through the houses their residents develop a discourse about society and about themselves. For the Paulista urban poor, the process entails not the purchase of a ready-made dwelling but a whole process of construction, both material and symbolic. They do not buy a home but literally build it themselves. There are no newspaper advertisements for working-class houses in São Paulo. In working-class neighborhoods, the real estate market relies almost exclusively on small local offices, interpersonal communication, and the distribution of pamphlets at busy traffic intersections. Newspaper ads appear only for middle- and upper-class homes, especially apartment buildings.

For the upper and middle classes, the construction of a home occurs through the mediation of advertisements and the real estate and construction industries. In the last twenty years, these ads have elaborated what they call "a new concept of housing" (um novo conceito de moradia) and transformed it into the most desirable type of housing.[13] This "new concept of housing" articulates five basic elements: security, seclusion, social homogeneity, amenities, and services. The image that confers the highest status (and is the most seductive) is that of an enclosed, fortified, and isolated residence, a secure environment in which one can use various facilities and services while living exclusively among equals. The advertisements present the image of islands to which one can return every day to escape the city and encounter an exclusive world of pleasure among peers. The enclaves are, therefore, opposed to the city, which is represented as a deteriorated world not only of pollution and noise, but, more important, of confusion and mixture, that is, social heterogeneity.

Closed condominiums correspond to the ideal version of this new concept of housing, an ideal in relation to which the other, less complete forms are always measured. Closed condominiums are supposed to be separate worlds. Their advertisements propose a "total way of life" superior to that of the city, even when they are built pretty much inside it. Portal do Morumbi was one of the first closed condominiums in São Paulo. On September 4, 1975, the complex was announced in a full-page advertisement. A series of small illustrations showed what the life of its residents would be like, hour by hour, from 7 A.M. to 11 P.M. People are shown in the swimming pool, the exercise room, the sauna, the playground, and the gardens. The main text reads: "Here every day is Sunday. Alfredo Mathias Developer. Playground, sports courts, medical center. Enjoying the outdoors at any time of the day and night can again be a pleasure completely possible and totally secure in Portal do Morumbi. Guards on duty 24 hours a day. Perfect security amidst the increasing insecurity of the city" (O Estado de S. Paulo, 4 September 1975).

The ad suggests a world clearly distinguishable from the surrounding city: a life of total and secure leisure. At least ten years before violent crime increased and became one of the main concerns of São ᴾaulo's residents, the insecurity of the city was already being constructed in real estate images to justify a new type of urban development and investment. This practice has persisted to the present day.

> Granja Julieta. Go there and live happily. Three bedrooms, two bathrooms, 1,000 m² of gardens, swimming pools, playground, ballroom, all with garage. . . . You do not have high[-rise] neighbors; far from environmental and visual pollution. Complete sunshine, pure air and a lot of silence. All the complex is surrounded by high protective fences. The garage gate ensures control. . . . Status, comfort. All the advantages of a closed residential complex with the charm of a sophisticated club. (*O Estado de S. Paulo*, 11 January 1976)

Making appeals to ecology, health, order, leisure, and, of course, security, the ads present the closed condominiums as the antithesis to the chaos, dirt, and danger the city. These images are shared by those who decide to leave the city center to inhabit the new complexes, even though the new complexes are sited in areas with precarious infrastructure that entail long commutes.

7.1

> I left Avenue Paulista because of the noise. . . . During weekends it was the movement around those restaurants, all of that. So, it started to become impossible to live there. . . . And the circulation of people all day long in front of the place I lived in, it was as if it were downtown: there were office boys, that permanent movement, permanent.
> *Housewife, fifty-two, lives in Morumbi with her husband,*
> *an executive at a multinational corporation, and their two children*

Seclusion and distance from the center of the city and its intense urban life are touted as promising a better lifestyle. Ads refer to the natural setting of the development, with green areas, parks, and lakes, and use phrases with ecological appeal. The condominiums are also frequently represented as islands set in the middle of noble surroundings.

> Who said that apartments do not go with nature? Here is the counterproof. . . . A perfect apartment where you and your family will feel in total harmony with nature. Two bedrooms, living room with two sitting

areas, spacious kitchen and service area. Sophisticated finishing, condominium enclosed by walls and iron fences, guardhouse with guards on
duty 24 hours a day, intercom, garage. Permanent tranquility: the green
around you will be permanent, an external view to rest the eyes and
the spirit. (*O Estado de S. Paulo*, 12 October 1986)

Wake up the free man who exists inside you. Move to Chácara Flora.
Here you will be able to be human the whole week and not only on
Saturday and Sunday. Here you will live surrounded by green, breath-
ing pure air. . . . Here you will change your life without leaving São
Paulo. . . . Total security with fences and guardhouse with intercom.
(*O Estado de S. Paulo*, 22 January 1989)

The right to not be bothered. We are offering you a totally new and
revolutionary housing concept. Townhouses with two bedrooms. Total
security for you and tranquility for your children. The residences
form a complex totally protected by walls. Access allowed exclusively
to residents. The reception controls everything. But you will never be
isolated. 5,000 m² of gardens and leisure area, with two swimming
pools. (*O Estado de S. Paulo*, 6 January 1980)

Only with "total security" is the new concept of housing complete. Security means fences and walls, twenty-four-hour guards, and an array of facilities and technologies—guardhouses with bathrooms and telephones, double sets of doors in the garage, and video monitoring. Security and control
are the conditions for keeping the others out, for assuring not only seclusion but also "happiness," "harmony," and even "freedom." To relate security exclusively to crime is to overlook its other meanings. The new systems of security not only provide protection from crime but also create
segregated spaces in which exclusion is carefully and rigorously practiced.
They assure "the right to not be bothered," probably an allusion to life in
the city and the encounters with people of other social groups, beggars, and
homeless people in its streets.

In addition to being distant, secluded, and secure, closed condominiums
are supposed to be self-contained worlds. Residents should be provided with
almost everything they need so that they can avoid public life in the city.
In keeping with this view, shared amenities transform the condominiums
into sophisticated clubs.

Verteville 4—in Alphaville—real solutions for current problems. . . .
View of two lakes and parks. Breathe deeply! Reduced population density. Sociability without inconvenience: complete and hyper-charming
common room. It's worth getting to know it: four swimming pools (the
big one, the heated one, the one for children, and the jacuzzi). Water

bar. . . . saunas. Room for ballet, fencing, and exercise. Massage and tanning room. Complete dressing room. Mini *drugstore* with books, magazines, tobacco, etc.[14] . . . Daily program of guided activities for children, sports, library, vegetable garden, breeding and care of small animals, etc. An independent administration: totally different from the conventional, creating new, amazing, and fundamental services such as: special assistance to children . . . optional cleaning service, optional supply service: you will have someone to do your grocery shopping. Car wash service. Transportation to other São Paulo neighborhoods. Absolute security, including electronic security. Three suites plus office and three garages, 420 m² of total area. (*O Estado de S. Paulo*, 4 October 1987)

Despite this determined marketing of the numerous shared facilities, in all high-rises and condominiums where I did research, their use is very low, with the exception of the playgrounds. Maybe this reflects the residents' uneasiness with the idea of sharing residential space, something the ads try to counteract by suggesting that sociability is possible without inconvenience, and that population density is low. The low use of the common areas might also indicate that the presence of all these amenities—some of them quite luxurious—is more a sign of social status and distinction than a necessary condition for a satisfying everyday life. In other words, these facilities are more ostentation than a sign of new patterns of sociability among neighbors or of new conceptions of private life. Only children seem to develop sociability in the condominiums, but even this seems not to survive after they engage in other relationships in their private schools or in clubs, which the families continue to join.

In addition to common amenities, São Paulo's closed condominiums offer a wide range of services: psychologists and gymnastics teachers for children, classes of all sorts for all ages, organized sports, libraries, gardening, pet care, physicians, message centers, frozen food preparation,[15] housekeeping, cooks, cleaners, drivers, car washing, transportation, and servants to do the grocery shopping. If the list does not meet your dreams, do not worry, "everything you might demand" can be made available.

It is not only in large condominiums that services rule. One of the types of housing that is becoming increasingly popular among the middle classes are labeled "flats." These are small apartments (one or two bedrooms) in buildings that offer all the services of a hotel. Because of their popularity, the price per square meter of these one-bedroom apartments has been higher than that of four-bedroom apartments in recent years (Embraesp 1994:4).

Nor is the expansion of domestic service exclusive to Brazil. As Sassen shows (1991: chapters 1 and 8), in global cities, high-income gentrification requires an increase in low-wage jobs: yuppies and poor migrant workers depend on each other. Any analysis of Los Angeles's West Side reveals the presence of innumerable immigrant maids, nannies, and gardeners working to maintain the luxury lifestyle of the houses protected, as signs warn, by "Armed Response" (see, for example, Rieff 1991). In São Paulo, however, domestic service in the closed condominiums is a modification of an old pattern. Services are an obsession among the Brazilian middle and upper classes. One of the most common reasons people give for moving into apartment buildings is the impossibility of finding "good services"; that is, the impossibility of having live-in maids who take care of the house and children. Elaborating on this theme, an ad for an apartment in Ibirapuera was illustrated with a picture of a fat, smiling black woman—the stereotype of a nice maid, alluding to the image of a slave—wearing a uniform and holding a feather duster. It read: "An apartment where there is no lack of good services for your family to live calmly. The first apartment to come with services" (O Estado de S. Paulo, 12 October 1986).

While the services offered by the condominiums emphasize the tradition of domestic servants, they introduce important changes. An arrangement in which "independent and different administrations" offer many different services is a long way away from the old, personalistic relations of domestic labor. The tasks are provided under multiple, temporary agreements, instead of by one or a few people employed on a permanent basis and living in the household: for example, a person who prepares frozen food once a month instead of a cook, or a cleaning person who comes once a week instead of a live-in maid. The services are managed by the administration of the condominium (including hiring personnel, negotiating payments and contracts, and controlling the employees), instead of through a personal relationship between the servant and the family (usually the housewife). Both changes render the provision of services more formal and impersonal, without necessarily affecting the nature of the tasks the middle and upper classes pay others to perform for them.[16]

As changes have evolved in traditional services, new ones have been created, the most obvious being private security (see chapter 5).[17] In the condominiums, this service combines new and old patterns. Although recently the industry of private security has increased considerably, in most of the condominiums to which I had access, these services take the form of "organic security": guards are hired directly by the condominium, often under other categories of services (for example, cleaning) or without a legal labor contract. Many of the condominium guards do not have formal training for the job and are working under illegal conditions (many are policemen performing private services in their off-duty time, using police weapons). Even so, the existence of an official market of security services—shaped by federal law, training courses, and labor obligations—frames the labor relationship in quite different terms from the traditional market of domestic services, and these differences introduce new problems and concerns. The dubious character of the labor arrangements is also becoming a source of high anxiety in some circumstances: residents have trouble firing guards with whom they have only verbal agreements but who learned a great deal about their habits and could use this knowledge against them by working with criminals or blackmailing their former bosses.

The new types of services have not eliminated traditional maids or personally negotiated labor contracts, but the framing of these relationships has also changed. In many middle-class residences the space for maids has diminished, and families can no longer afford live-in maids (much less two or three maids, common among the middle classes a generation ago). On the other hand, domestic service is now legally regulated. The 1988 Brazilian constitution extends to domestic servants the benefits of the labor law (paid time off, annual gratuity—the so-called thirteenth salary—social security, an eight-hour workday, and payment of overtime). As expected, resistance to this law was intense, and one of the ways to bypass it is to contract for multiple temporary services instead of one permanent employee. In general, maids under permanent arrangements now refuse to work without a contract and are learning to use the labor justice system, which is probably the only branch of the judiciary system in Brazil that may benefit the working classes. However, the limit on working hours continues to be disregarded, especially in the case of live-in maids, and contracts are not extended to casual workers (weekly cleaners, for example). Domestic employees hired by the administration of the condominium are more likely to have formal contracts and to be employed in conformity with the labor regulations.

Providing space for servants and services in the home has always been a problem for the middle classes. Solutions vary, but one of the most emblematic concerns the circulation areas of apartment buildings. Despite many recent changes, the tradition of separate "social" and "service" entrances to buildings and individual units seems to be inviolate: different classes are not supposed to mix or interact in the public areas of the buildings, even though this separation is now illegal.[18] The middle classes may give up their single-family houses, they may abandon central areas of the city, they may move to smaller spaces than they were used to, and they may have less permanent types of domestic help, but they do not give up the separation between their families and the people providing services. Sometimes the distinction seems ridiculous, because the two elevators or doors are often placed side by side. As spaces shrink, apartments that have totally separate areas of circulation capitalize on that fact by advertising "social hall independent from service hall" (for example, O Estado de S. Paulo, 24 January 1988). The idea is an old one: physical separation is a form of class distinction.

The so-called service area, traditional in Brazilian homes, has also changed. In apartments, the service area is usually adjacent to the kitchen; it includes the maid's room and bathroom, laundry facilities, and storage space. Apartments and houses also have a space called a copa, a kind of intermediary, informal area between the domestic and formal spaces of the apartment, where the family has breakfast and the children and the maids eat. All these areas have shrunk considerably in recent developments because of their high costs (they are usually tiled and feature lots of plumbing), and solutions like a shared laundry in the basement and a locker room for maids who do not live with the family are starting to appear in the newer developments. (The separate maid's bathroom in each apartment, however, is still included in even the smallest plans.) In upper-class developments, the existence of two or three maids' rooms is advertised as a luxury. What is remarkable is that whereas situations similar to these in other Western countries resulted in the reduction of domestic servants, development of labor-saving machines for household tasks, and increased involvement of all family members in domestic tasks, in Brazil ingenious solutions have been developed so that the traditional concept of domestic service—not to mention the gender division of domestic tasks—remains unchanged.[19]

As the number of workers per condominium increases, as domestic jobs change their character, and as services proliferate for the middle and upper classes who cannot do without them, so the mechanisms of control diversify. When the "creative administrations" of the new enclaves take care of labor management, they can impose forms of control that, if adopted in the more personal interaction between domestic servants and the families who employ them, would create impossible daily relationships. This more "professional" control may be advertised as a new service.

> The avant-garde style in a top class investment. Ritz Flat. Top class project. . . . Top class apartments. . . . Top class design. . . . Top class leisure and social life. . . . Top class location. . . . Top class equipment: internal sound system, collective TV and FM antenna, garage control,

electronic gates, central video, service entrance isolated from the social part, with specific controls. *Top class* administration and services. . . . *Top class* rentability. (*O Estado de S. Paulo,* 11 January 1987)

In this example, the servants are absolutely central to the whole "top class" business (the expression is given in English), since the development advertised is a flat. The method of "special controls" involves empowering some workers to control the others. In various condominiums, including at least two in which I did fieldwork, both employees of the condominium and maids and cleaning workers employed in individual apartments (even those who live there) are required to show identification to enter and exit the condominium. Often they and their personal belongings are searched when they leave work. These arrangements usually involve men exercising power over women.

The middle and upper classes are creating their dream of independence and freedom—both from the city and its mixture of classes and from everyday domestic tasks—by relying on services performed by working-class people. They give guns to poorly paid working-class guards to control their own movements in and out of their condominiums. They ask their poorly paid "office boys" to solve all their bureaucratic problems, from paying bills and standing in line to transporting astronomical sums of money. They also ask their poorly paid maids—who often live in the favelas outside the condominium wall—to wash and iron their clothes, make their beds, buy and prepare their food, and frequently care for their children all day long. The upper classes fear contact and contamination by the poor, but they continue to depend on their lower-class servants. They can only be anguished about finding the right way to control these people, with whom they have such ambiguous relationships of dependency and avoidance, intimacy and distrust.

In fact, the meaning of control extends beyond the management of servants. Since total security is essential for this type of residence, control is exercised continuously not only over servants but over all visitors, even one's own family. Although property owners may resist or bypass this control, visitors, and especially people from the working classes, usually must submit to it. Once in place, this control is in fact class control, which helps to maintain the condominiums as a separate and homogeneous world. Control completes the new concept of housing, that is, the image of the secluded, disciplined, fortified, homogeneous, and self-sufficient world of the condominiums that seems to synthesize the notion of an alternative lifestyle embodying what the Paulista elite of the 1990s call freedom.

These total and autonomous universes seem to be able to fulfill the strangest fantasies. One of these is the desire to bring back the past, in a postmodern retro fashion. For example, the horizontal closed condominium Aldeia da Serra has been totally conceived of as a revival of the past. It was built by the same developers who built Alphaville: it seems that they can play equally well with the construction of fictions of the past and of the future. Put on the market in 1980, Aldeia da Serra is a residential theme park meant for people "who miss 'the old days.'" It tries to imitate a colonial village (aldeia) by putting in its central square a bandstand and a colonial chapel, furnished with Baroque paintings and sculptures bought in antique stores or copied from Ouro Preto's churches. Antique farm equipment is distributed throughout the residential districts (moradas), the same districts that are protected by fences, armed guards, and security systems. The simulacrum of a historical village protected by armed guards constitutes a truly postmodern undertaking.

Aldeia da Serra, together with Alphaville and Tamboré, is among the most aggressive examples of real estate investment combining closed condominiums, shopping centers, and office complexes on the model of the new American suburbs.[20] In October 1993, an extensive advertisement campaign in São Paulo elaborated on the similarities of this area with enclaves in the United States. It was a campaign to sell the idea of an "edge city" (using the English expression) as a way of increasing the appeal and price of specific enclaves. One of the main proponents of the campaign was Joel Garreau, an American journalist and the author of the book *Edge City: Life on the New Frontier*. His photograph appeared in full-page ads in national magazines and newspapers, he came to São Paulo to talk to a select group of realtors, and he was one of the main participants in a thirty-minute television program marketing the new developments as if they were a piece of the first world that had been dropped into metropolitan São Paulo.

As chapter 6 shows, the western zone in which these developments are located is the part of the metropolitan region most dramatically transformed by socioeconomic changes in the last two decades. Since the 1970s, real estate developers have invested heavily in this area, benefiting from the low price of land and advantages offered by local administrations, and attracting rich residents and important tertiary activities to their developments. The 1993 campaign relied on many already old images of closed condominiums, but added a touch of novelty with the name "edge city"—a name that failed to capture the attention of Paulistanos, who continue to refer to the area by the name of the oldest development, Alphaville.[21]

The advertising program broadcast in São Paulo by Rede Manchete on Saturday, 16 October, 1993, explicitly illustrates the connections with the

U.S. model as well as local peculiarities. The program combined scenes from U.S. edge cities (Reston, Virginia, and Columbia, Maryland)[22] and the three developments being advertised in São Paulo. Garreau—speaking in English with Portuguese subtitles—described edge cities as the predominant form of contemporary urban growth and used Los Angeles and its multicentered form as an example. There were interesting differences in the way the program presented Brazilian, as opposed to U.S., edge cities. Residents from enclaves in both countries were interviewed in front of swimming pools, lakes, and green areas, emphasizing the luxurious and antiurban character of the developments. However, where the U.S. edge cities have external walls and controls at their entrance gates, these are not shown, and neither are their security personnel. In the Paulista developments, however, security is emphasized. In one scene, shot from a helicopter, the private security guards of a Brazilian condominium intercept a "suspect car" (a popular vehicle, a Volkswagen bus) outside the walls; they physically search the occupants, who are forced to put their hands up against the car. Although it is completely illegal for a private security service to perform this kind of action on a public street, this, together with scenes of visitors submitting identification documents at the entrance gates, reassures the rich residents (and spectators) that "suspect" (poor) people will be kept away. Another revealing scene is an interview in English with a resident of a U.S. edge city. He cites as one of his reasons for moving there the fact that he wanted to live in a racially integrated community. This observation is suppressed in the Portuguese subtitles, which say instead that his community has "many interesting people." In São Paulo, the idea of a racially integrated community would jeopardize the whole development.

To import first world models and to use them to sell all sorts of commodities is obviously a common practice in third world countries. The parallel between the Brazilian and the American examples suggests that although the degree of segregation varies, it uses similar devices in both cases. Put side by side with the U.S. cases, the Brazilian methods of segregation (high walls, armed guards everywhere, ostensible private policing of the poor) appear obvious and exaggerated. Nevertheless, they reveal in caricature some of the features of the original U.S. model. The issue of racial segregation also offers an interesting contrast. Pointing out racial integration as an advantage in an American common-interest development is anomalous, given the long history of restrictive covenants and racial segregation in this form of housing in America (cf. McKenzie 1994, especially chapter 2). In Brazil, it would be unthinkable given the traditional etiquette of racial relations, in which the issue is never mentioned. As in everyday life, the advertisement simply silenced the reference to race; and under the pretense that it is not an issue, blacks continue to be harassed and sent to the service entrance.

KEEPING ORDER INSIDE THE WALLS

The ideal of the closed condominium is the creation of a private order in which residents can avoid the city's problems and enjoy an alternative lifestyle with people from the same social group. The advertisement of a luxury development in Morumbi makes this concept unmistakably clear. Called Place des Vosges, it is a replica of the famous Parisian square. Its largest apartments have four bedrooms and 268 square meters (plus four garages and external areas of up to 539 square meters per unit), and they sell for U.S. $476,000. In 1993, when construction began, it was announced with the phrase "Condominium Place des Vosges. Another like it only in Paris" (*O Estado de S. Paulo,* 17 October 1993). The development's ads focused on the similarities between the two until 1996, when they started to highlight differences. The new ad shows a photograph of the Parisian square and a drawing of the Morumbi enclave and states: "Place de Vosges. The only difference is that the one in Paris is public and yours is private" (*O Estado de S. Paulo,* 15 March 1996).

Although the new enclaves valorize a private universe and reject the city, to organize a common life inside the walls of these collective residential areas has proved complicated. Many people I interviewed in the condominiums agree that they have solved most problems associated with the outside world, but they are continuously struggling with internal conflicts. The condominiums are indeed secure, if by this one means that they are able to prevent crime and to control external interference. However, life among equals seems to be far from the harmonious ideal that some advertisements construct.

Social equality and a commonality of interests do not automatically constitute the basis for a public life. Agreeing on rules appears to be one of the most difficult aspects of life in the collective residences. Moreover, even if rules are agreed on, enforcing them can be hard, especially in dealing with children and teenagers. The central problem of the condominiums and highrises seems to be how to function as a society with some type of public life. Many residents seem to treat the entire complex like a private home in which they can do whatever they like. They interpret freedom to mean an absence of rules and responsibilities toward their neighbors.

It is again revealing to make some comparisons with American enclaves. In the United States, "community" is a common designation of condominiums of various types. In São Paulo, developers do not think of themselves as "community builders," and ads do not present closed condominiums as a new type of communitarian life, but only as a place of residence for homogeneous social groups. In other words, the ads do not insist on a community of shared values and interests, do not try to create any special sense of belonging to a community, and do not appeal to the importance of a space that can facilitate face-to-face interaction. For Brazilian developers and their clients, the advantages of social homogeneity do not imply the desirability of a local sociability. Although Blakely and Snyder's study of gated communities in the United States (1997, especially chapter 6) reveals that residents have little interest in engaging in local sociability and collective activities, and although the level of participation in homeowners' associations is low, the reference to community is both a rhetorical device to sell planned developments and an ideological criterion for evaluating life inside the walls.[23] In what follows, I criticize common life inside the walls, though not for failing to create a "sense of community." Rather, I criticize it for failing to create a public life ruled by democratic principles, public responsibility, and civility.

A second important difference between Brazilian and American condominiums, and one that also reveals the problems with building a public and democratic life within the São Paulo enclaves, lies in the internal rules and the ways in which they are applied. All Paulista condominiums have covenants, some drafted by the developers, some by the residents. They are a frequent subject of discussion in condominium meetings and are constantly being rewritten. Enforcing these rules, however, is a big problem, and the justice system is not routinely used to solve it. All disputes tend to be treated as private matters among residents. It is only in extreme cases that a dispute reaches the justice system (usually cases of nonpayment or forcing a resident to repair damages in his or her unit that affect other residents). In other words, although in both Brazil and the United States disputes among condominium residents are quite common (McKenzie 1994:12–23), in São Paulo they tend to be dealt with privately and not as matters of public interest or public law.

Residential meetings are the main arenas of conflict, although arguments between neighbors are quite common as well. My observation of various meetings in different condominiums and high-rises revealed that conflicts and aggression were inevitable in the process of arriving at any decisions that would affect everyday routines. People could be nasty and disrespectful if they failed to impose their will. Residents would stand up and shout at each other, pound on tables, verbally threaten their neighbors, and use what sounded to me like a good amount of derogatory language and insults. Although in all condominiums decisions are supposed to be made by vote, discussions could last for four or five hours before a vote was called. Instead of voting, people preferred trying to convince each other and enforce their own views. Disagreements at these meetings could generate long-standing bitterness.

Discomfort with democratic procedures, such as voting and respect for the person disagreeing, are not found only among the Brazilian elite. It has been observed, for example, in the meetings of working-class social movements (Caldeira 1987 and 1988). In these situations, discomfort with disagreement was expressed in an ideological preference for consensus (whose origins can be traced to Marxist organizations) and in a valorization of the notion of community that is rare in Brazilian political life. Various movements, especially those organized by the Catholic Church under the form of Christian Base Communities (CEBs), have relied on the idea that they represent a local community of people supposed to be equal; if differences emerged, they had to be leveled to maintain the strength of the political community (Durham 1984). The meetings of social movements could also be endless as they tried to build consensus. Although this process was frequently passionate, it did not seem to involve the same level of aggressiveness and disrespect among the participants as the condominium meetings. In any event, São Paulo residents, especially the elite, have a hard time accepting democratic procedures, respecting other people's views, and accepting differences and disagreements as a normal part of social interaction. The authoritarian desire of imposing one's will without recognizing other possibilities seems strong indeed.

One of the main issues that reveals the difficulty in creating and respecting common rules is the behavior of adolescents, especially adolescent boys. The resident in charge of security at one of the condominiums in Alto de Pinheiros (a mid-level executive with a wife and two children) began his interview by saying: "What affects us the most is internal security, our own children. The problem of external security was solved a long time ago." In fact, the association of the central problems of the condominiums with "our own children" expresses a kind of commonsense knowledge. It was repeated to me by two people in charge of organizing security, several residents, and one administrator. The offenses of the children vary, running from small thefts or the vandalizing of collective equipment (such as fire extinguishers) to the consumption of drugs and driving without a license.

One of the most common problems, and probably that with the most serious consequences, is the increasing number of car accidents caused by unlicensed teenage drivers (on both public and private streets). The legal driving age in Brazil is eighteen, but the number of elite children driving before that age has increased considerably in the last decade, frequently with the compliance of their parents. For the Brazilian elite, it is easy to break the law and it can even be fashionable. No one is prosecuted for driving without a license, even if they are involved in an accident. According to the law, parents are responsible for the behavior of their minor children, but enforcement of the law is lax, even in relation to accidents and deaths.[24]

Inside the condominiums, disrespect of the law is almost a rule. People feel freer to break the law because they are in private spaces from which the police are kept out, and because they perceive the complex's streets as extensions of their own backyards. In fact, when people have weak notions of public interest, public responsibility, and respect for other people's rights to start with, it is unlikely that they will acquire these notions inside the condominium walls. Rather, life inside the private worlds only further weakens their notions of public responsibility. If traffic in general is marked by a disregard of regulations, the situation inside the condominiums brings it to absurd levels. The case of Alphaville, for which I obtained statistics, clearly exemplifies this. Between March 1989 and January 1991, the police registered 646 car accidents, 925 injuries, and 6 deaths in Alphaville. Eighty percent of the accidents occurred inside the residential areas, that is, inside the walls and on the private streets to which only residents and their visitors have access. The majority of the accidents were caused by teenagers, and the majority of the victims were either children or teenagers playing in the streets (only one of the people who died was over eighteen).[25] The accident rate has been impossible to control. The difficulty is associated with the permissiveness of some parents, who continue to give cars to their children, and with the fact that residents prefer to keep the police out; thus, those in charge of enforcing internal order are private security guards. The elite teenagers regard these people as their servants and refuse to obey them: they threaten the working-class security guards with dismissal by their parents if the guards insist on enforcing regulations about driving and drugs. Although statistics are not available, in various interviews residents remarked that drugs are common inside the condominiums. (The same is true in elite private schools.)[26]

Problems such as adolescents' breaking the law are controversial inside the condominiums. Some residents fear that making such problems public will decrease the value of their property. Moreover, they see such issues as a matter of private order, to be dealt with internally: a matter of discipline, not of the law. Secrets are kept, especially in the case of condominiums such as Alphaville, famous for its internal security, where property values have risen spectacularly over the last decade. Sometimes, however, residents brave this risk, and the disapproval of their neighbors, to offer information to the press. One resident of Alphaville spoke to *Folha de S. Paulo* in 1990, and his comments capture the essence of the problems of a community that considers itself separate from the rest of society. He said that the police do not enter Alphaville because they are kept out by the residents. "They inhibit the police. They use the old phrase 'Do you know who you're talking to?' Everything here is covered up. There is a law for the mortal people, but not for Alphaville residents" ("Alphaville, o 'Condomínio-Paraíso' de São Paulo, agora Teme os Assaltos," *Folha de S. Paulo*, 20 April 1990).[27]

Reactions are quite different when an "external" security problem changes the life of the condominium, and reports throw light on some of the problems of the enclosed worlds. Such an "external" problem brought Alphaville to the crime pages of all newspapers in February 1991. An eighteen-year-old girl who had grown up there was kidnapped in the parking lot of the condominium's tennis club, raped, and killed. The unfolding of the events reveals paradoxical aspects not only of the maintenance of order inside an elite place like Alphaville but also of Brazilian society as a whole. Immediately after the case was made public, the crime was blamed on construction workers who had access to the condominium. Because the victim was an upper-class girl, the police acted quickly, and the media presented every aspect of the investigations, along with photographs of the girl and her family. Three men (who were not construction workers) were eventually accused of the crime and jailed. The following day, newspapers published their photographs: they had clearly been beaten, and their eyebrows and mustaches had been shaved off. The newspapers and magazines informed the population that this was a sign they had been raped by other prisoners, and that this was a "common treatment" for people accused of rape. Nothing has been done, either to investigate how these abuses happened or to punish the people responsible, nor were any measures taken to prevent them; everything was reported as routine. The paper *O Estado de S. Paulo,* with a readership that includes the elite, commented that "an old code of honor shared by the prisoners was applied during the weekend to two of the people involved in the death of the student. Joanilson, the Big, and Antonio Carlos, the 'Cota,' were beaten and raped (sodomized) by their cellmates in Jandira's prison. Among the prisoners the rapist is rejected and should be punished by the crime he committed" (*O Estado de S. Paulo,* 26 February 1991).

Folha da Tarde, whose readers are primarily from the lower middle and working classes and which gives special attention to crime, informed readers about the fate of the third suspect:

> Edgar, in the same way as his companions, did not go unpunished: through the law of the prison, the rapist becomes the woman of the other prisoners. When asked if he had been raped, "Baianinho" answered with a nod of the head. "Baianinho" was not beaten as hard as his companion Joanilson de Lima, "the Big," because he did not resist the rape, according to a prison guard. Despite this, his face and arm were covered in blue marks. "They beat me only a little," said "Baianinho." . . .
>
> A cardinal of the Civil Police—director of a department—who did not want to identify himself, said the day before yesterday that any perpetrators of rape and murder will not remain alive more than two days inside an institution such as the Casa de Detenção. "They will get him during daytime or at night," he said. (*Folha da Tarde*, 27 February 1991).[28]

"Terror as usual," as Michael Taussig would put it (1992: chapter 2). Torture, rape, beating of prisoners, sexism, and disregard for the law and for human rights are treated as trivial by the press. The trivialization of these facts makes them seem so natural that their reporting generates no further response.

Since beating and rape are not routine for the upper classes, the event shook the security of Alphaville. It seems that the girl's murder and the subsequent events showed those who had decided to live above the law that they had problems to face. A few days after the murder, a group of residents from all parts of the complex went to the public security secretary of the state of São Paulo, asking for his help in solving the problem of internal crime that had been downplayed until that moment. They created Conseg (Conselho de Segurança), a security council formed by representatives of the community and the civil and military police. The residents simultaneously created the Associação de Mães de Alphaville (Association of Alphaville Mothers) which promoted conferences and discussions among the residents. All those I talked to, or whose opinions appeared in the press, seemed to blame the problems on the disintegration of the family. From the developers' representatives to the mothers' association and the police, all agreed that the origin of adolescent misbehavior is a "lack of love and attention." The main solution proposed is more love and attention, stronger families, and more control, that is, a solution in accordance with commonsense beliefs about preventing the spread of evil (see chapter 2). To discuss the question in terms of public order or public responsibility is unheard-of. Judge Mariano Cassavia Neto, addressing the residents at a meeting just after the events of February put things this way: "I don't want to transform this into a Gestapo, but you should follow the everyday life of your children. In the drug dealer's mind, they are the consumption market. Let's try to protect our children. Spend more time with them. Prevention starts inside the home. . . . Do you know who they go around with? When was the last time you kissed them?" ("Alphaville Vive 'Dia de Twin Peaks' em Debate sobre Drogas e Violência," *Folha de S. Paulo*, 10 April 1991).

In other words, the problems are domestic and must be solved privately. Internal (domestic, private) control should be enforced, and thus society's general law does not have to intervene. This notion is so strong that no one thinks of the police enforcing public order inside the condominium: their job is only to keep drug dealers, rapists, and murderers away. The representatives of public order finally came, called in by the mothers, but only to advise. The judge, however, seemed to be conscious of the paradoxes of the situation. In the same speech, he said:

> It seems that there are other laws around here. I started saying that I would put into jail parents of young defaulters [law-breakers], and the telephones did not stop ringing. One wanted amnesty because he was a judge as well, the other was a cousin of a judge, another was a mayor, another said he was the cousin of a judge of the Court of Appeals—the only thing missing was to say that they were brothers of Romeu Tuma and of Minister Zélia Cardoso de Mello.[29]

He was applauded. Nevertheless, the episode only exemplifies the status quo in Brazil: the creation of private rules; the private manipulation of the public order by the elite; and the nonenforcement of the law: in fact, the judge only threatened parents with the idea that he would enforce the law!

This case also reveals the complexities of the relationships between public and private domains in Brazilian society, which is marked by vast social inequality and a tendency to explicitly devalue the public sphere. This happens not only because private enclaves have proliferated but also because spaces that used to be public, and in which a certain respect for collective interest was previously enforced, are being privatized. As public parks are fenced, streets closed by chains and controlled by private guards, and as neighborhoods are transformed into closed enclaves with the help of city officials, the possibility of fair treatment in the public sphere shrinks. Although Brazil has always been an unequal society, the privatization of the public sphere that I have been describing is something new, and the tendency to create private islands of privilege seems to have grown stronger.

Residents of City Boaçava, an area in the western part of town with its own private security service, are trying to achieve a consensus to apply to Emurb (the city agency in charge of urban problems, which authorizes the enclosures of neighborhoods) for construction of barriers on the streets leading to their neighborhood. In this case crime is not the main reason, for they consider their private security system to be efficient. The problem is that a new city park is being constructed nearby, and they want to prevent its visitors from parking their cars on Boaçava's streets. According to the president of the neighborhood association, the enclosure is the only way to relieve residents of this "problem."[30] Until now, streets have still been considered public space, even by the elite. For example, one of the richest neighborhoods in central São Paulo, Pacaembu, developed in the 1930s under the inspiration of the Garden City model, contains the municipal soccer stadium. To this day, inhabitants of the luxury residences have never thought of closing the streets to the tens of thousands people attending games and other events (from rock concerts to religious gatherings). Neither have the residents of the mansions of Morumbi, who live around the biggest soccer stadium in the city. Maybe they will try to in the future, and maybe the city administration will help them out, as the PT administration did in the early 1990s. Nevertheless, the fact that this has not been an issue before indicates the extent of the transformations.

All these tendencies toward privatization and rejection of the public order became especially visible in Brazil during the period of consolidation of democratic rule. This change embodied attempts to create a more egalitarian public sphere and in fact expanded the political citizenship of the working classes, who, through their social movements, were for the first time participating effectively in political life. It is therefore possible to interpret the elite's retreat to private enclaves as a form of resistance to democratization.[31] However, similar, widespread processes of privatization happening in other parts of the world, such as those in the United States, where there is a consolidated democracy, should caution us about the limits of a political interpretation. The comparison suggests, however, that even if the issue is not democratization per se, it may be the inclusion of people previously excluded or marginalized, both politically and socially. In the United States, for example, the white flight to the suburbs in the 1960s and 1970s and to gated communities in the 1990s may be related to the expansion of citizenship rights of the black population and to the incorporation into American society of an increased number of immigrants. In Europe, the increase of racism and of new patterns of segregation seem to be similarly associated with the expansion of citizenship rights to immigrants.[32]

Although the tendencies toward privatization and secession by the rich are clear, especially in new areas and developments, São Paulo is not yet ruled by them. These ideas and practices are powerful, in part because they are associated with the elite, but they also generate ambiguities and resistance, especially as other social groups engage them.

RESISTING THE ENCLAVES

The enclosed condominium is the most prestigious type of residence in contemporary São Paulo. References to its elements appear in all types of developments. Security, enclosure, seclusion, amenities, and services integrate a code of distinction that residents of the city from all social classes understand and use to elaborate, transform, and signify their spaces. However, the ways of using and interpreting the elements of the code vary across the city. They reveal situations in which this code is resisted or adapted to coexist with opposing values, generating ambiguous and contradictory results. The rejections and ambiguities occur especially in relation to opinions about collective housing, as opposed to detached houses; about central and well-urbanized areas of the city, in contrast to distant areas; and about closed versus open residences. The different evaluations frequently combine and reveal different class perspectives on housing arrangements.

Selling Collective Housing

The upper and middle classes constitute the majority of residents of apartments and closed condominiums. They are already used to collective housing and are continuously moving to such enclaves for security, financial, and status reasons. The idea that apartments are more secure than houses is so prevalent in contemporary São Paulo that many advertisements for detached houses use phrases like "Exquisite residence with the security of an apartment" (*O Estado de S. Paulo*, 16 January 1983). Nevertheless, negative perceptions of apartments persist and can be noticed even in advertisements for middle-class high-rises.

> Maison Adriana. Between Santo Amaro Avenue and Ibirapuera Park. Around you will always be the mansions of a strictly residential area, without the inconvenience of another high-rise. (*O Estado de S. Paulo*, 6 February 1977)

The first two-bedroom apartments without neighbors . . . Moema. . . . .
It distinguishes itself by its advanced architectural design in the form
of a cross, which allows each apartment on the floor to remain isolated.
(*O Estado de S. Paulo,* 2 September 1979)

Morumbi Kings Ville. Definitely the most incredible development in
Morumbi. . . . A new concept of housing has just appeared: the system
double stair side-by-side which allows the construction of two-story
apartments (duplex) side by side, with private entrances, both social
and service. Thus we have one apartment per floor, because the social
accesses alternate: even-numbered apartments on the first floor, odd-
numbered on the second, utilizing in this way a single social elevator.
(*O Estado de S. Paulo* 12 October 1986)

Indeed, it requires great creativity and verbal dexterity—if necessary
with resort to foreign languages—to reconcile apartments, with multiple
units on the same floor, with the image of detached houses. Proximity is a
sensitive issue among Paulistanos, even the proximity of people who are
supposedly social equals. This attitude is strongly sustained by the Morumbi residents of detached houses I interviewed. Their houses are small
fortresses. All of them have dogs and electronic alarm systems (in one of
them, the pads of the alarm were put at 20-centimeter intervals over the entire external wall); one house has immense bars over all the windows, making them look like prison windows, and an iron door separating the bedrooms
from the rest of the house, which is locked every night. Residents of these
individual fortresses prefer their paraphernalia of security to living close to
other people in closed condominiums or apartments: only in their detached
homes do they feel sufficiently isolated and in control, especially of their children's encounters. The residents of detached houses outside closed condominiums seem to have a deeper need for isolation and control—what they
call freedom—and a strong fear of strangers, even children and neighbors
from the same social class. They take further than condominium residents
the perception that fortresses can protect them from crime and from undesirable social interactions and contacts.

In Moóca, where the obsession with the *cortiços* and with differentiating oneself from them is strong, the view of apartment buildings is still
more negative and widespread. When people move from a house into an
apartment, they feel that their quality of life has deteriorated, and in some
cases (see chapter 1) they perceive the move as a social decline. They feel
that they are losing independence and control over their own lives, as well
as the status they associate with owning a single-family house. Moóca is

still a neighborhood of houses. In 1990, 63.2 percent of the constructed residential area consisted of houses, but the area of vertical constructions almost doubled between 1986 and 1990 (São Paulo—Sempla 1992:148–49 and Seade 1990:42).

Thus, in spite of their objections, Moóca´s residents are increasingly moving into apartment buildings, some of them closed condominiums (less luxurious ones than those of Morumbi). These new buildings exemplify the gentrification that began in the 1970s and is associated with the opening of subway lines and major improvements in infrastructure. This process, which is mirrored elsewhere in northern and eastern parts of town that used to be lower middle-class neighborhoods, is changing the local real estate market and bringing places like Moóca, Santana, and Tatuapé to the newspaper pages as "fashionable" locales. The new high-rises bring simultaneously the meanings of imprisonment and security, decline and prestige.

In the poor periphery there are few apartment buildings, and most residents live in autoconstructed houses. In the entire São Miguel Paulista old district, for example, only 2.76 percent of the constructed residential area consisted of apartments in 1990 (São Paulo—Sempla 1992:148–49).[33] Apartments for the working classes are usually built by a state agency in charge of affordable housing such as Cohab (Companhia Metropolitana Habitacional); they are extremely devalued and are associated with high criminality and drug use. According to the 1991 census, these apartments represent 3 percent of the total number of households, and the majority of them (66.5 percent) are located in districts on the eastern and poorest periphery.[34] In Jardim das Camélias, also on the eastern periphery, there are no apartments, and all residents live in houses. They value their space and consider moving to something like a Cohab apartment as a very undesirable option. In addition to the stigma of criminality and the fear of proximity to "bad influences," Camélias' residents value being able to design their own houses according to their taste and personality, and resent the idea of having to submit to a patterned, ready-made design. Not only that which is collective, but also that which is uniform, is considered bad and ugly—a perception once shared by the middle classes living in houses. In these negative evaluations of apartment buildings, aesthetic judgments intertwine with views of social mobility and a moral discourse about the dangers of proximity, the necessity of self-control, and the value of individuality. This confluence of discourses and meanings is shared by people in Jardim das Camélias, Moóca, and Morumbi. It is the reason that patterned houses for the elite are rare, even inside condominiums, and that developers of middle- and upper-class apartments strongly emphasize originality of design in their advertisements. Nowadays, however, the majority of property owners of de-tached houses outside condominiums are from either the working classes or the lower middle classes, and they are the ones who explicitly sustain the discourse about the moral values embedded in the ownership of a detached house, frequently turning against the upper classes the same kind of judg-ments and prejudices that the elite once elaborated to stigmatize the poor and their collective dwellings.

When the City Is Still Desirable

The second issue over which there is much ambiguity and disagreement is the opposition to "the city" and the abandonment of the well-equipped and central areas of town. Not everybody is willing to abandon the city to derive status from the negation of urban life. Some, in fact, are struggling to re-main in their neighborhoods, both traditional, central, middle- and upper-class areas where luxury apartment buildings have been common for a long time, and the intermediary and even peripheral neighborhoods where tradi-tionally the lower middle classes or the working classes have lived, and which are undergoing gentrification. In both cases, there is an appeal to the old style of life offered by the city and to tradition rather than transformation.

Ads for new high-rises in old, valorized middle- and upper-class areas like Jardins, Higienópolis, or Pinheiros praise exactly the urban qualities op-posed by the closed condominiums, reinforcing the view of these neigh-borhoods as "noble" and sophisticated:

> Mansão de Itu [in Jardins] . . . In a time in which one saves even with locks, we present the best in every detail. In a place absolutely inside civilization. (*O Estado de S. Paulo,* 11 January 1976)

> Ed. Villa Velasquez. Jardins are today the pole of maximum attraction in São Paulo. . . . . The *beautiful people* circulate there. . . . Live where things happen. (*O Estado de S. Paulo,* 8 September 1985)

> The good times are back. You can already live as in the past. In a high-quality apartment in one of the noblest neighborhoods of São Paulo: Higienópolis. A neighborhood which has not lost its character. Nowa-days Higienópolis combines an aristocratic neighborhood with an all-modern infrastructure. (*O Estado de S. Paulo,* 28 October 1990)

> Live in a Madrid Villa in the middle of Pinheiros. For those who do not want to escape. Everything in Mansões de Pinheiros helps you surpass the obsession with roads. They are apartments that bring back the pleasure of staying at home. (*O Estado de S. Paulo,* 2 September 1979)

To be in the heart of the city still seems to be attractive to some, especially if the place can be—in the same way as some condominiums—valorized by its proximity to the rich, their mansions, aristocratic style, and civilization (whatever that means), or simply their beauty. However, the ads reveal the power of the "new concept of housing" by including negative references to escape and distance.

Since the closed condominiums embody prestige, it is not surprising that ads for other high-rises make references to them. In advertisements for apartment buildings in traditional lower-middle-class or even working-class neighborhoods it is impossible to claim Morumbi´s luxury, but some gestures toward its model are there.

> Two and three bedrooms. . . . Assure your place in this intelligent project. 72 m² of private area. Living room for two sitting areas. Children's swimming pool. Adult swimming pool. Sauna. Dressing room. Squash court. Jogging track. Playground. Ballroom. Children's room. Barbecue. Kiosk. Exercise room. Gardens and squares. Underground garage. Collective laundry. Maid's WC. Central video. Individual storage. Message service. The Residencial Ilhas Gregas (Greek Islands) is located in an excellent part of Tatuapé. It is 200 m from the subway, and in addition to various green areas nearby has a panoramic view of the municipal park. (*O Estado de S. Paulo,* 28 October 1990).

Even when the area of each apartment is only 72 square meters, all the possible requirements of the "new concept of housing" have to be squeezed into the development, from two swimming pools to a separate maid's bathroom in each apartment. However, to appeal to the lower middle classes and working classes, the ads have to change some of their emphasis. For example, they frequently refer to the existence of public transportation—a valuable asset for people who may not have a car—and to public services and urban infrastructure: the view of the public park replaces the area of the private condominium.

Advertisements for apartments in neighborhoods such as Moóca have to address the ambivalence among the lower middle classes about collective housing and about abandoning the center of town and its style of public space. Some of them attempt to make the new housing blend with traditional local values, looking more like a continuation of than a rupture with the past. These ads appeal not to outsiders moving in—as Morumbi's ads do—but to upwardly mobile local residents. The properties are frequently presented as a new step in the tradition of the neighborhood.

Piazza de Capri—the new way of living in the traditional Moóca. . . .
Swimming pool, solarium and lawn bowling green. Reception 24 hours
a day, complete laundry service. Playground and gardens. Space for
your kids to be truly children. Ballroom, playroom, and an exclusive
movie theater for your family. Nursery: you go out and leave your
baby in security. Piazza de Capri, the most comfortable and secure way
to live in Moóca. . . . Moóca: history and tradition. Piazza de Capri:
the most complete infrastructure of services and leisure. (*O Estado de
S. Paulo*, 24 January 1982)[35]

Set your family free in Jardim Tropical. Vila Carrão, the neighborhood
which brings people together. It makes them create roots. Because here,
fortunately, people still cultivate friendships, the family, traditions. For
all that, it is natural that those who live in V. Carrão do not want to
change their neighborhood. . . . For your security, the development is
totally walled, with a single entrance and guard. (*O Estado de S. Paulo*,
2 September 1984)

Alto de Santana . . . four bedrooms, two suites, two spaces in the
garage. Ed. Piazza Navona. . . . To live in Santana is a privilege. Who
has it does not exchange it for anything. This is a neighborhood complete in terms of commerce, services, schools, restaurants, etc., with the
typical tranquility of tree-lined streets and easy access to all parts of
town. (*O Estado de S. Paulo*, 12 October 1986)

We can read in these ads a dislike for the central part of town and for
some ideas associated with city life but an appreciation of other aspects of
public and urban life and of local sociability. These ads attempt to capitalize
on urban and public infrastructure, services, and proximity to the city center (exactly the qualities Morumbi lacks). These urban qualities come together with old values (which central neighborhoods presumably lack): tranquility and local, traditional, and family values that can compensate for the
supposed absence of these values in the rest of the city. Even "friendships"
may be presented as an advantage, suggesting that proximity is good if it is
of the traditional type. The ads imply that people should not move to new
areas of town to show off their status, but should stay where their roots are.
This appeal is particularly meaningful in neighborhoods such as Moóca and
Santana, which suffered an exodus of the younger generation during the
1970s. Now that these neighborhoods are being gentrified and can offer the
same type of developments as Morumbi, it may be advantageous again to
live there, and tradition becomes fashionable.

A development in São Miguel Paulista, one of the poorest working-class
areas of São Paulo, was advertised as follows:

> The two-bedroom apartment with the highest standard in São Miguel
> Paulista . . . . The finishings were taken care of in the smallest details:
> aluminum window frames, decorated tiles, carpet in the color of your
> choice. In addition, the Jardim Independência is totally closed, guaran-
> teeing your family's security, including the children playing in the play-
> ground. There even your car has the protection of a garage. *(O Estado
> de S. Paulo,* 3 October 1982)

"Independence Garden" is the name of this development. For people
used to living in extremely small spaces and not having cars, the protection of the car is really "something special." In another ad, also for a
working-class neighborhood in the eastern zone, where people usually dislike collective housing, the reason for the "independence" becomes more
explicit:

> Take advantage of the new plan for home ownership. . . . Get to know
> the new conditions: smaller installments. . . . More accessible family
> income requirements. Use your FGTS to further diminish the monthly
> payment. Financed by the *Nossa Caixa.* We, the residents of the Con-
> junto Residencial Jardim Centenário, are preparing a wonderful party
> to welcome you and your family. Everybody living here is already
> free from the torment of rent. Here everything is nice, everyone is
> a friend. . . . Security: you will live in a closed condominium, totally
> surrounded by walls and with a centralized guardhouse. . . . Leisure . . .
> Comfort: here you will be close to everything: . . . bakery, supermarket,
> pharmacy, bus stop. . . . The best of Sapopemba is here. *(O Estado de
> S. Paulo,* 24 January 1988)

To be free from rent is the general dream that was made more difficult
after the end of BNH financing and the economic recession. The emphasis
on financing is typical for both working-class and upper-class ads of the period. What is atypical is the image of a community welcome, which would
probably be considered in bad taste, even frightening, in Morumbi. It was
only in ads for the working classes and for the lower strata of the middle
classes that I found positive references to sociability inside the condominium.
This is the closest the ads came to the idea of community that is widespread
in the American context. In Brazil this idea is manipulated by developers as
a value of the "others," not of the elite.

The above ad includes another element that would probably not appear
if it were meant for the upper classes: the proximity to the local bakery,
pharmacy, and bus station, things that appeal to working-class people without a car and which until a decade ago were not common in any peripheral
neighborhood. The not-so-rich are not ready to leave the city and its pub-

lic facilities; they are eager to become even more urbanized, both by becoming property owners and by joining more fully in the consumer lifestyle it offers. Paulistanos of the lower middle and working classes want to be part of society, not to escape it. When they feel that they cannot enjoy the city space and its public life as they want, they feel restricted and imprisoned. To withdraw from the city's public life and from the use of its public spaces is seen as a privilege only by those whose participation in it is taken for granted and who can dream of creating better and more exclusive universes.

Closed Doors

Enclosure of residences is the third issue generating contradictory and ambivalent feelings among São Paulo's residents. Whether they are detached family houses or collective apartment buildings and condominiums, all types of housing in contemporary São Paulo have gone through processes of enclosure largely in response to the fear of crime. The necessity of enclosing has affected poor and rich residents alike and transformed the way they live and the quality of public interactions in the city. Nevertheless, feelings about these enclosures seem to differ considerably.

Neither the residents of Morumbi's detached houses nor those of collective residences seem to evaluate their enclosures negatively. Upper-class occupants of closed condominiums and high-rises felt that to live inside of one of these fortresses conveyed feelings of freedom and protection, not to mention a high quality of life. People living in detached houses express the same feelings about their individual fortresses, and they cannot imagine that condominiums could offer the same. In neither case, however, do residents show much regret or nostalgia for a more open type of housing or for a more diversified public sociability. To live in isolation is considered best; they are doing what they want, and thus they have a feeling of freedom. Interestingly, the people I interviewed in Morumbi never use arguments of privacy, individuality, or intimacy to justify their preferences. Morumbi residents seem to fear the spread of evil more than they value individualism.[36]

Whereas residents of closed condominiums think of their fortified enclaves as spaces of freedom, and see their moves and house transformations as positive achievements, people who continue to live in houses in Jardim das Camélias and especially in Moóca feel that their houses have been turned into prisons. They tend to evaluate transformation in a negative way, expressing a sense of loss.

7.2

Do you live in a house?

I do, but it is a prison. There are bars everywhere, and given the way things are now one cannot leave the door open, not even to wash the sidewalk in front of the house.

Housewife, late forties, lives in Moóca; married to a bar owner

One of the most common images used to describe feelings of insecurity and ways of dealing with them was that of closed doors.[37] This image conveys not only people's fears but also the reality of restrictions caused either by the economic crisis or by the fear of crime. Residents in all neighborhoods think that they need fences, walls, bars on the windows, special lights, and intercoms, but many do not appreciate their more secure houses in the same way that they enjoyed the open ones and the social space they created. In many cases the façades are now hidden; to approach a neighbor means to go through locked doors and intercoms, even in the poorest areas of town. In older neighborhoods—that is, those at least fifteen years old—the signs of transformation are obvious: the fences and walls offend the original design of the houses and apartments. Many houses are less comfortable and cozy than before.

7.3

There is always a first time, the burglaries, the thefts. . . . Those iron bars did not exist. The wall was normal, as in any house, one and a half meters, more or less; there was a parking space for one car—today it is for two cars—and I used to leave one car on the street, covered, well locked. . . . It was on a Wednesday, twelve years ago. I had two new cars, one Maverick and one pickup. I used to leave the pickup that I used for work in the garage because the ownership papers weren't ready. At that time the living room was bigger: I've diminished the living room in order to fit in the cars, to enlarge the garage. It was on a Wednesday. . . . They took the new car. . . . From that day on I started to enclose the house. . . . I started to do things . . . the iron bars which you see in the door. . . . We started to close the house: we would build a piece and then another . . . and as I was building, I was building it more secure. Iron, aluminum, concrete. A matter of security. But, thank God, it is not too frightening yet. We keep holding on, right?

Owner of a small foundry, late fifties,
lives in Moóca with his wife and two children

Once again the narrative is divided into times before and after a crime that, in this case, initiated a process of house transformation. Inventories of changes to make a house more secure, and many narratives describing the change of residence from houses to apartments, are accompanied by the expression of feelings of imprisonment that jeopardize the sense of pleasures that a house of one's own should offer. How is it possible to enjoy in the same way a house whose living room had to be made smaller to accommodate a garage to protect one's cars? Or in which the light of the bedroom is completely blocked by the new wall? Or in which the view from all the windows is framed by bars? How is it possible to enjoy in the same way one's backyard and the common areas of an apartment building? The transformation of the house into a prison adds to the feelings of restriction and loss associated with the economic crisis and anguish about social decay. The closed door is a strong metaphor.

Although various groups of Paulistanos resist and resent such transformations, the "new concept of housing" dominates the city. In addition to being universally understood, it influences people's decisions and options and shapes the transformations they make in their homes and their lifestyles. It has become a model of the most appropriate, most prestigious, and for many the most desirable style of residence. Among all the characteristics of this model, the most conspicuous is security. To live behind walls and fences is the everyday experience of Paulistanos, and the elements associated with security constitute a language through which people of every class express not only fear and the need for protection but also social mobility, distinction, and taste. While this language has many class dialects, it also has some general features that cut across all social classes. For all social groups today, security is an element through which they think of their place in society and materially create their social space.

AN AESTHETIC OF SECURITY

Fences, bars, and walls are essential in the city today not only for security and segregation, but also for aesthetic and status reasons. All the elements associated with security become part of a new code for the expression of dis-

PHOTO 9.   High-security façade in Morumbi, 1994. The opening in the wall, covered with bullet-proof glass, indicates the presence of private guards. Photo by Teresa Caldeira.

tinction, a code I call the "aesthetics of security." This code encapsulates elements of security in a discourse of taste and transforms it into a symbol of status. In contemporary São Paulo, fences and bars become elements of decoration and of the expression of personality and invention. They are elements of a new aesthetic code. These elements have to be sophisticated not only to protect inhabitants from crime but also to express the social status of the residents: sophisticated cameras, intercoms, and electronic gate openers, not to mention defensive design and architecture, become statements about social class. They are investments in public appearance and must allow comparison between neighbors, to show who is doing better and who has more sophisticated tastes.

A couple of years ago, residents of middle- and upper-class areas saw security as something imposed on the architecture in an artificial way. This is still the feeling of residents of Moóca and Jardim das Camélias. When added to a design conceived without it, security may still look and feel strange. But now that security features are part of the building design, residents view them differently. In 1980, there were still debates in São Paulo's newspapers about the rights of apartment owners to add fences and walls to their

PHOTO 10.   Autoconstructed houses in Jardim das Camélias, 1994. Residents
carefully choose the style of the fence and try to avoid replicating their neighbors'.
Photo by Teresa Caldeira and James Holston.

buildings, sometimes changing the original design.[38] This debate seems to
have died. Very few high-rises or houses lack fences, and no one would ad-
vertise a building without fences and security devices! By the early 1990s,
the new "architecture of security" was making its way into newspaper articles.[39] This architecture creates explicit means of keeping away undesirables, especially the homeless.[40] After twenty years of elaboration and of
experiments in a new mode of segregation, the language of social distancing and isolation is becoming increasingly explicit and spread across the city
(see photos 9 and 10).

    House transformations that increase security represent significant in-
vestment in a time of hardship. But although the investment may represent a burden for a family of modest income, it is considered absolutely necessary. The man who makes fences and window bars for the residents of
Jardim das Camélias, in a small workshop in front of his house, showed me
the long list of his clients in the neighborhood, explained to me how expensive the fences are for his poor clients, and told me how he works out
installment plans and ways of playing with inflation to make his services
more affordable. He also proudly showed me the portfolio with his designs

PHOTOS 11, 12, AND 13. In Moóca (1989) one finds at least three genera-
tions of façades. Photo 11 shows old working-class row houses built right to the
sidewalk. In the next generation, houses usually had a front yard open to the
street. Photos 12 and 13 show examples of these second-generation houses next
to others modified according to the new security requirements. The older and
more open houses are now dwarfed by the new style that mandates that the front
yard be enclosed. Photos by Teresa Caldeira.

of fences and gates and talked about his efforts to decorate them and to transform the simplest fence into something attractive. This is his contribution
"to make the neighborhood more beautiful," he told me. He knows his business indeed, and he is conscious that fences are not only about security but
also about aesthetics and distinction.

At its most basic level, a well-enclosed house with an aura of place definitively marks the distance between a house and a *cortiço* or a favela. However, more extensive comparisons are possible because residents of São Paulo
of all social classes are now literate in the new code of distinction. Of course
variations are enormous between rich and poor neighborhoods, but, in all
of them, the more ostensibly secure and enclosed the property, the higher
its status. It seems that the residents of São Paulo are learning to transform
restriction, limitation, uncertainty, and fear to advantage by manipulating
the aesthetic of security: they are making their houses into prisons, but their
prisons make statements about their social position.

Looking at neighboring houses or apartments in any neighborhood of
São Paulo demonstrates clearly how fences and walls talk of distinction and
constitute styles of design. In rich areas such as Morumbi, the individual
architecture of each building and competition for the most original detail
to single out a development try to create feelings of distinction. Neighborhoods constructed in earlier periods, such as Moóca and Jardim das Camélias,

display the changes in fashion in every street. Older façades with more discreet fences and an open design are dwarfed by the new style of security architecture (see photos 11, 12, and 13).

Walls, fences, and bars speak of taste, style, and distinction, but their aesthetic intentions cannot distract us from their main message of fear, suspicion, and segregation. These elements, together with the valorization of isolation and enclosure and the new practices of classification and exclusion, are creating a city in which separateness comes to the forefront and in which the quality of public space and the possibility of social encounters have already changed considerably.

CHAPTER 8
The Implosion
of Modern Public Life

São Paulo is today a city of walls. City residents will not risk living in a house without fences and bars on the windows. Physical barriers enclose both public and private spaces: houses, apartment buildings, parks, squares, office complexes, shopping areas, and schools. As the elites retreat to their enclaves and abandon public spaces to the homeless and the poor, the number of spaces for public encounters between different social groups shrinks considerably. The everyday routines of those who inhabit segregated spaces—guarded by walls, surveillance systems, and restricted access—are quite different from their previous routines in more open and mixed environments.

Residents from all social groups argue that they build walls and change their habits to protect themselves from crime. However, the effects of these security strategies go far beyond self-protection. By transforming the urban landscape, citizens' strategies of security also affect patterns of circulation, habits, and gestures related to the use of streets, public transportation, parks, and all public spaces. How could the experience of walking on the streets not be transformed if one's environment consists of high fences, armed guards, closed streets, and video cameras instead of gardens and yards, neighbors talking, and the possibility of glancing at some family scene through the windows? The idea of going for a walk, of naturally passing among strangers, the act of strolling through the crowd that symbolizes the modern experience of the city, are all compromised in a city of walls. People feel restricted in their movements, afraid, and controlled; they go out less at night, walk less on the street, and avoid the "forbidden zones" that loom larger and larger in every resident's mental map of the city, especially among the elite. Encounters in public space become increasingly tense, even violent, because they are framed by people's fears and stereotypes. Tension, separation, discrimination, and suspicion are the new hallmarks of public life.

This chapter analyzes the changes in public space and in the quality of public life that result from expanded strategies of security: segregation, social distance and exclusion, and the implosion of the experience of public life in the modern city. First, I discuss the modern notion of the public, framed by ideals of openness and accessibility both in the city space and in the polity. I analyze two critiques of industrial cities that remain committed to modern values: modernism and the Garden City. Both have influenced the fortified enclaves. Next, I compare the spaces of the new enclaves with those of modernist city planning, showing that the former use modernist conventions with the intention of creating what the latter produced unintentionally: segregation and fragmentation. Third, relying on ethnographic data and on my own experiences in São Paulo, I discuss the relationship between changes in the built environment and changes in the everyday life in the city, showing how the latter is increasingly shaped by incivility and enforcement of social distance. A comparison with Los Angeles shows that São Paulo's pattern of segregation is in fact not unique. In both cities the new urban experience is structured not by the modern values of openness and tolerance to heterogeneity but rather by separation and the control of boundaries. Finally, I address some of the political consequences of these spatial changes in terms of the expansion and restriction of democracy itself.

Of course, the public spaces of cities and the types of relationships that exist there represent only one aspect of public life. Pervading the discussions in this chapter is one of the most challenging questions in urban analysis: how to conceive of the relationships between urban form, politics, and everyday life. These relationships are very complex and usually disjunctive: simultaneous processes with opposite meanings may take place in the same public sphere. São Paulo offers a compelling example of disjunction: its walling process has coincided with the organization of urban social movements, the expansion of citizenship rights for the working classes, and political democratization. By emphasizing this type of disjunction, I differ strongly from environment determinists who would see in the walls and the pattern of segregation crystallized in the urban environment the determinant origin of political processes.

Nevertheless, the built environment is not a neutral stage for the unfolding of social relations. The quality of the built environment inevitably influences the quality of the social interactions that take place there. It does not determine them completely; there is always room for diverse and sometimes subversive appropriations of spaces and for the organization of social actions that counter those shaped by spatial practices. However, the material spaces that constitute the stage for public life influence the types of social relations possible on it. Against a backdrop of walls and technologies of surveillance, life on the sidewalks is quite different from what Jane Jacobs described in her famous defense of urban public space (1961:50–54). The "metaphorical" cities people construct in their everyday practices of space (de Certeau 1984:93) are inevitably different in an open modern city and in a city of walls. Usually it takes organized political action to resist walls or to dismantle patterns of segregation. In everyday life, it is a difficult matter to contest walls and rituals of suspicion and humiliation, as the residents of São Paulo know so well.

THE MODERN IDEAL
OF PUBLIC SPACE AND CITY LIFE

Streets open to the free circulation of crowds and vehicles represent one of the most vivid images of modern cities. Although there are various and sometimes contradictory accounts of modernity in Western cities, the modern experience of urban public life is widely held to include the primacy and openness of streets; free circulation; the impersonal and anonymous encounters of pedestrians; spontaneous public enjoyment and congregation in streets and squares; and the presence of people from different social backgrounds strolling and gazing at others, looking at store windows, shopping, sitting in cafes, joining political demonstrations, appropriating the streets for their festivals and celebrations, and using spaces especially designed for the entertainment of the masses (promenades, parks, stadiums, exhibition spaces).[1] These are elements associated with modern life in capitalist cities at least since the remodeling of Paris by Baron Haussmann in the second half of the nineteenth century. Haussmann's state-promoted transformation of Paris was strongly criticized and opposed by citizens and analysts alike, but no one denied that the new boulevards were readily appropriated by huge numbers of people eager to enjoy both the street life, protected by anonymity, and the consumer possibilities that came with it. The flaneur described by Baudelaire and the consumer of the new department stores became symbols of the modern use of urban public space, as Paris became a prototype of the modern city.

At the core of this concept of urban public life are two related notions: city space is open space to be used and enjoyed by everyone, and the consumer society it houses is accessible to all. As Young puts it, in the ideal of modern city life "borders are open and undecidable" (1990:239). Of course, this has never been entirely the case in Paris or anywhere else. Modern cities have always been marked by social inequalities and spatial segregation, and their spaces are appropriated in quite different ways by diverse social groups, depending on their social position and power. Paris itself demonstrates the perpetuation of inequality: the remodeling of the city under the Second Empire was in fact a transformation in the mode of spatial segregation and of the organization of class differences, as Engels (1872) noted early on (see also Harvey 1985). As a result, the literature on modern cities has often emphasized their negative aspects, from crime and violence to the danger of the mob, anomie, excessive individualism, congestion, and disease. However, in spite of persisting inequalities and social injustices, Western cities inspired by this model have always maintained signs of openness in circulation and consumption, signs that sustained the positive value attached to an open public space. Moreover, the sometimes violent appropriations of public spaces by different categories of excluded people—the most obvious example being the barricades erected during workers' rebellions—also constituted the modern public and simultaneously contributed to its expansion. Contestation is an inherent component of the modern city.

Some analysts of modern city life have been especially compelling in enumerating the positive values of the city and in defending modern public space. In general, they neglect the fact that the contemporary notion of the public is, in fact, a type of space and an experience of city life that was constituted only in the process of nineteenth-century industrial urbanization. The historical specificity of this notion of the public is essential in understanding its current transformation.

Jane Jacobs is one of the most famous advocates of the values of modern public life in cities. Her analysis of the use of sidewalks emphasizes not only openness and accessibility but also the etiquette and the conditions that make interactions among strangers possible and secure. These conditions include the complex and voluntary control exercised by city dwellers that she labels the "eyes upon the street" (Jacobs 1961:35); density; continuous use; a wide diversity of uses; and a clear demarcation between public and private space. When these conditions disappear, she argues, the freedom of the city and its civilization are threatened. This happens, for example, when the "institution of the Turf" (1961:47–50) orients urban constructions and people build barriers that enclose some areas and fence the others out. It also happens when the separation between public and private is confused. Privacy, Jacobs argues, is "indispensable" in cities (1961:58). "Civilized public life" is maintained on the basis of dignified, formalized, and reserved relationships—what we can call civility—kept separate from people's private lives. Where no vivid sidewalks and public spaces exist, and when relationships in public start to extend into private life and require close sharing among neighbors, then city freedom is threatened; people tend to enforce common standards, creating a sense of homogeneity that leads to insularity and separation. When public life is absent, the alternative to sharing too much may be sharing nothing, and suspicion and fear of neighbors are the expected outcomes. For Jacobs, both the drawing of lines and boundaries in city space and the extension of the private into the public threaten the values of a good urban public life.[2]

Iris Marion Young (1990) starts from Jacobs's analysis to construct a "normative ideal of city life," which she conceives as an alternative to existing cities and as one way of redressing their many social injustices. Young creates her model as an ideal and therefore does not elaborate on its historic and specific modern character. However, her arguments and criticisms of some Enlightenment views reveal its modern character. Young defines city life as "the being together of strangers," whose ideal is "an openness to unassimilated otherness." "As a normative ideal," she argues, "city life instantiates social relations of difference without exclusion" (Young 1990: 237, 227). By principle these ideals are incompatible with any kind of hierarchical order (such as the medieval, status-based order) and can be conceived only under the assumption of a universal equality of citizens that constitutes modern Western societies.

Young conceives her model of city life as an instrument to criticize communitarianism, that is, the ideal of the fusion of subjects with one another and of the primacy of face-to-face relations as a primary model of democratic politics. This is exactly the model used to justify building fortified enclaves and retreating to suburban life. Using arguments that parallel those of Jacobs, Young argues that the ideal of community "denies the difference between subjects" and "often operates to exclude or oppress those experienced as different. Commitment to an ideal of community tends to value and to enforce homogeneity" and therefore has exclusionary consequences (Young 1990:234–35). She claims that her normative ideal is an elaboration of the virtues and unrealized possibilities of the contemporary experience of cities. The main virtues are four: (1) social differentiation without exclusion; (2) multi-use differentiation of social space; (3) eroticism, understood broadly as "an attraction to the other, the pleasure and excitement of being drawn out of one's secure routine to encounter the novel, strange, and surprising"; and (4) publicity, which refers to public space as being by definition a place open and accessible to anyone and where one always risks encountering those who are different (Young 1990:238–41). "In public life the differences remain unassimilated. . . . The public is heterogeneous, plural, and playful" (Young 1990:241). Although social reality in any contemporary city is full of inequalities and injustices, the ideal allows us to consider, criticize, and formulate alternatives to them.

Modern ideals of the public do not refer only to city life but are always coupled with conceptions of politics. The promise of incorporation into modern society includes not only the city and consumption but also the polity. Images of the modern city are in many ways analogous to those of the liberal polity, consolidated on the basis of a social contract among equal and free people. The ideal of the social contract based on a principle of universality is quite radical—like that of the open city—and it helped destroy the feudal social order that preceded it. But, clearly, it is only through struggle that the definition of "free and equal" has been expanded. As with the open city, the polity that truly incorporates all citizens equally has never existed. Yet its founding ideals and its promise of continuous incorporation have retained their power for at least two centuries, shaping people's experience of citizenship and city life and legitimating the actions of various excluded groups in their claims for incorporation.[3]

In contemporary politics, the unfulfilled liberal promises of universal citizenship and, simultaneously, the reaffirmation of some of these promises have been articulated best through social movements. These have taken various forms, either affirming the rights of specific groups (such as blacks, indigenous populations, gays, and women) or trying to expand the rights of excluded social groups (as in the case of São Paulo's movements of poor residents of the peripheries demanding their "rights to the city"). In general, especially in their liberal incarnations, social movements have mounted what one might call a positive attack on modern liberal ideals: their aim is still to expand rights, freedom, justice, and equality, and they search for models that include the excluded and, therefore, achieve those goals in a more effective way. In other words, their attack maintains and reinforces basic liberal values, especially those of universality and equality. What distinguishes these liberal social movements from a second type is the treatment of difference.[4] In the liberal version, which Charles Taylor calls a "politics of universalism," social movements mark differences in order to expose injustice. For social movements that emphasize "the equal dignity of all citizens," to call attention to difference means to struggle for the expansion of rights and "the equalization of rights and entitlements" (Taylor 1992:37). Ultimately, their goal is the erasure of difference by the incorporation of the groups discriminated against into full citizenship. These movements aim at a public life and a polity in which equal respect for everybody's rights would eliminate the need to stress differences and inequalities. Because of their emphasis on universal principles, they do not view difference as something to be maintained and valorized.

A second type of social movement has brought to the forefront the question of difference. In this second category, which Taylor calls a "politics of difference," minority groups, especially feminists, argue that liberal notions of universalism have always been constituted on the basis of the exclusion of some. They insist that the rights of minority groups can be addressed only if approached from the perspective of difference rather than that of sameness.[5] Although they still refer to a principle of universal equality, they demand recognition of the unique identity of each group and its distinctiveness from all others (Taylor 1992:38–39). Iris Young's understanding of a politics of difference and of city life as the realm of social relations of "difference without exclusion" represents one version of this criticism (Young 1990). In her model, differences should remain unassimilated; they should not disappear under any fiction of a universal belonging. Although the break with liberalism in this view is explicit, it still constitutes an attack based on the principles of rights, freedom, justice, and equality and, therefore, within the parameters of modernity.

Other theorists of democracy such as Claude Lefort, Chantal Mouffe, Ernesto Laclau, and Étienne Balibar offer similar analyses. What they have in common, in addition to an emphasis on the nonassimilation of differences, is an insistence on a democratic polity and on a public space founded on uncertainty and openness and marked by the negotiation of meaning. As Lefort puts it, democracy is instituted and sustained by "the dissolution of the markers of certainty" (Lefort 1988:19). In a democracy, the basis of power, law, knowledge, and social interactions is indeterminate, and the public space is the locus for negotiation about the meaning of the social and the legitimate.

These ideals of the democratic polity—openness, indeterminacy, fluidity, and coexisting, unassimilated difference—have found some of their best expressions in the public spaces of modern cities.[6] Such spaces promote interactions among people who are forced to confront each other's anonymity on the basis of citizenship and therefore to acknowledge and respect each other's equal rights. Of course, there are many ways of subverting that equality and invoking status and hierarchy. Nevertheless, the modern city space, more than any other, forces their confrontation and therefore has the potential to challenge and level those hierarchies. In the space of the modern city, different citizens negotiate the terms of their interactions and socialize despite their differences and inequalities. This ideal of the open city, tolerant to social differences and their negotiation in anonymous encounters, crystallizes what I call the modern and democratic public space.

Cities such as contemporary São Paulo and Los Angeles display a strikingly different type of public urban space. The difference is not of the kind expressed by the demands of social movements (of either type) or by criticisms of the numerous dysfunctions of modern cities, which aim to improve the modern public space and make it live up to its promises. Rather, the public spaces being created in these cities negate the main characteristics of the modern democratic ideal of urban public space. They represent a type of public space that makes no gestures toward openness, indeterminacy, accommodation of difference, or equality, but rather takes inequality and separation as organizing values. It contradicts the principles of modern city space and brings into existence some of Jacobs's and Young's worst scenarios of incivility, inequality, and privatization of public space. Cities of walls and fortified enclaves are cities of fixed boundaries and spaces of restricted and controlled access.

GARDEN CITY AND MODERNISM: THE LINEAGE OF THE FORTIFIED ENCLAVE

The fortified enclaves and the type of public space being created in São Paulo and Los Angeles are the result of complex and heterogeneous influences. Some of them can be traced to a number of critiques of inequalities, segregation, and social injustices that have plagued industrial cities. Two of these views especially influenced the new segregation of enclaves: the notion of the Garden City, and modernism. This analysis will help us to understand how what once constituted a critique of the problems of industrial cities became the source of the destruction of its democratic ideals.

The Garden City model was first articulated by Ebenezer Howard in nineteenth-century England.[7] Considering the problems of large industrial cities insoluble, he proposed replacing them with small towns. Residents, especially the poor, would live close to nature, on a basis of mutuality and collective ownership of land. Howard imagined the Garden Cities as self-reliant and therefore different from traditional suburbs where workers go only to sleep. In fact, the cities he imagined, with their combination of office and industry jobs and residences, are closer to the idea of the new suburbs.[8] Howard envisioned his towns as round, encircled by a greenbelt (like those adopted by many British cities), and connected to other small towns to form another circle (as in the concept of satellite cities). Economic activities, residence, and administration were to be separated by green areas. At the center, public buildings would be clustered to create the "civic spirit." The town was to be planned as a totality—according to a concept that became the synonym for planning itself—and would be controlled by the public authority to prevent speculation and irrationality in its use. Garden Cities were to be governed by a democratically controlled, corporate technocracy, and its main members were to be elected by the renter-residents.

The Garden City model has been extremely influential, generating numerous "new towns" both in England and in the United States since the early twentieth century (Fishman 1988: chapter 1). Contemporary Paulista closed condominiums and American common interest developments (CIDs) exemplify the influence of the Garden City model and also the extent to which it has been modified. The enclosing walls and the private character of today's developments, the absence of a preoccupation with urban order, and the exclusive and exclusionary lifestyle directly contradict the original ideals. However, the Garden City imagery is still significant. In the United States, this model has been frequently associated with communitarian political ideals, although these were not necessarily a part of Howard's vision.[9] It is not difficult to trace to this concept the origins of the CID, administered by a homeowner's association, which is becoming the main type of middle-class residence in the outer cities of the United States.[10] Similarly, as my analysis of advertising shows, Brazilian closed condominiums were inspired by the Garden City model. In contrast with American CIDs, however, Brazilian condominiums do not emphasize the values of community. In São Paulo, communitarianism is not an important ideology, and the Garden City inspiration is expressed in a cruder way. Without the (presumably positive) discourse on the values of local community, its discriminatory intentions are the only ones to stand out.

Le Corbusier and modernist city planning represent another critique of the industrial city and its modern public space that has been appropriated and transformed by the new enclaves. In spite of many differences, Le Corbusier's Radiant City had some links with the Garden City model. In fact, he himself described it as a "vertical garden city" (Jacobs 1961:22).[11] His ideas about density were the opposite of Howard's, and he introduced the skyscraper into his plans; he also brought in the automobile and considerations about the rapid flow of traffic. Nevertheless, his plans reveal a dislike of the street and destruction of its unity; spatial segmentation of functions; emphasis on the city as a park and on the existence of green areas intercalated among built ones; and the need of a total plan that is continuously controlled by public authorities.

Modernist planning and design were influential everywhere in the world, but especially so in both modern Brazil and Los Angeles. As Holston shows (1989), the construction of modernist Brasília in the late 1950s crystallized an international modernism in its transformation of public space and communicated it to the rest of the country.[12] Modernism has been the dominant idiom of Brazilian architecture and planning to this day. As such, it is associated with prestige and has been helping to create elite spaces and sell residences for the Brazilian elite since the 1950s.[13] In the closed condominiums, however, modernist architecture becomes not only a status symbol for the bourgeoisie, for whom this architecture is still fashionable, but also a principal device of segregation. To achieve their goals of isolating, distancing, and selecting, the fortified enclaves use instruments of design drawn from modernist city planning and architecture. One striking characteristic of both modernist city planning (and the Garden City) and the fortified enclaves is the attack on streets as a form of public space. In Brasília, as Holston shows (1989: chapter 4), as in new parts of São Paulo and Los Angeles, modernist conventions of architectural and urban design eliminate pedestrians and anonymous interactions from the streets, which become dedicated to the circulation of motor transport. The street as a central element of modern public life in the city is thus eliminated. However, even if the results tend to be the same, the original projects of modernism and current enclosures are radically different. It is worth investigating how such different projects have ended up using similar strategies and producing similar effects.

Modernist architecture and city planning arise from a criticism of industrial cities and societies, which they intend to transform through the radical remodeling of space. Their ambition is clear: the erasure of social difference and the creation of equality in the rational city of the future, designed by the avant-garde architect. In this scheme the corridor street is perceived as a source of disease and an impediment to progress because it fails to accommodate the needs of the new machine age. Moreover, modernist architecture attacks the street because it opposes the architectural organization of the public and private embedded in the corridor street (Holston 1989:103)and its related system of public spaces, including sidewalks and squares: a solid mass of contiguous private buildings frames and contains the void of public streets. Modernist planning and architecture invert these solid-void/figure-ground relationships. In the modernist city, "streets appear as continuous voids and buildings as sculptural figures" (Holston 1989:125). By subverting the existing code of urban order, modernist planning aims at and succeeds in blurring the representational distinction between public and private. The result is the subversion of modern public space.

Modernist city planning aspired to transform the city into a single, homogeneous, state-sponsored public domain, to eliminate differences in order and create a universal, rationalist city divided into sectors by functions:

residential, employment, recreational, transportation, administrative, and civic. Brasília is the most complete embodiment of this new type of city.[14] The result, however, has turned out to be the opposite of the planner's intentions. Brasília is today not Brazil's most egalitarian city but its most segregated (Holston 1989: chapter 8; Telles 1995a). In destroying the street as the space for public life, modernist city planning has also undermined urban diversity and the possibility of the coexistence of differences. The type of space it creates promotes not equality, as was intended, but only a more explicit inequality.

Ironically, then, the instruments of modernist planning, with little adaptation, are well suited to producing inequality. Streets designed for vehicles only, the absence of sidewalks, enclosure and internalization of shopping areas, and spatial voids isolating sculptural buildings and wealthy residential areas effectively generate and maintain social separation. These modernist creations radically transform public life. In the new fortified enclaves, they are used not to destroy private spaces and produce a total, unified public, but explicitly to destroy public spaces. Their objective is to enlarge some private domains so that they will fulfill public functions, but in a segregated way.

Contemporary fortified enclaves use essentially modernist instruments of design, with some notable adaptations. The treatment of circulation and commerce is quite similar: pedestrian circulation is discouraged, vehicular traffic is emphasized, sidewalks are absent, and shopping areas are kept away from the streets, discouraging meaningful public interaction. The large spaces separating sculptural buildings are another common feature. The surrounding walls are the clearest departure from the modernist idiom, but their effects are not strange to the modernist city. In modernist planning, as in Brasília, residential, commercial, and administrative areas were to have no fences or walls but were to be delimited by green areas and expressways, as in the Garden City model and in various contemporary American suburbs. In São Paulo, walls are considered essential to demarcate all types of buildings, especially the new enclaves. However, this demarcation of private property does not create the same type of (nonmodernist) public space that characterizes the industrial city. Because in contemporary enclaves the private universes are kept apart by the voids of open spaces (as in modernist design), they break the street line and no longer generate street corridors. Moreover, when there is a street line created by walls and enhanced by sophisticated technologies of security, the residual public space it produces is at odds with modern public life.

A significant difference between modernist design and the fortified enclaves occurs in the use of materials and forms of individual buildings. The plain modernist façades might be eliminated in favor of ornaments, irregularities, and ostentatious materials that display the individuality and status of their owners. The technologies of security can also help assure the exclusivity of the already isolated buildings. The architecture of these buildings is also at odds with modernist notions of transparency and disclosure of private life, expressed in its use of glass façades. In other words, contrary to modernist publicness, the enclaves enhance internalization, privacy, and individuality, but they are disconnected from its modern counterpart, the formal public sociability, as the building façades no longer constitute a solid frame for meaningful public life in the streets.

The surviving elements of modernist architecture and city planning in the new urban form are those that destroy modern public space and social life: dead streets transformed into highways, sculptural buildings separated by voids and disregarding street alignments, walls and technologies of security framing public space as residual, enclaves turned inward, separation of functions, and destruction of heterogeneous and diverse spaces). The devices that have been abandoned are those intended to create equality, transparency, and a new public sphere (glass façades, uniformity of design, absence of material delimitations such as walls and fences). Instead of creating a space in which the distinctions between public and private disappear—making all the space public, as the modernists intended—the enclaves use modernist conventions to create spaces in which the private quality is enhanced beyond any doubt and in which the public, a shapeless void treated as residual, is deemed irrelevant. This was exactly the fate of modernist architecture and its "all public space" in Brasília and in all cities that have used modernist urban planning to make and remake themselves (Holston 1989). However, while in Brasília the result was a perversion of initial premises and intentions, in the closed condominiums and fortified enclaves it represents a deliberate choice. In the enclaves, the aim is to segregate and change the character of public life by transferring activities previously enacted in heterogeneous public spaces to private spaces that have been constructed as socially homogeneous environments, and by destroying the potential of streets to provide spaces for anonymous and tolerant interactions.

Today, in the new spaces in cities such as São Paulo or Los Angeles, we tend to find no gestures toward openness and freedom of circulation, regardless of differences, nor a technocratic universalism that aims to erase differences. In São Paulo, the old modern urban design has been fragmented by the insertion of independent and well-delineated private enclaves (of modernist design) that are focused entirely inward. The fortified fragments are not meant to be subordinated to a public order kept together by ideologies of openness, accessibility, tolerance for differences, or promises of incorporation. Heterogeneity is now to be taken more seriously: fragments express irreconcilable inequalities, not simple differences. Public space expresses the new intolerance. The modernist conventions of design used by the enclaves help to ensure that different social worlds meet as infrequently as possible in city space: that is, they belong to different spaces.

In a city of walls and enclaves such as São Paulo, public space has undergone a deep transformation. Experienced as dangerous, framed by fences and walls, fractured by the new voids and enclaves, privatized with chains closing off streets, armed guards, and guardhouses, public space is increasingly abandoned by the well-to-do. As the spaces for the rich are enclosed and turned inward, the remaining space is left to those who cannot afford to go in. Because the enlarged, private worlds of the better-off are organized on the principles of homogeneity and exclusion of others, they are by principle the opposite of the modern public space. Yet neither can the leftover public spaces, territories of fear, aspire to modern ideals. Everyday life in the city of walls reinforces exactly the opposite values: incivility, intolerance, and discrimination.

In the ideal modern city life, "borders are open and undecidable," suggests Young (1990:239). Fixed boundaries create nonmodern spaces, an undemocratic public space. However, the relationships between urban form and politics are complicated, as are the effects of a nonpublic space on civil life. My reflections on these complexities are all framed by the fact that the consolidation of the city of walls in São Paulo has coincided with the process of political democratization. It was exactly at the moment when social movements were booming in the periphery, when trade unions were paralyzing factories and filling stadiums for their meetings, when people were voting for their leaders for the first time in twenty years, that city residents started building up walls and moving into fortified enclaves. While the political system opened up, the streets were closed, and the fear of crime became the talk of the city.

STREET LIFE: INCIVILITY AND AGGRESSION

In São Paulo, as in any city, the urban environment is heterogeneous and shows the signs of different layers of construction, uses, and interventions. The current process of building up walls affects all types of spaces in the city but transforms them, and the experiences of public life, in different ways. I describe different types of material transformation caused by the walling process and discuss how they affect the quality of public life. Although the changes are of different types and have diverse effects, they all reinforce boundaries and discourage heterogeneous encounters. They all create policed borders and consequently leave less space for indeterminacy in public encounters. They all promote intolerance, suspicion, and fear.

As people move around the city, they use the space in individual and creative ways and, as de Certeau reminds us, make fragmented trajectories that elude legibility (1984: chapter 7). Therefore, any account of these spatial practices can be only fragmentary and particular. I draw here on what people have told me and on what I have read and seen, but I rely mostly on my own observations, experiences, and memories of the city. I want to indicate changes and suggest different experiences in the use of the city, but I have no pretension to being exhaustive.

In contemporary São Paulo, the public space is emptiest and the use of streets, sidewalks, and squares rarest exactly where there are the most fortified enclaves, especially residential ones. In neighborhoods like Morumbi, streets are leftover spaces, and the material quality of public spaces is simply bad. Because of the inward orientation of the fortified enclaves, many streets have unpaved sidewalks or none at all, and several streets behind the condominiums are unpaved (photo 6). The distances between buildings are large. Walls are high, out of proportion to the human body, and most of them are topped by electric wires. Streets are for cars, and pedestrian circulation becomes an unpleasant experience. The spaces are intentionally constructed to produce this effect. To walk in Morumbi is a stigma: the pedestrian is poor and suspicious. People on foot may be workers who live in nearby favelas and who are treated by their richer neighbors with distance and disdain—and, evidently, with fear. Since middle- and upper-class people circulate in private cars while others walk or use public transportation, there is little contact in public among people from different social classes. No common spaces bring them together.

The paths inside the favelas are spaces for walking, but the favelas too end up being treated as private enclaves: only residents and acquaintances venture in, and all that is seen from the public streets are a few entrances. The favelas can be seen in their entirety only from the windows of the exclusive apartments above them. When both rich and poor residents live in enclaves, passing within the walls is obviously a carefully policed activity, in which class signs are interpreted in order to determine levels of suspicion and harassment. Empty streets of fixed boundaries and scrutinized differences are spaces of suspicion and not of tolerance, inattention to differences, or wandering around. They are not enjoyable urban spaces.

Various strictly residential neighborhoods for the upper classes (older

parts of Morumbi, Alto de Pinheiros, and Jardim Europa, for example) tend
to have empty streets as well, but older neighborhoods, some of them designed as garden cities, have good streets and sidewalks. In these areas, however, other devices restrict circulation. Residents have privatized public
streets and closed them off with gates, chains or, less ostensibly, with gardens, vases, and plants. In the United States, the same practice is becoming
common; the spaces thus produced are called "security zone communities"
by Blakely and Snyder (1997). Because the street is still considered open
space, its privatization still generates opposition. A few years ago, when this
trend started in São Paulo, the city government reacted and removed the
chains. However, as support for the practice grew, the city incorporated enclosure into its policies: in 1990, the city government of the PT started offering the services of its architects and construction workers to middle-class
neighborhoods interested in the enclosures.[15]

Although these neighborhoods still have nice streets full of trees and sidewalks, a form of entertainment enjoyed by my family when I was a child
has now become impossible: to go around the streets of Jardim Europa ad-
miring the mansions of the rich. They are no longer visible; the houses have
been concealed behind walls and protected by electric wires and other security equipment. To walk in the area has become unpleasant, as the streets
are now dominated by private guards installed in guardhouses, trained dogs
barking at passers-by, and devices blocking circulation. The few people walking become suspects. I tried it, with my camera, and drew many guards aggressively in my direction, in spite of my middle-class appearance. The sense
of being under surveillance is unavoidable, because the guards position
themselves on the sidewalks (instead of inside the buildings, as in Morumbi);
they observe everyone passing by, and directly address anyone they find
suspect. Well, they are paid to suspect and to keep away strangers. This private army is there to privatize what used to be reasonable public spaces.

I spent my childhood in the late 1950s and early 1960s in a new middle-
class neighborhood, Sumaré, which since the late sixties has been completely
urbanized and is today a central neighborhood. When we moved there, the
streets were unpaved; there was no sewage system and no telephone. We were
just two blocks away from the headquarters of the city's department of trash
collection, that is, the stable for the horses that pulled the collection carriages
through our street every morning, to the great amusement of the children.
Sometimes when it rained, my father's beautiful blue '54 Chevrolet, directly
imported from the United States and designed for other roads, got stuck in
the mud, and he had to walk the one kilometer from our house to the School
of Medicine of the University of São Paulo, where he was a professor. There

weren't many houses on our street; some resembled little *chácaras* (country houses), with their vegetable gardens and chickens. Although it was a middle-class neighborhood, in the late 1950s it was still in the process of becoming, like Jardim das Camélias, on the periphery, when I first went there in the late 1970s. The city grew so rapidly, and Sumaré is today so urban, that it is strange to remember that not too long ago it was so undeveloped.

For many years my family's house was separated from the street by a low fence. The gate was only closed at night. In the 1970s, when the neighborhood was built up, the sidewalks became full of people, and traffic increased considerably, my parents built a wall and started to close the gate during the day. They were bothered by passers-by looking into their living room. But we always walked around freely and without fear, even at night. In the early 1980s, my father's house was robbed, and after that the gate was kept locked. Today my father has a private guard inside the walls during the night, and the gate is locked twenty-four hours a day. He asks us to call him in advance when we visit at night so that the guard can be prepared to open the gate promptly and we do not have to wait outside. All the surrounding houses and apartment buildings have been remodeled and have added gates and walls. There are several other private guards on the block. The street, which today combines residences, offices, and commerce, is intensively used during the day (in fact, parking has become a problem), but I would feel uneasy walking around after dark.

A working-class neighborhood such as Jardim das Camélias still has an intense street life, although it has changed in many ways since the late 1970s. On the one hand, the neighborhood has expanded, the houses have improved, the trees have grown, and the streets have been paved, illuminated, and equipped with sidewalks (see photos 3 and 4). But as the neighborhood was urbanized and its material quality improved, fences went up as well, and people became more scared and suspicious. Crime increased in the late 1980s, from thefts to homicides, some of these involving boys who had grown up together playing on the streets. Nevertheless, everyday life is still marked by a public sociability among neighbors, the kind of formal and polite interchange on the sidewalks that gives life to a neighborhood and makes public space meaningful.[16] Traffic is light, and the streets are still constantly used by groups of children and adolescents playing, people who stop for a little chat and maybe sit down on the sidewalks to watch those passing by, people taking care of their cars or building something, people who stop at a little shop to catch up on the local news or, if they are men, to play *sinuca* or have a drink on their way home. The houses are enclosed, but by fences that allow visibility and interaction, not by high walls. This is the kind of neighborhood kept safe by intense use, mixed functions, and the "eyes upon the street" (Jacobs 1961: chapter 2). In other words, safety is maintained by engagement, not by isolation.

In spite of the continuing local sociability, people do not feel the neighborhood is as safe as it used to be.[17] They have fortified their houses, are more suspicious, talk to strangers on the street from behind their bars, more carefully choose the people they relate to, and control their children. Many children are now prohibited from playing outside the fences of their houses, and adolescents are restricted from going out. As everywhere else, people focus their concerns on the poorest areas; they are especially afraid of the favela nearby and another area recently invaded by participants in the Movimento dos Sem Terra. Suspicion toward people seen as "other" or as "inferior" is not exclusive to the upper classes, as chapter 2 makes clear. The frequency of public parties and celebrations sponsored by the local associations has decreased, and the activities of social movements have slowed down. Collective life and political activities have weakened in the last decade, but the public space of the streets still sustains local interactions and public interchanges.[18]

Most central neighborhoods of São Paulo, those with good urban infrastructure that the elite have maintained for themselves, have traditionally had mixed functions and maintain a relatively intensive and heterogeneous use of public space. Some of these neighborhoods are quite sophisticated, with luxury shops and restaurants (especially Jardins, but also Higienópolis and Itaim-Bibi). In these areas the streets are still used by people of various social backgrounds, and the rich rub elbows with the poor. Now, however, the streets are policed by an army of private guards and video cameras (each building has at least one), and interclass relationships have become nastier. Moreover, in this kind of neighborhood, as well as downtown, property owners have been creative in installing devices to keep undesired people away. In entranceways and *marquises*, sprinklers come on at odd times to discourage the homeless from lingering; chains are placed across patios, entryways, and sidewalks, and public parks are fenced off. The main target of these techniques is the increasing number of homeless people inhabiting the streets. Nevertheless, because the streets are generally crowded, the effects of the constant suspicion are not as severe as in emptier areas.

In these areas of intensive mixed use, the material obstacles at street level are complemented by a series of less visible practices of surveillance that reinforce social differences. The residents and users of these areas are not interested in indeterminacy. Their tools include video cameras, electronic pass systems at the entrances of any major office building, metal detectors at bank doors, and guards who demand identification of anyone entering office buildings and, increasingly, residential condominiums.[19] Systems of identification, screening, and control of circulation are considered central to good business management and feed the rapidly growing industry of private security services. These systems are a matter not only of security but also of discipline and social discrimination.[20] The image of the suspect is made up of stereotypes, and therefore systems of screening discriminate especially against poor and black people. The entrance guards do not bother people with the right class signs, but they give a hard time to everyone else.

Thus for many people everyday life in the city is becoming a daily management of barriers and suspicion, marked by a succession of little rituals of identification and humiliation. These including forcing office boys, who are invariably stopped by metal detectors in bank entrances, to open their backpacks in front of a long line of people waiting to get in; sending workers to the "service" doors; and physically searching maids when they leave their jobs at the condominiums. It is true that rich people also have to identify themselves and that they too are under surveillance, but the differences in the levels of control exercised over different people are obvious. Managers do not wear the same kind of ID tags, and upper-class people know how to use their class signs (including arrogance and disrespect) to avoid interrogation and go quickly past the guards, who respond with deference instead of the disdain they reserve for poorer people. In a city in which systems of identification and strategies of security are spreading everywhere, the experience of urban life becomes one of social differences, separations, exclusions, and reminders of the limitations of one's possibilities in the public space. It is, in reality, a city of walls, the opposite of the boundless public space of the modern ideal of city life.

São Paulo's streets may still be full of people, especially in central neighborhoods of commerce and service and in regional centers,[21] but the experience of the crowd and the quality of anonymous interactions have changed. People are afraid of being robbed, and their fear of *trombadinhas* (muggers) is taken for granted. Nobody wears jewelry or valuable watches; people carry limited cash and if possible only photocopies of documents, for their replacement requires hours of dealing with various bureaucracies. Women carry their purses tied in front of their bodies, and people embrace their backpacks on their chests. People in cars drive with closed windows and locked doors. They are especially afraid of stopping at traffic lights, for the news is filled with tales of muggers who use knives or pieces of glass as weapons to rob drivers, especially women. It is hard to distinguish these muggers from the increasing number of beggars and street vendors disputing the same street corners.

Not only are the attitudes in the crowd changing, but so is the crowd itself. The middle and upper classes try to avoid the crowded streets and sidewalks, preferring to shop at enclosed shopping centers and hypermarkets.[22] As the middle and upper classes circulate by car, the use of public transportation is becoming a lower-class experience. Still, it remains a mass experience, since the elite constitutes hardly 5 percent of the population of the metropolitan region.

The centers of public transportation—subway and train stations and the hubs of bus lines—have a culture of their own. They are mostly working-class spaces, filled with the sounds of popular music and the smell of fruits and all kinds of food. Every day, masses of people pass through these stations and spend a considerable amount of time commuting on public transportation.[23] These always packed areas are great spaces to sell anything, from religions to food, from cures to electronic gadgets, from herbal medicines to lingerie. This intense informal commerce of the *marreteiros* or *ambulantes*—as the street sellers are called—takes up most of the sidewalk space downtown, filling it with small stands. The experience of taking a bus, a train, or the subway at rush hour (something the middle and upper classes have stopped doing) entails fighting for space in crowded cars and being squashed against others. This is nothing new; if anything, the quality of public transportation in São Paulo has improved, especially as far as the subway is concerned. Nevertheless, frequent users of public transportation, such as the residents of Jardim das Camélias, feel that things today are more tense and unpleasant than in the past: there is little courtesy and a lot of aggression. And there is certainly more prejudice, as the middle classes teach their children that buses are dangerous and hire private drivers for them.

Traffic is by consensus considered to be one of the worst aspects of public life in São Paulo. Disregard of rules and of other people's rights is the norm.[24] There is no civility, as a significant part of the population seems to consider traffic regulations merely as obstacles to the free movement of individuals. The media has investigated and reported frequently on behavior in traffic. The findings are amazing, not only because of the extent of the disrespect they reveal, but also because they have become routine and lost the capacity to provoke any reaction. DataFolha, the *Folha de S. Paulo* research agency, found in April 1989 that 99 percent of São Paulo's drivers consider its traffic dangerous and that one in every four drivers had been involved in at least one accident the year before.[25] Another survey from DataFolha, in April 1986, found that city residents saw the main cause of car accidents as "the lack of responsibility and imprudence of drivers."[26] In October 1989, the research department of *O Estado de S. Paulo* interviewed a sample of drivers and discovered that 85 percent of them agreed that São Paulo's drivers do not respect pedestrian crosswalks and frequently make prohibited turns. Moreover, eight in ten people interviewed thought that drivers park in prohibited areas, double park, go through red lights, and ignore speed limits.[27] In 1991, DataFolha decided to observe an important intersection of the city (Avenue Paulista and Brigadeiro Luís Antonio). There were an average of thirteen prohibited left turns per hour, in spite of physical obstacles on the road, and most of the drivers never got a ticket because most of the time no policemen were there. They also found that one car ran one red light in every five, that 41 percent of the cars that stopped for a red light disregarded the pedestrian crosswalk, and that only 3 percent of the drivers used seat belts.[28] An additional problem is that of teenagers driving before they legally qualify for a license. Until the 1970s, middle-class adolescents like myself used public transportation to go to school and run their errands around the city. Today this is considered too dangerous or too uncomfortable for the kids, and they are transported exclusively by car, driven by private drivers or their parents—or else they are simply allowed to drive themselves.

São Paulo's traffic reveals that people use the public streets according to their private convenience and do not seem to be willing to conform to general rules or respect other people's rights. There is little respect for others or for the public good. There is also some sense of omnipotence in this behavior, for people do not seem to fear being injured by the same kind of transgressions they commit.[29] The results are dramatic: during the 1980s, more than two thousand people died in car accidents every year in the municipality of São Paulo. Between 1992 and 1994, the numbers decreased, but not significantly. In addition, more than fifty thousand people are injured in car accidents annually in the metropolitan region of São Paulo. In 1996, there were 195,378 reported car accidents in the MSP, which means an average of 535 accidents per day. Of these, 13.16 percent resulted in injuries. According to one source, the total number of accident victims was 59,679, and of these 1,113 were fatalities.[30] Very few people responsible for accidents are prosecuted.

Traffic is a strong indicator of the quality of public life. In Brazil, traffic behavior constitutes only the most obvious example of the routine disrespect for the law and the difficulties in enforcing it. Traffic policemen disregard some violations simply because they have become the norm. When they issue tickets, traffic enforcers usually hide in places where they cannot be seen by drivers. They try to avoid confronting upper-class people, who do not hesitate to challenge their authority. This is done on the basis of manipulation of class signs, but sometimes, when the signs are ignored or misunderstood, drivers resort to violence. The most violent attacks seem to be made against parking wardens, usually women, who control the restricted parking areas called the *zona azul* (blue zone). Some have been beaten by men when they refuse to void tickets, and one ended up in the hospital after an enraged motorist ran his car over her. These behaviors indicate how violent people can become when they are asked to conform to the law and cannot use their class position as a source of privilege, that is, to evade the law. Since the working classes usually cannot avoid the law, these behaviors reveal once more how class differences not only rule public interactions but also are reproduced by the elements that shape the public space.

Traffic is obviously not exclusively São Paulo's problem, but it is a national problem. In 1996, around twenty-seven thousand people died in car accidents in Brazil. The situation has acquired such dramatic dimensions that the federal government decided to revise the national traffic code *(código nacional de trânsito)*. After six years of debate in Congress, the new code took effect in January 1998. It establishes high fines and serious penalties and a system of demerit points that may lead to suspension of one's license. All violations, from not carrying the car registration to drunk driving, earn points and entail a fine (from R$40 to R$800). A more severe code is expected to increase civility in traffic. But it remains unclear whether the authorities can enforce these regulations, especially in a context in which public civility is deteriorating, not improving.

EXPERIENCING THE PUBLIC

Different social groups experience the transformed public spaces of the city in contradictory ways. The young middle-class and upper-class children who are coming of age in the city of walls do not seem unhappy with their experience of public spaces. Nor should they, perhaps, with private drivers on hand and no need to fight their way in crowded public buses. Moreover, they seem to love the secure spaces of shopping malls and fast food stores, of discotheques and video-game arcades. These are for them "cool" spaces in which to display their knowledge of a global youth culture of style labels and fashion trends. They connect to "global youth" but not to the youth of their own periphery. The Paulista working-class youth does not have the privilege of avoiding public transportation or the congested streets on which they commute and where some of them work. They do, however, share with rich kids some of the signs of a global youth culture, especially in clothes: sneakers, blue jeans, T-shirts. Nevertheless, they gather not in the upper-class malls but in spaces on the periphery itself (including malls), and they favor some subcultures (punk, skinhead) and some styles of music and dance (especially funk) not shared by the middle classes. Moreover, they experience violence and harassment in their use of the city and in their neighborhoods. In their musical gatherings themes such as police abuse, murders, and disrespect are constant.[31] For working-class kids, the experience of the city is one of injustice, not of privilege.

In contrast to the experience of these younger groups, older people, who grew up in São Paulo when progress was the goal and the use of streets and parks was more open, are nostalgic in their discussions of public space. Their descriptions of the city in the past have a quality similar to those recalling the period before the trauma of a crime. The old city is remembered as better, more beautiful, and more civilized than it is now. I spoke to two sisters about changing habits, specifically going to the movies.

8.1

People don't go to the movies anymore?

L: They don't. Now, after the video, they won't really go.

W: And it is too difficult! It all starts with parking: there is no place to park: parking is as expensive as the movie. If you leave the car on the street, either it is stolen or there are the "owners of the street" to take care of it.[32] So it is a problem to go out with the car, we cannot relax. You go to a shopping mall; sometimes we go to the movie in a shopping center.

L: We park the car inside. When we go to movie theaters, it is in the Lar Center, Center Norte, because it is more convenient.

W: Thirty, forty years ago we could go out. We used to dress well to go out, with gloves, all beautifully arranged, to go to the city, the downtown. Ipiranga, Metro. . . . Metro was the greatest . . . [33]

L: Lido, at the Lido a man could not enter without a tie. Would not enter.

When was this?

W: Like forty years ago.

L: I think it was thirty years ago. We would only go to the movies downtown. We used to go to the movies, and then go out, look at some shop windows—Barão de Itapetininga was a good street, with good stores. You would have a snack . . . would have dinner out. Nowadays you cannot go downtown on a Sunday, on weekends, it is impossible because there are the homosexuals, the transvestites . . . the little stalls *(barraquinhas)*. Well, downtown is horrible now with all those street vendors *(marreteiros)*.

> *L and W are both widowed and in their fifties. They spent their lives in Moóca and now live together to allow W's son to live with his family in her house without paying rent.*

Older people recall with nostalgia the formality involved in the enjoyment of the public space, the gloves and the ties they wore, the distinctiveness of the old movie theaters, and the "good" streets of old downtown in which one walked among elegant people—"It was so chic!" said the woman whose narrative I analyze in chapter 1. These are signs of distinction and rules of class separation that have been lost. In today's downtown, the "chic" population has been replaced by "marginals," nothing guarantees distinction, and the feeling that remains is uneasiness with the proximity of the poor. Many years ago, when the downtown area was used by the upper classes, joining the crowd (through the use of the right clothes and accessories, for example) was a matter of identification with social superiors, a sign of distinction for the working-class residents of Moóca. Today, however, the same people feel the need to promote distance rather than identification with the downtown crowd, for it is now made up of poor and marginalized people—vendors, street children, transvestites, prostitutes.

The expansion of mass consumption makes matters of distinction more complicated. Easy symbols of superiority, such as gloves and ties, have disappeared, and frequently the middle and upper classes feel irritated by poor people's consumption of goods considered to carry some form of status but which are no longer exclusive (see chapter 2). It is more difficult for the elite to impose their own code of behavior—including rules of deference—onto the city. Moreover, with democratization, the poor forced the recognition of their citizenship, and they occupied spaces—physical and political—previously reserved for the elite. With fewer obvious signs of differentiation at hand and with more difficulty in asserting their privileges and codes of behavior in the public space, the upper classes turn instead to systems of identification. Thus, spaces of controlled circulation (such as shopping centers) come to assure that distinction and separation are still possible in public. Signs of social distance are replaced with material walls.

The transformations in the various spaces in the city all seem to lead to more rigid and policed boundaries, and consequently less indeterminacy and fewer spaces for contact between people from different backgrounds. These experiences engender fear and intolerance rather than expectation and excitement. Experiences in public space seem to run counter to a modern and democratic public life. However, the politics of urban public spaces in São Paulo are still more complex, and two uses of public space contradict the dominant tendency of boundaries and segregation.

The few major parks in the city are intensively used in quite a democratic way. When a park is located on the periphery, such as Parque do Carmo, its users are mostly from the working classes, but the parks of Ibirapuera and Morumbi, both in rich neighborhoods, are used by people from all social classes. Although most of them are fenced, they are large, and they are the few green areas remaining in the city. In the last few years, the parks have been appropriated by thousands of people who go there, especially on weekends, to jog, bicycle, roller-skate, play ball, or simply be outside. These oases of intensive and mixed use are very few in São Paulo, and it is interesting that they are usually spaces used for the leisure of the masses. If what happens in other areas of the world is any indication, spaces for leisure and entertainment continue to have a mixed massive use—as in American waterfront areas, rebuilt historical districts, and theme parks, for example—even when all other public spaces deteriorate.

The second example is Praça da Sé, São Paulo's central square. Praça da Sé is the powerful symbol of the center of the city, whence all roads and streets are imagined to radiate.[34] Today, the landmarks of this big square are the Catholic cathedral, the central subway station, and the "zero mark" of the city, indicated by a stone erected on top of a compass engraved on the ground. The square is mainly a working-class space. Every day, a mass of commuters crosses Praça da Sé. Many people work there: vendors of every type of popular product, preachers of different religions, musicians, and policemen—the same types of people who fill any major hub of public transportation. The square has many residents, too: a contingent of street children and homeless people. Men dressed in suits and carrying briefcases, usually lawyers who have to reach the Central Forum next door, are frequently seen in the square, but they no longer give the place its identity. Praça da Sé is fundamentally a space for poorer residents, both in its everyday uses and in its symbolism. Residents of Jardim das Camélias I interviewed in the late 1970s considered going to Praça da Sé a special activity for the holidays, such as New Year's Day: it was their way of enjoying the city and feeling that they belonged in it. Today, they feel that the square has become a dangerous space, and although they still use it, for leisure they instead go somewhere like a shopping mall. As the working classes rule the square with their sounds and smells, the wealthy avoid it as a dangerous and unpleasant space.

But Praça da Sé has a second layer of symbolism: for both rich and poor Paulistanos it is the main political space of the city, a meaning that has been fixed by various events in the process of democratization. During the military years, the few political demonstrations that took place were held in Praça da Sé mainly because of the presence of the cathedral. The Catholic Church was at that time the only institution able to offer a relatively safe space for protests against the abuses and human rights violations practiced by the military regime. For the same reason, Praça da Sé became the site of numerous demonstrations by social movements during the *abertura* process, most visibly the huge gatherings of the Movimento do Custo de Vida in the second half of the 1970s. When the movement for free elections was organized in the early 1980s, it was only natural that mass demonstrations be held in the square. On 25 January 1984, the day of the city's anniversary, around three hundred thousand congregated in Praça da Sé to demand free elections. Middle- and upper-class people who had not been downtown for years (the main economic activities and all luxury commerce had moved southwest) found out how to take the subway and emerged in the middle of the square to demand democracy. Demonstrations were moved to Vale do Anhangabaú on only two occasions, when the square was too small for the expected crowd of one million: the last rally for direct elections in April 1984, and the demonstration for the impeachment of President Collor in September 1992.[35]

On the one hand, Praça da Sé symbolizes the political reappropriation of public space by the citizens in the transition to democracy. On the other hand, it represents the deterioration of public space, danger, crime, anxieties about downward mobility, and the impoverishment of the workers who continue to use it for commuting, working in the informal market, and consuming its cheap products. It symbolizes both the strength and the deterioration of public space and, therefore, the disjunctive character of Brazilian democracy (Holston and Caldeira 1998).

The example of Praça da Sé is another indication that political democratization is not contradictory to the deterioration of public spaces. In fact, democratization may have helped to accelerate the building of walls and the deterioration of public space. This does not, however, occur in the simplistic way some right-wing politicians want us to believe it does: that democracy creates disorder and crime and therefore generates the need for walls. If democracy gave rise to walls, it was because the democratization process was unexpectedly deep. Until the end of the military regime, politics had been the exclusive realm of the elite. With the *abertura*, however, the poor residents of the periphery became important political players, taking Praça da Sé to present their demands and assert their rights to the city. Their trade-union movements and social movements surprised everybody; and they were able to claim a political space that was being opened, but not necessarily for them. In the imagination of those who prefer to abandon the city, the fear of crime intertwines in complex ways with other anxieties provoked by change, as I showed in chapter 2. It intertwines with the fear of electoral results (especially the fear that the PT might win elections, as it did); the fear that one might decline socially because of inflation and economic crisis; the fear that certain goods no longer serve to create social distance or confer status; and the fear that the poor can no longer be kept in their places.

The coincidence of democratization with the deterioration of public space and more obvious processes of social segregation, as well as the ambiguous symbolism of Praça da Sé, precludes any easy associations between the material public spaces of cities and forms of polity. São Paulo shows that the polity and the public space of the city can develop in opposite directions. This disjunction between the political process and urban form is meaningful. On the one hand, because recent urban transformations are mostly not the result of imposed state policies but rather of the way in which the citizens engage with their city, they can be seen as the result of a democratic intervention. Although this engagement may be seen as a form of democratic action, it has produced mainly undemocratic results. The perversity of this engagement of the citizenry is that it leads to segregation rather than to tolerance.[36] On the other hand, as citizens build all types of walls and controls in the city space, they create limits to democratization. Through the creation of walls, residents re-create hierarchies, privileges, exclusive spaces, and rituals of segregation where they have just been removed from the political sphere. A city of walls is not a democratic space. In fact, it counters democratic possibilities. Fortunately, however, this process is not monolithic, and there is always the possibility that spaces such as Praça da Sé will fill again with people from all classes, as it did when they gathered to overthrow the military regime.

THE NEO-INTERNATIONAL STYLE:
SÃO PAULO AND LOS ANGELES

In contemporary São Paulo, disjunctive processes do not diminish the fact that rigid and policed boundaries and the increasing segregation of social

groups create a type of urban environment that impairs openness and freedom of circulation and jeopardizes anonymous and impersonal interactions
of people from different social backgrounds. These and similar transformations may be detected in many other cities around the world, although not
always with the same intensity or obviousness. From Johannesburg to Budapest, from Cairo to Mexico City, from Buenos Aires to Los Angeles, similar processes occur: the erection of walls, the secession of the upper classes,
the privatization of public spaces, and the proliferation of surveillance technologies are fragmenting the city space, separating social groups, and changing the character of public life in ways that contradict the modern ideals of
city life.[37] In the same way that these ideals have shaped cities all around
the world, transformations of that ideal, similar to those occurring in São
Paulo, are now affecting the character of urban space and public life. Thus
it is important to broaden the discussion and include some comparison.

Los Angeles is an interesting case for this comparison for two reasons.
First, several of the new instruments used to enforce segregation in cities
around the world seem to have been first developed in Los Angeles and its
metropolitan region. Some of these instruments are even considered to give
the region its distinctive character. Consequently such devices are more evident in L.A. than in other places and may help us to understand the process
that is still evolving in cities such as São Paulo. Second, Los Angeles's nonmodern public space is less explicitly uncivil than São Paulo's, and some of
its practices of segregation may not be immediately readable. In this regard,
São Paulo offers the clearer form and may guide the perception of L.A.'s
characteristics. The juxtaposition of the two cases therefore illuminates both
and suggests more general trends in the transformations of public space.[38]

Until the second half of the nineteenth century, Los Angeles and São
Paulo were insignificant towns. Industrialization and migration from the
turn of the century onward made them into large metropolitan regions. Spatially, however, they were laid out in completely different ways. São Paulo
grew according to a center-oriented urban model of European lineage that
has been modified only recently. Los Angeles, in contrast, has always been
dispersed and decentralized, favoring the suburbs. It has always been what
Fogelson (1967) calls a fragmented metropolis. Los Angeles epitomizes
American antiurban sentiment, the valorization of nature, and a preference
for small-scale communities, even within a global metropolis (Banham 1971;
Weinstein 1996).[39] The metropolitan region expanded under the form of a
fragmented "patchwork quilt of low-density suburban communities stretch-
ing over an extraordinarily irregular terrain of mountains, valleys, beaches,
and deserts. Both tying the fabric together and giving it its unusual elastic-

ity was first a remarkable network of interurban electric railways and then an even more remarkable freeway system" (Soja 1996a: 433–34).[40]

Although the city has always had a center, which grew around the original eighteenth-century pueblo and continues to accommodate the main administrative structures and a dynamic financial district, the center's relationship to the rest of the city is not that of a traditional downtown. The Los Angeles metropolitan region does not have a single center but rather a network of dynamic nuclei. The renovated downtown is only one of the region's economic and financial centers.[41] Everything in the metropolitan region, from housing to industry, has always been dispersed, and it decentralized further as the city grew. As a result, contemporary Los Angeles is "polynucleated and decentralized" (Soja 1989:194). This pattern, which is not new but is certainly not common for industrial cities, has sometimes been evoked to characterize its urbanism as postmodern (Dear 1996:85; Soja 1989 and 1996a). As a similar formula of urban expansion and urban structuring appears in other metropolitan regions, it becomes a model. This is suggested, for example, by Garreau's assertion that "every single American city that *is* growing, is growing in the fashion of Los Angeles, with multiple urban cores" (Garreau 1991:3; emphasis in original).

Although Los Angeles's urbanism has never been dense and concentrated, until the 1940s the expansion of residence and manufacture was essentially contained within the limits of the county. Between 1940 and 1970, the population of Los Angeles's metropolitan region tripled to almost ten million. This growth, however, occurred in the form of mass suburbanization, as is attested by the boom in the incorporation of cities, some of them already gated and walled in the 1960s (Soja and Scott 1996:8–9). Much of this expansion was sustained by the growth of the military-industrial complex. After 1970, although the rates of population growth were not as high, they were still the highest of all American metropolitan regions. Moreover, they were much higher in the outer counties, especially Orange County, than in L.A. (Soja and Scott 1996:11). Characterized by Soja as a "peripheral urbanization," this expansion created a multicentered region on the basis of high-tech, post-Fordist industrialization, luxury residential enclaves, huge regional shopping centers, programmed environments for leisure (such as Disneyland), links to major universities and the Department of Defense, and various enclaves of cheap labor, mostly immigrants (Soja 1989: chapters 8 and 9). Development during the last three decades in Los Angeles's metropolitan region is a departure from the pattern of residential suburbanization with dependency on downtown jobs. It exemplifies a new "exopolis" in which not only residences but also employment, production, and consumption expanded on the periphery and created relatively independent nuclei. The same type of development started to be detected in São Paulo's metropolitan region in the 1980s, although on a rather smaller scale.

The urban restructuring of Los Angeles accompanied an accelerated economic restructuring during the 1970s and 1980s, which transformed it into the largest industrial center in the United States. While the rest of the country was deindustrializing, L.A.'s industrial sector continued to expand. This expansion, however, involved a "shift in industrial organization and technology from the Fordist-Keynesian practices of mass production and mass consumption . . . to what is increasingly described today as a post-Fordist system of flexible production and corporate development" (Soja 1996a:438). In other words, the region went through a complex process of simultaneous deindustrialization and reindustrialization. Moreover, this happened concomitantly with a pronounced expansion in the service sector. From 1969 to 1989, "the service sector increased its dominance, from 45 percent to 58 percent of all jobs, making Los Angeles a more service-oriented economy than the nation as a whole" (Ong and Blumemberg 1996:318). This shift toward service indicates both a transformation in the region's economic structure and the new international role of Los Angeles, which became the site of massive foreign investment, the major urban center on the Pacific Rim, and the second largest banking center in the United States. These transformations occurred as the region also received a massive influx of immigrants from Asia and Latin America, which transformed the region's ethnic and racial composition. The population of Los Angeles County "shifted from 70 percent Anglo to 60 percent non-Anglo between 1960 and 1990, mostly living in ethnic enclaves" (Soja and Scott 1996:14). By 1980, L.A. was the most racially segregated of all American cities (Soja and Scott 1996:10).

As in many other global cities (Sassen 1991), Los Angeles's economic restructuring accentuated a bifurcation in the labor market between a growing high-wage, high-skill group of workers and a mass of low-wage, low-skill workers, often undocumented. It is not surprising, then, that economic disparity, always a characteristic of the city, deepened. Although the same happened throughout the country, reversing the social gains of previous decades, it was accentuated in Los Angeles. Ong and Blumemberg (1996) show that between 1969 and 1989 both the per capita income and the median family income increased in the city and were higher than the national averages. However, in Los Angeles the income distribution was more unequal. The GINI coefficient for Los Angeles increased from .368 in 1969 to .401 in 1979 and .444 in 1989, whereas the national rates were, respectively,

.349, .365, and .396 (Ong and Blumemberg 1996:319). At the same time, the income ratio—that is, the percent of income going to the poorest fifth of all families as a percentage of the income going to the richest fifth— dropped from 11.8 percent in 1969 to 9.7 percent in 1979 and to 7.8 percent in 1989).[42] The poverty rate increased, jumping from 2.8 percent of the population in 1969 to more than 15 percent in 1989 and an estimated 23 percent in 1993 (Ong and Blumemberg 1996:318–19, 322, 328). Homelessness became a feature of the region as jobs were lost in the economic restructuring process, the welfare state was dismantled, and the cost of housing escalated (Wolch and Dear 1993; Wolch 1996). Given the ethnic and racial makeup of the contemporary city, it is no surprise to verify that the economic disparity "coincide[s] with racial and ethnic divisions, leaving African-American, Latinos, and Asians disproportionately represented at the bottom of the economic ladder" (Ong and Blumemberg 1996:312). Although Los Angeles's indicators of inequality are still lower than São Paulo's, disparities and inequalities in both metropolitan regions increased as the regions went through economic crises and economic restructuring. We can only wonder if Los Angeles's pattern coincides with that of São Paulo, where the most severe rates of inequality are exactly in those areas where economic performance and restructuring have been most successful and where the wealthiest are moving into fortified enclaves.

After the 1980s, it was clear that another type of urbanization was happening in L.A.'s metropolitan region, one that differed markedly both from previous centered urban forms and from the traditional residential suburbanization. Various expressions have been coined to describe the new phenomenon: "peripheral urbanization," "outer cities," "exopolis," "edge cities," "postsuburban," and so on. For Edward Soja, who uses the first three expressions, the decentralization of Los Angeles surpasses the region itself and becomes "globalized" (1996a: 435). He argues that the new urban dynamics require completely new analytical perspectives. They should, for example, be able to make sense of L.A.'s role as "the world's most productive and influential center for the manufacturing and marketing of hyperreality" (1996a: 453). This specialized role of the region would translate into comprehensive theme-parking and "scamscape."[43]

Among the many characteristics of L.A.'s peripheral urbanization that separate it from traditional industrial urbanism, particularly notable is the absence of a densely built urban environment. Even in the central districts of L.A., which are largely laid out according to modernist design, there is no dense urban fabric whose solids would generate spaces able to frame the public and promote a meaningful pedestrian street life. Streets are wide and empty, and cars circulate rapidly. Walking is discouraged, and urban crowd do not congregate. Circulation in the public space is always mediated by the automobile—usually individual and private, since public transportation is limited and is certainly not a realistic alternative for the majority of the population. The primacy of the automobile constructs streets as the modernist, machine-oriented space of circulation and, therefore, as spaces for drivers, not for pedestrians. The typical streets in the Los Angeles region are obviously not corridor streets: they are usually wide, may have high speed limits, are truncated by large, empty spaces and gardens, and have empty or sometimes nonexistent sidewalks. These are the kinds of streets created by modernist devices, in which what is public is what is left over. As a result, "the city is experienced as a passage through space, with constraints established by speed and motion, rather than the static condition of solids, of buildings that define the pedestrian experience of traditional cities. The resulting detachment further privatizes experience, devalues the public realm, and, by force of the time spent in travel, contributes to isolation" (Weinstein 1996:35).

Even where corridor streets do provide a frame, as in the downtown area, street life is limited: people's activities are contained in the corporate buildings and their under- and overpass connections to shops, restaurants, and hotels. In other words, many functions of the street have been transferred to more sanitized, controlled, and privatized spaces, and the separation between the universe of wealth and business and that of poverty and homelessness becomes vast.[44]

Obviously, Los Angeles still has open and nonprivatized areas of relatively intense public use, in which something like a crowd can congregate. However, these areas seem to be mainly of two nonmodern types. One is the increasingly segregated and socially homogenized space in which people of only one social group circulate (Latino parks and Beverly Hills luxury shopping areas, for example). Such spaces do not favor heterogeneous, anonymous encounters. The other is specialized spaces mainly for leisure and consumption that have been transformed into a kind of theme park, like the Promenade in Santa Monica or the Venice boardwalk. These constitute the most significant category of spaces that still allow anonymous and heterogeneous encounters, and so one can only wonder what happens to the urban experience of encountering the other when it becomes something extraordinary—that is, something done only on weekends and in special spaces—and not a matter of routine.

Most of L.A.'s public life takes place in segregated, specialized, and enclosed environments such as malls, gated communities, entertainment centers, and theme parks of all sorts, whose creation Los Angeles pioneered.[45]

They are all privatized spaces, administered by enterprises or homeowners' associations whose interests are at odds with public administrations. Moreover, as Davis shows (1990: chapter 3), these private administrations may engage in various NIMBY ("not in my backyard") strategies to "protect their investment," passing all sorts of segregationist legislation to guarantee the exclusivity of their enclaves. These enclaves, usually for the better-off, exist in relation to the spaces left for the impoverished population—the parks and streets occupied by the homeless, the poor and ethnically diverse inner-city neighborhoods, the gang territories, the migrant camps and shanty-towns.[46] In other words, the wealthy, the poor, and those from different ethnic groups do not encounter each other in proximate spaces in contemporary Los Angeles.

Los Angeles exemplifies the new urban form in a much more explicit way than São Paulo, where the old center-oriented urbanism still provides a stage for anonymous and heterogeneous encounters. In L.A., streets are emptier, and the new types of decentered spaces produce apartheid zones for different social groups. Postsuburbia as a type of urban form is not about "open and undecidable" borders; it is not about the creation of spaces for the vitality of the heterogeneous public. Postsuburban spaces are about clear delimitations and separations, rigid boundaries, and predictable, policed encounters. Los Angeles is not only fragmented but enclaved. Its postsuburban pattern has created a metropolitan region that is more unequal and more segregated than most American cities. Separation is guaranteed more by modernist design devices than by walls, but although these are more subtle than São Paulo's, they generate what Soja calls the "carceral city" and Davis labels "fortress L.A." (Soja 1996a: 448–50; Davis 1990: chapter 4).

Compared to that of São Paulo, however, Los Angeles's fortification is mild. Where rich neighborhoods like Morumbi use high walls, iron fences, and armed guards, the West Side of L.A. uses mostly electronic alarms and small signs announcing "Armed Response." While São Paulo's elite clearly appropriate public spaces—closing public streets with chains and other physical obstacles and installing private armed guards to control circulation—L.A.'s elite still show some respect for public streets. However, walled communities that appropriate public streets are proliferating, and one wonders if Los Angeles's more discreet pattern of separation and surveillance is not in part related to the fact that the poor already live far from the West Side, whereas in Morumbi they live right across the street. Moreover, the Los Angeles Police Department—although considered one of the most biased and violent police forces the United States—still seems effective and non-violent compared to São Paulo's police.

Two analysts of Los Angeles have captured the transformations in the character of its built environment and public life in quite opposed and significant ways. Charles Jencks defends the new urbanism and the need to segregate spaces. In contrast, Mike Davis reads in the new configuration "the end of public space." I disagree with both while supporting many aspects of Davis's analysis.

Charles Jencks analyzes recent trends in Los Angeles's architecture in relation to a diagnosis of the city's social configuration. In his view, L.A.'s main problem is its heterogeneity, which inevitably generates chronic ethnic strife and explains episodes such as the 1992 uprising (1993:88). Since he considers this heterogeneity as constitutive of L.A.'s reality, and since his diagnosis of the economic situation is pessimistic, he predicts that ethnic tension will increase, the environment will become more defensive, and people will resort to increasingly diverse and mean-spirited measures of protection. Jencks sees the adoption of security devices as inevitable and as a matter of realism. Moreover, he discusses how this necessity is being transformed into art by styles that metamorphose hard-edged material needed for security into "ambiguous signs of inventive beauty and 'keep out'" (1993:89), and which design façades with their backs to the street to camouflage the contents of the houses. For him, the response to ethnic strife is a gimmicky stylistic slogan: "Defensible architecture and riot realism" (1993:89); this realism lies in architects' looking at "the dark side of division, conflict, and decay, and represent[ing] some unwelcome truths" (1993:91). Among these "truths" is the assertion that heterogeneity and strife are here to stay, that the promises of the melting pot can no longer be fulfilled. In this context, boundaries must be both clearer and more heavily defended. "Architecturally it [Los Angeles] will have to learn the lessons of Gehry's aesthetic and en-formality: how to turn unpleasant necessities such as chain-link fences into amusing and ambiguous signs of welcome/keep out, beauty/defensive space. . . . Defensible architecture, however regrettable as a social tactic, also protects the rights of individuals and threatened groups" (Jencks 1993:93).

Jencks identifies ethnic heterogeneity as the reason for Los Angeles's social conflicts and sees separation as a solution. His arguments resemble a form of reasoning that Balibar, following P. A. Taguieff, calls differentialist racism. It is a type of argument that naturalizes not racial belonging, but culture and racist conduct. It assumes that since cultural or ethnic differences are insurmountable, the attempt to abolish them would generate interethnic conflict and aggression. As a result, the argument goes, to avoid conflict people must "respect the 'tolerance thresholds', maintain 'cultural distances' or, in other words, in accordance with the postulate that individuals are the exclusive heirs and bearers of a single culture, segregate collectivities" (Balibar 1991:22–23). What Jencks proposes and admires in the intervention of some architects and planners in L.A.'s urban environment is the development of an aesthetic of separation and of a built environment that precludes unprogrammed and heterogeneous encounters. He is obviously not interested in fostering any of the ideals of the modern public, but exactly their opposite.

But Los Angeles's defensible architecture also has critics, and the most famous of these is Mike Davis. For Davis (1990, 1991, 1993), social inequality and spatial segregation are central characteristics of Los Angeles, and his expression "Fortress L.A." refers to the type of space presently being created in the city.

> Welcome to post-liberal Los Angeles, where the defense of luxury lifestyles is translated into a proliferation of new repressions in space and movement, undergirded by the ubiquitous "armed response." This obsession with physical security systems, and, collaterally, with the architectural policing of social boundaries, has become a zeitgeist of urban restructuring, a master narrative in the emerging built environment of the 1990s. . . . We live in "fortress cities" brutally divided between "fortified cells"' of affluent society and "places of terror"' where the police battle the criminalized poor. (Davis 1990:223–24)

Davis ascribes the increasingly segregated and privatized Los Angeles to a master plan of the postliberal (i.e., Reagan-Bush Republican) elite, a theme he reiterates in his analysis of the 1992 riots (Davis 1993). To Davis, contemporary Los Angeles represents a new "class war at the level of the built environment" and demonstrates that "urban form is indeed following a repressive function in the political furrows of the Reagan-Bush era. Los Angeles, in its prefigurative mode, offers an especially disquieting catalogue of the emergent liaisons between architecture and the American police state" (Davis 1990:228).

Davis's writing is marked by an indignation fully supported by a wealth of evidence. Nevertheless, he sometimes collapses complex social processes into a simplified scenario of warfare, which his own rich description defies. Moreover, the coincidence of São Paulo's current segregation with political democratization advises skepticism in affirming direct correspondences between political intentions and urban transformations. In spite of this limitation, Davis elaborates a remarkable critique of social and spatial segregation and associates the emerging urban configuration with the crucial themes of social inequality and political options. For him, there is nothing inevitable about "fortress architecture," and it has deep consequences for the way in which public space and public interactions are shaped.

In both São Paulo and Los Angeles the public space created by enclaves and devices of the "defensible" style fosters the reproduction of inequalities, isolation, and fragmentation.[47] As urban orders based on enclosure and on the policing of boundaries, these cities deny the modern ideal. Realizing how Los Angeles's contemporary urban environment is at odds with the modern public, Davis treats it as the "destruction of public space" (Davis 1990: chapter 4). Yet this unqualified phrase evades many questions. Are we dealing with the destruction of public space in general or with the creation of another type of public space, one that is undemocratic, does not tolerate indeterminacy, and negates the modern ideals of openness, heterogeneity, and equality? After all, the soviet type of monumental, modernist space in Moscow or Warsaw and the modernist type of Brasília are still public.[48] In the same way that the industrial city did not invent public space but only its modern version, today's destruction of modern public space is leading not to the end of public space altogether but to the creation of another kind. Privatization, enclosure, and distancing devices offer means not only of withdrawing from and undermining a certain public space (modern) but also of creating another public sphere: one that is fragmented, articulated, and secured by separation and high-tech devices, and in which equality, openness, and accessibility are not organizing values. The new spaces structure public life in terms of real inequalities: differences are not to be dismissed, taken as irrelevant, left unattended, or disguised in order to sustain ideologies of universal equality or myths of peaceful cultural pluralism. The new urban environment enforces inequalities and separations. It is an undemocratic and nonmodern public space.

Of course, many of those who have analyzed the new features of Los Angeles urbanism, such as Edward Soja (1996a and b) and Michael Dear (1996), would simply call it postmodern. However, they thereby emphasize certain aspects of L.A. life, such as flexibility, cultural syncretism, "social heterodoxy," and borderlessness, that directly contradict the aspects I have been emphasizing. Although these aspects are also part of L.A.'s public life, they are not the main features by which the built environment is organized. The notion of the postmodern is usually associated with experiences of fluidity and borderlessness; L.A.'s present urban environment is marked by opposite characteristics.[49]

São Paulo and Los Angeles probably have as many differences as similarities. Nevertheless, the juxtaposition of the two cases is especially suggestive. Their similarities suggest that patterns of segregation and urban restructuring cannot be understood only as local responses to local processes. Different cities constitute their particular built environment and public spaces in a broad dialogue, using instruments that are part of a common repertoire. The Garden City model, modernist design and city planning, and now the fortified enclaves, "outer cities," and theme parks are part of the repertoire from which different cities around the world are now drawing. At earlier times, there have been other elements in this repertoire, such as the Laws of the Indies, the corridor street, and Haussmann-style boulevards. The use of forms from the contemporary repertoire articulates a strong separation of social groups in a process that transcends the built environment. The fear of crime and the production of stereotypes of dangerous others (the poor and the migrant, for example) are other dimensions of the same process. Paulistanos' intense fear of crime and the city's high rates of violence and its high walls might tell us about similar, as yet less extreme tendencies in Los Angeles. In São Paulo tensions are higher than in L.A. because the ghetto is not as enclosed, inequalities are more pronounced, violence is greater, and the old urban model still keeps crowds on the streets.

The differences between the two cities, however, point up the specific histories and choices of each society. While Los Angeles is a metropolitan region that seems always to have favored dispersion, suburbanization, and privatization, São Paulo developed according to an European model that valued the center, where the main economic activities and the residences of the elites were concentrated. When the city expanded, the poor were sent further out, but the elite remained in the center. Although the center's importance has been an organizing principle in the city since its origins as the colonial village, São Paulo's urban environment is composed of various layers of experiments. It has expanded quickly and without much concern for historical preservation. For example, during this century Avenida Paulista has had two incarnations: as a street of mansions for the coffee producers and as an agglomeration of modernist buildings for corporations. The cityscape bears various inscriptions: an old downtown framed by neoclassical plans and architecture; the Garden City plan of upper-class neighborhoods; the Haussmann-inspired avenues; the vernacular architecture of the autoconstructed houses; the improvisation of the slums; and the postmodern-inspired design of the contemporary fortified enclaves. Some of these elements left a stronger mark on the built environment, as they were able to dictate its restructuring. The most important effect of the fortified enclaves seems to be exactly this: they alter the principle of centrality that has always organized the city space. After the radical opening toward the periphery in the 1940s (inspired by Haussmann), the present investment in "outer cities" and enclaves is probably the most radical change to the built environment, one that inaugurates a new pattern of segregation. The juxtaposition with Los Angeles indicates that the instruments causing this new pattern in São Paulo are not exclusively local but are part of a broader repertoire. It also suggests that we are dealing not only with a change in design styles but with a change in the character of public space. The new urban form challenges the modern and democratic public space.

Although political projects may not always be read directly into the urban environment, especially given its multilayered quality, the instruments available in the urban environment are related to different political projects. To use them, however, may not necessarily fulfill the intended goal. In fact, the authoritarian Haussmann created democratic spaces in Paris (Clark 1984), and the socialist modernists created undemocratic, empty spaces in Brasília and many other places around the world (Holston 1989). In what ways do urban form and political processes coincide in cities such as São Paulo and Los Angeles, and in what ways do they diverge? What democratic processes might be counteracting urban transformations and vice versa? If social inequalities seem to organize the urban environment instead of being put aside by a tolerance for differences and undecidable borders, what kind of model can we adopt for the public realm? Is democracy still possible in the new city of walls? What kind of polity will correspond to the new, fragmented public sphere in which interests are privately expressed—by homeowner associations, for example—and in which it becomes difficult to defend the common good?

CONTRADICTORY PUBLIC SPACE

In spite of their specificities, São Paulo and Los Angeles are today more socially unequal and more dispersed than they used to be, and many of the changes to the urban environment are causing separation between social groups, which are increasingly confined to homogeneous enclaves. Privatization and rigid boundaries (either material or symbolic) continuously fragment what used to be more open spaces and serve to keep groups apart. Nevertheless, the experience of the urban environment is not the only experience of the residents of theses cities, and it is certainly not their only experience either of social difference or of democracy. One of the qualities of Los Angeles repeatedly emphasized by its analysts is its multiculturalism, the presence of expressive numbers of different ethnic groups changing the makeup of a once predominantly Anglo city. These are the characteristics highlighted by those who, like Soja and Dear, look at its postmodern urbanism from a positive perspective instead of emphasizing its bleaker side, as Davis tends to do. Soja, for example, talks about a new cultural syncretism (Latino, Asian American), cross-cultural fusion, and coalition building (1996a). There is also talk about hybridity and border cultures. Some mention the importance of the mass media and new forms of electronic communication and their role in blurring boundaries and bridging distances, not just in L.A. but everywhere. In São Paulo, opposition to the segregationist and antidemocratic impulses of the built environment comes partly from the media but mainly from other sources: the democratization process, the proliferation of social movements, and the expansion of citizenship rights of the working classes and of various minorities.

In both São Paulo and Los Angeles, therefore, we can detect opposing social processes, some promoting tolerance of difference and the melting of boundaries, and some promoting segregation, inequality, and the policing of boundaries. In fact, we have in these cities political democracy with urban walls; democratic procedures used to promote segregation, as in the NIMBY movements; and multiculturalism and syncretic formations with apartheid zones, promoted by segregated enclaves. These opposing processes are not unrelated but rather tensely connected. They express the contradictory tendencies that characterize both societies. Both are going through significant transformations. Both have been unsettled by the opening and blurring of boundaries (migration and economic restructuring in Los Angeles, and democratization and economic crisis and restructuring in São Paulo). If we look for a moment at other cities around the world where enclaves are increasing, we see that some are going through similar processes of deep transformation and democratization: Johannesburg and Buenos Aires, for example. The unsettling of social boundaries is upsetting, especially for the elite. Their movement to build walls is thus understandable. The problem is that the consequences of fragmentation, privatization, and walling are severe. Once walls are built, they alter public life. The changes we are seeing in the urban environment are fundamentally undemocratic. What is being reproduced at the level of the built environment is segregation and intolerance. The space of these cities is the main arena in which these antidemocratic tendencies are articulated.

Among the conditions necessary for democracy is that people acknowledge those from different social groups to be co-citizens, having similar rights despite their differences. However, cities segregated by walls and enclaves foster the sense that different groups belong to separate universes and have irreconcilable claims. Cities of walls do not strengthen citizenship but rather contribute to its corrosion. Moreover, this effect does not depend directly on either the type of political regime or on the intentions of those in power, since the design of the enclaves and walls itself entails a certain social logic. The new urban morphologies of fear give new forms to inequality, keep groups apart, and inscribe a new sociability that runs against the ideals of the modern public and its democratic freedoms. When some people are denied access to certain areas and when different groups do not interact in public space, then references to ideals of openness, equality, and freedom as organizing principles for social life are no longer possible, even as fiction. The consequences of the new separateness and restriction of public life are serious: contrary to what Jencks (1993) thinks, defensible architecture and planning may promote conflict instead of preventing it, by making explicit the social inequalities and the lack of common ground. In fact, we may argue that the Los Angeles uprising was caused by social segregation rather than by the lack of separation and defenses.[50]

If the experiences of separateness expressed in the urban environment become dominant in their societies, people will distance themselves from democracy. However, given the disjuncture between different types of experiences in cities such as Los Angeles and São Paulo, there is also hope that the reverse could happen: that the experiences of the blurring of boundaries and of democratization will one day extend into the built environment.

PART 4

Violence, Civil Rights, and the Body

CHAPTER 9

Violence, the Unbounded Body, and the Disregard for Rights in Brazilian Democracy

The experience of violence is an experience of violation of individual or civil rights, and therefore it affects the quality of Brazilian citizenship. I have analyzed the increasing violence and fear of crime in São Paulo from a series of interconnected perspectives, and I conclude by considering them from the point of view of Brazilian democracy. Violence and disrespect for civil rights constitute one of the main dimensions of Brazil's disjunctive democracy. By calling it disjunctive, James Holston and I (1998) call attention to its contradictory processes of simultaneous expansion and disrespect for citizenship rights, processes that in fact characterize many democracies around the world today (Holston, forthcoming). Brazilian citizenship is disjunctive because, although Brazil is a political democracy and although social rights are reasonably legitimated, the civil aspects of citizenship are continuously violated.[1]

In this chapter I focus on one of the crucial aspects of the disjunction of Brazilian citizenship: the association of violence, disrespect for civil rights, and a conception of the body that I call the unbounded body. I analyze two interconnected issues that surfaced *after* the beginning of democratic rule in the early 1980s. The first issue is the widespread opposition to defenders of human rights. The second is a campaign for the introduction of the death penalty in the Brazilian constitution. These two issues have as their background the increase in violent crime and fear, and the urban tendencies toward fortification and new modes of discrimination that I have analyzed in the previous chapters. In these debates, a principal theme is the limits (or lack of limits) to intervention in the criminal's body. By discussing people's ideas about how the body of the criminal should be treated and punished, I hope to illuminate more widespread conceptions of the body and of rights.

My interest in exploring the association of violence, rights, and bodies derives from two sets of related concerns. First, I seek to understand the character of Brazilian democratic citizenship and the role violence plays in it. Second, I want to make this understanding talk back to theories of citizenship and rights. I approach these subjects as an anthropologist. I analyze citizenship and violence as lived experiences of the residents of São Paulo, that is, as specific ways in which Paulistanos engage available notions of rights, justice, punishment, and pain, and by doing this create a certain type of body politic as they reproduce a certain type of body. I build this analysis as a dialogue with theories of rights and violence, a dialogue whose expected result is not only to illuminate São Paulo's experience but also to problematize notions of citizenship and democracy. Because these notions are formulated on the basis of a specific Western European or American experience, to apply them directly to a country like Brazil results only in seeing it as a failed or incomplete modernity. Rather than consider only one model of citizenship, democracy, or modernity, I suggest that different societies have diverse ways of engaging the elements generally available in a common repertoire of modernity to create their specific nations, citizenries, and democracies. The peculiarity of the Brazilian engagement comes from the fact that social rights (and secondarily political rights) are historically far more legitimated than individual and civil rights, and that violence and interventions in the body are broadly tolerated. This tolerance for the manipulation of bodies, the proliferation of violence, and the delegitimation of justice and civil rights are intrinsically connected.

HUMAN RIGHTS AS "PRIVILEGES FOR BANDITS"

Disrespect for human rights is widespread in Brazil, as the absurd record of police abuses indicates. Although this disrespect is by no means restricted to police abuse or to the universe of crime, I focus on these areas because it is in this context that human rights have come to be explicitly opposed by many Brazilians.[2] While the violation of human rights is common in the contemporary world, opposing human rights and conceiving of them as bad, even reproachable, in the context of a political democracy is unique. To understand how this became possible and how human rights were transformed from legitimate rights into "privileges for bandits" is revealing of various elements of Brazilian culture and political life. I focus on São Paulo, but because some of the issues I address are certainly broader, I sometimes refer to Brazil in general.

Although human rights are in theory a self-proclaimed ideal and a universal value, in fact they are culturally and politically interpreted and modified, as are civil rights in general. This interpretation is not predetermined: in São Paulo, the defense of human rights has helped both to enlarge the recognition of rights (during the military regime) and to contest them (under democratic rule). In other words, the meaning of human rights depends on how the concept is politically articulated in specific contexts.

Defenders of human rights were not stigmatized when the cases concerned middle-class political prisoners and when the so-called *abertura* process was just beginning. On the contrary, respect for human rights was an important demand of the political movement that ended the military regime. At that time (the late 1970s), rights for political prisoners were demanded by various groups following the leadership of intellectuals, center to left politicians, the Catholic Church and its Commission of Justice and Peace, and civil associations such as the Movimento Feminino Pela Anistia (Women's Movement for Amnesty) and the OAB (Ordem dos Advogados do Brasil, the Brazilian Bar Association).[3] Attention to common prisoners' rights was not included in the demands, although violation of their rights was routine. The campaign for amnesty of political prisoners—many of whom were imprisoned, and also tortured, without a trial or even a judiciary mandate—became intertwined with other political movements demanding the return of constitutional rule, free elections at all levels of government, freedom of expression, freedom of the press, freedom of organization for political parties and trade unions, and so on, which culminated in the overthrow of military rule.

After the Amnesty Bill was approved in 1979 and political prisoners were freed, and as the electoral democracy started to consolidate, groups defending human rights (those mentioned above, plus the newly created Centro Santos Dias and Comissão Teotônio Vilela) turned their attention and action toward regular prisoners, who have continued to be tortured and forced to live in degrading conditions to the present day.[4] By changing their focus, groups defending human rights significantly broadened the scope of their activities. This trend runs counter to that in other Latin American countries and other newly democratized societies, where human rights debates remain tied to the activities of the overthrown authoritarian regimes.[5] However, the idea of guaranteeing human rights to "criminals" proved unacceptable to the majority of the residents of São Paulo.

In the 1980s, therefore, it was not the idea of rights per se that was contested, nor even the idea of human rights in general. Human rights were contested only when they were associated with nonpolitical prisoners. We must therefore look to the image of the criminal and of the justice system to understand how human rights were interpreted and then rejected by the population. This investigation reveals the fragility of individual and civil rights in Brazil.

The main attack on human rights, which consolidated the still-pervasive negative images to which the population refers, was first articulated during Franco Montoro's term as governor in the state of São Paulo. Montoro, the first elected governor after military rule, campaigned by guaranteeing the return of the rule of law *(estado de direito)*, and once elected he tried both to control police abuses and to ameliorate prison conditions in São Paulo (see chapter 5). During his administration (1983–1987) , violent crime increased significantly in São Paulo, and the concern with crime came to the forefront of political debates. Political opposition to Montoro and to his political parties (initially the PMDB and then the PSDB), as well as resistance to the process of democratic consolidation, began to center on human rights. While Montoro was supported by human rights groups and by center to left political parties, right-wing politicians accused him and his allies of protecting criminals. In this campaign, human rights were called "privileges for bandits."

Montoro selected a well-known defender of political prisoners and human rights, José Carlos Dias, to be his secretary of justice. During his three years in office (1983–1986), Dias and his policy of "humanizing the prisons" met intense opposition; this was articulated by and expressed in the mass media, especially through such newspapers as *O Estado de S. Paulo* and the radio programs on which crimes are renarrated (such as Afanasio Jazadji's). Among Dias's most controversial measures to defend the rights of prisoners were the creation of officially elected commissions of representatives of prisoners; the installation of mailboxes inside prisons for inmates to send complaints directly to the disciplinary office *(corregedoria)* without the mediation of the prison administration; and the institution of "intimate visits" *(visita íntima)* for prisoners (during which they could have sexual relations with their partners). Moreover, the secretary was criticized for his direct approach to inmates, including his participation in a televised debate with them. The defense of human rights for common prisoners thus became a publicly discussed issue and a matter of government policy. The administration's approach was summarized in the idea that prisoners had (human) rights to be protected. According to Dias, one of the most important achievements of his administration was to transmit to the prisoner "our conviction that he is a citizen, although with his rights restricted by a condemnatory sentence. He was condemned to lose his liberty, but only that, and in accordance with the limits of the sentence. He was not condemned to the humiliations and other types of violence that occur inside the prison" (interview, 10 September 1990).

Opponents of this view skillfully articulated in the mass media a series of prejudices, stereotypes, and beliefs shared by large parts of the population. Three examples follow. The first is part of a manifesto of the Associação dos Delegados de Polícia (Association of Police Chiefs) of the state of São Paulo, addressed to the population of the city on 4 October 1985. The manifesto appeared one month before São Paulo's mayoral elections and in the context of Montoro's attempts to reform the police (see chapter 5).

> The situation today is one of total anxiety for you and total tranquility for those who kill, rob, rape. Your family is destroyed and your patrimony, acquired with a lot of sacrifice, is calmly being reduced. Why does this happen? You know the answer. Believing in promises, we chose the wrong governor, the wrong political party, the PMDB. How many crimes have occurred in your neighborhood, and how many criminals were found responsible for them? You also know this answer. They, the bandits, are protected by the so-called human rights, something that the government considers that you, an honest and hardworking citizen, do not deserve.

The second example comes from an article in the newspaper *Folha de S. Paulo* on September 11, 1983. It was written by Antonio Erasmo Dias, the former secretary of public security during military rule, an active member of the "security bloc" supporting a violent police, and a lobbyist for the private security industry.

> The population's dissatisfaction with the police, including their demand for tougher action, in what can be considered the responsibility of Montoro's government, originates from the inflated philosophy of "human rights," applied in a unilateral mode in favor of bandits and marginals. This philosophy gives preference to the marginal, giving him the "right" of going around armed, robbing, killing, and raping.

The third example comes from the daily radio program of Afanasio Jazadji, one of the most popular radio stars in São Paulo. Jazadji defines himself as a police reporter and used to host a program in which he renarrated crimes. He is known by his deep voice, the disrespectful way he refers to suspected criminals, his defense of the police and of the death penalty, and his radical opposition to human rights. He opposes humanizing prisons, police reform, and some other innovations of Montoro's government, like the women's police stations. His influence is evident: people I interviewed often mentioned him to justify their views, and in 1986, in a campaign based entirely on attacking human rights and Montoro's policies, Jazadji received the highest number of votes of any candidate for State Congress (three hundred thousand votes in the city of São Paulo and more than half a million in the state). He is also a member of the "security bloc." The following quotation comes from a program on Rádio Capital on 25 April 1984, the day the National Congress voted to deny the population the right to vote for president.

> Someone should take all those irredeemable prisoners, put them against the wall and fry them with a blow torch. Or instead throw a bomb in the middle of them: boom!, end of the problem.[6] They have no family, they don't have anything, they don't have anything to worry about, they only think about doing evil, and why should we worry about them? . . .
> Those bastards, they consume everything, millions and millions a month. Let us get this money and transform it into hospitals, nurseries, orphanages, asylums, and provide a respectable life for those who really deserve to have this dignity. Now, for those type of people . . . people? To treat them as people! We're offending humankind!

These opponents of human rights operate within the categories, prejudices, and strategies of the talk of crime. Their discourses articulate clearcut, stereotypical categories associated with the opposition of good and evil. In contrast, people who defend prisoners' rights on the basis of a humanitarian discourse (such as José Carlos Dias) rely on relativizations and insist on considering the various dimensions of a situation: "They are citizens, although with their rights restricted"; "They have to be punished, but only within the limits of the law." The first type of discourse has proved infinitely more popular.

These discourses against human rights use three principal strategies. The first is to deny the humanity of criminals. Prisoners are represented as those who have committed the most violent crimes (murder and rape) and thus as people who have violated human nature, are dominated by evil, and who belong only to the space of crime: they have no family, no ties to others, they "offend humankind." The discussion never refers to less serious crimes, although it is obvious that prisons are not populated exclusively by murderers and rapists. Moderate examples do not serve the talk of crime nor the radical classifications by which the criminal is put on the fringes of humanity, society, and the polity. Both the talk of crime and the discourse against human rights rely on simplifications and stereotypes to create a symbolic criminal who is the essence of evil. On the other side of the debate, arguments in favor of human rights try to confront these well-established stereotypes. Their strongest challenge is to affirm that criminals are fully human—something many people disagree with.

A second strategy used by those attacking human rights is to associate the state administration's efforts to enforce the rule of law, to control the police, to reform prisons, and to defend human rights with the fact that crime has increased. In other words, democratization itself is held responsible for the increase of crime and violence. The success of this association was responsible not only for the rise of opposition to Montoro's administration but also for making it more difficult for his administration to guarantee the rule of law.

A third line of attack, and the core of the argument, is to compare the policies of humanizing prisons to the concession of privileges for bandits. This is a popular position because it resonates with the dominant experience of the justice system for the majority of the population. Although the working classes are beginning to use the law, and the legal arena has been the site of new experiments that are for the first time benefiting them, these experiences are not enough to change people's negative perceptions of the institutions of order and the widespread lack of confidence in the justice system.[7] Most people believe that "justice is a joke"; they believe that both the police and the judiciary favor the upper classes and rarely dispense justice to the working classes. Justice becomes a privilege of the rich. Opponents of human rights make use of this point, asking why criminals should have this privilege if the majority does not have its rights respected. Sometimes, as in Jazadji's comment, conservative politicians set the human rights of prisoners in opposition to the social rights of the majority of the population: they argue that to assure decent treatment to prisoners is to spend money that would be better used to provide much-needed services for the majority of the population. In sum, the good of many citizens is always opposed to the privileges of some noncitizens who are "barely humans." The defenders of human rights are transformed, consequently, into people working against the rights of honest citizens and in favor of criminals.[8]

The same anti–human rights discourse has led to demands for severe punishment for criminals, including the death penalty, summary executions, and sometimes torture. Humanitarian methods and restrictions on police behavior are considered to have contributed to an increase in crime. In the context of the increase in crime and fear of crime, the population has asked for tougher punishments and a more violent police, not for human rights. When the police have acted violently, as in the 1992 massacre at the Casa de Detenção or in summary executions, a considerable part of the population has supported them.

As I described in chapter 5, Montoro was followed by two governors who abandoned any idea of respect for human rights and who supported instead a tough policy of public security that made police abuses escalate. It was only almost a decade later that human rights came back into the discourse and policies of state administrators. After Fernando Henrique Cardoso became president and Mário Covas governor in 1995, both the federal and the state government of São Paulo tried to curb human rights violations. These two administrations, which were reelected in 1998, have been trying to implement plans guaranteeing human rights. Although the difficulties have been immense, in the last decade resistance to the defense of human rights has diminished. Although the same kind of anti-rights discourse continues to be formulated by the same politicians, and although the population continues to repeat these arguments (as some of my interviews confirm), the defense of human rights causes less passionate opposition now. Probably this change is related to the fact that democracy has consolidated since the late 1980s and is now routine rather than threatening, as it was considered by the right wing in the early 1980s. Moreover, during the last decade human rights has become an important issue internationally and is a more common theme in the mass media, where it is not always represented in derogatory terms. Although these are positive signs of transformation, there are plenty of signs of continued support for police abuses, private and violent revenge, and the death penalty.

DEBATING CAPITAL PUNISHMENT

Current debates about the legalization of capital punishment in Brazil have as their background the contrast between the de facto violence exercised against alleged criminals and legislation that prohibits violent forms of punishment. Although police violence and private violence (by the so-called *justiceiros* or vigilante groups) have been extremely common in Brazil, capital punishment for nonpolitical crimes has not been legal for the last century.

Hanging was legal in Brazil during the imperial period (1822–1889) in cases of slave insurrection, murder, and felony murder (robbery followed by murder), but not for political crimes. Brazil's last legal execution, which occurred in 1855, was a clear miscarriage of justice.[9] Thereafter the emperor granted clemency to everyone sentenced to death. The death penalty was eliminated in 1890, with the beginning of the Republic, except for war crimes, as determined by the military code. Prohibition of the death penalty was confirmed in similar terms by all four constitutions written under democratic rule.[10]

The two constitutions written under authoritarian regimes, however, constitute exceptions. In 1937, Getúlio Vargas inaugurated his dictatorship by imposing a new constitution that called for capital punishment for six types of crimes. Five were political crimes, and the sixth was homicide involving extreme perversity. (Despite this, the death penalty was not included in the penal code of 1940, still in effect.) In 1969, the military regime reintroduced the death penalty through Institutional Act 14, but reserved it exclusively for political crimes. The regime saw itself waging a war against terrorism and extended military legislation to the cases of the so-called urban guerrilla. During these two periods, however, there were no legal executions of political prisoners. In the Brazilian Republic, capital punishment has been an instrument conceived but not used by dictatorships to deal with political prisoners. In contrast, it has been prohibited but used illegally (in the form of summary executions) and with relative frequency to deal with common crime and political opposition.

The idea of a death penalty was reintroduced into public debates in the late 1980s—during the democratization process—when fear of crime, violent crime, and police violence started to increase. It is frequently proposed as a punishment for felonies: robbery followed by murder, rape followed by death, kidnapping followed by death, and crimes involving cruelty (these are terms from bills discussed in the National Congress). The defenders of capital punishment are primarily right-wing politicians, more or less the same ones who attack human rights; many of them are supporters of the military regime and the police. In 1987, during the Constitutional Assembly, a proposal to introduce the death penalty was rejected by 392 votes to 90. The 1988 constitution establishes that there will be no death penalty (article 5, insert 47), prohibits life imprisonment, and sets the longest possible prison term at thirty years.

This defeat has not kept right-wing politicians from renewing their proposal whenever a well-publicized violent crime occurs. This group dominates public debates about capital punishment, and supporters of human rights frequently find themselves in a defensive position. In spite of the efforts of the many lawyers and intellectuals who write on the subject, the public debate is dominated in the media by the imagery of the talk of crime.[11] A few simple arguments are repeated over and over, with extremely prejudiced opinions often expressed on both sides. Although the debate in newspapers and news programs is essentially a debate among the elite, both sides frequently invoke "the people" to justify their arguments and adopt a paternalistic, even disrespectful, way of talking about them. One of the most frequent arguments in favor of capital punishment is that it reflects popular sentiment.[12] This argument is substantiated by public opinion polls indicating that around 70 percent of the population supports the death penalty.[13]

Right-wing politicians argue that, in the context of widespread violence and the failure of the judiciary system, only an extreme measure like the death penalty can provide a solution. They think of the death penalty more in terms of revenge than in terms of the law or reducing crime. They do not say that capital punishment would solve the problem of violence in general, and only a minority argues that the death penalty would deter others from committing similar crimes. However, they insist that because people who commit violent crimes are irredeemable and dominated by evil, executing them forestalls further crimes they might commit and, to cite their own rhetoric, "saves innocent lives." They also use economic arguments, claiming that it is too expensive to keep an irredeemable criminal in prison and that the money should be used for social policies to benefit the poor. Their central point, however, is to avenge crime. Although they are trying to adopt the death penalty legally, the references in their discourses are those of personal vengeance, and it is in these terms that the popular debate is framed.[14]

Death penalty defenders and human rights opponents display impressive skill in manipulating the imagery that makes up the repertoire of the talk of crime. They always argue in empirical terms, relying on examples and individual cases. Their campaigns peak whenever a highly publicized crime occurs, and they retell the events with all the simplifications allowed by the repertoire of good versus evil. The following two examples are from January 1993, following two famous murders: that of Daniella Perez, a soap opera actress from the Globo network, who was killed by a fellow actor, her estranged boyfriend on the show; and that of Míriam Brandão, a five-year-old girl who was kidnapped and then killed, allegedly because she cried too much. The first quotation is from Amaral Netto, the federal deputy from PDS (Partido Democrático Social) of Rio de Janeiro, who has repeatedly proposed adopting the death penalty at the National Congress.[15]

> Do not believe in the rehabilitation of the murderers who killed
> that teacher in Rio Grande do Sul, Adriana from Alphaville,[16] and
> Míriam from Belo Horizonte. . . . You know that we have millions
> of adolescents on the streets who are victims of murder and drugs.
> Do you think we have money to resocialize this type of bandit, when
> we don't have money to feed those people? [We don't] have money
> to generate employment and housing either. What is the best way to
> invest? To invest in the criminal, or in children who don't have any-
> thing to eat? . . . You know that the cost of maintaining a man impris-

oned for life is very high. It's not a case of killing in order to save money. It's a case of saying: Let's execute him according to certain parameters in order to prevent him from running away and committing the same crime again. (*Jornal da Tarde*, 18 January 1993)

At the end of this interview, Amaral Netto was asked if the idea of taking someone's life had ever tormented him. His response was a gem of the logic of private revenge: "Not me. I would be the first executioner to assassinate the young man who killed that girl. I, the father of seven children, thirteen grandchildren, and two great-grandchildren, would take the greatest pleasure in killing him."

The second example comes from a newspaper article by Alberto Marino Júnior, a São Paulo state judge.

A small child, victim of kidnapping, is executed by her tormentor because away from her parents she was crying too much. The homicide, committed with refined perversity, touched the nation and reopened the polemic about the death penalty. . . .

As far as human rights are concerned, it is necessary to pay more attention to the human rights of the man of goodwill rather than—as has been done—to those of the beasts disguised as people, who randomly slaughter their defenseless victims. Our people are naturally docile and ready to sacrifice. They are content with a little bread, soccer, carnival, a place to live, and a simple and honest job. Nevertheless, recently people have been feeling cornered by the criminals. Many times they have even resorted to lynching, which is the immediate form of the death penalty, without trial and sentence, that is, they have adopted a very bad solution which may give occasion to irreparable mistake. . . .

It is necessary to prevent dozens of defenseless victims from being massacred by a little gang of coward villains, spared by questionable "human rights." It is necessary to punish in exemplary faction the bastard who kidnapped the little girl and gave himself the right to kill her. (*Folha de S. Paulo*, 16 January 1993)

The choice of words always highlights the horror of the case—the little child executed because she was crying for her parents—and the inhuman character of the criminals. They are "beasts" dominated by evil, "villains," "bastards." As such, they become natural candidates for execution—the only "solution" given the impossibility of their rehabilitation—and absurd candidates for protection in the name of "debatable 'human rights.'" Criminals are also frequently set in opposition to "the people," as evil is opposed to good. As Amaral Netto hints obliquely, to kill them would mean saving money to take care of the needy. Judge Marino Júnior contrasts the "beasts" with a traditional, elitist view of "our people": docile, content with a few things, but, it seems, exasperated by increasing criminality that leads them to take justice into their own hands.

The logic of personal revenge is taken for granted. For the judge, the lynching of criminals is not acceptable; but because killing them makes sense, the death penalty should be made legal, allowing the death of the "beast" and the satisfaction of vengeance. Amaral Netto takes the logic of personal revenge to the limit. He sees himself as the avenger: a man from an honorable family who would willingly be the first Brazilian executioner *(carrasco)* and personally "assassinate" Míriam's killer. There is no talk of law here. A congressional representative, Amaral Netto is pushing to establish the death penalty in law, but the popular discourse with which he supports it relies on the references of personal vengeance that dominate the talk of crime.

Many more people oppose the death penalty in the newspapers than defend it. All the people and institutions who publicly defend human rights are also against the death penalty, because for them the two issues are inseparable. This principle is clear in an article by Fábio Konder Comparato, a lawyer, law professor, and member of the Justice and Peace Commission.

> There is no democracy without respect for the fundamental rights
> of the human being. The regime of popular democracy, when it is dis-
> connected from human rights, is not democratic. . . . The death penalty
> does not imply the disrespect of any common right, but means the nega-
> tion of the most fundamental of human rights, that which constitutes
> the root or source of all rights: the right to life.
>   The idea of human rights originated from a demand for individual
> protection against acts of public power. The fact that a penalty may
> have been created by law or applied in a regular due process does not
> mean that it should be considered legitimate when it violates a funda-
> mental right of the human being. *(Folha de S. Paulo,* 21 March 1991)

Many participants in this debate argue similarly that the death penalty violates a basic human right and as such is illegitimate, even if codified in law. They also argue that the causes of violence and crime are social and structural and cannot be addressed by a measure like the death penalty. Accordingly, they propose reforms whose purpose is to transform society, the state, and the judiciary system: their concern is to guarantee that the institutions in charge of crime work better (they insist on judiciary and prison system reforms) and that the main causes of social problems, such as poverty, are addressed. One version of this argument was articulated by José Bisol, a federal deputy from the PSB, in the debate with Amaral Netto.

> The Brazilian state is falling apart, has no efficacy. It's a state that does not have enough authority and is dissociated from society. And since Brazilian society is cruelly disorganized, it is visible and palpable that we will not be able to establish a relationship of legitimation between the application of the death penalty by this state and in this society and the justice system. . . . When we have a more just and organized society and a more just and productive state, evidently violence will be controlled. (*Jornal da Tarde*, 18 January 1993)

Not surprisingly, social and structural arguments against the death penalty also draw on the vocabulary of the talk of crime. Moreover, these arguments have an evolutionist touch: since society and the state are at fault for the increased violence, when they become more just and organized, violence will naturally be controlled. Expressed by a member of the socialist party, this view can be seen as a version of the traditional Marxist argument that social life will improve naturally after the revolution. But arguments that associate crime with poverty and marginality reinforce the stereotype linking criminality to poverty, a link that is taken for granted even when it is being explained. In fact, one of the most striking aspects of arguments against the death penalty (especially those of left-wing politicians identified with popular interests) is how easily they reproduce stereotypes of the working classes. Poor people are commonly portrayed as being incapable of knowing and reasoning or of judging things for themselves, and therefore as easily influenceable—but only by the wrong arguments, it seems, as the majority of the working classes favor the death penalty.

Another, related argument in which sociological reasoning reinforces negative stereotypes is the claim that life is cheap in Brazil. Articles from both sides of the debate assert that people have become so used to poverty, terrible living conditions, and violence that they are insensitive to the value of life. In the article cited above, Fábio Comparto argues that the death penalty debate exposes a "traditional disdain for human life" among Brazilians and concludes that defenders of the death penalty exploit a "mental and social malformation" that characterizes Brazilian society. He writes that "in a country in which 60 percent of the population vegetate below the level of tolerable poverty, . . . man in fact is worth very little" (*Folha de S. Paulo*, 21 March 1991). Some people argue that because of this devaluation, the death penalty would have no effect: people (especially criminals, who are seen as having no feelings) would be undeterred by it. An opponent of capital punishment, the criminal judge Roberto Caldeira Barioni, has said: "The criminal is not afraid of dying, especially the Brazilian criminal, an offspring of misery. His life is not life, it is simply outliving, so miserable, so bad that death does not scare him" (*O Estado de S. Paulo,* 15 May 1991).

Another common way of arguing against capital punishment is to bring up miscarriages of justice or its implementation in the United States. Statistics are used to demonstrate the possibility of racial bias and to insist that this form of punishment does not deter crime. José Carlos Dias, one of the many lawyers to express this opinion, thinks the main deterrent to criminal activity is the certainty of punishment and not the duration or type of penalty. For the certainty of punishment to become a reality in Brazil, he contends, it is necessary "to change the judiciary system and the prison system, because nowadays in Brazil you only have the certainty of impunity" (*Folha de S. Paulo,* 18 January 1993). This argument of impunity, which is certainly an accurate description of what happens in Brazil, has been used by defenders and opponents of the death penalty alike. José Carlos Dias, the secretary of justice who tried to reform the prison system in São Paulo, thinks that changes should go in the direction of the respect for human rights and the rule of law. Right-wing politicians in favor of capital punishment, however, use the argument of impunity to call for stricter laws and to attack the 1988 constitution. Among them is the former president José Sarney, who opposes the death penalty on religious grounds but still uses the rhetoric favoring punishment. "Before talking about the death penalty we should extinguish the permissive and unjust legislation that favors the criminal and which was consecrated in the Constitution. . . . Nowhere in the world is there a single legislation more feeble, more unjust, more in favor of the criminal than the Brazilian legislation. It stimulates crime and ignores the victim, who has only one right—to die" *(Folha de S. Paulo,* 15 January 1993).

The idea that the 1988 constitution—written and promulgated during Sarney's presidency—should be modified is common among representatives of the right wing and people of all classes who think it protects criminals by redefining the requirements for arrest. These were introduced in the 1988 constitution with the intention of preventing police arbitrariness. However, when people feel that to refrain from arresting—or even killing—criminals right away leaves the citizenry vulnerable and unprotected, legal procedures that slow down the process are condemned. In general, whereas defenders of capital punishment criticize legal institutions when they create impediments to immediate revenge, its opponents denounce them for their retrograde character. Criminal lawyers critical of the Brazilian penal system, which relies almost exclusively on imprisonment, argue that "modern countries" use more subtle and less violent methods of punishment, and therefore it makes no sense to regress to violence. For them, violence is not a remedy for violence but only the cause of more violence, and it can even send the message that it is good to kill. Finally, some people point to the widespread illegal killing of alleged criminals by police and vigilante groups in Brazil and assert that if killing criminals were able to put an end to violence, it should have already done so.

Religious beliefs are often cited in the debate on capital punishment. In Brazil, the Catholic Church is one of the main institutions that defends human rights and attacks capital punishment, a position it links with opposing legal abortion. Representatives of the Jewish community have also written against the death penalty.[17] However, most religions fail to exercise a strong influence on this subject. In the survey by O Estado de S. Paulo on the death penalty in January 1993, there was little variation by gender, education, or socioeconomic position, although the survey did show stronger support among the poorest social strata (74 percent of the two lowest income strata were pro–death penalty, compared to 63 percent of the two highest). The only religion that seems to influence opinions about death penalty is Pentecostalism. Only 37 percent of Pentecostalists were in favor of capital punishment, compared to 74 percent of all Catholics (the highest percentage) and 68 percent of Umbandistas (a syncretic Afro-Brazilian religion).[18]

In the early 1990s a proposal was made that capital punishment be decided by plebiscite. The proposal was made by the supporters of the death penalty who calculated that they would not be able to garner enough votes in Congress to pass a constitutional amendment but felt they had enough popular support for a successful plebiscite.[19] The irony is that among those calling for implementation of this democratic instrument, just incorporated by the new constitution, are various politicians who not only criticize that constitution for its "protection for bandits" but who were also long-term supporters of the military regime. In fact, this debate seems to invert political logic in many ways. It forced opponents of capital punishment into a defensive position from which they had to oppose the democratic procedures they had struggled to introduce into the constitution. Although they had strong legal support for their position, they were vulnerable to accusations of being antidemocratic and elitist while their rivals appeared genuinely "popular."

Three fundamental arguments are used against a plebiscite: that it is unconstitutional, inopportune, and inadequate. The basis for the first are two articles of the 1988 constitution: article 5, which guarantees the "inviolability of the right to life" and establishes that there will be no death penalty (insert 47); and article 60, regarding constitutional amendments, which establishes in paragraph 4, insert 4, that there will be no deliberation of proposals aimed at "abolishing individual rights and guarantees." The plebiscite is called inopportune because it could be proposed at "emotional moments"—either when people are shocked by notorious crimes and influenced by television propaganda, or when they are suffering the effects of a serious social crisis. Under these circumstances, common people would not be able to decide rationally. Moreover, they would not have reliable information and would be under the negative influence of television, which makes them accustomed to violence and to the idea of the death penalty. Once again, these positions deny poor people's ability to consider arguments rationally and decide by themselves: "They are not rational, do not plan, do not save." They were expressed, for example, by Miguel Reali Júnior, a lawyer and secretary of public security during Montoro's administration.

> To submit the nation to an emotional clash, passing to each Brazilian at this moment of profound social crisis the decision to introduce or not the death penalty, is an irresponsibility. . . . With the plebiscite will come a climate of passion in relation to a theme whose analysis requires, first of all, exemption, contemplation, and peace of mind; that is, exactly what is most lacking among Brazilians at this moment of serious privations.
>
> The dramatization of violence, especially by the mass media, will allow the avalanche of instincts and the satisfaction of the worst of feelings, which is resentment. . . . Moreover, if the state has a monopoly on the legitimate use of violence, that is of punishment, this should be done rationally. But with the plebiscite, reason will submit to the emotional and unreflective opinion of the individual, and the result may be the authorization for official assassination, the passionate approval of a bureaucratic and cold extermination of life. (*Folha de S. Paulo,* 20 April 1991)

The third argument against the plebiscite is that it is an inadequate means to decide such a serious topic. Human rights cannot be abolished legitimately, even by the majority, argues Dyrceu Aguiar Dias Cintra Júnior, judge in the state of São Paulo and member of the Associação Juízes para a Democracia (Association of Judges for Democracy). "The respect for human rights should never depend on public opinion. Torture would never be admissible even if it had been approved in a plebiscite. To invoke popular sovereignty in this case constitutes demagogy taken to its furthest extremes. In fact, the juridical principles consecrated by humankind were not established by the number of votes" (*O Estado de S. Paulo*, 15 January 1993).

Capital punishment is rarely opposed in Brazil on the grounds of cruelty, which is the argument set forward by Amnesty International. In Brazil's debate, I could find this argument expressed only by a foreign envoy of Amnesty International, Ezat Abdel Fattah, who maintains that democracy and the abolition of capital punishment come together, and that, like slavery, this form of penalty has only a past, not a future. According to him, "The death penalty is a cruel, inhuman, and degrading penalty which violates all the international conventions on human rights. There is no place for it in a modern juridical system, administered by human beings and therefore fallible."[20] Although the absence of an association of capital punishment with cruelty may be striking, it makes sense in the context of the unbounded notion of the body and the support for painful forms of punishment that are common in Brazil.

PUNISHMENT AS PRIVATE
AND PAINFUL VENGEANCE

The debates on both human rights and the death penalty reveal a central tension between two views of punishment. The first is the perspective of law, justice, and the judiciary system. The second is the perspective of vengeance, of the body, and of pain as an instrument of punishment. These two references are articulated in quite different ways by people on either side of these debates. The defenders of human rights and critics of the death penalty speak from the perspective of legality and the judiciary system and are opposed to any form of punishment that inflicts pain. However, the vast majority of the population experiences the judiciary system as ineffective and unjust. The defenders of human rights know this well, and they concentrate on criticizing and reforming the judiciary and the prison system. But they never abandon the vantage point of law and the legal order. For them, crime should always be dealt with by the public system of revenge, and only the judicial system can stop cycles of vengeance. However, because they speak exclusively from the perspective of the judiciary system and are the only ones doing so in a context in which that system does not enjoy legitimacy, the defenders of human rights and reforms are cast as apologists for the system as it functions now, and they are treated accordingly, with disbelief and cynicism. Although they criticize the legal and prison systems, they are seen by the majority of the population as trying to further distort the judicial system by guaranteeing privileges for bandits.

People who attack human rights and defend the death penalty enjoy the support of the majority of Brazilians and usually speak in the polar imagery of the talk of crime. They, too, assert that the judiciary system is not working. However, instead of proposing legal reforms (which would mean legitimating it), they articulate a discourse and a politics that bypass the legal order, and they think of punishment as inflicting suffering on the body. Their reference, therefore, is the universe of private, immediate, and usually very physical revenge. This universe reveals a specific conception of the body, and especially of the infliction of pain as a means to moral and social development. This conception applies not only to criminals but to many spheres of Brazilian social life. Therefore, by addressing the question of how criminals should be punished, one is led to examine broader dimensions of Brazilian society.

In my conversations with residents of São Paulo about the death penalty and human rights, it became clear that people go back and forth between the two references: the legal system and private, violent vengeance. The dominant discourse is that of private revenge, a system that uses pain and interventions on the body as a means of creating order.

9.1

Would you vote in favor of or against the death penalty?

I have never thought whether I would vote for or against it. Sometimes you see certain things happening, and you think: "Well, if there were a death penalty, they wouldn't do this." But, on the other hand, when you see those people who are really into heavy violence, for them it does not matter, they don't have any love of life. It does not make much difference whether there is or there isn't a death penalty. I think it wouldn't change anything. . . . I don't see that it would be a threat for them. I think that for a creature of real violence, the death penalty does not intimidate, it is not going to help. I think I would vote against it.

And what about the question of human rights for prisoners?

Well, that I'm radically against. I'm totally against them, because they create a climate as if the person who did something horrible, when he gets to prison he becomes an angel. In general, those people have serious problems, serious psychological problems. . . . I have the impression that a criminal of this kind would be more afraid of a severe prison system than of the death penalty. In a way, the death penalty doesn't punish anything.

And what would be a severe prison?

Look, one thing that I think is wrong in this issue of human rights is to protect, to say they are nice, and so on. Come on! You cannot be nice with a creature like that. Now, I also think that those tortures, etc., that is out, out of consideration. . . . It's very difficult to know what is the limit.

> *Housewife, age fifty-two, Morumbi, two children;*
> *her husband is an executive of a multinational industry*

9.2

Are you in favor of or against the death penalty?

I'm in favor of it. . . . I think that the death penalty should be applied in all horrible crimes, barbarian crimes: rape, especially those people who get innocent children. The guy who does that I think is an abnormal person, with mental problems or something. Or he is perverse by nature.

Do you think that human rights would apply to them?

Human rights, they end when someone takes yours. So, when someone takes your right, his is finished. If a person comes and takes the life of someone in your household, he takes his right away. You have the right, he doesn't have rights anymore. I think that he has to pay in the same way as he did it [the crime].

What do you understand by human rights?

I think that human rights would be for political cases because each one has an ideology, and as long as someone is not doing any damage, is not a terrorist, has an ideal, is struggling for something, this one has the right to human rights. . . . I think that human rights in a democracy have to be respected through idealism and dialogue.

> *Businessman, age fifty-nine, Moóca, married, lives with his wife*

9.3

What do you think about this question of human rights?

A: I don't think such a thing exists. Human rights and the constitution don't exist for the poor; they exist for the rich.

There are many people who think that the rights of prisoners should be respected . . .

A: What? To respect the rights of prisoners? Prisoners do not respect our rights.

B: When they get out of there, they want to kill us.

A: Something that I think is wrong in the constitution, I don't know if it is in the constitution, is that prisoners can have sex in prison. Because of that AIDS is increasing in the jails. It should be like Afanasio [Jazadji] says: someone has to stop that.

Do you think that Afanasio is right?

A: I think he is right. He said, "Someone must stop this shameless behavior," in that way that he talks.

Do you like the way he talks? Don't you think he exaggerates?

A: No, I think he is just. "Bastard," as he starts to call those guys "bastards." [He imitates the way in which Afanasio talks.] Many times a bandit enters a worker's house, the worker defends himself and kills the bandit, he [Afanasio] defends the worker. But the bandit, he has to die, it must be the death penalty, it should be. But here in Brazil we never have anything.

> *Two brothers who live in Jardim das Camélias. A is twenty-two,*
> *an auto mechanic, and married; B is sixteen, an unskilled factory worker.*

9.4

The (Catholic) Church is against the death penalty, they are not in favor of it. . . . I think that when they talk about human rights, they think that nobody should be killed. But I don't agree, because why can a bandit kill a head of a household, but a head of a household cannot kill a bandit? . . .

And what about the prisons? The church also says that prisoners should be better treated . . .

Come on! They, with *mordomia* [privileges]! Then they would really take advantage of the thing! With all the *mordomia*, then they would

really rob! They would rob, kill, rape, do whatever they pleased. Because they would have everything they wanted, the *mordomias*, even
women, who are now allowed, color TV and everything. Then they
would do whatever they pleased!

> *Housewife from Jardim das Camélias, age thirty-three, with four children;*
> *she has participated in various social movements and local associations.*
> *Her husband is a skilled worker in a small textile factory.*

In the same way as the public figures who attack human rights—and frequently using their very expressions and examples—residents of São Paulo
from different social groups claim both that respecting the rights of prisoners is an absurd idea, even a bad joke, and that it promotes crime. In fact,
these citations and the following analysis of punishment only complement
those of previous chapters about the character of criminals, the spread of
evil, the role of authorities, the violent police, and the dysfunctions of the
justice system. The people I interviewed think that criminals—always portrayed as perverse, inhuman, with no family ties, and so on—should be
treated harshly, not necessarily tortured but punished with the death
penalty or "severity," which for many means painful chastisement. It is a
common opinion that the death penalty may not be severe enough because
those executed do not suffer.

Like the majority of Paulistas, the interviewees can accept the idea of human rights for political prisoners, but not for "criminals." To highlight the
absurdity of guaranteeing human rights to "criminals," they cite the lack
of rights of the majority of the population, especially the workers, for whom
"human rights and the constitution do not exist" (quote 9.3). In other words,
reactions against human rights always refer to the notion that rights in Brazil
are the privilege of a few rather than universal. In quote 9.4, a working-
class woman uses the word *mordomia*. This is a term for the excessive money
and services that upper-echelon public servants spend on entertaining and
housekeeping, that is, taxpayers' money used for private, often superfluous,
expenses. These kinds of elite privileges (like the idea of justice) are regarded
with cynicism and seen as mocking the living conditions of common citizens. To associate prison reforms with *mordomia* is to regard them as excessive and even disrespectful of ordinary citizens.

Defenders of human rights have been unable to question and dismantle
the population's association of rights with privileges. While they insist that
everybody, even a prisoner, has rights that must be respected, they have not
effectively addressed the fact that individual rights in Brazil are largely disregarded and that the judiciary system is not effective in solving conflicts

and distributing justice, especially for working-class victims. The defenders of human rights have failed to convince the population that prisoners would not be the only ones having their rights respected and that other policies should assure that rights are not the privilege of a few but available to all. Their efforts to enforce the rule of law, to make the police less violent, were associated with protecting the privileges of a few—the common image of the law—against the interests of the many. By failing to challenge the view of rights as privileges, they not only failed to instill respect for rights in reforming the police and in guaranteeing the rule of law but also failed to expand the legitimacy of the notion of rights in general, and of human and individual rights in particular.

At this point we must address an apparent paradox: if people consider the judiciary system to be weak, biased, and ineffective, why would they choose to enlarge its power by giving it the prerogative of executing people? If justice does not work in general, why would it work in deciding about life and death? If the judiciary system is known to be violent toward workers and soft on criminals, wouldn't the death penalty be only another instrument used to repress workers?

Many Brazilians see no paradox here because they think of capital punishment as summary execution and not as a juridical process. In their distrust of the justice system, they think that evil should be eliminated without mediation, by killing those who have been contaminated by it. Many people think that if someone is caught committing a violent crime, he or she should be killed immediately. Moreover, many people support the death squads and *justiceiros* by arguing that they are not as corrupt as the police are, and that their methods are effective: they do a good job "because they only kill." In sum, both private actions and violence are regarded as legitimate in the urgent fight against the spread of evil.

In the discussions of how the death penalty should work and against whom, and of how to establish some kind of social order, it is clear that the judicial system is considered largely irrelevant. Vengeance is conceived in personal and immediate terms, even when the responsibility of carrying it out is lodged in an institution, the police. In quote 5.17, I cited a young, working-class man who wished that the Esquadrão da Morte still existed. In his view, the best way to dispense justice is to allow the police to kill. "Why should we get a guy and kill him?" he asked. "What do we pay taxes for? For this, to be protected. . . . It is not worth it for us to lynch, they [the police] should have the right, they have the duty, because we pay taxes for this. . . . The law must be this one: if you kill, you die."

When I asked another working-class man who defended the Esquadrão da Morte (in quote 5.18) who would decide which people would be killed, he answered:

9.5

> It's the guy you catch in the act. If you know that the guy is dangerous, then go get him. Get him, kill him, no one to arrest. To arrest is out!
>
> *But weren't you saying that what is necessary is to have law?*
>
> Yes. There should be law. So, a law to kill bandits. If the guy robs, he knows he's going to die, and he won't rob heads of household making the minimum salary. You get the guy, take him to the gallows just in the middle of the avenue, hang the guy there. . . . So, you hang that one, you have distributed order for the whole Brazil, people won't want to rob anymore. Do you understand?
>
> > *Driver, Jardim das Camélias, age thirty-two, married with four children; used to be a taxi driver and now works for a public institution*

In addition to reminding us of Foucault's descriptions of punishment in the ancien régime, these opinions display two striking features. The first is the realization that for some people, justice means allowing the police to exercise immediate vengeance, without the mediation of the justice system. The second is the ease with which people talk about private vengeance and the taking of life, which is associated with their ready acceptance of the idea of physical punishment in general.

As I pointed out in chapter 5, support for summary executions and a violent police implies an implosion of the legal models of both the police and of justice. The logic of this view is rooted in the everyday abuse and injustice practiced by institutions of order and in people's desire for justice and vengeance. The ambiguities in the quotations above also indicate the complex imbrications of the public (legal) and the private (illegal) systems of revenge. People want the police to fulfill their obligation, they think the law is necessary, but because they know that these institutions do not work, they imagine private, violent, and illegal means of accomplishing the same things. This ambivalence between references to the judiciary system and to a private system of revenge reappears even in the opinions of people who reject illegal methods, and even among interviewees opposed to the death penalty.

A few people I interviewed opposed capital punishment. Some believed that nobody should take another person's life. Others expressed fears that it would become yet another instrument of injustice either at the hands of judiciary system bureaucrats or among the police.

9.6

Are you against the death penalty?

Oh, yes! I don't think it has any effect. Everything which affects my conscience I try to avoid. I think the following: something which affects me is something which reaches my mind, which makes me grind again wondering if I have done something I shouldn't have. This would be to put obstacles in my path. . . . I think the following: I'll never forget the wrong things. I avoid any attitude which would be a mistake. So, I may say that I have the right to kill the man who tormented my mother, I give him some blows, but if he had tormented my mother and I do the same with him, I don't know, my conscience would be heavy.

Skilled worker, Jardim das Camélias, age forty-eight, married with four children; makes fences and window bars; has a workshop and store in front of his house

9.7a

It's a vicious circle: people are extremely revolted because of the barbarities the robbers, the criminals commit. And they do commit them. At a personal level, I think that if someone killed someone in my family, and I saw that the guy wasn't tried, wasn't found guilty, I would kill or order someone else to kill him. This is at a personal level, with the interference of a lot of emotion; but at a theoretical level, from the perspective of how a rule of law works, how the jurisprudence works, then I think that things should be another way. Human rights are the basis of a civilization.

What do you think of the death penalty?

No! Absolutely not! No way! You can understand the human feeling of revolt, but you cannot go to the extreme of extinguishing human rights. The person then ends her own rights.

If there is the plebiscite about the death penalty, what do you think will happen?

I think that the death penalty will win. Unfortunately. People don't have in their minds this theoretical perspective of the rule of law. They follow the path of emotion, survival, panic, fear . . . the path of willingness to extinguish all bandits, kill everybody.

Real estate agent, age fifty-six, started working in 1990,
lives in Alto de Pinheiros with one daughter

References to private vengeance are made even by people totally opposed to capital punishment. The speaker in quote 9.6 opposes the death penalty but thinks of it only as a private matter, something to be decided between himself and his conscience and to be executed personally. He is against the use of violence under any circumstances and believes in the values of education and respect as sources of good social relationships. For him, the only institution that could play a crucial role in preventing violence and creating the conditions for a good social life is the family. Quote 9.7a is one of the few examples of a discussion of the death penalty that refers to the justice system. For the interviewee, private vengeance and personal sentiment are opposed to the rule of law and universal human rights, both of which she endorses. However, although she values the principle of human rights and opposes the death penalty, she also recognizes that if the justice system failed, she herself would consider the path of private vengeance.

The naturalness with which people talk about private vengeance and taking a life is associated with the naturalness with which they deal with physical punishment in general. I asked everyone I interviewed what they thought about beating children. Whereas the feminist movement has succeeded in stigmatizing the beating of women, and violence against street children is publicly opposed, the beating of one's own children for disciplinary reasons is taken for granted. It therefore offers a good means of approaching the question of violent punishment in the context of everyday life, that is, removed from the exceptional context of crime. The interviews confirmed the general practice: even people in favor of human rights and against the death penalty, such as the woman just cited in quote 9.7a, felt the hitting of children may be advisable in some circumstances.

9.7b

I think that in order to educate it is OK. To smack, to give a big slap, to punish or pull their ears when they are small, I did this with my children sometimes, I really did, because patience has its limits, but beating is different. There is a saying that chicken's wings don't kill little chicks. . . . I think that a little bit of superego is always necessary.

The need to establish limits and set an example are ways of justifying the beating of children. What is not clear is why setting limits means hitting a child rather than using some other punishment. It is striking as well that the logic in this discussion about the disciplining of children is the same as that used to justify the death penalty: making an example, setting limits. This analogy was explicitly made to me:

9.8

> People say the death penalty isn't effective, but I'll give you an example. You take a two-year-old child and say: "Don't touch the stove, because you'll get burned." She goes and touches it. But if she goes to touch it and gets a big slap, she won't touch it, because she is afraid—so, it's the same thing with the death penalty. . . . You have to explain things to children, but when they don't have enough responsibility, they cannot understand. . . . The example works. . . . People argue that developed countries have abolished the death penalty. But we are a third world country and what is the limit? . . . It's necessary to have a limit. As the slap that you give your child, the death penalty would be a limit.
>
> *Engineer, Morumbi, high-ranking technician*
> *working for the police, fifties, married with five children*

The shocking analogy between capital punishment and child beating reveals that the death penalty is considered pedagogic: a definite, bold example of what happens to people who do not behave as society demands. It also reveals that the model of the family, the institution in charge of disciplining people and preventing their contamination by evil, is applied directly to the public sphere. These opinions and the following discussions are complementary to and make sense in the context of the conceptions about the spread of evil and the role of the authorities in preventing it that I analyzed in chapter 2. But maybe the more striking element in the above quotation is the ease with which this man (like other interviewees) talks about beating children. People seem to take for granted that children must be beaten to be disciplined: this reasoning is so obvious that it can be used to justify capital punishment. Most people who admit that they beat or have beaten their children seem to hold the view that children are not reasonable enough to understand everything a parent says. However, they believe that they can understand violence (a term never in fact used in the references to the disciplinary beating of children). Unable to understand language, children nevertheless are clearly believed to understand pain. Since fear of pain generates obedience, provoking such fear is considered good pedagogy. The marking of the body by pain is perceived as a more forceful statement than mere words could make, and it should be used especially when language and rational arguments would not be understood. In general, the people I interviewed think that children, adolescents, and women are not totally rational (or not always rational), in same way that the poor and, obviously, criminals are not. Toward such people the use of violence is necessary; it is a language anyone can understand, which has the power to enforce moral principles and correct social behavior. Pain is understood as a path to knowledge (especially moral knowledge) and reform. Violence is considered to be a language closer to truth.

This association of pain, knowledge, and truth becomes especially clear in discussions about torture. People generally describe torture as bad, though a few see it is a necessary evil. But nobody doubts its efficacy. The same sentiment was repeated to me by totally different people. One was a left-wing intellectual who had been tortured during the military regime and who said, over a dinner where the death penalty was being debated, "I can say that because I was tortured myself: torture works. If a person kidnaps my daughter and the police put their hand on someone who can lead them to the kidnappers, I would not hesitate to tell the police to torture them to get information." This is the same argument that Afanasio Jazadji uses publicly.

> The police don't have a crystal ball. They don't. . . . You have to extract the truth in one way or another. What do you do to extract the truth from the guy? There is no other way, no way. It's beating. . . . There is no persuasion, there is no interrogation which works, there isn't, in the whole world. . . . There is no other method for you to extract the truth from somebody, the real truth. [Suppose a] guy was in a robbery with five others, he killed someone, the others escaped, and he is arrested. Then he comes and says: "I have my constitutional rights, nobody touches me." How does a policeman behave? There isn't any other way, there isn't. . . . The bandit, he knows that it is the law of the jungle; he knows that if he made a mistake, it is the role of the policeman to make the truth come out, and that there is no other method for this. (Interview, 20 December 1990)

This association of torture and truth is in no way unique to Brazil. On the contrary, it belongs to a long Western tradition of judicial torture and of Christian religious practices.[21] What is striking is how Jazadji and others conceive of torture as an everyday resource in the hands of the police, a technique that produces results when all others fail. By expressing this opinion, however, Jazadji is only reflecting the well-known modus operandi of São Paulo's police. His opinion is thus parallel with that of the man who makes the casual analogy between beating children and the death penalty: in their direct assessment of the issue of the use of pain, they reveal that those practices are so embedded in everyday life that they can be taken as the norm.

In contemporary São Paulo, however, the associations of pain, truth, and order do not derive their meaning from the inquisitorial tradition alone. They also find their pedigree in the colonial encounter and what Michael Taussig calls its culture of terror (1987). This colonial culture, which entangled colonizer and colonized in the reproduction of violence, is a culture in which narrative reproduces terror (as with the fear of crime) and in which meaning is produced in the body of the dominated.

Some critics of torture, notably Elaine Scarry, have deconstructed the way in which it is represented as a means of producing truth. Such analysis helps us to understand some of the dimensions of the kind of power relationship that seems to have been reproduced in Brazil. Scarry demonstrates that what is central in torture is not knowledge or truth, but power. She shows that "intense pain is world-destroying"; that is, it unmakes meaning. What is crucial for torturers in compelling a confession is not so much the content of what is said, but rather the ability to force a confession (1985:28–29). In other words, what is crucial is the creation of a "fiction of absolute power" (1985:27): the infliction of pain demands and receives a response. Those who torture, Scarry reminds us, do so because they are weak, not because they need knowledge.[22] The discourses I have just analyzed apparently operate with opposite meanings to Scarry's view, as they still insist that torture leads to truth. However, their logic seems to coincide with that of people who are in a position to inflict pain. Both Scarry and the interviewee I just cited think of language and pain as opposed. However, while interviewees generally believe that pain can produce discipline, order, and knowledge, Scarry argues that pain only destroys signification. In fact, both in the disciplining of children, women, and other "weak" people and in the infliction of torture, pain is an instrument of authority used to induce submission and compliance. The meaning created by pain in people's bodies is the will of absolute authority, an authority unwilling to engage in debates or acknowledge dissent, an authority that disregards language. A world of negotiated signification is created by language, not by pain.

I would like to comment on one last point: people's fascination with the role of the executioner and with an economy of intervention in the body of the executed. Amaral Netto has claimed on more than one occasion that he would like to be Brazil's first legal executioner (see also *Folha de S. Paulo,*

2 July 1991). He is apparently not the only one: he has claimed publicly that many people have written to him to volunteer for the position. Some have been interviewed and had their pictures published in the papers (see, for example, *Folha de S. Paulo*, 3 August 1991). People have also offered suggestions for the best methods for execution (a popular choice is an injection of rat poison), and on how to dispose of the bodies of the executed. The most popular option for the latter seems to be using their organs for transplants, and some people have even created elaborate tables relating different organs to the kind of crime committed (*Folha de S. Paulo*, 3 August 1991). Other people propose mutilation and castration as punishments for certain crimes.

These stories add another dimension to what seem to be two interconnected features of Brazilian culture: the centrality of the body in considerations of punishment, and acceptance of the use of pain in disciplinary practices not only against alleged criminals, but also against all categories of people considered in need of special control (including children, women, the poor, and the insane). The body is thus perceived as being a field for various interventions. This notion of a manipulable body relates to the delegitimation of civil rights and is at the heart of debates over democratizing Brazilian society.

BODY AND RIGHTS

Clearly, the body is conceived of as the locus of punishment, justice, and example in Brazil. It is conceived by most as a proper site for authority to be asserted through the infliction of pain. On the bodies of the dominated—children, women, blacks, the poor, and alleged criminals—those in authority mark their power, seeking, through the infliction of pain, to purify the souls of their victims, correct their characters, improve their behavior, and produce compliance.[23] To understand how these conceptions, and their consequences, can be accepted as natural in everyday life, it is not enough simply to unveil the associations of pain and truth, pain and moral development, or even pain and a certain type of authority. These conceptions of punishment and chastisement are associated with other notions that legitimate interventions in the body and with the absence of respect for individual rights.

The naturalness with which Brazilians view the infliction of pain as a corrective is consistent with other perceptions of the body. Interventions and manipulations of other people's bodies, or one's own body, are seen as relatively natural in many areas of social life. These interventions are not nec-

essarily painful or violent. In fact, some are perceived as desirable and attractive features of Brazilian culture. Nevertheless, what all interventions
reveal is a notion of an unbounded body. On the one hand, the unbounded
body has no clear barriers of separation or avoidance; it is a permeable body,
open to intervention, on which manipulations by others are not considered
problematic. On the other hand, the unbounded body is unprotected by individual rights and, indeed, results historically from their absence. In Brazil,
where the judicial system is openly discredited, the body (and the person)
is in general not protected by a set of rights that would bound it, in the sense
of establishing barriers and limits to interference or abuse by others.

A full account of the ways in which the body is unbounded in Brazilian
society would probably require revisiting both colonial relations and the
legacy of slavery and is outside my scope. Nevertheless, I want to add two
examples that lie outside the field of punishment and crime. The first comes
from medicine, in principle a field in which interventions in or on the body
are considered legitimate. There are, however, various issues on which one
might question the extent of the interventions. One of these is reproduction, which affects primarily the bodies of women. Birth via cesarean section is becoming more common than vaginal birth in Brazil. In the state of
São Paulo, in 1992, 53.4 percent of all births were by cesarean (Berquó
1993:471). According to Elza Berquó (1993), this increase is associated with
the prevalence of sterilization (tubal ligation) as the main contraceptive
method in Brazil: it is used by 45 percent of women and is performed mostly
during a cesarean section.[24] In the northeast, Brazil's poorest region, 63 percent of women use it, and recent data indicate that 19 percent of women in
this area were sterilized before the age of twenty-five (as compared to 10
percent in São Paulo; PNUD-IPEA 1996:67).

These data illustrate, first, a serious public health problem and the existence of a medical class that performs cesarean sections far more often than
is medically necessary and provides few alternative means of birth control.
Second, they indicate that this trend is strongest in the poorest region of
the country. Third, and most important from the perspective of women's
control of their bodies, the data indicate that Brazilian women are taking
radical steps to control reproduction, selecting a method that is invasive and
irreversible more often than a noninvasive procedure. In other words,
women's reproductive decisions are being made in ways that normalize drastic interference in the body. Reproduction is not the only area in which this
interference occurs. Plastic surgery of all types is also extremely common
among the middle classes.[25]

The second arena where interventions are taken for granted refers to one of the features that, as the saying goes, "makes Brazil Brazil": the open sensuality and display of the body on the beaches, the so-called flexible sexuality, the valorization of the proximity of bodies, Carnival with its mixture of bodies, and so forth. Carnival is an occasion for displaying the body and playing with transformations of the body. It as also an occasion for open sensual play. During Carnival performances people expect to touch and be touched: it is considered in bad taste to repel such interventions because one is out there to play, and the mingling of bodies is the essence of the play. Not only is Carnival a realm for the merging of bodies, their manipulation, and display, but it is also one where the threat of violence and actual violence are always present.

Carnival is obviously not a Brazilian invention. But in the European cultures that used to celebrate it, the carnivalesque has been largely relegated to the past. Some of the most compelling interpretations of the history of modern Europe help us to understand why. These interpretations, in fact histories of modernity, describe the interconnections of the formation of nation-states, the establishment of the liberal tradition and notions of citizenship and rights, and the control of violence and its monopoly by the state. In this context, the carnivalesque, with its mixture of bodies—what Bakhtin (1984) has called "grotesque images of the body"—and widespread violent behavior, including violent punishment, were buried with the birth of the "age of rights" and the primacy of the individual. They became things of the past, things associated with other cultures or displaced and reenacted in the colonies by the same imperial administrations who were learning to put them aside at home. The genocide of the native population that occurred during the Conquest in the Americas, the continuous marking of bodies in the process of colonization, and the creation of a culture of fear in Latin America (Taussig 1987) coincide with the internal pacification of European states and their increase in the sophistication of mores and the control of violence.

The passage from the dominance of the grotesque body to that of the individual body in Europe is crucial to the formation of modernity: it signifies the prevalence of new sensibilities and cultural values, the triumph of new forms of social relations and social organization, and the establishment of new forms of control and subjection. In the long term it affected all dimensions of social life and has been described from many different perspectives. Norbert Elias (1994 [1939]), in his essays on the civilizing process, describes the change as a long-term process that created the modern nation-states, with their monopoly of the use of force and theories of citizenship and rights.[26] Moreover, Elias's fascinating analysis reveals how these macroprocesses intertwined with the refinement of manners and the microprocesses through which bodily functions were controlled and removed from the public sphere. As a result of this process, the "civilized" person learned to enclose his or her body, to control its fluids, to avoid mixing with others or with the exterior, and to control his or her aggressiveness. The civilized person is the self-contained, bounded individual.

Another interpretation of the same process is developed by Michel Foucault in his history of punishment. It is the passage from public rituals of physical punishment to the private punishments and moral exercises of the penitentiary system; it is the passage from the marking of bodies to the discipline of the soul as the main form of exercising power. This transition parallels the change in dominant modes of political organization and legitimation of political power: monarchies whose source of power was the body of the king, and whose power was exercised suddenly, violently, and in a discontinuous way (Foucault 1977:208), gave way to states inspired by the notion of social contract, which have as a guiding principle the idea of universal citizenship and its rights.

Foucault argues that the formation of the disciplinary society is connected with various broader historical processes—economic, juridico-political, and scientific (Foucault 1977:218–28). He stresses the links between the formation of the disciplinary society and the development of new juridico-political structures.

> The general juridical form that guaranteed a system of rights that were egalitarian in principle was supported by those tiny, everyday, physical mechanisms, by all those systems of micro-power that are essentially non-egalitarian and asymmetrical that we call the disciplines. . . .
> The real, corporal disciplines constituted the foundation of the formal, juridical liberties. The contract may have been regarded as the ideal foundation of law and political power; panopticism constituted the technique, universally widespread, of coercion. It continued to work in depth on the juridical structure of society, in order to make the effective mechanisms of power function in opposition to the formal framework that it had acquired. The "Enlightenment," which discovered the liberties, also invented the disciplines. (Foucault 1977:222)

The combination of the disciplines with the juridical apparatus of the contract society in Europe resulted in the docility of bodies and the bounding of individuals. Although they used totally different techniques, both the disciplines and the juridical apparatus of modern society enforced the notion of the isolated individual and bounded self. Moreover, although their promises were mutually antagonistic—the social contract promising equality and the disciplines reproducing hierarchy and domination—both helped to legitimate ways of exercising power, in relation to the body and the individual, that repressed violence. The infliction of pain as a way of exercising power had been a characteristic of monarchy; the new form of political power was legitimated by the idea of consent and a free contract among equal individuals. In the new system, individual citizens were not only bounded but were also the possessors of a whole range of rights. Among all the rights constituting citizenship, those protecting the male individual, his body, and his privacy were the first to be developed and are those which to this day constitute the core of the liberal tradition (Marshall 1965 [1949]). Moreover, modern disciplines are productive, not repressive, and aim at molding the soul and the character through exercise rather than pain.

The association of the development of the disciplines with that of individual rights and liberal democracies and with the control and enclosure of the body, as well as the progressive abandonment of violence as either a pedagogic method or a form of punishment, is clear in the history of the countries that invented the liberal-democratic model (France, England, and the United States).[27] Scholars of citizenship have tended to generalize this history so that it becomes the history of the development of rights and discipline in general and the model of what citizenship and democracy should look like. One of the effects of this generalization is to link certain elements as if they always occur together and in a certain sequence. Countries such as Brazil, but also others with different histories (usually colonial histories) and that today have disjunctive democracies, force us to dissociate the elements of that history and to question their sequence. They force us to see the possibility of political citizenship without the control of violence, of a rule of law coexisting with police abuses, and of electoral democracies without civil rights or a legitimate justice system. Moreover, disjunctive democracies accustom us to different histories of citizenship, histories like Brazil's, where social rights are highly developed but civil rights are not protected, or where political rights have a convoluted history of being guaranteed only to be taken away again by a new regime. Looking at these histories, we realize that what we think of as the norm—the European history of the control of violence and development of citizenship rights—is only one version of modernity, and probably not even the most common one. When we look at other histories we realize that multiple modernities are produced as different nations and peoples engage with the various elements of the repertoire of modernity (monopoly of the use of force, citizenship, liberalism, and so on).

Fernando Coronil and Julie Skurski (1991) offer an example of another type of culture and history in which modernity and democratic politics have always been entangled with violence. They show how political violence in Venezuela is regularly enacted in democratic contexts. They argue that violence is "wielded and resisted" (1991:28) in terms of a society's distinctive history, in relation to which, therefore, it has to be analyzed. Contemporary violence in Venezuela, they suggest, continues to be framed "in Conquest terms," mobilizing notions of a barbaric people and a civilizing government (of elites). Taussig (1987) demonstrates a similar process for Colombia in his study of the use of violence in the rubber boom and the creation of what he calls a "culture of terror and space of death."

In Brazil, every constitution has promulgated the principles of universal citizenship since the first constitution in 1824 and long before the abolition of slavery in 1888. Yet the associations of disciplines, individual rights, and enclosure of the body that we find in the European model have never taken hold. Individual rights are neither legitimated nor protected, and the body is not respected in its individual enclosure and privacy. Bodies and civil rights are entangled with each other, both in countries like Brazil and in those with bounded bodies and respected civil rights. In Brazilian society, what dominates is the unbounded notion of the body and of the individual. To this day, and regardless of the political regime, it is on the unbounded bodies of the dominated that relationships of power are structured, that meanings circulate, and that the establishment of order is attempted. When the marking of bodies prevails, the realization of civil rights is unlikely, though there may be an electoral political democracy and a relatively broad respect for social rights. Civil rights, though, seem to depend on the bounding of the body and the individual, and on the recognition of their integrity.

As I have shown, Brazil has a disjunctive democracy that is marked by a delegitimation of the civil component of citizenship: the justice system is ineffective, justice is exercised as a privilege of the elite, individual and civil rights are delegitimated, and human rights violations (especially by the state) are routine. This specific configuration does not arise in a social and cultural vacuum: the delegitimation of civil rights is deeply embedded in a history and culture in which the body is unbounded and manipulable and pain and abuse are seen as instruments of moral development, knowledge, and order. This specific configuration allows us to suggest that the cultural and political logic that creates unbounded bodies is not the same logic that generates the bounded individual in the liberal tradition of citizenship. These two logics have been in dialogue for a long time in places such as Brazil, as they have in North America and Europe. However, these dialogues have produced quite different results. By pointing out the different paths of development of European and North American citizenship rights and democracies and of

Brazilian citizenship, I do not intend to minimize the danger that the weak civil component represents for Brazilian democracy. Rather, I wish to suggest that to understand the peculiar disrespect for civil rights in Brazilian democracy and to consider how it could become less violent and more respectful of people's bodies and rights, we may have to focus more on conceptions of evil, the punishment of children, the overuse of cesarean sections, and the practice of Carnival than on electoral procedures and political party formations. In fact, nothing indicates that political democracy and the rule of law will bound bodies and generate respect for individuals or vice versa. Indeed, in Brazil, violence and human rights violations increased under democratic rule, and at the same time the desire to inflict pain on the body of the dominated has led to challenges against the rule of law. It is not by chance, I think, that the main attack on São Paulo's first elected governor was articulated through the bashing of human rights and the defense of capital punishment (and summary executions). We could suggest, then, that through the issue of violent punishment and crime, Brazilians articulate a form of resistance to the expansion of democracy into Brazilian culture, social relations, and everyday life.

The elaboration of prejudice in the talk of crime, the symbolic re-creation of inequalities just as democracy took root, the support of police violence and of private and illegal measures of dealing with crime, the walling of the city, the enclosure and dislocation of the rich, the creation of fortified enclaves and changes in public space toward more explicitly separated and undemocratic patterns, the disrespect of human rights and their identification with "privileges for bandits," and the defense of the death penalty and summary executions all run counter to, and sometimes counteract, democratization and the expansion of citizenship. Because all of these trends increased under democratic rule, I have pointed out Brazilian democracy's disjunctive character. Moreover, because many of these elements indicate civil rights problems, they expose the sphere of justice and individual rights as one of the most problematic of Brazilian citizenship.

Nevertheless, I do not necessarily advocate for Brazil any of the existing models of citizenship rights or expect it to follow those models. Individual rights in Brazil must be shaped in the context of its own history and culture, which includes the unbounded conception of the body in both the legal and the experiential sense. Although I believe that without the reform and legitimation of the justice system there will be no end to the cycle of violence or any increase in the respect for individuals and their rights, this system must be reformed and bodies bounded with respect to distinctively Brazilian conceptions of the body.

How can Brazilians create protection and respect for people's bodies, individual rights, and privacy, and at the same time maintain the features of Brazilian culture that are seemingly valued and appreciated by many, such as those symbolized in Carnival? I do not have an answer to this question, but the following may help shape the discussion.

The feminist theorist Jennifer Nedelsky argues (1990) that the prevalent notion of rights in the American constitutional tradition is that of rights as boundaries, and that it derives from the property model. In this tradition, individual rights are conceived of as proprietary rights to one's own body and the protection of individuals and their autonomy as the erection of walls. In her critique of boundary images as the models for conceptions of rights, self, and autonomy, Nedelsky argues that they cannot be useful for women and their bodies, given elementary facts like pregnancy and intercourse. She argues instead for a more flexible model for the body and the self, a model focused on connection, contact, relationship, and permeable boundaries that has some resemblance to the flexible Brazilian model. I am skeptical of Nedelsky's alternative for the Brazilian case because I have come to believe that its more flexible and unbounded model is the counterpart of much violence in various areas of social life and also is itself inherently violent, especially against women, children, and the poor—that is, in conjunction with the imposition of authoritarian will. Moreover, as flexibility combines with great inequality in social relations, the permeability works only in one direction, from dominant to dominated, without any institutional restraints or boundaries. Thus I advocate more rather than less boundedness for the body, especially when it involves relationships between unequals. This stance, however, seems to contradict my argument about public space, in which I criticize the fortification of the city for destroying a type of democratic public space where borders are undecidable and negotiable. In fact, it does not, because the walls fortifying São Paulo are walls generated both by the disregard of civil rights and by the absence of desire among wealthier people to respect the rights of those they see as inferior and will not admit as co-citizens in the same public space.

Advocating more flexible models for the body means completely different things when civil rights and justice are legitimated (as in the United States, in Nedelsky's analysis) and when they are delegitimated (as in Brazil). In fact, a society's attitude toward these rights is inseparable from certain conceptions of the body: the society that produces unbounded bodies is unlikely to have strong civil rights, and vice versa. How, then, can we envision a model of citizenship and individual rights that is more protective of the dominated without imposing a male and maybe non-Brazilian model of the contained individual body? Can such a model provide boundaries for women's bodies, protecting them from sexual harassment and not penalizing them for becoming pregnant (by forcing them, for example, to conceive of their more flexible bodies in terms of disability, as U.S. labor legislation)?[28] How can we think of rights and autonomy in the contexts of social inequality and gender oppression without using the imagery of limits? Can we conceive of a model that can leave space for the proximity of bodies and sensuality and yet enforce respect for privacy, individuality, and human rights? Does the control of violence and abuse require rigid, clearly defined boundaries? Can we develop a model of citizenship and individual rights that is flexible and at the same time efficient at controlling violence? Is there a model that protects people's bodies and enforces individual rights while maintaining the indeterminacy of borders that constitutes the democratic public space? How do we establish the limits of what constitutes an alternative formation of democracy and rights and not a different order of being? Brazilian democracy will probably continue to be unique, but if it aspires to be less violent, it must not only legitimate the justice system but also stop playing out its games of power and abuse of authority on the bodies of the dominated. It will have to find ways to democratize public space, renegotiate borders, and respect civil rights.

APPENDIX

MAP 3. Districts of the municipality of São Paulo.

1. Água Rasa
2. Alto de Pinheiros
3. Anhangüera
4. Aricanduva
5. Artur Alvim
6. Barra Funda
7. Bela Vista
8. Belém
9. Bom Retiro
10. Brás
11. Brasilândia
12. Butantã
13. Cachoeirinha
14. Cambuci
15. Campo Belo
16. Campo Grande
17. Campo Limpo
18. Cangaíba
19. Capão Redondo
20. Carrão
21. Casa Verde
22. Cidade Ademar
23. Cidade Dutra
24. Cidade Líder
25. Cidade Tiradentes
26. Consolação
27. Cursino
28. Ermelino Matarazzo
29. Freguesia do Ó
30. Grajaú
31. Guaianazes
32. Iguatemi
33. Ipiranga
34. Itaim Bibi
35. Itaim Paulista
36. Itaquera
37. Jabaquara
38. Jaçanã
39. Jaguara
40. Jaguaré
41. Jaraguá
42. Jardim Ângela
43. Jardim Helena
44. Jardim Paulista
45. Jardim São Luís
46. José Bonifácio
47. Lajeado
48. Lapa
49. Liberdade
50. Limão
51. Mandaqui
52. Marsilac
53. Moema
54. Moóca
55. Morumbi
56. Parelheiros
57. Pari
58. Parque do Carmo
59. Pedreira
60. Penha
61. Perdizes
62. Perus
63. Pinheiros
64. Pirituba
65. Ponte Rasa
66. Raposo Tavares
67. República
68. Rio Pequeno
69. Sacomã
70. Santa Cecília
71. Santana
72. Santo Amaro
73. São Domingos
74. São Lucas
75. São Mateus
76. São Miguel
77. São Rafael
78. Sapopemba
79. Saúde
80. Sé
81. Socorro
82. Tatuapé
83. Tremembé
84. Tucuruvi
85. Vila Andrade
86. Vila Curuçá
87. Vila Formosa
88. Vila Guilherme
89. Vila Jacuí
90. Vila Leopoldina
91. Vila Maria
92. Vila Mariana
93. Vila Matilde
94. Vila Medeiros
95. Vila Prudente
96. Vila Sonia

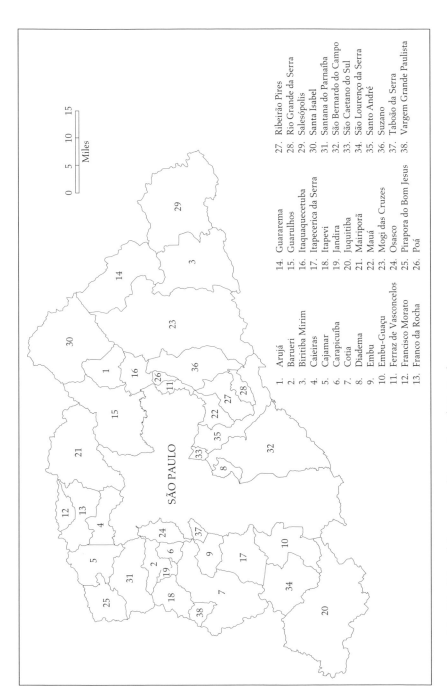

1. Arujá
2. Barueri
3. Biritiba Mirim
4. Caieiras
5. Cajamar
6. Carapicuíba
7. Cotia
8. Diadema
9. Embu
10. Embu-Guaçu
11. Ferraz de Vasconcelos
12. Francisco Morato
13. Franco da Rocha
14. Guararema
15. Guarulhos
16. Itaquaquecetuba
17. Itapecerica da Serra
18. Itapevi
19. Jandira
20. Juquitiba
21. Mairiporã
22. Mauá
23. Mogi das Cruzes
24. Osasco
25. Pirapora do Bom Jesus
26. Poá
27. Ribeirão Pires
28. Rio Grande da Serra
29. Salesópolis
30. Santa Isabel
31. Santana do Parnaíba
32. São Bernardo do Campo
33. São Caetano do Sul
34. São Lourenço da Serra
35. Santo André
36. Suzano
37. Taboão da Serra
38. Vargem Grande Paulista

MAP 4. Municipalities of the metropolitan region of São Paulo.

NOTES

INTRODUCTION

1. The Laws of the Indies, proclaimed in 1573 by Philip II of Spain, established uniform standards for the planning of towns in the colonies.

2. The distinction between anthropologies of "nation-building" and anthropologies of "empire-building" is elaborated by Stocking (1982). He also opposes an "international anthropology" that constitutes the Euro-American tradition and the "anthropology of the periphery." This distinction makes evident the power relations and the inequalities shaping the classification of different anthropological traditions. I use this terminology here between quotes to emphasize the framing of the traditions in which I have been formed, not to give to the Euro-American anthropologies a privileged epistemological position. For a discussion of various "national anthropologies," see Ethnos 1982. For discussions from the perspective of Brazilian anthropology, see Oliveira 1988 and 1995 and Peirano 1980.

3. The talk of crime and practices of segregation operate by constituting "others" to be criminalized and kept at a distance.

4. The critique of anthropology that took place in the past decade in American anthropology has provoked a reassessment of the work of classic ethnographers and of the experience of fieldwork. As a consequence, ethnographic research has become a highly problematized and self-conscious undertaking, and relationships with "the other" have been submitted to detailed deconstruction and criticism. Yet, so far, this trend has not changed the dominant preference for fieldwork abroad and for the study of "the other." For a recent critical review of this subject, see Gupta and Ferguson 1997.

5. For a history of the public life of Brazilian intellectuals, see Martins 1987 and Miceli 1979. I do not consider here all the historical variations in this public role or in the specific concerns that frame it.

6. I do not conceive of citizenship in formalist terms. I assume that residents of a city, whatever their official nationality, tend to engage with everyday urban life as citizens, as people engaged with the city's present and future conditions.

7. Methodological and theoretical discussions about ethnographers who study their own society and the type of knowledge they produce are extensive in Brazilian anthropology (see especially Caldeira 1981, R. Cardoso 1986, DaMatta 1978, Durham 1986, Velho 1978 and 1980, and Zaluar 1985 and 1986). However, these discussions usually do not challenge either the principle of otherness as a methodological device or the dominant imagery it creates in methodological discussions. The most common strategy is to try to adapt this imagery to local realities, as in DaMatta's suggestion (1978) that anthropology in one's own society is like a shamanistic trip, "a drastic movement in which paradoxically one does not change places" (1978:29), in contrast to the trip of the "international anthropologist," which DaMatta compares to the voyage of the Homeric hero. While the "heroic" ethnographer transforms the exotic into the familiar, the "native" ethnographer transforms the familiar into the exotic. Ruth Cardoso offers one of the most interesting critiques of the way in which anthropologists of the 1980s were trying to solve the question of otherness as they studied social movements. She argues that they dealt with social distance by identifying politically with the working classes of these movements. But although they articulated this political identification, anthropologists left untouched their positivist epistemological assumptions about the nature of their data. They continued to conceive of the data as "something objective, with an existence of their own and independent of social actors" (1986:99).

8. This position of leadership and untouchability has been strengthened by discourses legitimating intellectuals' work. In addition to being members of social elites, public intellectuals have frequently envisioned privileged positions for themselves, such as members of the avant-garde, educators of the masses, designers of master plans, social visionaries, voices of the subaltern, and so forth. They have legitimated these roles with metanarratives such as modernization, Marxism, developmentalism, and modernism. Although they frequently place themselves on the left and on the side of the subaltern, they do not always interrogate their ambiguous position of speaking for those who supposedly have no voice.

9. For a discussion of how class differences framed my fieldwork among working-class people, see Caldeira 1981.

10. The clearest exception to this localism in Brazilian intellectual history is the formulation of dependency theory in the 1970s. However, in contrast to what happened in the other social sciences, its influence in anthropology was reduced.

11. Both national and Euro-American anthropologists contribute to this situation. Because they identify with the international style and do not question their elite position, national anthropologists have a hard time conceiving of themselves as subalterns. Consequently, they have difficulty in facing the subalternity of their language, their production, and their country. Who reads Portuguese, who cares about scientific production in Latin American journals, who respects a Brazilian doctorate? Hence, they prefer to focus on the national arena.

12. The interviews in other neighborhoods on the periphery of São Paulo

were done by a research team based at Cebrap (the Brazilian Center for Analysis and Planning), an institution with which I have been affiliated in different capacities since 1980. The interviews were part of the research project "The Periphery of São Paulo and the Organization of Urban Social Movements," coordinated by Ruth Cardoso and initiated by a request from the Commission of Justice and Peace of the Archdiocese of São Paulo. This research was conducted in Cidade Júlia, Jaguaré, Jardim Míriam, Jardim Peri-Peri, and Jardim Marieta (the last in Osasco, in the metropolitan region of São Paulo), and in Jardim das Camélias, where I was responsible for the investigation. Publications in English about the results of this research include Caldeira 1987, 1988, and 1990.

13. In Moóca, I had a research assistant, João Vargas; in others I did not. In Vargas 1993, dealing with Moóca, João Vargas extends the discussions about how recent urban transformations affected residents and shaped their fears and views of crime.

1. TALKING OF CRIME
AND ORDERING THE WORLD

1. All the information I give about the people I interviewed dates from the time of the interview.

2. Literally, small palace.

3. A set of shacks built on seized land. Although people own their shacks and may transport them, they do not own the land, since it was illegally occupied. From the point of view of urban infrastructure, favelas are extremely precarious. The shacks are crammed together, there is no sewage service and frequently no piped water, and generally people obtain electricity by illegally tapping into existing electrical lines.

4. A *cortiço* is either an old house whose rooms have been rented to different families or a series of rooms, usually in a row, constructed to be rented individually. In each room a whole family sleeps, cooks, and entertains. Residents share external or corridor bathrooms and water sources.

5. *Nordestino* translates literally as someone from the northeast of Brazil. The term may be used to refer to people from any state north of and including Minas Gerais. Although this classification is geographically imprecise, in São Paulo it usually refers to migrants (mostly poor) who came to the city in large numbers between 1940 and 1980. The term, commonly used in a derogatory fashion, may also have a color basis, for *nordestinos* are considered to be *morenos* or *pardos:* colored, not white.

6. Praça da Sé is São Paulo's central square and rua Direita one of the most famous streets of the oldest downtown area. The financial institutions and the most sophisticated commerce and entertainment were located in this part of town until the early 1960s, when they moved southwest to the Avenida Paulista region.

7. I translate as "to infest" the expression *empestiar*, repeated many times

in the narrative to refer to the *nordestinos*. It derives from the verb *empestar*, which literally means to infect with plague and also to demoralize, to deprave.

8. *Nortista* means someone from the north of Brazil (usually from Amazonas, Pará, Maranhão, Piauí, or Ceará). However, it is used interchangeably with *nordestino*. Again, the classification is not geographically precise, but in São Paulo it always refers to (poor) migrants.

9. That the individuals had a "good face" *(eles tinham cara boa)* means in this case that they did not fit criminal stereotypes. See chapter 2 for a detailed analysis of these.

10. The narrator implies that children of mothers who "do not think" and have children they cannot care for, either because they are too poor or because the children are born out of wedlock, will certainly become criminals. She does not elaborate on this idea because it is quite common. I analyze the association of single mothers, poverty, and crime in chapter 2.

11. Where names are used in the narration, I substitute fictitious ones.

12. According to Fipe (1994:7–9), in 1993 Moóca had 9.0 percent of the city's almost twenty-four thousand *cortiços* but 16.12 percent of the families living in this kind of dwellings. The average number of families per *cortiço* in Moóca was 12.1, almost double the city average.

13. See Daniel 1996: chapter 5 for an ethnographic analysis of torture and terror that corroborates Scarry's hypothesis. Discussions about torture always refer to the production of meaning, as torture is commonly associated with questions of truth and law. I discuss these issues in chapter 9.

14. On national-developmentalist economic theories in Latin America, see F. H. Cardoso 1980. On the history of industrialization, see Dean 1969 and Singer 1984. For an analysis of the creation of Brasília and its symbolism, see Holston 1989; for analyses of Kubitschek's government and of developmentalism, see Benevides 1976 and M. L. Cardoso 1978.

15. All demographic data are from Brazilian censuses. These metropolitan areas are Belém, Fortaleza, Recife, Salvador, Belo Horizonte, Rio de Janeiro, São Paulo, Curitiba, and Porto Alegre. These are all state capitals. There are also other, noncapital cities with more than one million inhabitants, such as Santos and Campinas in the state of São Paulo.

16. See Faria 1983 and 1991 for analyses of the pattern of urbanization in the last fifty years, the consolidation of a national "system of cities," and changes in the structure of employment.

17. During the 1970s, according to Rocha, "per capita income evolved at 6.1% per year, the illiteracy rate declined from 40% to 33%, and the urban population increased from 55% to 68%. Although income and regional inequalities clearly deepened in the seventies, this was offset by the fact that most people were nonetheless better off. From the angle of income, absolute poverty fell sharply: the proportion of poor is estimated to have declined from 53% in 1970 to 27% in 1980" (1996:2).

18. Data on fertility rates are from PNUD-IPEA (1996:65–67). For a dis-

cussion of the radical types of birth control adopted by Brazilian women, see Chapter 9.

19. See Hamburger 1999 for an analysis of Brazilian television and its role in modernizing Brazil.

20. The last industrial census in Brazil took place in 1985.

21. According to Dieese-Seade, rates of unemployment were around 6 percent in the late 1980s and around 8.5 percent in the first half of the 1990s.

22. Recent studies on poverty and income distribution include Barros and Mendonça 1992; Barros, Camargo, and Mendonça 1996; Barros, Machado, and Mendonça 1997; Barros, Mendonça, and Duarte 1997; Leme and Biderman 1997; Lopes 1993; Lopes and Gottschalk 1990; and Rocha 1991, 1995, and 1996.

23. Poverty lines vary in different cities and regions of the country. Rocha presents her methodology for calculating them in Rocha 1996. She calculated the poverty line of the metropolitan region of São Paulo in 1990 at a monthly per capita income of U.S.$43.29. This is the country's highest poverty line. In the metropolitan region of São Paulo, the proportion of poor was 22.0 percent in 1981, 34.4 percent in 1983, 16.9 percent in 1986, and 20.9 percent in 1989 (Rocha 1991:37). These data indicate that the worst years of the recession were 1981 to 1983, a view confirmed by Lopes and Gottschalk (1990:104).

24. PNAD refers to the Pesquisa Nacional por Amostra de Domicílios (national research by domicile sample). These are periodic national household surveys undertaken by IBGE (Instituto Brasileiro de Geografia e Estatística), the census bureau. All data above about income distribution come from the PNADs.

25. The GINI coefficient is a widely used measure of income distribution that varies between zero and one. It would be zero if everyone had the same income and one if one person received the whole national income. In other words, the larger the value, the greater the level of inequality. For Brazil, the GINI coefficient was 0.580 in 1985, 0.627 in 1989, and 0.6366 in 1991 (Rocha 1991:38 and 1991 census).

26. As in the rest of Brazil, in the state of São Paulo and in the metropolitan region wealth is highly concentrated in the richest decile. While the difference between the first and the second deciles is around 75 percent, and that between the second and the third is around 38 percent, the difference between the ninth and the tenth deciles is 180 percent (Leme and Biderman 1997:198).

27. The Brazilian census uses the racial categories *branca, preta, parda,* and *amarela* (white, black, colored or mestizo, and of Asian origin). Usually analyses of racial relations consider *preta* and *parda* together because it has been demonstrated that they share equally bad social conditions. In 1991, whites constituted 55.3 percent of the population, *pardos* 39.3 percent, blacks 4.9 percent, and Asians 0.5 percent.

28. Although the PT candidate for president did not win, the political and social changes that the party represents have taken root in Brazilian society. PT has been successful in local politics, and its candidates became the mayors of various capital cities, including São Paulo. Luísa Erundina, a woman from

the northeast and a migrant to São Paulo, was São Paulo's mayor from 1989 to 1992.

29. The concept of disjunctive democracy does not apply only to Brazilian society but points to processes of contradictory development that may occur in any democracy (see Holston and Caldeira 1998). However, very clear disjunctions seem especially to characterize countries that have undergone recent transitions to democracy (Holston, forthcoming).

2. CRISIS, CRIMINALS, AND THE SPREAD OF EVIL

1. The transcribed interviews generated thousands of pages that were difficult to manage. I therefore developed the following technique for analyzing the material: first, on the day of each interview, I wrote a detailed account of the situation of the interview. This was a preliminary interpretation, dealing both with the nonverbal elements of the interaction and with some of my reactions to the themes discussed. These exercises were important not only for understanding the interview but also for generating questions for future ones. Second, each interview was transcribed verbatim. Third, after I finished all the interviews and had an overview of the material, I went back to each interview and wrote a detailed analysis of the structure of the narrative and the speaker's opinions about different themes. This type of analysis is similar to the example presented in chapter 1. Its intention was to imprint on my mind the individuality of each narrative and its articulations before I began to think in terms of comparison, juxtapositions, and generalizations. In fact, to deal with qualitative material is to focus on the richness of the details. Fourth, I generated a list of themes that seemed to be central and recurrent. These themes expressed associations of issues (for example, evil versus authority, instead of evil and authority separately). Fifth, I went back to the electronic file of each interview and indexed the themes I had identified. Sixth, I produced an index for each interview. Seventh, I produced a general index of indexes. Those two types of indexes guided me throughout the writing process and allowed me to navigate with a certain confidence through the interviews. The first version of the comprehensive analysis had all the pertinent citations for each theme analyzed. It was almost unreadable because of the length, amount of repetition, and attention to details. The present version is the third rewriting, in which I try to establish a compromise between the requirements of readability and reference to the material.

2. The "basic basket" was a notion of what a worker's family needed to survive. It was used by the government to calculate the minimum salary. Recently, it has been used to refer to a set of food basics. Because of the decreased purchasing power of salaries, many employers distribute these foods to their workers along with their paychecks.

3. For an extensive discussion of what working-class people think of Vargas

and his rule, and especially of the corporatist state he created, see Caldeira 1984: chapter 4.

4. This theme had many other expressions at the time. For example, in a famous song of the late 1980s, Caetano Veloso asks: "Quando é que em vez de rico ou polícia ou mendigo ou pivete serei cidadão, e quem vai equacionar as pressões do PT, da UDR e fazer dessa vergonha uma nação?" (Where will I be a citizen instead of a rich man, or a policeman, or a beggar, or an urchin; and who is going to equate the demands of the PT and the UDR [party of the rural elite] and make of this shame a nation? (Caetano Veloso and Tony Costa, "Vamo Comer").

5. This tension between a modern ideal and the backward reality of the nation surfaces in the most disparate models invented by Brazilian social sciences. It is present in the racial discussions of the late nineteenth century about "whitening the population" (see Skidmore 1974) and in the debates about the relationship between liberalism and slavery (see Schwarz's famous discussion [1977] about "ideas out of place"). It is also obviously present in the discussions about national developmentalism and the need to skip stages of development and accelerate industrialization (see Furtado 1969 and F. H. Cardoso's discussion (1980) on the "originality of the copy"), and about dependency theory (F. H. Cardoso and Faletto 1967). The most famous anthropological model articulating a tension between local specificities and full modernity in Brazil is that by DaMatta (see especially 1991).

6. Some of these images are as old as the country itself. Brazil is often described as "a land where whatever you plant grows and blooms." This phrase was used in 1500 by the scribe Pero Vaz de Caminha, who traveled to the Brazilian shores to describe the new land to the king of Portugal.

7. Illusion is also a good metaphor for what happens under inflation and the financial spiral that accompanies it: one thinks one has made money in financial speculation, but it is only an illusion, for purchasing power still declines; one thinks that one's salary has increased, but it has only just kept up with inflation.

8. He uses here the expression *querendo ter os direitos* (seeking to have rights respected). It has been a popular motto of the labor movement since Vargas and one much emphasized by the contemporary social movements and the PT. Thus this young man, who votes for the PT, interprets Rambo in these political terms.

9. See chapter 7 for an analysis of real estate development. This opinion about luxury developments was quite common at that time in the press and among realtors.

10. James Holston and I are conducting the research project "Working-Class Interiors: The Aesthetics of Autoconstructed Houses in São Paulo," in which we analyze the architectural and consumer aesthetics of the working classes—aesthetics that provide them with a public idiom with which to evaluate their experiences of building the city and becoming modern citizens. See Caldeira 1986 and Holston 1991a for an analysis of working-class taste and a critique of Bourdieu's view with respect to Brazil.

11. Del Rey and Caravan are large, expensive cars.

12. These types of prejudices are widely manifested. In recent years they have resurfaced in opposition to a program called Renda Mínima (literally, minimum income). This is a program adopted by some municipalities in Brazil that provides a cash stipend to families below the poverty line and without income on the condition that they keep their children in school. This program has been opposed by various sectors of the population—including various philanthropic institutions and left-wing organizations—on the grounds that poor people should not be given cash because they will make the wrong spending decisions. They have proposed that poor people receive food rather than money. In spite of the opposition, the program was successfully adopted in various cities, such as Brasília and Campinas, where, together with members of NEPP (Núcleo de Estudos de Políticas Públicas) and Unicamp students, I researched its effects in 1995.

13. When I first arrived in Jardim das Camélias in 1978, I was asked to organize a women's discussion group. We held meetings between 1978 and 1980 and were joined by the sociologist Cynthia Sarti, who was also doing research in the neighborhood. The central theme of these meetings was female sexuality, and Cynthia and I were frequently asked to explain birth control methods and say where the women might obtain them. One of the most important social movements in the periphery demanded the construction of child-care centers so that women could hold regular jobs, and not only domestic positions, where their schedules are flexible and they can sometimes bring their children but where the pay is low and exploitation high.

14. Programs that renarrate crimes are a popular radio genre. In the 1980s and early 1990s, two such programs were always mentioned in my interviews on the periphery. One was by Gil Gomes, who in the mid-1990s introduced the genre to television (with the program *Aqui, Agora,* on SBT). The other was by Afanasio Jazadji, a crusader against human rights whose opinions I discuss in chapter 9. These programs had the effect of reproducing fear and promoting a violent police force and a disrespect for civil rights (see chapters 5 and 9). They were often invoked as a form of proof: if Gil Gomes discussed it, then it was a real and serious crime.

15. AI-5 refers to the "Institutional Act 5" that initiated the most repressive period of military rule in December 1968.

16. Interviews in Cidade Júlia in 1981 and 1982 were done by Antonio Manuel Texeira Mendes, a member of Cebrap's team.

17. Interviews in Jaguaré were done by Maria Cristina Guarnieri, a member of Cebrap's team.

18. I witnessed several of these surprise visits to City Hall. The mayors appointed by the military government preferred to receive individual leaders rather than large groups of people. In general, the people who went individually were identified with center- to right-wing political parties, whereas those who went in large numbers were affiliated with the PT. The first mayoral election in the city of São Paulo occurred only in 1985, although São Paulo's first gubernatorial election was in 1982.

19. For an analysis of different types of neighborhood leadership, especially among women, and their different tactics to mobilize neighbors and approach the city administration, see Caldeira 1990.

20. The play with words here is lost in translation. The word used to assert the favelados' humanity is *gente*. It means people, or folk. However, in spoken Portuguese, *a gente* is a pronoun used instead of *nós* (we), and includes the person who is speaking. So, the phrase *eles são gente tanto quanto a gente* means "they are people (human beings) as much as we are." *Ser gente* also means to be a good person, a sensitive person. Usually *gente* carries positive connotations. The interviewee chose to use this expression and to pun on it with *indigente*, which carries only the negative connotations of indigent, needy, and beggar.

21. For an analysis of poor people's efforts to master the dominant narratives and distance themselves from their stereotypes, see Caldeira 1984: chapter 4 and 1987. See also de Certeau 1984.

22. The literature on Brazilian "racial democracy" is extensive. I list here some works available in English. For a history of the Brazilian myth of racial democracy and social relations, see Andrews 1991, Degler 1971, and Skidmore 1974. For a history of the contemporary black movement, see Gonzalez 1985 and Hanchard 1994. The denial of racial categories is shared by other Latin American countries with a legacy of slavery and which at the end of the nineteenth century adopted the theory of "whitening the population." These are countries that usually do not register race in their census (Hasenbalg 1996). On Venezuela, see Wright 1990; on Colombia, see Wade 1993; and on Cuba, see Helg 1990.

23. Interviews in Jardim Peri-Peri were conducted in 1981 by Célia Sakurai, a member of Cebrap's research team.

24. Another version is the popular saying "Idleness is the root of all evil."

25. See Zaluar (1983, 1985, 1987, 1990, 1994). For the conceptions of work in Jardim das Camélias, see Caldeira (1984: chapter 4).

26. The equivalence of woman and prisoner in this quote from a "macho" man should not go unnoticed.

3. THE INCREASE IN VIOLENT CRIME

1. The significance of crime in the understanding of modern urban life is revealed not only in the development of social statistics but also in urban sociology, as the work of the Chicago School exemplifies. For an analysis of how, in the second half of the nineteenth century, crime and criminals began to be seen as normal facts of social life, see Leps 1992.

2. In addition to censuses, IBGE carries out periodic national household sample surveys to gather basic socioeconomic information. These surveys are called PNAD—Pesquisa Nacional por Amostra de Domicílio (National Research by Domicile Sample). The questionnaire of the 1988 PNAD included questions about victimization of crime and use of the justice system. I thank Márcia Bandeira de Mello Leite from IBGE for making available to me the data on the met-

ropolitan region of São Paulo (still unpublished). The results of the PNADs are available only for metropolitan regions, not for individual municipalities.

3. IBGE did not use the legal classifications of crimes: instead of *lesão corporal dolosa* (aggravated assault), it used a generic category *agressão física*, which can include various types of crime, such as rape. I translate *agressão física* as physical assault.

4. The number of people who are victims of physical violence is probably higher, but this abuse may not be considered wrong or worth reporting, or it may not be declared because people feel ashamed. Although the beating of children is commonplace among Brazilians of all social classes, and can be observed on the streets, the percentage of people younger than nine years of age reported as victims of physical assault in the PNAD was only 3.78 percent of the total number of assault victims.

5. Whereas in Brazil men are victimized mainly in public spaces (54.73 percent of the cases occurred on streets), women are mostly victimized inside their homes (48.2 percent). This information is not available for the metropolitan region of São Paulo.

6. Data on use of the justice system are available only for Brazilian regions. The southeast is the most developed and urban area of the country: it includes the states of Minas Gerais, Espírito Santo, Rio de Janeiro, and São Paulo.

7. In Brazil, the state administration mirrors the federal administration but changes the titles of functions. At the state level, the equivalent of the ministers is called a secretary. Therefore, when I refer to the secretary of public security, I am referring to the state secretary.

8. *Pau-de-arara*, or parrot's perch, seems to be the most common form of torture used by the police in São Paulo. It was also the most common torture used against political prisoners during military rule. The prisoner is suspended from a bar by the back of his or her knees, hands tied in front of the legs. Descriptions of this and other common methods of torture are found in Archdiocese of São Paulo 1986: chapter 2; Americas Watch 1987: chapter 5; and Amnesty International 1990.

9. In Portuguese there is a verb, *apanhar*, to designate the act of suffering a beating inflicted by somebody else, whereas in English there is no specific verb, and the passive voice has to be used: to be beaten up.

10. Lima's analysis of the police in Rio de Janeiro also indicates that police statistics are distorted, especially on thefts, robberies, vagrancy, and *jogo do bicho* (1986:124).

11. The expression *papel de bala* carries a pun lost in translation. The police call the unofficial record *papel de bala* "*pois não serve para nada, só para embrulhar.*" Literally it means that a candy wrapper is not useful for anything, only for wrapping. In Portuguese, however, *embrulhar* means both to wrap and to deceive.

12. For an analysis of the stereotypes that bias trials of violent crime in which the victim is a woman, see Ardaillon and Debert 1988, Americas Watch Com-

mittee 1991a, and Correa 1981 and 1983. On violence against women, see Gregori 1993.

13. For an analysis of the women's police stations, see Ardaillon 1989 and Nelson 1995. Data on the number of police stations from the press office of the department of public security.

14. The information that the deaths caused by military policemen are not counted as homicides was officially confirmed by the department of public security.

15. Deaths registered by the civil registry are classified according to the categories of the World Health Organization ICD (International Classification of Disease. Version 9 was used until 1996).

16. Although the boundaries of what is officially called the Metropolitan Region of Greater São Paulo have remained constant, the boundaries of the Police Region of Greater São Paulo have changed at various times during the period considered. All criminal statistics refer to the police region and consequently have a slightly different geographical basis depending on the year. The changes do not affect the municipality of São Paulo. From 1973 to 1985 the police region excluded the municipalities of Cajamar and Salesópolis (which are part of the MRSP) and included the municipality of Igaratá (not part of the MRSP). In 1986, Salesópolis was included; in 1987, the region included Cajamar and excluded Igaratá, and in this year it coincided with the MRSP; in 1988, Guararema, Salesópolis, and Santa Isabel were excluded, and this configuration continues up to the present. For all types of crime, I give in the text the most recent information available, usually from 1996.

17. A Forum of Presidents of Councils on the Feminine Condition elaborated a feminist proposal for reformation of the civil and penal codes and presented it to the National Congress in March 1991. This proposal suggests eliminating the category "crimes against custom" and including rape in the category "crimes against persons." A similar proposal circulating among feminist groups advocates criminalizing sexual harassment and family violence and legalizing abortion. A version of this proposal appears as "Women's Manifesto against Violence: Proposal for Changes in the Brazilian Penal Code," *Estudos Feministas* 1[1] (1993): 190–91). For a feminist proposal for legislation concerning violence within the family, see Pimentel and Pierro (1993:169–75). As of March 2000, reformation of the penal code is still under discussion. It seems there is a consensus among the members of the commission on eliminating the category "crimes against custom." However, the majority of the commission members, of whom only one is a woman, opposes legalizing abortion. On March 8, 1996, the Brazilian president and the National Council for the Rights of Women announced a series of measures to celebrate Women's Day. These included sending a proposal to the National Congress to include rape among "crimes against persons." As of December 1999, the proposal has not been voted on. For an analysis of the feminist lobby during the works of the Constitutional Assembly, see Ardaillon 1989.

18. Data from the civil police show that between 1981 and 1996, car accidents accounted for an average of 12 percent of the total police reports in the metropolitan region, and 40 percent of the reports of crimes against persons. The civil police records show a lower incidence of traffic fatalities than the other available records. I use them here for consistency because for all other types of crime, data from the civil police are the only ones available.

19. Separate data for the municipality of São Paulo are available only from 1976 onward. Unless otherwise noted, all criminal data cited are from Secretaria de Segurança Pública do Estado de São Paulo, Delegacia Geral de Polícia, Departamento de Planejamento e Controle da Polícia Civil, Centro de Análise de Dados, organized by Seade—Fundação Sistema Estadual de Análise de Dados. Seade is also in charge of the official publication of data in its annual collection of statistics for the state of São Paulo, the *Anuário Estatístico do Estado de São Paulo*, from which I quote. I thank Dora Feiguin and Renato Sérgio de Lima from Seade for making data available to me and for helping me navigate through the statistics. Unless otherwise noted, in all calculations I consider rates of crime per 100,000 population. Annual population estimates are also based on Seade's data, and were corrected according to the results of the 1991 census and the 1996 *Contagem da População*.

20. It is difficult to know how much this pattern has changed in relation to previous periods because of the lack of studies, the difficulty in comparing data from different studies, and their contradictory results. According to Fausto 1984:445, of the total arrests for crimes (not including misdemeanors) in São Paulo from 1892 to 1916, 39.5 percent were for crimes against persons (Fausto calls them "blood crimes"), and 54.6 percent were for property crimes. However, for Rio de Janeiro between 1908 and 1929, Bretas (1995:108) argues that "violent crimes represent the greater proportion of crimes in Rio, mainly through cases of assault which constituted more than a third of annual crimes." For imperial Rio de Janeiro, Holloway (1993:213, 256) indicates that the proportion of arrests for property crimes was higher than that of crimes against persons in 1862, 1865, and 1875.

21. Data of death registration compiled according to the International Classification of Disease are also elaborated by Seade and published in the *Anuário Estatístico do Estado de São Paulo*. Since 1991, they have also been elaborated by Pro-Aim (Programa de Aprimoramento de Informações de Mortalidade no Município de São Paulo), which keeps the most detailed information, but only for the municipality of São Paulo. Data from death registration have a much more complex and accurate classification of causes of death than do those of the police: they allow one to differentiate, for example, the instrument used and the motive (intentional, unintentional, or undetermined). Usually, deaths intentionally provoked are labeled homicides in health statistics. However, since the categories included in this classification (E960 to E969) exclude unlawful deaths of undetermined intentionality, I name it murder, making it comparable to the civil police category of *homicídio doloso* (murder), which excludes manslaughter *(homicídio culposo)*.

22. According to the department of public security, in 1994 there were 19 *chacinas* in the city of São Paulo, with a total of 61 deaths. In 1995, there were 30 *chacinas* and 96 deaths. Although these numbers are elevated, they do not explain the difference between the police reports and the civil registry reports, which in 1994 was 473 and in 1995 was 894 in the city of São Paulo.

23. Feiguin and Lima (1995) use a special tabulation of homicides that differs from the data usually published by Seade that I use here. For civil police data, they group murder and manslaughter together. For civil registry data, they tabulate according to place of death rather than the victim's place of residence.

24. Feiguin and Lima (1995) analyze only data for the municipality of São Paulo but formulate this hypothesis for the other municipalities.

25. From the 1970s to the 1990s, while American rates have oscillated between 8 and 10 homicides per 100,000 population, European rates have oscillated between 0.3 and 3.5, and Japanese rates have remained at around 1 homicide per 100,000 population (Chesnais 1981:471). Chesnais analyzes the available statistics for Europe and the United States comparatively since at least the mid-nineteenth century. The lack of information and analyses for previous periods make it difficult to talk about the historical trends in homicide rates in Brazil, but there are indications that in the first decades of the twentieth century they were higher than in Europe and the United States. For São Paulo, Fausto (1984: 95) indicates that between 1910 and 1916 the rate of imprisonment for homicide per 100,000 population was around 10.7. According to Bretas (1995:111), the rates of homicide per 100,000 population in Rio de Janeiro between 1908 and 1929 oscillated between 3 (1918) and 12.33 (1926). The average was 8.09. According to Chesnais, the homicide rate for Paris between 1910 and 1913 was 3.4, and between 1921 and 1930 1.9 (1981:79). In France, the rate of murder (voluntary homicide) for 1901–1913 was 1.13, and for 1920–1933 it was 1.06 (Chesnais 1981:74). For the United States, the rate for 1901–1910 was 2.93, and between 1911 and 1920 it was 6.28 (Chesnais 1981:93).

Chesnais's contemporary data are based on statistics from the World Health Organization. According to this source (United Nations 1995:484–505), in the 1990s homicide rates were 9.8 in the United States (according to the FBI, the 1990 rate was 9.4); 1.1 in France (1991); 1.2 in Germany (1992); 2.9 in Italy (1991); 1.0 in Spain (1990); 0.9 in the United Kingdom (1992); and 0.6 in Japan (1992).

26. Data for American cities are from the *Uniform Crime Reports for the United States,* based on police reports and published by the FBI. Data for Latin America and the Caribbean are from United Nations 1995:484–505 and refer to death rates compiled by health authorities. Local situations may differ considerably from national averages. According to a study by the Population Crisis Committee, in 1985 some of the worst rates of homicide per 100,000 population were in Cape Town (64.6), Cairo (56.3), Alexandria (49.3), Rio de Janeiro (49.3), Manila (36.5), Mexico City (27.6), and São Paulo (26.0) (*Veja,* 28 November 1990, 66) . We should also be careful when looking at these international rates. For 1985, the rates shown in this study for the city of São Paulo al-

most coincided with those of police reports (26.98) but are quite different from those produced on the basis of death registration for both São Paulo (35.8) and Rio de Janeiro (41.0).

27. For São Paulo for 1880–1924, there is a study of criminal statistics by Fausto (1984). For Rio de Janeiro during 1907–1930, there is a study by Bretas (1995), which also analyzes statistics and written reports produced by the police. For Rio de Janeiro circa 1900, there is a study by Chalhoub (1986), which does not analyze statistics but tries to uncover from judiciary records a picture of the everyday relationships and conflicts of the working classes. For the colonial and imperial periods, see Aufderheide 1975, Chalhoub 1990, Franco 1974, Holloway 1993, Huggins 1985, and Lara 1988; but only Aufderheide, Holloway, and Huggins analyze statistics. For other countries in Latin America, see Johnson 1990, Rohlfes 1983, Taylor 1979, and Vanderwood 1981. On Brazilian social bandits of the early twentieth century, the classic study is Queiroz 1977.

28. The bibliography on those cases is vast. Interesting summaries are, for Colombia, *Comisión de Estudios sobre la Violencia* (1987), and, for Peru, *Comisión Especial de Senado* (1989).

29. Various of these studies were sponsored by the Ministry of Justice and the National Secretariat of Human Rights and are part of the project "Maps of Risk of Violence" coordinated by Cedec in São Paulo. For São Paulo, see Núcleo de Estudos de Seguridade Social (1995); and for Rio de Janeiro, see Cano (1997).

30. A recent study by Claudio Beato supports the interpretation I am offering. It could not find correlations between rates of violent crime and indicators of social inequality, availability of public services, unemployment, or quality of urban life. Partial results of this research, which is still in progress, were presented at the conference "Rising Violence and the Criminal Justice Response in Latin America: Towards an Agenda for Collaborative Research in the Twenty-first Century," University of Texas at Austin, May 1999.

4. THE POLICE

1. The above figure refers to total homicides calculated by the civil registry, which probably include killings by police. If we consider the homicide total reported by the civil police, the percentage of police killings would be 27.6 percent.

2. This tendency can be traced throughout the history of Brazilian and Brazilianist social sciences. It has sometimes been expressed as the idea of "two Brazils": one modern, industrial, and urban, the other retrograde and rural.

3. An earlier and similar interpretation appears in the provocative analysis by Antonio Candido (1970) of the novel *Memórias de um Sargento de Milícias*. He claims that imperial Brazilian society was marked by a dialectic of order and disorder.

4. Linger (1992) also develops a dualistic model to explain violence in a Brazilian city, São Luís do Maranhão. He opposes Carnival, a "bacchanalian festival," and *briga*, defined as a ritualized and potentially lethal street confrontation. Violence runs through both, and Linger explains it by reference to a folk theory

about the expelling of accumulated frustrations, resentments, and irritations he calls *desabafo*. In this theory, Carnival, *briga*, and *desabafo* supposedly form a "cultural cluster." Carnival would be a "good *desabafo*" and represent "self and society under control," whereas *briga* would be a "bad *desabafo*" and represent "self and society out of control" (1992:225). Thus *desabafo* is the "operator" between order and disorder, calm and violence. When it is managed successfully, as in an orderly Carnival, it produces *communitas;* when it goes awry, it leads to *briga* and death. Linger goes to the point of claiming that *desabafo* is the "raison d'être of Carnival" (234), thus reducing considerably the many dimensions of this complex social festival—a reduction probably needed to make it pair with *briga*, a social event of rather less cultural significance. Linger's analysis is restricted to a psychological folk theory of the management of aggression and does not offer any sociological explanation for the spread of violence. Thus, he reproduces a view that violence is both extraordinary and an individual matter of self-control. This view precludes the understanding of violence as a regular element of power relations in everyday social interactions. None of the people I interviewed about the increase in crime and violence in São Paulo mentioned *desabafo* in their efforts to make sense of them.

5. These oppositions are all found in DaMatta (1991). See, for example, the chart on page 177, in which he lists oppositions between the characteristics of the individual and the person.

6. Although police institutions in Brazil have always been split, there is a tendency to talk about the police without specifying which force is being analyzed. This happens, for example, in Bretas 1995, Cancelli 1993,and Lima 1986, which analyze only the civil police but refer to it as "the police" without explaining that they are not considering other, very important parts of the police institutions. Fernandes 1974 studies only the military police in São Paulo.

7. A broad and flexible definition of the police is characteristic of the formation of the police everywhere, not only in Brazil. Schwartz (1988:4), for example, argues that in eighteenth-century France, "police" should be understood in a comprehensive way associated with the idea of governance. Holloway (1993) provides the main analysis of the history of the police forces during the Empire.

8. The rhetoric used to express the need for violence also seems to have a striking continuity. In 1888, a *delegado* is quoted as saying: "An arrested person has a right to be protected from the authority in whose custody he finds himself. But this does not mean that [the police] should not put into effect all due energy when respect for the law is not obtained by other means" (Holloway 1993:245). As we shall see, for more than a century "due energy" has continued to mean brutality.

9. For discussions of the connections between the development of a repressive state machinery and attempts to control the urban poor in Western Europe during early industrialization, see Schwartz 1988, Chevalier 1973 [1958], Davis 1991, and Jones 1982: chapters 5–7. For an analysis of the continuous decline of imprisonments for victimless crimes in the United States between 1860 and 1920, see Monkkonen 1981.

10. During the redemocratization years of 1945 to 1964, the structure of the police forces seems to have remained the same—at least in São Paulo, where police forces continued to be divided into the civil police, the Força Pública, and the Guarda Civil. However, the history of the police in this period has still to be written.

11. For an analysis of the history of the military police and its illegal practices since military rule, see Pinheiro 1982, 1983, and 1991b, and Pinheiro et al. 1991.

12. For an account of abuses during the military regime, see Archdiocese of São Paulo 1986. For the military conception of national security that structured the whole repressive apparatuses, see Stepan 1971 and 1988.

13. From the colonial period until well into the twentieth century, violence was also pervasive among the "free men" as the means used to solve interpersonal conflicts, as Franco 1974 shows. See chapter 9.

14. In 1910, sailors in Rio de Janeiro revolted against punishment by whipping. This revolt (Revolta da Chibata) had the support of Rio's working classes. After a few days, the sailors surrendered in exchange for amnesty; instead, they were tied with iron chains into a boat and sent to the Amazon. At the same time, the police took the opportunity to "clean" the city prison of all people it considered inconvenient and sent to the Amazon at least 292 common prisoners classified as vagabonds, 105 sailors, 44 female prisoners, and 50 army recruits (Pinheiro 1981:42). In other words, a revolt against physical punishment ended up not only punishing those who had been promised amnesty but also served as a pretext for a totally illegal "cleansing" of the city prison. The sailors and prisoners were sent to work in the Amazon on the installation of telex cables with Marechal Rondon.

15. The Brasil Nunca Mais (Brazil Never Again) project secretly undertaken by the Archdiocese of São Paulo photocopied and analyzed the military court proceedings of 707 complete trials held from 1964 to 1979 and fragmentary records of dozens of other trials. The documents are now in various archives around the world. A summary of the conclusions, from which I quote, was published in Brazil in 1985. An edited version of this summary has appeared in English as Torture in Brazil (1986). The deaths and disappearances mentioned by BNM are only those documented either directly or indirectly in the trials; they do not include victims of abuses that were never connected to trials, as in cases of rural violence. Sigaud 1987:7–8 calculates that between 1964 and 1986, 916 peasants were killed for political reasons, but only 93 of those deaths were committed by representatives of the state.

5. POLICE VIOLENCE UNDER DEMOCRACY

1. For a broader discussion of the disjunction between respect for political and social rights and disrespect for individual rights in contemporary Brazil, see Holston and Caldeira 1998.

2. In this sense, the present situation is totally different from that of the military regimes in the Southern Cone from the 1960s to the 1980s and of the po-

litical struggles in Central America in the 1970s and 1980s, which could be described as situations of high political violence. There have been repression and violence against participants of social movements, especially in rural areas (against the Movimento dos Sem Terra, for example), but nothing on the scale of what happened during the military regimes in Latin America.

3. *Relatório Trimestral da Ouvidoria da Polícia do Estado de São Paulo*, December 1995–February 1996, 44.

4. In São Paulo, for each police officer who dies, there are an average of seventeen wounded. But as far as civilians are concerned, the ratio is the opposite of what is expected.

5. These percentages refer to the total number of homicides recorded by the civil registry. If we consider the civil police reports, the percentages are 15.93 percent in 1991 and 27.4 percent in 1992.

6. The candidate supported by the party of the military regime, Reynaldo de Barros, received 25.2 percent of the votes. The rest were distributed among three other opposition parties. For analyses in English of the 1982 elections, see Caldeira 1987, F. H. Cardoso 1987, and Lamounier 1989.

7. As far as I know, the history of the Montoro government has not yet been written. Nevertheless, the opposition to José Carlos Dias, which started the day he disclosed his intentions, is extremely well documented by the press.

8. This explanation coincides with Bretas's argument about the autonomy of the civil police during the Old Republic (1995: conclusion).

9. Pinheiro (1982:90) reproduces a document of a Rota chief attesting that it was impossible to identify the guns used by a team of Rota because of the way the guns were issued.

10. Interview, 25 July 1990.

11. Pinheiro 1982:77. Pinheiro has written extensively on Rota's abuses. For an article in English, see Pinheiro 1991b.

12. "Rota, a Mística, os Métodos e as Mortes," *Folha de S. Paulo*, 10 October 1982.

13. "População Quer a Rota," *Folha de S. Paulo*, 3 December 1982.

14. "Para os Eleitores, Segurança É o maior Problema de São Paulo," *Folha de S. Paulo*, 8 September 1985.

15. One of the first very serious violations of human rights occurred during Carnival in 1989. Eighteen of the fifty prisoners kept in a cell *(cela forte)* of three square meters died of asphyxiation in the Forty-second Police District of São Paulo. This episode reveals the effects of the different systems of accountability to which civil and military policemen are subject. The civil policemen involved were prosecuted, eventually found guilty, and given unusually long prison terms (adding up to 516 years). The military policemen, however, have not yet been brought to trial by the military justice.

16. Data from the Corregedoria da Polícia Civil (Secretaria da Justiça e da Cidadania, Report prepared for the Fiftieth Session of the Commission on Human Rights of the United Nations, Geneva, 1994, Appendix D-3).

17. The massacre was extensively documented by the Brazilian media. It is

also recorded in Amnesty International 1993, Machado and Marques 1993, and Pietá and Pereira 1993. Various other massacres involving military policemen subsequently occurred in Rio de Janeiro. They include the killing of eight minors sleeping by the Candelária Church on 23 July 1993 and the killing of twenty-one residents of the favela Vigário Geral on 30 August 1993.

18. I analyzed press coverage of the massacre at Casa de Detenção in five newspapers and two magazines, all published in São Paulo, for a period of ten days following the massacre. The sample includes the two biggest Paulista newspapers with national circulation, *Folha de S. Paulo* and *O Estado de S. Paulo,* and three local papers, *Jornal da Tarde, Folha da Tarde,* and *Notícias Populares.* The latter two are considered sensationalist. The magazines are *Veja* and *IstoÉ,* both of national circulation. I did this analysis at Cebrap for the research project "Politics, Democracy, and the Mass Media."

19. The Casa de Detenção is São Paulo's largest prison, part of the Carandiru complex. It was built in the early 1960s, in what used to be a peripheral part of town, to house 3,250 prisoners. On the day of the massacre, however, it held more than 7,100 prisoners (statistics are not exact, but all reports mention more than 7,000). Such overcrowding is common at the Casa de Detenção and other Brazilian prisons, where conditions are dangerous and degrading. (See, for example, Amnesty International 1993 and Americas Watch 1989). Revolts at Casa de Detenção, considered to be one of Brazil's worst prisons, are relatively common, and the previous biggest one, in 1987, resulted in thirty-one deaths. On the day of the massacre, Pavilion 9 was lodging 2,069 prisoners instead of the 1,000 for which it was planned. This pavilion is considered especially violent.

20. Although every magazine and newspaper criticized the authorities and the police, there were significant differences among them. *Notícias Populares,* a sensationalist newspaper specializing in crime and news with sexual content, wrote one of the strongest critiques of the governor and the police. *Jornal da Tarde,* a newspaper of the group *O Estado de S. Paulo,* known for its concern with the rule of law, surprisingly gave more space to police views than other newspapers did and published various reports in which police officers justified their actions.

21. It is interesting to compare the reactions of Paulista state authorities after the massacre with the reactions of President Fernando Henrique Cardoso after the massacre of nineteen members of the Movimento dos Sem Terra in the interior of Pará in April 1996. Cardoso condemned in very explicit terms the action of the military police and asked Congress to consider a law that would allow the civil justice system to try military policemen.

22. In contrast to what happened in São Paulo, the state administration in Rio adopted a very explicit "tough" policy that produced a dramatic increase in killings by the military police. After General Nilton Cerqueira took office as secretary of public security in 1995, the number of civilians killed increased from an average of 3.2 per month to 20.55 (Human Rights Watch/Americas 1997:15)

23. The Covas administration also started publishing the numbers of killings by the civil police, which were not available before: 47 in 1996 and 18 in 1997. The numbers of civil police officers killed were 17 in 1996 and 11 in 1997.

24. This group includes the following state representatives: Afanasio Jazadji, who defends torture and attacks human rights in his radio programs, and who received the greatest number of votes in São Paulo in 1986; Erasmo Dias, former secretary of public security under the military rule; the ex–military policeman Conte Lopes, the most active in defending the PM after the 1992 massacre; and the *delegado* Hilkias de Oliveira.

25. Conte Lopes was elected with 66,772 votes; Afanasio Jazadji was elected with 58,326 votes; Erasmo Dias was elected with 28,178 votes. Guimarães, with 26,156 votes, and Hilkias de Oliveira, with 11,799 votes, were not elected.

26. This discussion refers to a famous crime involving two upper-class people who appeared frequently in the newspapers' social columns. Doca Street was acquitted of killing his girlfriend, Angela Diniz, during a controversial trial in which his lawyers argued that he had acted in "legitimate defense of honor." The trial garnered a strong reaction from feminists, who challenged the juridical argument of "legitimate defense of honor," which has been used to acquit men who kill their wives. For a history of this argument and the ways in which its use has been changing, see Ardaillon and Debert 1987 and Americas Watch 1991a. This argument was finally outlawed in 1991 by the Brazilian Supreme Court. The working-class woman I quote does not refer to this crime as it is usually discussed—as proof of a male-biased judiciary system—but as proof of a class-biased justice system.

27. Interview by Antonio Flávio Pierucci, a member of Cebrap's research team.

28. According to Martins (1991:22), between 1979 and 1988 the press reported 272 lynchings in Brazil, 131 of them in the state of São Paulo. In April 1991, a lynching was broadcast on national television.

29. Interview by João Vargas.

30. It is widely acknowledged in Brazil that the law discriminates by class: the poor suffer criminal sanctions from which the rich are generally immune, while the rich enjoy access to private law (civil and commercial) from which the poor are systematically excluded. On the consequences of this double bias and other aspects of judicial discredit in Brazil, see Holston and Caldeira (1998).

31. Some enterprises selling security equipment in São Paulo are branches of multinational corporations. In the United States there are more than sixteen million residential security systems in use. Between 1986 and 1991, the sales of alarm systems increased by 80 percent (*New York Times*, 9 February 1991).

32. For analyses of private policing in developed countries, see Bayley and Shearing 1996, Johnston 1992, Ocqueteau 1997, Ocqueteau and Pottier 1995, and Shearing 1992.

33. Coincidentally or not, this shift happened just after the first directly elected governors took office and followed the shift of all political archives (DOPS) from the state secretary of public security to the federal police. At that point, the military retained control of the federal government but had lost elections for governor in all major states. The control of private security services shifted to a special commission at the Ministry of Justice, the Comissão Exe-

cutiva para Assuntos de Vigilância e Transporte de Valores do Ministério da Justiça, as regulated on 12 December 1986 (Portaria 601 of Ministry of Justice).

34. Complemented by Decree 1,592 of 10 August 1995 and by Portaria 992 of the federal police of 25 October 1995.

35. This commission was originally created in 25 February 1991 (Portaria 73 of the Ministry of Justice), and reformed by Portaria 1545 of 8 December 1995.

36. According to José Luiz Fernandes, president of Abrevis (Associação Brasileira de Empresas de Vigilância e Segurança), the national association of private security enterprises, and of the employers' trade union in the state of São Paulo (Sindicato das Empresas de Segurança Privada e Cursos de Formação do Estado de São Paulo), the private security market grew about 20 percent per year after 1980, and in both 1989 and 1990 it had a U.S.$500 million profit (interview, 12 June 1991, and *Gazeta Mercantil*, 10 July 1990).

37. Unpublished statistics, Comissão Executiva para Assuntos de Vigilância e Transporte de Valores.

38. Even the 1:1 ratio of 1996 can be considered low relative to that of developed countries, where private security guards tend to outnumber public law enforcement officials. In 1990 in the United States there were 1.5 million people employed in private security enterprises and approximately 600,000 public (law enforcement) employees, that is, a ratio of 2.5 private guards per policeman. In 1993, it was estimated that by the year 2000 private security officers would outnumber public law enforcement officers three to one (U.S. House 1993:97, 135).

39. Following the Brazilian corporatist labor legislation, the legal segment of private security in the state of São Paulo is organized into two trade unions, one for employers (Sindicato das Empresas de Segurança Privada e Cursos de Formação do Estado de São Paulo) and one for employees (Sindicato dos Empregados em Empresas de Segurança, Vigilância, Cursos de Formação de Vigilantes, Transporte de Valores e Segurança Privada de São Paulo). Moreover, business owners have their own national association, Abrevis. There is still a national association of the enterprises of transportation of valuables, ABVT (Associação Brasileira das Empresas de Transporte de Valores).

40. Recently, members of the registered firms have also been writing in the press about the dangers of what they call "clandestine" private security (for example, article by José Luiz Fernandes in *Gazeta Mercantil*, 30 July 1996).

41. Brazilian private security entrepreneurs are expanding their business to the Mercosul countries and have formed an association to this end. Brazil is the only country in the Mercosul to have specific legislation governing private security, and its executives are preparing to influence laws to be created by other countries. They are especially concerned about labor legislation, arguing that the cost of a private guard in Brazil is 40 percent higher than in Chile and 30 percent higher than in Argentina because of Brazilian regulations (interviews with representatives of the association, July 1996).

42. Pires Serviços de Segurança Ltda. is probably one of the most sophisti-

cated security companies in Brazil. I visited Pires's installations, had access to their large training facilities, and interviewed five of its directors. Their expansion plans are clearly stated in their newsletter, *Jornal da Pires.*

43. Interview, 12 June 1991.

44. Dias is part of the "security bloc" that supported the Casa de Detenção massacre.

45. Interview, 17 December 1990 and *Folha de S. Paulo,* 23 September 1990.

46. See Fernandes 1991 for analysis of the case of Cabo Bruno and other *justiceiros.*

47. This problem is certainly not exclusive to highly unequal societies. Western democratic societies, argue Bayley and Shearing, "are moving inexorably, we fear, into a Clockwork Orange world where both the market and the government protect the affluent from the poor—the one by barricading and excluding the other by repressing and imprisoning—and where civil society for the poor disappears in the face of criminal victimization and government repression" (1996:602).

48. Borneman (1997) has recently applied Girard's hypothesis on the role of the justice system in preventing cycles of violence to the fate of Eastern European countries and their "invocation of the rule of law" in the aftermath of socialism. He concluded that the states that are able to transform and establish themselves as legitimate moral authorities, providing justice and invoking the principles of the rule of law, "will not disintegrate into cycles of violence." The key to such a transformation is "the state's assumption of accountability for retributive justice" (Borneman 1997:165). The state that typifies this process, in Borneman's analysis, and which, according to him, was most successful in controlling violence and institutionalizing the rule of law, is East Germany. This example is, however, quite particular, since East Germany was essentially incorporated into the existing institutional framework of West Germany. Focusing mostly on this very specific case, Borneman does not consider how the rule of law may be legitimated in a context in which it did not exist or was abusive before, that is, a context in which the terms of the "invocation of the rule of law" have no institutional representation and little resonance among the population. This seems to be the challenge of various postsocialist states as well as of Brazil.

6. SÃO PAULO

1. The historical analysis of São Paulo for the period 1890–1940 relies on the following studies: Bonduki 1982 and 1983; Langenbuch 1971; Morse 1970; Rolnik 1983, 1994, and 1997. Ribeiro (1993) develops a similar analysis for Rio de Janeiro.

2. The new inhabitants of the city arriving to work in the just-built factories were mainly European immigrants. They were attracted to Brazil under the incentives of a policy aimed at importing white workers to replace the black ex-

slaves and "whiten" the Brazilian population. In 1893, foreign-born people represented 55 percent of the population of the city, according to the city census. This was the peak of foreign immigration; after 1900, the rate of population growth started shrinking. In 1920, foreigners represented 36 percent of the population (Fausto 1984:10).

3. In 1900, the average number of people per building in São Paulo was 11.07 (Bonduki 1982:85).

4. One of the main popular revolts at the time originated not in the workplace but in the government's decision to vaccinate the population against smallpox and to send sanitary agents to poor areas of Rio de Janeiro to disinfect their homes and destroy those allegedly infested. The Revolta da Vacina Obrigatória (revolt against obligatory vaccine) occurred in 1904, precisely when the mayor, Pereira Passos, launched a radical program of urban reform of the Haussmannian type, opening huge avenues through working-class neighborhoods and destroying many houses.

5. Municipal Law 1,874, of 1915, created the first division of the city into four zones (central, urban, suburban, and rural) and required that construction plans be approved by city officials. Act 849, of 1916, regulated construction. Municipal Law 2,611, of 1923, established minimum dimensions for an urban lot (300 square meters) and rules for paving the streets. It also established that for developments larger than 40,000 square meters, developers should donate spaces for streets and green areas. It seems that this law was influenced by the City of São Paulo Improvements and Free Hold Land Co., Ltd, a developing company that had been launching new developments inspired by the British Garden Cities since 1912. These developments produced the neighborhoods called "Jardins" (gardens), which have housed the upper and middle classes since the 1920s. (São Paulo—Sempla 1995:15). In 1929, the city passed its first Código de Obras (building code: Municipal Law 3,427, Código Arthur Saboya), which systematized most of the previous legislation and established a minimum of three floors per building in the central area, thereby encouraging vertical build-up. This code was reconsolidated in 1934. See Morse (1970:366–67) for a common critique of this plan.

6. See Holston 1991b for an analysis of the relationship between illegal practices and land occupation in Brazil, especially on the periphery of São Paulo. See Rolnik 1997 for an analysis of the urban legislation and the same legal/illegal dynamic between 1886 and 1936.

7. Although important decisions based on the plan began to be made in the late 1920s, its main work was done after 1938, during the administration of Prestes Maia.

8. In 1937, the federal government created the *institutos de previdência* (social welfare institutes) and in 1946, the Fundação da Casa Popular (Popular House Foundation) to construct houses for workers to buy. This plan was never realized: the few houses that were built were distributed according to clientelistic criteria. Vargas also renewed the *caixas econômicas* (government-run credit institutions), which started to finance houses for the middle classes.

9. For an analysis of the various dimensions of the *Lei do Inquilinato*, see Bonduki 1983 and 1994. For an analysis of Vargas's labor policy, see Santos 1979.

10. Since 1934, various restrictions have applied to foreign migration. Over the same period, droughts in northeast Brazil brought many people to São Paulo. Between 1935 and 1939, 96 percent of the 285,000 migrants to the state of São Paulo were Brazilians (Morse 1970:302).

11. The analysis that follows is based on Brant et al. 1989, Bonduki 1983, Caldeira 1984, Camargo et al. 1976, and Langenbuch 1971.

12. Population growth is shown in table 7. Between 1950 and 1960, more than one million people settled in the metropolitan region. Between 1960 and 1970, the number of migrants surpassed two million. A similar number arrived in the following decade (Perillo 1993:2).

13. Cf. Langenbuch 1971. Real estate speculators bought most of the lots sold before the 1930s, and they remained unoccupied. For the history of a peripheral neighborhood first opened in the 1920s but occupied only in the 1960s, see Caldeira 1984.

14. In 1948, only 4.2 percent of the urban commutes on public transportation were made by train; during the 1950s and 1960s, the percentage of train commutes was never higher than 6.6 percent of the total (R. Velze, cited in Kowarick and Bonduki 1994:153).

15. This monopoly was broken at the end of the 1920s, when the city decided not to renew the contract with Light and to deny it a monopoly of the bus system. At the same time, the city government decided to start opening Avenida 9 de Julho, the first of the new radial avenues.

16. In 1948, public buses accounted for 31.0 percent of the commutes, and private buses for 12.6 percent. By 1966, however, the situation had reversed, with private buses carrying 75.7 percent of all commuters and public buses only 15.5 percent (R. Velze, cited in Kowarick and Bonduki 1994:153).

17. All these forms of illegality or irregularity affect people who buy their lots in good faith and pay for them. They constitute a different case from the favelas, which are formed by land invasion and in which people usually do not buy their lots (although they may buy their shacks).

18. In 1977, in the eastern zone of the city, where Jardim das Camélias is located, residents who traveled to work by bus spent an average of thirteen hours a day outside the home, commuting to work and working. In 1987 the situation was unchanged (Caldeira 1984:62; Metrô 1989:41).

19. For 1920, Bonduki 1982:146; for 1960 and 1991, Brazilian census.

20. I thank Cebrap's Laboratório de Espacialização de Dados, and especially Ciro Biderman and Anderson Kazuo Nakano, for the invaluable assistance in the elaboration of the maps used in this chapter.

21. Ferreira's source is the registration of elevators in the city of São Paulo. Since 1940 the law has required all elevators to be registered with the city government. These records contain the address of each building and the year it was put on the market.

22. Decree 5,481, of 25 June 1928, regulated the selling of individual apart-

ments in buildings with more than five floors (Ferreira 1987:72). In the United States, condominium ownership was regulated only in 1961 (McKenzie 1994:94).

23. The original Ibope polls can be found in the Arquivo Edgard Leuenroth at Unicamp. The figures cited above are in volume 2 of the 1945 surveys. Documents are identified only by date.

24. This law was inspired by Anhaia Melo, São Paulo's mayor and planner, who was in favor of controlling the vertical expansion and population density of the city. He used the English expression "floor space index" to refer to the *coeficiente de aproveitamento* (Rolnik 1997:197). I use a more literal translation.

25. See Sachs 1990 for an analysis of housing policies in Brazil during the existence of BNH. Because of Brazil's high rates of inflation, incomes are usually expressed in terms of minimum salaries to facilitate comparisons. In 1998, a minimum salary was U.S.$108.00.

26. The number of apartment buildings registered each year in the municipality of São Paulo jumped from an average of 265 between 1959 and 1969 to 580 between 1970 and 1976 (Ferreira 1987:25). For analyses of Rio de Janeiro showing a similar pattern, see Ribeiro 1993 and Ribeiro and Lago 1995.

27. PUB was the basis for the first general urban plan of the city, the Master Plan on Integrated Development (Plano Diretor de Desenvolvimento Integrado) approved in 1971 (Municipal Law 7,688).

28. Detailed documentation of social and spatial inequalities in the city and in the metropolitan region in the mid-1970s is given in Camargo et al. 1976. See Caldeira 1984 for an analysis of the peripherization process and for a case study of São Miguel Paulista, on the eastern periphery, in the late 1970s.

29. São Paulo had 63,000 motor vehicles circulating in 1950; in 1966 there were 415,000 and in 1993 4.1 million (Morse 1970:373; São Paulo—Sempla 1995:89).

30. Political organization in the neighborhoods on the periphery was influenced by the Catholic Church and its local organizers, inspired by liberation theology. Organization was also facilitated by the political opening that led to the end of the military regime. See R. Cardoso, 1983, Singer and Brant 1983, and, in English, Kowarick 1989 and Stepan 1989. For an overview of this process in Latin America, see Escobar and Alvarez 1992.

31. The 1980 census presents data for fifty-six districts and subdistricts of the city of São Paulo; the 1991 census presents data according to ninety-six districts. The new districts are not subdivisions of the old ones but have totally different boundaries. The planning bureau of the city of São Paulo (Sempla—Secretaria Municipal de Planejamento) has produced one table that estimates the 1980 population according to the new districts. This is the only comparable information tabulated according to the new districts for the period 1980–1991. Moreover, Emplasa (Empresa Metropololitana de Planejamento da Grande São Paulo) has produced a few comparable indicators according to the old districts. The 1996 *Contagem*, which has data organized by the new districts, is restricted to a few demographic indicators.

32. One alternative source of information would be the Pesquisas OD

(Pesquisas Origem-Destino, origin-destination surveys). They are sample surveys undertaken by the Companhia do Metropolitano de São Paulo (Metrô) in 1977 and 1987. They show results for small subdivisions of the city called traffic zones. Although the subdivisions are also different for the two dates, the department of planning (master plan team) of the planning department of the municipality of São Paulo created comparable units during the administration of Luiza Erundina. Although I used these data in my dissertation, I decided to abandon them after the publication of the census because the data for 1987 differ considerably from the census data for 1991. The Pesquisa OD-87 used population estimates that the census proved to be completely wrong (for example, for the city of São Paulo, the Pesquisa OD estimated an annual population growth of 3.2 percent instead of the 1.1 percent observed by the census). As a consequence, most of the information I had relied on before the publication of the census (and which used population density as a variable) was inaccurate. The discrepancies were especially high for some neighborhoods central to my analysis, such as Moóca, which had a negative annual population growth (−1.6 percent) according to the 1991 census but a significant annual growth according to the Pesquisa OD-87 (2.0 percent). In the present analysis I do not use any data from the Pesquisa OD that depend on population estimates. Nevertheless, I use its data on construction based on the municipal records of urban property (TPCL—Cadastro de Propriedade Urbana). The results of the Pesquisas OD, published in aggregated form for São Paulo and the metropolitan region, are included in São Paulo—Emplasa 1978; Metrô 1989; and Rolnik et al. n.d. Data by traffic zones were not published. I thank the Department of Planning of the municipality of São Paulo (Erundina's administration), and especially Raquel Rolnik and Heloísa Proença, for making the unpublished data available to me.

33. The city of São Paulo has a total area of 1,509 square kilometers.. The total area of the metropolitan region is 8,051 square kilometers.

34. Seade's calculations are given in São Paulo—Emplasa 1994:136.

35. For the following analysis of population growth according to the ninety-six new districts, I use the population estimate for 1980 made by Sempla, the city of São Paulo Planning Bureau, on the basis of census data, the 1991 census, and the 1996 *Contagem*. See in map 3 (in the appendix) the 96 districts of the city of São Paulo.

36. 7.5 percent of the city's districts lost population in the 1970s. These had 1.87 percent of the population in 1980. For an analysis of population growth according to the old districts of the city during the period 1940–1980, see Caldeira 1984: chapter 1.

37. The average annual population growth rates between 1980 and 1991, and 1991 and 1996, respectively, were: −0.61 and −3.80 in Itaim Bibi, −1.90 and −3.57 in Santo Amaro, −1.35 and −2.53 in Consolação, −1.67 and −2.43 in Pinheiros, −0.68 and −1.33 in Vila Mariana, −0.69 and −0.95 in Perdizes.

38. For example, in Cidade Tiradentes (previously part of the old district of Guaianazes on the eastern border), which had the highest annual population

growth in the 1980s (24.55 percent) and the second highest between 1991 and 1996 (11.06), 90.3 percent of the population live in areas classified as rural. Marsilac (previously part of Parelheiros on the south border), the district with the worst urban conditions, is classified as totally rural.

39. For the subdivision of the Metropolitan Region into municipalities, see map 4 in the appendix. In addition to São Paulo, the industrial cities of Osasco, Santo André, São Caetano, and Salesópolis had emigration between 1980 and 1991 (São Paulo—Emplasa 1994:136).

40. In July 1997, the only information about income from the 1991 census available according to city districts refers to the income of heads of households. Information about the labor force and economically active population are not available by district. Unfortunately, the information about the income of heads of households is not available for the 1980 census, which again makes comparisons and diachronic analysis difficult. In 1991 (September), the value of the minimum wage was Cz$36,161.60, or U.S.$65.00; in 1997, it was R$112.00, or U.S.$100.00.

41. The TPCL data is organized according to the old district limits. For the 1991 census, I use a special tabulation of domiciles according the old districts by Emplasa (São Paulo—Emplasa 1994:349).

42. TPCL registered 19,537 residential units in Guaianazes in 1990, while the census registered 104,155 domiciles in 1991. For the city as a whole, the census noted 2,539,953 domiciles, whereas the TPCL in 1990 noted 1,684,994— a difference of 50.74 percent. This problem is an old one. Rolnik found high proportions of irregular construction in the late nineteenth and early twentieth centuries (1997:60, 77).

43. The residential constructed area corresponds to the total number of constructed square meters registered at the municipality (TPCL). TPCL data according to the old districts for 1990 are in São Paulo—Sempla 1992:148–50; for 1977 and 1987 they are not published and originated in the Pesquisa OD. Other examples of large differences on the periphery are 198 percent in Itaim Paulista, 189 percent in Jaraguá, 186 percent in São Mateus, 172 percent in Itaquera, and 163 percent in Capela do Socorro.

44. Some of the differences are: 1.18 percent in Cerqueira César, 1.92 percent in Jardim América, and −6 percent in Jardim Paulista. In several central districts the difference is negative: that is, the TPCL registers more units than the census does. This discrepancy may be due to the existence of unoccupied legal residences (especially apartments) and to the transformation of old residences into business.

45. The twelve precarious districts of 1980 are Brasilândia, Capela do Socorro, Ermelino Matarazzo, Guaianazes, Itaim Paulista, Itaquera, Jaraguá, Parelheiros, Perus, São Mateus (sometimes included in Itaquera-Guaianazes), São Miguel Paulista and Vila Nova Cachoeirinha. The corresponding twenty-eight districts of 1991 are Anhanguera, Brasilândia, Cachoeirinha, Cidade Dutra, Cidade Tiradentes, Ermelino Matarazzo, Grajaú, Guaianazes, Iguatemi, Itaim Paulista,

Itaquera, Jaraguá, Jardim Ângela, Jardim Helena, Jardim São Luís, José Bonifácio, Lajeado, Marsilac, Parelheiros, Parque do Carmo, Perus, Ponte Rasa, São Mateus, São Miguel, São Rafael, Socorro, Vila Curuçá, and Vila Jacuí.

46. As R. Cardoso 1985 shows, the state apparatuses were already becoming sensitive to the necessity for new social policies when they were addressed by the social movements. Thus, they were able to respond to demands relatively quickly.

47. According to calculations of the Municipal Planning Bureau, in 1981 there were 3,567 illegal developments on the periphery of São Paulo, corresponding to 35 percent of its urban area. In 1990, the illegal developments had dropped to 16 percent of the urban area (Rolnik et al. n.d.: 94–95).

48. Interviews with young residents of the periphery analyzed in chapter 2 confirm their feelings that to retrace their parents' steps in the city was impossible.

49. The same process seems to be occurring on the periphery of Rio de Janeiro, as indicated by Ribeiro and Lago 1995.

50. One *cortiço* usually has many rooms. On average, there are 6.7 families per *cortiço*, but in some areas, such as Moóca, the number is higher (12.1).

51. These districts are Jardim Paulista, Moema, Alto de Pinheiros, Morumbi, Consolação, Pinheiros, Itaim Bibi, Santo Amaro, Perdizes, Campo Belo, and Vila Andrade. It is worth remembering that São Paulo, like Brazil in general, is an unequal society with a small, extremely rich elite and a large impoverished population. Social inequality increased during the 1990s. As a consequence, it is not surprising that the richer population is quite small. Only 7.16 percent of the heads of households in the city made more than 20 minimum salaries (MS) in 1991.

52. The ratio of heads of households making more than 20 MS in relation to those making less than 3 is 4.59 in Jardim Paulista and 3.98 in Moema. Only in eleven districts of the city is this ratio higher than 1.0.

53. Apartments represented 20.8 percent of the total number of domiciles in the city of São Paulo in 1991, according to the census.

54. The sources for the number and locations of apartment buildings put on the market between 1976 and 1996 are annual reports from Embraesp (Empresa Brasileira de Estudos de Patrimônio S/C Ltda.).

55. During the 1980s, one of the most constant themes in newspaper articles on real estate was the association of the economic crisis with "luxury apartments." This seems to be the sector of the apartment building market that has fluctuated the most in the last fifteen years. Four-bedroom apartments represented 30.77 percent of the apartments put on the market in 1985 and 20 percent in 1984 and 1986. However, this proportion dropped to an average of 6.8 percent for the years 1987 to 1993 (Embraesp 1994:6). It increased again after 1994, and the average for 1994–1996 was 20.47 percent (Embraesp 1997:11). There was also a tendency for the average size of bigger apartments to diminish after 1985. In spite of that, the average area of apartments with four bedrooms is almost double of that of apartments with three bedrooms (185 square meters of usable floor space compared to 85.57 square meters). Moreover, while

the average area of three-bedroom apartments remained constant between 1990 and 1997, the average area of four-bedroom apartments varied considerably (Embraesp 1997:9).

56. There were fifty-five districts from the 1950s to the 1980s.

57. TPCL data for 1980 are unpublished; for 1990 they appear in São Paulo—Sempla 1992. Utilization rate *(coeficiente de aproveitamento)* can be calculated separately for horizontal and vertical residential areas and is a relatively reliable indicator of vertical housing, usually registered construction. In 1990, the TPCL registered 566,466 apartments, whereas the 1991 census registered 529,991 in the city of São Paulo, a difference of 6.9 percent. However, the TPCL registered 1,118,531 houses in 1990, whereas the 1991 census registered 1,984,710, a difference of 77.4 percent. The districts in which the difference between registered property and domiciles noted by the census is small are those with the highest proportion of apartment buildings and rich families (Consolação, Jardim Paulista, Jardim América, Cerqueira César, Pinheiros, and Perdizes).

58. The annual rates of population growth for 1980–1991 and for 1991–1996 are 2.33 percent and −0.75 percent in Morumbi, and 5.93 percent and 4.93 percent in Vila Andrade.

59. From 1980 to 1987, there were 217 new developments in Morumbi, corresponding to 4,972 units, mostly luxury. From 1993 to 1996, there were 177 developments and 8,849 units.

60. Outside Morumbi, the highest average incomes of heads of households in 1991 were 22.53 in Jardim Paulista, 21.44 in Alto de Pinheiros, and 22.08 in Moema.

61. It is impossible to give exact figures for either Morumbi or Vila Andrade alone because the results of the *Censo de Favelas* are given according to still another geographic classification: the regional administrations of the city. For the estimate presented in the text, I considered the population living in favelas in the regional administrations of Butantã and Campo Limpo, which include the areas of Morumbi and Vila Andrade but are larger than these districts.

62. In Portal do Morumbi, for example, which is situated on a narrow street and has only two exits, at rush hour, especially in the morning when everybody is leaving for work, it may take more than half an hour to cross the walled community and reach the avenue that connects it to the city.

63. In São Paulo, as elsewhere in Brazil, the middle and upper classes send their children exclusively to private schools. The upper classes have always done so, but since the 1970s it has become a general practice for the middle classes also. With the exception of universities, the public education system—like most of the public services—degenerated quickly as it turned into a service only for those who could not afford private schools. Attracted by cheap land and the possibility of building huge facilities, many of the traditional private schools of São Paulo either moved to Morumbi or opened new branches there even before the middle classes were living there. These schools are sometimes mentioned as a motivation for people to move there.

64. Total value added corresponds, in each municipality, to the value of mer-

chandise exports from the municipality plus the value of services paid within the municipality, minus the value of merchandise imported into the municipality in each fiscal year. It is calculated by the state department of treasury.

65. In the state of São Paulo, the participation of the industrial sector in total production dropped from 47.1 percent in 1980 to 41.3 percent in 1991. Simultaneously, the participation of tertiary activities increased from 49.7 percent to 54.6 percent.

66. It was 34.7 percent in 1960 (Seade 1990:24) and 39.6 percent in 1970 (Gonçalves and Semeghini 1992).

67. The studies of the urban economy I cite consider only two sectors: the industrial and the tertiary. Therefore, the percentage of the tertiary sector in the economic activities is the complementary percentage: 67.9 percent for the city in 1991.

68. The area of the city affected by the movement of tertiary activities follows the Pinheiros River on both sides, from Lapa through Butantã and Morumbi to Campo Limpo on the west side, and from Alto de Pinheiros to Santo Amaro through Ibirapuera and Vila Olímpia on the east side. In all these areas we can observe the combination of upper-class closed condominiums with favelas, and of residential enclaves with office and commercial centers.

69. Between 1980 and 1990, the average rate of growth of the total value added decreased in industrial municipalities such as São Paulo (−3.75 percent), Osasco (−2.19 percent) and those of the ABCD region: −4.46 in Santo André, −2.96 in São Bernardo, −7.27 in São Caetano, −0.26 in Mauá, and 1.23 in Diadema (Araújo 1993:35).

70. Only 2.85 percent of the heads of households in the other municipalities of the metropolitan region make more than 20 MS. From this total, 40.69 percent are still concentrated in ABCD, with another 7.26 percent in Osasco (see map 2).

71. Total value added rates of growth for the period 1980–1990 for municipalities in the eastern and northern regions were −2.58 in Mogi das Cruzes, −1.99 in Suzano, −1.60 in Biritiba Mirim, −0.59 in Guarulos, −4.49 in Santa Isabel, −2.95 in Franco da Rocha, and −1.91 in Caieiras (Araújo 1993:35).

72. The poorest municipalities are all in the fringes of the metropolitan region and most are still significantly rural.

73. Between 1980 and 1990, the total value added increased considerably in Barueri (12.62 percent), Santana do Parnaíba (5.87 percent), and Cajamar (8.68) (Araújo 1993:35).

74. Population growth between 1991 and 1996 was 8.7 percent. In 1991, 14.0 percent of the heads of households had an income higher than 20 minimum salaries. It is the only municipality (except São Paulo) in which more than 10 percent of the heads of household are in this category. In 1991, the average income of the heads of households (in minimum salaries) in the northwestern municipalities was 9.8 in Santana do Parnaíba; 6.2 in Barueri; 5.9 in Cotia; and 3.2 in Cajamar.

75. In 1980, only 1.5 percent of the economically active population of San-

tana do Parnaíba made more than 20 MS, whereas 53.7 percent made less than 2 MS.

76. The second highest is Barueri, at 0.6480. The GINI coefficient for the city of São Paulo is 0.5857 and for the metropolitan region 0.5748. Cajamar, which had a good economic performance but not rich residents, has a significantly lower GINI coefficient of 0.4635. Most municipalities in the eastern region have comparably low GINI coefficients.

7. FORTIFIED ENCLAVES

1. *Estorvo* is a fantastic chronicle of contemporary Brazilian life expressed in terms of economic crisis, urban transformation, and social disarticulation, including feelings of disorientation and uncertainty about the future.

2. See Cenzatti and Crawford 1998 for an interesting discussion of "quasi-public spaces," that is, the privately owned but publicly used interior spaces of shopping malls, hotels, airports, and so on. They do not discuss the residential version of the enclaves.

3. Some of the recent condominiums have more than 100,000 square meters for collective use and resemble sophisticated clubs. A few contain more than twenty thousand inhabitants and various internal streets. They are invariably enclosed.

4. See McKenzie 1994 for an analysis of common-interest development housing in the United States. According to McKenzie, CIDs share three characteristics that distinguish them from other types of housing: common ownership of property; mandatory membership in the homeowner association; and a private regime of restrictive covenants enforced by the residents. Such housing may be of three types: planned unit developments, or PUDs, which consist of single-family detached homes built according to a master plan, generally in the suburbs; condominiums, usually multifamily buildings; and co-ops, that is, cooperative apartments in which residents own a share of stock in the entire building, not simply a unit (1994:19).

5. Blakely and Snyder (1997:7, 180) estimate that 19 percent of the 190,000 community associations that are members of the CAI (Community Association Institute) were gated communities in 1996. These would account for more than three million units. No estimates are available of the number of closed condominiums in São Paulo.

6. I have been studying working-class housing transformations with James Holston. One of the neighborhoods in our study was first built by a developer in the 1970s, with patterned houses. The houses have been altered to such an extent that after twenty years it is almost impossible to identify the original plans and façades.

7. For the American case, see Jackson 1985 and McKenzie 1994.

8. These Garden Cities, which exist to this day, originated the richest areas of town, called "Jardins" (gardens). Featuring the famous circular streets, the

first one, Jardim América, was planned in England by the firm of Barry Parker and Raymond Unwin.

9. Data by Construtora Albuquerque, Takaoka S/A, published in the Alphaville newsletter (*Jornal de Alphaville*, 14 [3]: 5, 1991). In the late 1990s, the resident population seems to have grown to thirty thousand and the average fluctuating population to eighty thousand (oral communication with the developers).

10. See Augé 1989 for an analysis of a "system of real estate advertisement."

11. My sample was made by selecting two issues, generally from Sundays, from each year (one for the first half of the year and one for the second), and examining all the real estate advertisements in each issue.

12. See, for example, the classic analysis by Bachelard (1964) of the relationship between house and memory; by Bourdieu (1972) of the Kabyle house; and by Cunningham (1964) of the Atoni house.

13. There are many possible approaches to the ads. I chose to emphasize the symbolism of the home, but an alternative approach would be to identify how they express the variations of housing policies and construction codes analyzed in chapter 6. Although the ads do not talk about zoning codes, restrictive regulations, economic crisis, or difficulties of financing, all these issues can be read in the advertisements' specific language. In fact, the "new concept of housing" is a response to the real estate developers' need to construct apartment buildings away from the city center and in immense lots because of restrictive zoning codes and the increasing price of land. In the ads, however, this practical motivation is parlayed into a choice of lifestyle. In the same way, if apartments are constructed with smaller internal areas both because of the buyers' decreased purchasing power and because of the necessity of maintaining a certain utilization rate, the reduced space is announced as a "rational solution" perfectly adapted to the "modern life of dynamic people." Although the ads offer material for a rich interpretation of middle-class domestic life among Paulistano families (for example, through an analysis of the distribution of space and function, the use of materials, and so on), I focus here primarily on the public statements these residences make in the city space.

14. In the text of the advertisements I italicize expressions that originally appeared in foreign languages, but I do not italicize foreign proper names. Foreign expressions (often meaningless) are used as marks of status and to convey exclusiveness. I do not italicize foreign words that have been integrated into Portuguese, are in current use by people from different social groups, and do not connote distinction. A typical example of the latter is the English word "playground."

15. Brazilian middle-class families who can no longer afford a live-in cook have developed a compromise solution: they hire a cook who in one day prepares and freezes several days' worth of meals for the household.

16. This change is reflected in new data about the labor force. From 1980 to 1991, the domestic services sector of the urban labor force decreased by 0.3 percent annually in the city of São Paulo, while all the other tertiary sectors in-

creased. In particular, personal services and repair and maintenance services increased 3.3 percent and 4.2 percent. This may indicate a change in the way services are performed rather than a decrease in the use of domestic services. For example, house-cleaning services performed by employees of a cleaning company are not classified as domestic services but as maintenance and repair (Leme and Meyer 1997:66).

17. From 1980 to 1991, private security services increased 4.9 percent annually in the city of São Paulo (Leme and Meyer 1997:66).

18. In 1995, the city of São Paulo passed a law prohibiting discrimination in the use of elevators. Although the text of this law must be posted in all buildings, in practice the distinction between social and service elevators continues. See Holston (1989:174–81) for an analysis of spatial segregation in the modernist apartments designed by Oscar Niemeyer in Brasília.

19. For a revealing discussion of how little the professionalization of middle- and upper-class Brazilian women has affected the organization of domestic life, see Ardaillon 1997.

20. I use the expression "old suburbs" to refer to those that were primarily residential, from which residents traveled to downtown jobs. I use "new suburbs" to refer to those that combine residences with office and commercial developments. There are many labels for these new types of suburbs in the American context, such as "edge cities," "outer cities," and "exopolis." In Brazil, the phenomenon still does not have a label, in spite of the efforts of some developers. For a critique of the notion of "edge city," see Beauregard 1995.

21. Maybe one of the reasons why the label did not stick is that the Portuguese translation used in the ads, *cidade de contorno*, does not make much sense. *Contorno* literally means contour, outline, or periphery.

22. These are both new towns, privately financed and constructed and among the largest of this type of ventures (McKenzie 1994:100). By the 1990s, however, they had been assimilated into the greater Washington, D.C., suburban sprawl. They cannot be considered typical examples of the 1980s edge cities.

23. Blakely and Snyder's book (1997) evaluates life inside gated communities in relation to an ideal of community defined by two criteria: a sense of belonging and public participation (chapters 2 and 6). Sharing with suburbanites an antiurban sentiment and emphasizing nostalgically an idealized community life of "decades past—neighborhoods where people knew each other and watched out for each other" (1997:166), these authors criticize gated communities not for the segregation they may enforce but for failing to produce good communities. Their advice for replacing the gates aims at the creation of "better communities" and includes recipes for "neotraditionalism" and "defensible space" (chapter 8).

24. An egregious case occurred in Brasília in August 1996. A young man driving a sport utility vehicle at high speed hit and killed a working-class man walking on the side of the road. He did not stop or offer any help. The next day, the driver was identified as the son of Odacir Klein, at that time the minister of transportation. The minister was in the car at the time. When this news became public, the minister had to resign, but his son walked away unpunished. The judge,

Maria Leonor Leiko Agueno, known in Brasília for being soft on crimes committed by the elite, decided not to press charges of failing to render aid, arguing that "since the mason was dead, he did not need help" (*O Globo*, 21 January 1997). Moreover, she suspended the process against Klein on the basis of a special provision that allows judges to suspend trials for crimes in which the foreseen penalty is less than one year of imprisonment.

25. "Alphaville Vive 'Dia de Twin Peaks' em Debate sobre Drogas e Violência," *Folha de S. Paulo*, 10 April 1991. The numbers are probably underreported, since the residents have no interest in bringing the police in or in reporting crimes that occur inside their walls.

26. Drug use is a persistent problem in both private and public schools. The latter, especially those in poor neighborhoods on the periphery, are stigmatized as sites of drug trafficking. It is expected that expensive private schools should be able to control the practice, but this has not been the case.

27. See DaMatta 1979 for an analysis of the use of the phrase "Do you know who you're talking to?" as a way of enforcing social distance and the recognition of social inferiority.

28. The coverage of this event reveals the routine and unproblematized way in which Brazilian journalists use highly sexist phrases, such as defining a male who is forcibly sodomized as the violator's "woman," and phrases reproducing stereotypes, such as justifying the rape of a rapist as behavior in accordance with a "code of honor."

29. Romeu Tuma was at that time the chief of the federal police and Zélia Cardoso de Mello the most powerful minister, in charge of the economy. Most of these examples of manipulation of personal relationships to avoid the law refer to someone in the judiciary system.

30. "Bairros Residenciais Querem Fechar Ruas," *O Estado de S. Paulo*, 18 June 1991.

31. This democratization was not accomplished without problems. In fact, its effects have been quite limited in various spheres, especially in relation to what we call the civil component of citizenship (Holston and Caldeira 1998). Yet democracy, and especially political democracy, expanded during the 1980s, sending a message that various sectors of the elite interpreted as threatening.

32. For the United States, see Massey and Denton 1993 and McKenzie 1994. For Europe, see Wieviorka 1991 and 1993 and Wieviorka et al. 1992.

33. This percentage overestimates vertical construction: the data from TPCL on which it is based refer only to legally registered construction, which constitute a small percentage of the domiciles in such an area.

34. In the eastern region of the city, apartments in Cohab-type complexes make up 9.36 percent of the total of domiciles, according to the 1991 census.

35. Lawn bowling is rare in other areas of town but an obsession in Moóca. The frequent mention of lawn bowling greens in the ads for the area always signals that the development is meant for Mooquenses. The reference to a nursery in this ad may be directed toward people who do not have their own full-time maids.

36. Arguments that stress privacy, individuality, and intimacy are often associated with the spread of individualism in modern Western societies and with the destruction of public life (for example, see Sennett 1974). In addition to not mentioning these ideas when discussing their housing options, Morumbi residents explicitly reject any notion that privacy and individuality should be extended to their children, creatures they feel should be closely and directly controlled and who should not choose their own friends. Many men employ similar discourses of control with reference to their wives (see chapter 9).

37. The association of open doors with order and security, and of closed doors with disorder and insecurity, is not specific to Paulistanos alone. This image structures the novel *Open Doors* by the Sicilian writer Leonardo Sciascia. This is a dialogue between two judges:

> "As you know, it is a common wisdom that since fascism arrived into power we can sleep with our doors open . . . "
> "I continue to close mine," said the judge.
> "Me too. But we cannot deny that the conditions of public security have improved considerably in the last 15 years. Even here in Sicily. Whatever are our opinions about the death penalty, we should admit that it is useful to enforce in people's mind the notion of a State fully concerned with the citizen's security; that is, the idea that they sleep with the doors open." (Sciascia 1987:17)

38. Nelson Kojranski, a lawyer who writes frequently for the newspaper *Folha de S. Paulo* on legal issues related to life in apartment buildings, asserted that there was "no juridical injunction able to prevent the implantation of fences enclosing the terrain of a high-rise, even though this may break the architectural harmony of the façade, if it is determined by the majority of the homeowners" (January 28, 1980).

39. For example, "A Arquitetura do Medo Domina São Paulo" (The architecture of fear dominates São Paulo), *Jornal da Tarde*, 30 September 1991. This article reports that the IAB—Brazilian Institute of Architects—is holding meetings to discuss the incorporation of security into designs not only of houses and apartments but also of parks and squares. In the United States there is a more elaborate discourse about "defensible architecture," which I discuss in chapter 8.

40. For example, "Cerca em Árvore Pretende Evitar Medigos" (Fence around tree intended to prevent bums), *Folha de S. Paulo*, 10 September 1994. It reports on various strategies to prevent homeless people from loitering in certain areas: fencing trees, installing sprinklers in covered areas in buildings *(marquises)*, putting chains across entrance areas, and so on.

8. THE IMPLOSION OF MODERN PUBLIC LIFE

1. Analyses of various dimensions of modern urban life are found in Benjamin 1986, Berman 1982, Clark 1984, Harvey 1985, Holston 1989, Jacobs 1961, Rabinow 1989, Schorske 1961, Sennett 1974, Simmel 1971 [1903], Vidler 1978,

Wirth 1969 [1938], and Young 1990. I restrict my discussion to Western cities in both Europe and the Americas.

2. Other analysts of modern urban life make similar arguments. Richard Sennett anchors his thesis of the "fall of public man" (1974) on a description of the loss of formality in public interactions associated with the interiorization of the individual and the tyrannies of intimacy that mark contemporary societies. T. J. Clark (1984: chapter 1) describes modern Paris as a public space constituted to guarantee "inattention" to the other, that is, anonymity and the possibility of interactions with strangers in which privacy is always maintained.

3. A powerful image of progressive incorporation is offered in the classic essay by T. H. Marshall (1965 [1949]) on the development of citizenship. His starting point is the recognition that citizenship rights have never been equally distributed but have expanded considerably over time. After distinguishing the civil, political, and social dimensions of citizenship, Marshall argues that they evolved in succession, and that each took around one century to consolidate. The essay does not hide the long path that led to the recognition of each right, but this does not threaten its assertion of the progress of citizenship, supported by the history of its expansion. The image of progressive expansion of citizenship finds echoes in revisions of contemporary political thought announced as "radical" and not framed in terms of incorporation, as Marshall's is: for example, Laclau and Mouffe's analysis (1985) depicts democracy in terms of an imagery characterized by "equivalential displacement," and tries to consider the possibilities of its hegemony, in a radical form, in contemporary societies. For recent critiques of Marshall's optimistic and evolutionary view, see Hirschman 1991 and Turner 1992.

4. The civil rights movement and the feminist movement of the 1960s and 1970s in the United States, as well as the urban social movements in Latin America in the late 1970s and early 1980s, are examples of what I call "liberal" social movements.

5. For a feminist critique of the social contract theory, see Pateman 1988; and for a critique of the legal understanding of equality as sameness, see Eisenstein 1988. Scott 1997 offers an analysis of the paradox that has marked the history of French liberal feminism: its need both to accept and to refuse sexual difference in politics. See also the debates on multiculturalism and, especially, the demands for indigenous rights in some Latin American countries examined as rights for nations inside the nation-state (Stavenhagen 1996; Findji 1992) and the debate on Quebec's nationalism (Kymlicka 1996).

6. It is interesting to observe that instead of formulating a model of democracy in purely abstract terms, Young anchors it in the modern experience of city life. Although she points up the various social injustices and segregation found in cities, it is still from their experience that she derives a model of a democratic space in which differences remain "unassimilated" and heterogeneity, tolerance to others, openness, and flexible boundaries exist in some way and can be rescued as positive values. See Deutsche 1996 for a critique of conceptions of

public space with reference to the role of public art in a democratic public; Deutsche argues, inspired by Lefort, that the role of this art should be exactly to unsettle boundaries and identities.

7. Howard's book *To-Morrow: A Peaceful Path to Social Reform* was first published in 1898. It was retitled *Garden Cities of Tomorrow* in 1902. In England, his main followers were Raymond Unwin and Barry Parker, who planned the first Garden City and helped to create its idiom. They also designed São Paulo's first garden city neighborhood. For different accounts of Howard's influence in city planning, see Fishman 1982: part 1; Girouard 1985:351–63; Jacobs 1961:17–25; Kostof 1991:75–82, 194–99; and McKenzie 1994:1–6.

8. See Jackson 1985 for a view of the suburbanization of the United States, and Fishman 1995, Beauregard 1995, Soja 1996a, and Garreau 1991 for different views of changes in the character of American suburbia.

9. See above and Young 1990:227–36 for a critique of communitarianism and its antiurban and exclusionary character.

10. For an analysis of the expansion of common-interest developments, see McKenzie 1994. The association of antiurban sentiments with communitarian ideals is explicit in Blakely and Snyder's analysis of gated communities in the United States (1997). Although these authors criticize the gates, their antiurban bias and their concern with "community" prevent them from capturing the profoundly antidemocratic character of the gated communities.

11. For the affinities between Le Corbusier and Howard, see Fishman 1988:178 and chapter 21; Jacobs 1961:21–25; and Girouard 1985:360.

12. See Holston 1989 for an analysis of Brasília, the affiliation of its plan to the CIAM, and the inversions and perversions generated as the project was constructed and the city inhabited. My considerations of Brasília are based on this analysis.

13. Modernism thus could not be absent from the advertisements for closed condominiums. In 1982, a complex of seven high-rises in Morumbi was advertised as follows:

> L'Abitare—the planned success . . . introduced one of the most modern and victorious tendencies in architecture and urbanism. . . . L'Abitare returns to the residents the space for life experience and reflects a concern both with man and with quality of life, considering the specific necessities of Paulistana middle-class families, and with the experiences which, in the language of the famous architect Le Corbusier, resulted in the conception of the "neighborhood units." . . . All enclosed and protected by an entrance guard with permanent surveillance. (*O Estado de S. Paulo*, 3 October 1982)

Chico Buarque captured this use of modernist architecture as a form of status in the novel *Estorvo*. The sister's residence in the closed condominium is a modernist project. It is "a glass pyramid" that has to be encircled to be made a fortress. The result is weird, as the narrator observes: "I have always thought that such prize-winning architecture would prefer to inhabit another space" (1991:14–15).

14. Brasília was a comprehensive design created from scratch. Many exist-

ing cities around the world, however, were substantially modified by the intervention of modernist planning. Moreover, modernism became the standard design principle in cities under the influence of the Soviet Union. Through the use of monumental spaces and modernist buildings, soviet planning created a type of public space that is totally different from the Western modern one: a space for parades, demonstrations by large crowds, and state-sponsored spectacles, but not for the daily interaction of pedestrians.

15. The dispute between the city of São Paulo and the residents who have closed their streets with chains was reported in the newspapers *O Estado de S. Paulo* and *Folha de S. Paulo* (for example, during January 1985). The change in the public's conceptions and in the attitude of the city government toward the enclosures are registered in "Bairros Residenciais Querem Fechar Ruas," *O Estado de S. Paulo*, 18 June 1991. In the United States, the gating of streets has also provoked opposition. One of the most famous disputes occurred in Whitley Heights in Los Angeles, where the gates built by residents were ruled illegal and ordered never to be closed. In many other areas, however, the use of gates has been sanctioned. The Whitley Heights case has been discussed in numerous issues of the *Los Angeles Times* (especially in 1994 and 1995) and by Blakely and Snyder (1997:104–8).

16. See Caldeira (1984: chapter 3) for an analysis of the rituals of everyday life in the streets of Jardim das Camélias in the late 1970s and early 1980s.

17. In peripheral neighborhoods such as Jardim das Camélias we sometimes hear stories of control of access by some residents related to crime. Gangs of residents sometimes treat the neighborhood as their own territory and allow safe movement only to those residents who pay them a "security fee" monthly. Barricaded streets and control of circulation in ghettoes are not a novelty in the United States either.

18. On the organization of social movements and local associations in Jardim das Camélias and the periphery in the late 1970s and early 1980s, see Caldeira 1987 and 1990.

19. Control of the movements of workers and especially of their time at work has a long history. What is different about the use of the new technologies is the monitoring of anyone using public buildings, such as office buildings, where movement was uncontrolled a couple of years ago.

20. People who lived through the military regime know quite well how apparently innocent "security procedures" can be used to persecute people. Under the military regime, building superintendents had to fill out an information card for each new person moving into the building and send it to the police. Various superintendents were also among their collaborators. The cards disappeared with democratization, but the same people who opposed them during the military regime may favor contemporary screening methods.

21. Regional centers are the various areas on the periphery where commerce and services are clustered and which usually serve as public transportation centers: for example, Largo 13 on the southern periphery, or the center of São Miguel Paulista in the eastern zone.

22. The change here is not only from mixed to exclusive spaces but also from piecemeal consumption at various local vendors to monthly extended visits to one supermarket: that is, from relatively spontaneous to planned shopping. These changes have been accompanied by a corresponding transformation in domestic life, such as the use of additional appliances (freezers and microwave ovens), new ways of preparing and serving food, and new relationships.

23. In 1996, 69 percent of the trips on public transportation in São Paulo were made by bus, 26 percent by subway, and 5 percent by train. The subway alone transports more than one million passengers daily. (Seade, *Anuário Estatístico do Estado de São Paulo*, 1996).

24. For discussions of traffic, disrespect, and violence, see also DaMatta 1982 and O'Donnell 1986.

25. *Folha de S. Paulo*, 13 May 1989.

26. *Folha de S. Paulo*, 11 May 1986.

27. *O Estado de S. Paulo*, 8 October 1989.

28. *Folha de S. Paulo*, 21 May 1991. Use of seat belts increased after 1995, when the municipality started an aggressive campaign to enforce their use: people driving without them risked fines of more than 20 minimum salaries.

29. One of the best examples of this egocentric behavior is the traffic jams caused by middle-class parents double- or triple-parking when they pick up their children at school: they do not want to park a few blocks away and walk, and they do not hesitate to block traffic. Conflicts at middle-class school doors reach the newspapers frequently. The problem reached such dimensions that in 1991 the city of São Paulo mounted a campaign on television and street billboards to reeducate the parents.

30. Data on the number of victims are from the military police. As I argued in chapter 3, the military police data for fatalities are underestimated, and probably the data for injuries as well. According to the civil registry, the number of fatalities was 2,368.

31. There are various rock bands in the periphery that express this concern. One of them is called Pavilhão 9 after the sector of the Casa de Detenção in which the 1992 massacre occurred. See for example *Veja São Paulo* 30 (37): 15–21, September 1997.

32. The number of people on the streets offering such services as watching cars has increased in the last years of economic crisis, as has their aggressiveness: it is a common belief that if you do not give them money, they will damage your car. Moreover, since the number of vehicles stolen and the fear of crime have also increased, people feel it is hard to tell whether the person will steal the car or protect it.

33. Ipiranga, Metro, Lido, and Marrocos were sophisticated movie theaters until the 1960s. Today most downtown movie theaters are run-down and specialize in pornography.

34. São Paulo's space is chaotic ,and the city plan does not resemble a grid or any other rational form. In this chaos, the system of numbering buildings is based on the assumption that the beginning of any street is the end closer to

Praça da Sé. In the same way, the beginning of all railroads leaving the city is located at Praça da Sé. This indicates the power of the city's center-oriented model.

35. Smaller demonstrations have occurred in other areas, both in the center and on the periphery, but they have never had the same symbolism as those in Praça da Sé.

36. The type of undemocratic space produced in São Paulo by democratic means is similar to the various segregationist regulations formulated by NIMBY movements in California and analyzed by Davis (1990). However, if Davis reveals an acute sensibility to the disjunctive processes of democracy in this analysis, he does the opposite when he affirms that the fortress spaces that he finds in Los Angeles are a direct result of policies from Reagan-Bush era. The relationship between government policy and city space is more complicated than this, as the case of São Paulo indicates.

37. See, for example: on Johannesburg, Beavon 1998 and Mabin 1998; on Budapest, Ladányi 1998; on Buenos Aires, Lacarrieu 1997; on American cities, Blakely and Snyder 1997, Davis 1990, Dumm 1993, and Ellin 1997.

38. It is not my intention to give a detailed account of Los Angeles's history and pattern of urbanization. For details see Banham 1971; Cenzatti 1992; Davis 1985, 1987, 1990, 1991, and 1993; Fogelson 1967; Kling et al. 1991; Scott 1993; Scott and Soja 1996; and Soja 1989, 1992, 1996a, and 1996b.

39. "Los Angeles is the first consequential American city to separate itself decisively from European models and to reveal the impulse to privatization embedded in the origins of the American Revolution. . . . The absence of integrated hierarchical order in either the built or the institutional environment is in some sense the complete expression of the kind of democracy that accompanies an apotheosis of privatization in which the multiplicity of competing parts leads to a uniform texture of political activity" (Weinstein 1996:22, 30).

40. On L.A.'s transportation system, see Wachs 1996.

41. See Davis 1991 and Soja 1989: chapter 9 on the importance of downtown L.A. in the region.

42. The income rates for the United States as a whole were 13.8 percent in 1969, 12.5 percent in 1979, and 10.3 percent in 1989.

43. Soja's notions of hyperreality and simulacra, as well as descriptions of theme parks and scamscapes, are especially developed in his analysis of Orange County. See Soja 1992 and 1996b: chapter 8.

44. The creation of a maze of paths linking downtown buildings without using the streets is also a feature of Atlanta, Minneapolis–Saint Paul, and Toronto. See Boddy 1992 for an analysis of the "analogous cities" formed by underground and overhead passages and the kind of "spatial apartheid" they create. See Rutheiser 1996 for an analysis of the remaking of downtown Atlanta. On the reproduction of inequality in downtown L.A., see Davis 1990.

45. Sorkin (1992) provides an interesting collection of studies of different types of theme parks and elite spaces in various cities. See also Zukin 1991: chapter 8.

46. Arguing against what she calls a "narrative of loss" of public space, Margaret Crawford (1995) claims that Los Angeles's residents are continuously remaking public space. She does not think that empty spaces preclude sociability; she presents as examples of alternative or even subversive uses of public space in L.A. the street vendors (appropriating sidewalks, street corners, and parking lots) and the homeless. Although these examples are obviously uses of public space, they are not examples of heterogeneous uses but of segregation and exclusion. The spaces used by the street vendors and the homeless are leftover spaces, the only ones that the most marginalized groups—those excluded from walled and prestigious areas—can still appropriate.

47. I disagree with Sorkin's argument (1992: xii–xiii) that in the "new, recombinant city" social order cannot be read in urban form. Inequality and social separation are easily read in the new urban environment, although they are certainly expressed in a nonmodern vocabulary.

48. The idea of the "end of public space" appears in other recent books, as for example in the subtitle of the collection of essays organized by Sorkin 1992. Of the authors represented in this volume, Davis is the only one who approaches the theme directly. Nevertheless, various of the other analyses implicitly allude to the transformation of public space, considering the theme-park spaces they study as "analogue," "surrogate," "theatrical," and so on: that is, in some form fake public spaces. In these analyses there is a dehistoricization of public space, as its modern form stands for public space in general. To historicize the notion of public space helps both to avoid nostalgia and to understand current transformations. For a longer discussion of *Variations on a Theme Park*, see Caldeira 1994.

49. I do not enter here into the discussion about postmodern architecture, of which Los Angeles is always said to offer numerous examples. The focus of my analysis is urban forms, not architectural styles, although the apartheid public space may be partially shaped by buildings of postmodern architectural style.

50. Soja, for example, interprets the 1992 riots as the first movement of resistance to conservative postmodernism and post-Fordism (1996a:459).

9. VIOLENCE, THE UNBOUNDED BODY, AND THE DISREGARD FOR RIGHTS IN BRAZILIAN DEMOCRACY

1. I adopt Marshall's classic distinction (1965 [1949]) between civil, political, and social dimensions of citizenship. The civil dimension refers to the rights necessary for individual liberty, to the assertion of equality before the law, and to civil rights in general; the political dimension refers to the right to participate in political organizations, to vote, and to run for office; the social dimension refers to the entitlements of a citizen of the welfare state. (See chapter 8, note 3.) For the whole argument on disjunctive democracy, see Holston and Caldeira 1998.

2. Other dimensions of disrespect of human rights in Brazil, such as domestic violence, rural violence, slavery, and the abuse of children, homosexuals,

women, and indigenous groups, are documented by human rights organizations both nationally and internationally. They are also acknowledged by the Brazilian federal government in its Plan for Human Rights.

3. Disrespect of the human rights of political prisoners in Brazil during the military regime is documented in Archdiocese of São Paulo 1986.

4. Disrespect of human rights in Brazilian prisons is documented in Americas Watch Committee 1987 and 1989, Amnesty International 1990, and Comissão Teotônio Vilela 1986.

5. In countries such as Chile, Argentina, and South Africa, human rights movements have remained committed to dealing with the abuses of previous regimes. For a history of the human rights movement in Latin America, see Sikkink 1996. In Brazil, this kind of movement has been small. It was only after 1995 (twenty years after the beginning of the *abertura* process) that the Cardoso administration reopened cases of human rights violations against political prisoners and offered reparation to the families of people killed by the military regime.

6. This image recalls that used in the interview I analyzed in chapter 1, according to which kerosene and a match would solve the problem of the favelas and of crime.

7. For working-class uses of the judiciary system, especially after the 1988 constitution, see Holston and Caldeira 1998.

8. The people defending human rights were denouncing not only the deplorable prison conditions but also a series of abuses committed by the institutions of order, such as arrests without warrants, torture of suspects—not necessarily criminals—and summary executions. Most of those abuses were committed against people for whom there was no formal recognition of guilt. All these allegations, which expose various distortions of the justice system, were obscured by the emphasis on the "defense of criminals."

9. Manoel Mota Coqueiro was accused of and executed for ordering the massacre of a family of peasants. After the execution it was discovered not only that the trial had been conducted irregularly, ignoring evidence and under pressure from a mass of people demanding the death penalty, but also that he was not the instigator; the massacre was ordered by his wife.

10. These are the constitutions of 1891, 1934, 1946, and 1988.

11. The views of the principals involved in the capital punishment debate appear frequently in the newspapers. I base my discussion on analysis of newspaper articles from the late 1980s to the present, either pieces by or interviews with politicians or leaders of various associations. I gave preference to signed articles published in the op-ed pages of both *O Estado de S. Paulo* and *Folha de S. Paulo*, because they are not edited by the papers and are likely to better express people's opinions. Both these newspapers have written editorials against the death penalty, and *Folha* has engaged in a public campaign against it. The Globo network, owner of the newspaper *O Globo* (published in Rio de Janeiro) and broadcaster of the most popular news program on Brazilian television (*Jornal Nacional*), favors the death penalty.

12. For example, when Roberto Marinho, the owner and president of the

Globo network, was asked why he was in favor of the death penalty and was publicly promoting it through his newspaper and television station, he answered that he had only "reflected popular indignation." *Folha de S. Paulo,* 12 January 1993.

13. These polls are taken by and published periodically in newspapers. Data from both DataFolha and InformEstado for the city of São Paulo from 1986 onward show that between 66 percent and 75 percent of the population support the death penalty.

14. Defenders of capital punishment also have to deal with two arguments of their opponents: the possibility of a miscarriage of justice that could not be redressed after execution, and defense of the right to life as a basic human right. In response to the first, they maintain the possibility would be remote because the judicial process would provide for four levels of appeals. To the second argument they respond that they are interested in the lives of innocent people, and are defending the rights of victims and not those of bandits who, they insist, are being protected by the current constitution.

15. These comments by Amaral Netto were made during a debate with José Bisol, a federal deputy from PSB (Partido Socialista Brasileiro, the Brazilian Socialist Party).

16. I discuss this case in Alphaville in chapter 7.

17. For example, an article by Rabbi Henry I. Sobel appears in *Folha de S. Paulo,* 12 June 1991.

18. *O Estado de S. Paulo,* 17 January 1993.

19. Research conducted by DataFolha-Idesp in 1991 among members of the two houses of the National Congress showed that 73 percent were against the death penalty, 22 percent in favor of it, and 5 percent had other answers. Nevertheless, 51 percent were in favor of a plebiscite, 47 percent against one, and 2 percent had other answers. The preferences were split by party and along regional lines. The conservative parties (PDC, PRN, PFL, PDS, PTB) had a higher percentage of politicians in favor of the death penalty. They were also the majority of those in favor of a plebiscite. The parties in which the majority of members opposed the death penalty were those on the left (PT [100 percent against], PDT, and PSDB). They were also against the plebiscite. Those in favor of the death penalty were largely from the center-west, northeast, and north, while the majority of those from the south and southeast were against it (*Folha de S. Paulo,* 24 June 1991).

20. *Folha de S. Paulo,* 24 June 1991.

21. The use of pain in the determination of truth has a long history in Western cultures and their legal systems. See DuBois 1991 for an analysis of the relationship between torture and truth among the ancient Greeks. See Asad 1985 for an interesting discussion on the history of penance that shows how the use of pain, although always present in the Christian tradition, has been part of different practices of getting at the truth. In other words, the link between pain and truth has been articulated in different ways over time. In this sense, Asad

makes more complex Foucault's 1977 analysis of the ancien régime, which does not consider those variations. I have already discussed in chapters 3 through 5 the role of torture in Brazilian inquisitorial trial procedures; see also Lima 1986. For a discussion of Britain, where judicial torture was not as common as in continental Europe during most of the Renaissance, see Hanson 1991. See also Clastres 1978 for an analysis of the role of torture in primitive societies and its relationships with law and knowledge.

22. "The physical pain is so incontestably real that it seems to confer its quality of 'incontestable reality' on that power that has brought it into being. It is, of course, precisely because the reality of that power is so highly contestable, the regime so unstable, that torture is being used" (Scarry 1985:27). Scarry's analysis coincides with Hannah Arendt's interpretation of violence (1969), in which violence is seen as the instrument of those who do not have authority and are unable to rule by consensus.

23. See Scheper-Hughes 1992 for another interpretation of the routinization of violence in Brazilian society and for powerful descriptions of the unboundedness of poor people's bodies.

24. Most tubal ligations (75 percent in Brazil and 83 percent in the state of São Paulo) occur during cesarean sections. Sterilization is used by 38.4 percent of the women in São Paulo of reproductive age; the rate is higher in the north, center-west, and northeast of Brazil. It reaches 61.4 percent in Pernambuco and 71.3 percent in Goiás. The percentages of female sterilization are 15.7 percent for all countries worldwide and 7.6 percent for developed countries. In China, where the state has an aggressive policy of population control, the proportion is 49.1 percent (Berquó 1993:468, 463–65).

25. One of the indications of the popularity of plastic surgery, at least in the metropolitan areas, is the appearance in 1997 of a popular magazine called *Plástica: A Revista Que Vai Mudar Você* (Plastic [surgery]: the magazine that will change you). This magazine focuses exclusively on plastic surgery and gives tips about different techniques and services available (in addition to advertisements). Articles run the gamut from reportage on what Brazilians consider perfect buttocks to new laser technologies to how to get the perfect set of teeth. Plus, famous people reveal their own surgeries.

26. See also Tilly 1975 and Chesnais 1981.

27. In addition to Foucault's analysis, see Dumm 1987 for a discussion of the development of the penitentiary system in the United States in conjunction with the consolidation of American democracy. See also Nedelsky 1990 for a discussion of how the metaphor of boundaries (around selves and around state power) is central in the American tradition of constitutionalism.

28. Women's movements in Brazil have been among the few political movements demanding the expansion of individual rights (see Caldeira 1998). Although women's movements, in accordance with the specific pattern of legitimation of citizenship rights in Brazil, have framed many of their demands in terms of social rights, they have also addressed issues of individual rights and

the protection of women's bodies, which have always constituted the corner-stone of any feminist agenda. These concerns are especially clear in the intervention of feminists and nongovernmental organizations in the areas of reproductive rights (including the question of cesarean sections and sterilization), family law, violence against women, and racism against black women. In fact, women's movements represent one of the best examples I know of in Brazil of the potential for expansion of individual rights. Another example is the black movement, which unfortunately has not had the same level of efficacy in pressing its demands. For a critique of the classification of pregnancy as disability for purposes of leave and compensation in the United States, see Eisenstein 1988: chapter 3.

REFERENCES

Adorno, Sérgio.

1995.   "Discriminação racial e justiça criminal em São Paulo."
        Estudos Cebrap 43:45–63.

Americas Watch Committee.

1987.   *Police Abuse in Brazil: Summary Executions and Torture
        in São Paulo and Rio de Janeiro.* New York: Americas Watch
        Committee.

1989.   *Prison Conditions in Brazil.* New York: Americas Watch
        Committee.

1991a. Women's Rights Group. *Criminal Injustice: Violence against
        Women in Brazil.* New York: Americas Watch Committee.

1991b. *Rural Violence in Brazil.* New York: Americas Watch
        Committee.

1993.   *Urban Police Violence in Brazil: Torture and Police Killings
        in São Paulo and Rio de Janeiro after Five Years.* New York:
        Americas Watch Committee

Amnesty International.

1988.   *Brasil.* London: Amnesty International.

1989.   *When the State Kills: The Death Penalty versus Human
        Rights.* London: Amnesty International.

1990.   *Brasil: Tortura e Execuções Extra-Judiciais nas Cidades
        Brasileiras.* London: Amnesty International.

1993.   *"Death Has Arrived": Prison Massacre at the Casa de
        Detenção, São Paulo.* New York: Amnesty International.

Andrews, George Reid.

1991.   *Blacks and Whites in São Paulo, Brazil, 1888–1988.* Madison:
        University of Wisconsin Press.

Araújo, Maria de Fátima Infante.

1992.   "Uma Nova Centralidade da Região Metropolitana de São
Paulo." *São Paulo em Perspectiva* 6 (3): 55–59.

1993.   "Trajetória Econômica e Espacial da Metrópole Paulistana."
São Paulo em Perspectiva 7 (2): 29–37.

Archdiocese of São Paulo.

1986.   *Torture in Brazil.* New York: Vintage Books.

Ardaillon, Danielle.

1989.   "Estado e Mulheres—Conselhos dos Direitos da Mulher e
Delegacias de Defesa da Mulher." Research report. Fundação
Carlos Chagas.

1997.   *O Salário da Liberdade: Profissão e Maternidade, Nego-
ciações para uma Igualdade na Diferença.* São Paulo:
AnnaBlume.

Ardaillon, Danielle, and Guita Debert.

1988.   *Quando a Vitima é Mulher: Análise de Julgamentos de
Crimes de Estupro, Espancamento, e Homicídio.* Brasília:
Conselho Nacional dos Direitos da Mulher.

Arendt, Hannah.

1969.   *Da Violência.* Brasília: Editora da UnB.

Arquidiocese de São Paulo.

1985.   *Brasil Nunca Mais.* Petrópolis: Vozes.

Asad, Talal.

1985.   "Notes on Body Pain and Truth in Medieval Christian Ritual."
Economy and Society 12 (3): 287–327.

Aufderheide, Patricia Ann.

1975.   "Order and Violence: Social Deviance and Social Control in
Brazil, 1780–1840." Ph.D. diss., University of Minnesota.

Augé, Marc.

1989.   *Domaines et Châteaux.* Paris: Seuil.

Bachelard, Gaston.

1964.   *The Poetics of Space.* Boston: Beacon Press.

Bakhtin, Mikhail.

1984.   *Rabelais and His World.* Bloomington: Indiana University
Press.

Balibar, Étienne.

1991.   "Is there a 'Neo-Racism'?" In *Race, Nation, Class, Ambiguous
Identities,* ed. Etienne Balibar and Immanuel Wallerstein.
London: Verso, 17–28.

Banham, Reyner.

1971.   *Los Angeles: The Architecture of Four Ecologies*. Baltimore: Pelican.

Barcellos, Caco.

1992.   *Rota 66*. Rio de Janeiro: Globo.

Barros, Ricardo Paes de, and Rosane Mendonça.

1992.   "A Evolução do Bem-estar e da Desigualdade no Brasil desde 1960." *IPEA: Texto para discussão* 286.

Barros, Ricardo Paes de, José Márcio Camargo, and Rosane Mendonça.

1996.   "Pobreza no Brasil: Quatro Questões Básicas." Policy Paper 21, Fundação Friedrich Ebert/Ildes.

Barros, Ricardo Paes de, Ana Flávia Machado, and Rosane Mendonça.

1997.   "A Desigualdade da Pobreza: Estratégias Ocupacionais e Diferenciais por Gênero." *IPEA: Texto para Discussão* 453.

Barros, Ricardo Paes de, Rosane Silva Pinto de Mendonça, and Renata Pacheco Nogueira Duarte.

1997.   "Bem-estar, Pobreza e Desigualdade de Renda: uma Avaliação da Evolução Histórica e das Disparidades Regionais." *IPEA: Texto para Discussão* 454.

Batich, Mariana.

1988.   "A Criminalidade no Estado de São Paulo: Algumas Informações Quantitativas." *São Paulo em Perspectiva* 2 (3): 79–81.

Bayley, David H., and Clifford D. Shearing.

1996.   "The Future of Policing." *Law and Society Review* 30 (3): 585–606.

Beauregard, Robert A.

1995.   "Edge Cities: Peripheralizing the Center." *Urban Geography* 16 (8): 708–21.

Beavon, Keith S. O.

1998.   "Johannesburg, 112 Years of Division: From Segregation to Post-apartheid Community." Paper presented at the Conference "Social Geography of Divided Cities," International Center for Advanced Studies, New York University, February 26–27.

Benevides, Maria Victoria de Mesquita.

1976.   *O Governo Kubitschek: Desenvolvimento Econômico e Estabilidade Política*. Rio de Janeiro: Paz e Terra.

Benjamin, Walter.

1986. "Paris: Capital of the Nineteenth Century." In *Reflections: Essays, Aphorisms, Autobiographical Writings.*New York: Schocken Books, 146–62.

Berman, Marshall.

1982. *All That Is Solid Melts into Air.* New York: Penguin Books.

Berquó, Elza.

1993. "Contraception and Caesarians in Brazil: An Example of Bad Reproductive Health in Need of Exemplary Action." *Estudos Feministas* 1 (2): 461–72.

Bicudo, Helio Pereira.

1976. *Meu Depoimento sobre o Esquadrão da Morte.* São Paulo: Comissão de Justiça e Paz.

1988. *Do Esquadrão da Morte aos Justiceiros.* São Paulo: Edições Paulinas.

Blakely, Edward J., and Mary Gail Snyder.

1997. *Fortress America: Gated Communities in the United States.* Washington, D.C.: Brookings Institution Press and Lincoln Institute of Land Policy.

Boddy, Trevor.

1992. "Underground and Overhead: Building the Analagous City." In *Variations on a Theme Park: The New American City and the End of Public Space,* ed. Michael Sorkin. New York: Noonday Press, 123–53.

Bonduki, Nabil G.

1982. "Origens do Problema da Habitação Popular em São Paulo: Primeiros Estudos." *Espaço e Debates* 2 (5): 81–111.

1983. "Habitação Popular: Contribuição para o Estudo da Evolução Urbana de São Paulo." In *Repensando a Habitação no Brasil,* ed. Lícia do Prado Valladares. Rio de Janeiro: Zahar, 135–68.

1994. "Crise de Habitação e Moradia no Pós-guerra." In *As Lutas Sociais e a Cidade,* ed. Lúcio Kowarick. Rio de Janeiro: Paz de Terra/Unrisd, 113–46.

Borneman, John.

1997. *Settling Accounts: Violence, Justice, and Accountability in Postsocialist Europe.* Princeton: Princeton University Press.

Bourdieu, Pierre.

1972. "The Kabyle House, or the World Reversed." In *Algeria 1960.* Cambridge: Cambridge University Press.

1984.   *Distinction: A Social Critique of the Judgement of Taste.*
         Cambridge: Harvard University Press.

Brant, Vinícius Caldeira.

1986.   "O Trabalhador Preso no Estado de São Paulo (Passado, Pre-
         sente e Expectativas)." São Paulo: Cebrap, ms.

Brant, Vinícius Caldeira, et al.

1989.   *São Paulo: Trabalhar e Viver.* São Paulo: Brasiliense.

Bretas, Marcos Luiz.

1995.   "You Can't! The Daily Exercise of Police Authority in Rio
         de Janeiro, 1907–1930." Ph. D. diss., Open University, Milton
         Keynes.

Buarque, Chico.

1991.   *Estorvo.* São Paulo: Companhia das Letras.

Caldeira, Teresa Pires do Rio.

1981.   "Uma Incursão pelo Lado 'Não-respeitável' da Pesquisa de
         Campo." In *Ciências Sociais Hoje, 1: Trabalho e Cultura no
         Brasil.* Recife/Brasília: Anpocs/CNPq, 332–54.

1984.   *A Polítia dos Outros: O Cotidiano dos Moradores da Periferia
         e o que Pensam do Poder e dos Poderosos.* São Paulo:
         Brasiliense.

1986.   "Houses of Respect." Paper presented at the Thirteenth
         International Congress of the Latin American Studies
         Association, Boston.

1987.   "Electoral Struggles in a Neighborhood on the Periphery
         of São Paulo." *Politics and Society* 15 (1): 43–66.

1988.   "The Art of Being Indirect: Talking about Politics in Brazil."
         Cultural Anthropology 3 (4): 444–54.

1990.   "Women, Daily Life and Politics." In *Women and Social
         Change in Latin America,* ed. Elizabeth Jelin. London: Zed
         Books, 47–78.

1994.   Review of *Variations on a Theme Park: The American City
         and the End of Public Space,* ed. Michael Sorkin. In *Journal
         of Architectural Education* 48 (1): 65–67.

1996.   "Fortified Enclaves: The New Urban Segregation." *Public
         Culture* 8:303–28.

1998.   "Justice and Individual Rights: Challenges for Women's
         Movements and Democratization in Brazil." In *Women and
         Democracy: Latin American and Central and Eastern Europe,*
         ed. Jane S. Jaquette and Sharon L. Wolchik. Baltimore: Johns
         Hopkins University Press, 75–103.

Calvino, Italo.
   1974.   *Invisible Cities*. San Diego: Harvest Books.
Camargo, Cândido Procópio Ferreira de, et al.
   1976.   *São Paulo 1975: Crescimento e Pobreza*. São Paulo: Loyola.
Cancelli, Elizabeth.
   1993.   *O Mundo da Violência: A Polícia da Era Vargas*. Brasília:
             Editora da Universidade de Brasília.
Candido, Antonio.
   1970.   "Dialética da Malandragem." *Revista do Instituto de Estudos
             Brasileiros* 8:67–89.
Cano, Ignacio.
   1997.   *Análise Territorial da Violência no Rio de Janeiro*. Rio de
             Janeiro: ISER.
Cardoso, Fernando Henrique.
   1980.   "Originalidade da Cópia: a Cepal e a Idéia de Desenvolvi-
             mento." In *As Idéias e seu Lugar*. Petrópolis: Vozes, 17–56.
   1987.   "Democracy in Latin America." *Politics and Society* 15 (1):
             23–42.
Cardoso, Fernando Henrique, and Enzo Faletto.
   1967.   *Dependência e Desenvolvimento na América Latina: Ensaio
             de Interpretação Sociológica*. Rio de Janeiro: Zahar.
Cardoso, Miriam Limoeiro.
   1978.   *Ideologia do Desenvolvimento—Brasil: JK-JQ*. Rio de Janeiro:
             Paz e Terra.
Cardoso, Ruth Corrêa Leite.
   1983.   "Movimentos Sociais Urbanos: Balanço Crítico." In *Sociedade
             e Política no Brasil pós-64*, ed. Bernardo Sorj and Maria Her-
             mínia Tavares de Almeida. São Paulo: Brasiliense, 215–39.
   1985.   "Formas de Participação Popular no Brasil Contemporâneo."
             São Paulo em Perspectiva 1(3): 46–50.
   1986.   "As Aventuras de Antropólogos em Campo ou como Escapar
             das Armadilhas de Método." In *A Aventura Antropológica:
             Teoria e Pesquisa*, ed. Ruth Cardoso. Rio de Janeiro: Paz e
             Terra, 95–106.
Cenzatti, Marco.
   1992.   "Los Angeles and the L.A. School: Postmodernism and Urban
             Studies." *Los Angeles Forum in Architecture and Urban
             Design* 10.
Cenzatti, Marco, and Margaret Crawford.
   1998.   "On Public Spaces, Quasi-public Spaces, and Public Quasi-

spaces." In *Architecture and the (New) Public Sphere: Modulus* 24:14–21.

Certeau, Michel de.
1984.   *The Practice of Everyday Life*. Berkeley: University of California Press.

Chalhoub, Sidney.
1986.   *Trabalho, Lar e Botequim: O Cotidiano dos Trabalhadores do Rio de Janeiro da Belle Époque*. São Paulo: Brasiliense.
1990.   *Visões da liberdade: Uma História das Últimas Décadas da Escravidão na Corte*. São Paulo: Companhia das Letras.

Chesnais, Jean-Claude.
1981.   *Histoire de la Violence en Occident de 1800 à nos Jours*. Paris: Pluriel.

Chevalier, Louis.
1973 [1958].   *Laboring Classes and Dangerous Classes*. New York: Howard Fertig.

Chevigny, Paul.
1995.   *Edge of the Knife: Police Violence in the Americas*. New York: New Press.

Clark, T. J.
1984.   *The Painting of Modern Life: Paris in the Art of Manet and His Followers*. Princeton: Princeton University Press.

Clastres, Pierre.
1978.   "Da Tortura nas Sociedades Primitivas." In *A Sociedade contra o Estado: Pesquisas de Antropologia Política*. Rio de Janeiro: Francisco Alves, 123–31.

Coelho, Edmundo Campos.
1978.   "A criminalização da Marginalidade e a Marginalização da Criminalidade." *Revista de Administração Pública* 12 (2): 139–61.
1980.   "Sobre Sociólogos, Pobreza e Crime." *Dados* 23 (3): 377–83.
1988.   "A Criminalidade Urbana Violenta." *Dados* 31 (2): 145–83.

Comisión Especial del Senado sobre las Causas de la Violencia y Alternativas de Pacificación en el Peru.
1989.   *Violencia y pacificación*. Lima: Desco e Comision Andina de Juristas.

Comisión de Estudios sobre la Violencia.
1987.   *Colombia: Violencia y Democracia—Informe Presentado ao Ministerio de Gobierno*. Bogotá: Universidad Nacional de Colombia.

432   References

Comissão Teotônio Vilela.
1986.   *Democracia x Violência.* Rio de Janeiro: Paz e Terra.
Coronil, Fernando, and Julie Skurski.
1991.   "Dismembering and Remembering the Nation: The Semantics of Political Violence in Venezuela." *Comparative Studies in Society and History.* 33 (2): 288–337.
Correa, Mariza.
1981.   *Os Crimes da Paixão.* São Paulo: Brasiliense.
1982.   "As Ilusões da Liberdade—A Escola Nina Rodrigues e a Antropologia no Brasil." Ph.D. diss., Universidade de São Paulo.
1983.   *Morte em Família: Representações Jurídicas de Papéis Sexuais.* Rio de Janeiro: Graal.
Crawford, Margaret.
1992.   "The World in a Shopping Mall." In *Variations on a Theme Park: The New American City and the End of Public Space,* ed. Michael Sorkin. New York: Noonday Press, 3–30.
1995.   "Contesting the Public Realm: Struggles over Public Space in Los Angeles." *Journal of Architectural Education* 49 (1): 4–9.
Cunningham, Ian.
1964.   "Order in the Atoni House." *Bijdragen: Tot Taal, Land en Volkenkunde* 120:34–68.
DaMatta, Roberto.
1978.   O Ofíco de Etnólogo, ou como Ter "Anthropological Blues." In *A Aventura Sociológica: Objetividade, Paixão, Improviso e Método na Pesquisa Social,* ed. Edson de Oliveira Nunes. Rio de Janeiro: Zahar, 23–35.
1979.   *Carnavais, Malandros e Heróis: Para uma Sociologia do Dilema Brasileiro.* Rio de Janeiro: Zahar.
1982.   "As Raízes da Violência no Brasil: Reflexões de um Antropólogo Social." In Maria Célia Paoli et al., *A Violência Brasileira.* São Paulo: Brasiliense, 11–44.
1985.   *A Casa e a Rua: Espaço, Cidadania, Mulher e Morte no Brasil.* São Paulo: Brasiliense.
1991.   *Carnivals, Rogues, and Heroes: An Interpretation of the Brazilian Dilemma.* Notre Dame: University of Notre Dame Press.
Daniel, E. Valentine.
1996.   *Charred Lullabies: Chapters in an Anthropology of Violence.* Princeton: Princeton University Press.

Davis, Jennifer.
1991.   "Urban Policing and its Objects: Comparative Themes in England and France in the Second Half of the Nineteenth Century." In *Policing Western Europe: Politics, Professionalism, and Public Order, 1850–1940*, ed. Clive Emsley and Barbara Weinberger. New York: Greenwood Press, 1–17.

Davis, Mike.
1985.   "Urban Renaissance and the Spirit of Postmodernism." *New Left Review* 151:53–92.

1987.   "*Chinatown*, Part Two?" *New Left Review* 164:65–86.

1990.   *City of Quartz: Excavating the Future in Los Angeles.* London: Verso.

1991.   "The Infinite Game: Redeveloping Downtown L.A." In *Out of Site: Social Criticism of Architecture*, ed. Diane Ghirardo. Seattle: Bay Press, 77–113.

1993.   "Who Killed Los Angeles? Part Two: The Verdict Is Given." *New Left Review* 199:29–54.

Dean, Warren.
1969.   *The Industrialization of São Paulo, 1880–1945.* Austin: University of Texas Press.

Dear, Michael.
1996.   "In the City, Time Becomes Visible: Intentionality and Urbanism in Los Angeles, 1781–1991." In *The City: Los Angeles and Urban Theory at the End of the Twentieth Century*, ed. Allen J. Scott and Edward W. Soja. Berkeley: University of California Press, 76–105.

Degler, Carl N.
1971.   *Neither Black nor White: Slavery and Race Relations in Brazil and the United States.* Madison: University of Wisconsin Press.

Deutsche, Rosalyn.
1996.   *Evictions: Art and Spatial Politics.* Cambridge: MIT Press.

Dias, Erasmo.
1990.   *Doutrina de Segurança e Risco.* São Paulo: Ind. de Emb. Santa Inês.

Douglas, Mary.
1966.   *Purity and Danger: An Analysis of the Concepts of Pollution and Taboo.* London: Routledge.

434   References

DuBois, Page.
1991.   *Torture and Truth.* New York: Routledge.
Dumm, Thomas L.
1987.   *Democracy and Punishment: Disciplinary Origins of the United States.* Madison: University of Wisconsin Press.
1993.   "The New Enclosures: Racism in the Normalized Community." In *Reading Rodney King, Reading Urban Uprising,* ed. Robert Gooding-Williams. New York: Routledge, 178–95.
Durham, Eunice Ribeiro.
1984.   "Movimentos Sociais: a Construção da Cidadania." *Novos Estudos Cebrap* 10:24–30.
1986.   "A Pesquisa Antropológica com Populações Urbanas: Problemas e Perspectivas." In *A Aventura Antropológica: Teoria e Pesquisa,* ed. Ruth Cardoso. Rio de Janeiro: Paz e Terra, 17–38.
Eisenstein, Zillah R.
1988.   *The Female Body and the Law.* Berkeley: University of California Press.
Elias, Norbert.
1994 [1939].   *The Civilizing Process (The History of Manners* and *State Formation and Civilization).* Cambridge: Blackwell.
Ellin, Nan, ed.
1997.   *Architecture of Fear.* New York: Princeton Architectural Press.
Embraesp—Empresa Brasileira de Estudos de Patrimônio S/C. Ltda.
1994.   "Relatório Anual de 1993 e Prognóstico para 1994." *Informativo Imobiliário Embraesp.* São Paulo: Embraesp.
1997.   "Relatório Anual de 1996 e Prognóstico para 1997." *Informativo Imobiliário Embraesp.* São Paulo: Embraesp.
Engels, Friedrich.
1872.   *The Housing Question.* New York: International Publishers.
Escobar, Arturo, and Sonia Alvarez, eds.
1992.   *The Making of Social Movements in Latin America: Identity, Strategy, and Democracy.* Boulder: Westview Press.
Estudos Feministas,
various issues.
Ethnos.
1982.   47 (1–2).
Faria, Vilmar.
1983.   "Desenvolvimento, Urbanização e Mudanças na Estrutura do Emprego: A Experiêcia Brasileira dos Últimos Trinta Anos."

In *Sociedade e Política no Brasil pós-64*, ed. Bernardo Sorj and Maria Hermínia Tavares de Almeida. São Paulo: Brasiliense, 118–63.

1989. "Políticas de Governo e Regulação da Fecundidade: Consequências não Antecipadas e Efeitos Perversos." *Ciências Sociais Hoje* 1989:62–103.

1991. "Cinqüenta Anos de Urbanização no Brasil." *Novos Estudos Cebrap* 29:98–119.

Fausto, Boris.

1977. *Trabalho Urbano e Conflito Social, 1890–1920*. São Paulo: Difel.

1984. *Crime e Cotidiano: a Criminalidade em São Paulo, 1880–1924*. São Paulo: Brasiliense.

Feiguin, Dora.

1985. "Criminalidade Violenta: Algumas Hipóteses Explicativas." *Revista da Fundação Seade* 1 (2): 3–26.

Feiguin, Dora, and Renato Sérgio de Lima.

1995. "Tempo de Violência: Medo e Insegurança em São Paulo." *São Paulo em Perspectiva* 9 (2): 73–80.

Feldman, Allen.

1991. *Formations of Violence: The Narrative of the Body and Political Terror in Northern Ireland*. Chicago: University of Chicago Press.

Fernandes, Heloísa Rodrigues.

1974. *Política e Segurança—Força Pública do Estado de São Paulo: Fundamentos Histórico-Sociais*. São Paulo: Alfa-Omega.

1991. "Authoritarian Society: Breeding Ground for *Justiceiros*." In *Vigilantism and the State in Modern Latin America*, ed. Martha K. Huggins. New York: Praeger, 61–70.

Ferraz Filho, Galeno Tinoco.

1992. Considerações sobre a Oferta de Imóveis Novos na Década de 80 (Rio/São Paulo/Porto Alegre). In *Acumulação Urbana e a Cidade: Impasses e Limites da Produção Capitalista da Moradia no Brasil*, ed. Luiz César de Queiroz Ribeiro and Luciana Corrêa do Lago. Rio de Janeiro: IPPUR/UFRJ, 15–33.

Ferreira, Nádia Somekh Martins.

1987. A (Des)verticalização de São Paulo. M.A. thesis, University of São Paulo.

Findji, María Teresa.

1992. "From Resistance to Social Movement: The Indigenous Authorities Movement in Colombia." In *The Making of Social Movements in Latin America,* ed. Arturo Escobar and Sonia Alvarez. Boulder: Westview Press, 112–133.

Fipe (Fundação Instituto de Pesquisas Econômicas da Universidade de São Paulo).

1994. "Cortiços na Cidade de São Paulo: Relatório Gerencial." Research report.

Fishman, Robert.

1988. *Urban Utopias in the Twentieth Century: Ebenezer Howard, Frank Lloyd Wright, Le Corbusier.* Cambridge: MIT Press.

1995. Megalopolis Unbound. In *Metropolis: Center and Symbol of Our Times,* ed. Philip Kasinitz. New York: New York University Press, 395–417.

Flory, Thomas.

1981. *Judge and Jury in Imperial Brazil, 1808–1871: Social Control and Political Stability in the New State.* Austin: University of Texas Press.

Fogelson, Robert M.

1967. *The Fragmented Metropolis: Los Angeles, 1850–1930.* Cambridge: Harvard University Press.

Foucault, Michel.

1977. *Discipline and Punish: The Birth of the Prison.* New York: Pantheon Books.

Franco, Maria Sylvia de Carvalho.

1974. *Homens Livres na Ordem Escravocrata.* São Paulo: Ática.

Furtado, Celso.

1969. *Um Projeto Para o Brasil.* 5th ed. Rio de Janeiro: Saga.

Garreau, Joel.

1991. *Edge City: Life on the New Frontier.* New York: Doubleday.

Girard, René.

1977. *Violence and the Sacred.* Baltimore: Johns Hopkins University Press.

Girouard, Mark.

1985. *Cities and People: A Social and Architectural History.* New Haven: Yale University Press.

Goldani, Ana Maria.

1994. "Retratos de Família em Tempos de Crise." *Estudos Feministas.* Special issue. 303–35.

Gonçalves, Maria Flora, and Ulysses Cidade Semeghini.

1992. "A Modernização do Setor Terciário Paulista." *São Paulo em Perspectiva* 6 (3): 60–69.

Gonzalez, Lélia.

1985.   "The Unified Black Movement: A New Stage in Black Political
Mobilization." In *Race, Class and Power in Brazil*, ed. Pierre-
Michel Fontaine. Los Angeles: UCLA Center for Afro-
American Studies, 120–34.

Gregori, Maria Filomena.

1993.   *Cenas e Queixas: Um Estudo sobre Mulheres, Relações Vio-
lentas e a Prática Feminista.* São Paulo: Paz e Terra/Anpocs.

Guimarães, Antonio Sérgio Alfredo.

1997.   "Racismo e Justiça no Brasil: Porque a Discriminação Racial
Continua Impune." Paper presented at the Twentieth Interna-
tional Congress of the Latin American Studies Association,
Guadalajara, Mexico.

Gupta, Akhil, and James Ferguson.

1997.   "Discipline and Practice: "The Field" as Site, Method, and Location in Anthropology." In *Anthropological Locations: Boundaries and Grounds of a Field Science,* ed. Akhil Gupta and James
Ferguson. Berkeley: University of California Press, 1–46.

Gurr, Ted Robert.

1979.   "On the History of Violent Crime in Europe and America."
In *Violence in America: Historical and Comparative Perspec-
tives,* rev. ed., ed. Hugh Davis Graham and Ted Robert Gurr.
Beverly Hills: Sage, 353–74.

Hamburger, Esther.

1999.   "Politics and Intimacy in Brazilian Telenovelas." Ph.D. diss.,
University of Chicago.

Hanchard, Michael George.

1994.   *Orpheus and Power: The Movimento Negro of Rio de Janeiro
and São Paulo, Brazil, 1945–1988.* Princeton: Princeton
University Press.

Hanson, Elizabeth.

1991.   "Torture and Truth in Renaissance England." *Representations*
34:53–84.

Harvey, David.

1985.   "Paris, 1850–1870." In *Consciousness and the Urban Experience: Studies in History and Theory of Capitalist Urbanization.* Baltimore: Johns Hopkins University Press, 63–220.

Hasenbalg, Carlos.

1996.   "Racial Inequalities in Brazil and throughout Latin America:
Timid Responses to Disguised Racism." In *Constructing*

Democracy: Human Rights, Citizenship, and Society in Latin America, ed. Elizabeth Jelin and Eric Hershberg. Boulder: Westview Press, 161–176.

Helg, Aline.

1990.   "Race in Argentina and Cuba, 1880–1930: Theory, Policies, and Popular Reaction."In *The Idea of Race in Latin America, 1870–1940*, ed. Richard Graham. Austin: University of Texas Press, 37–69.

Hirschman, Albert O.

1991.   *The Rhetoric of Reaction: Perversity, Futility, Jeopardy.* Cambridge: The Belknap Press of Harvard University Press.

Holloway, Thomas H.

1993.   *Policing Rio de Janeiro: Repression and Resistance in a Nineteenth-Century City.* Stanford: Stanford University Press.

Holston, James.

1989.   *The Modernist City: An Anthropological Critique of Brasília.* Chicago: University of Chicago Press.

1991a.   "Autoconstruction in Working-Class Brazil." *Cultural Anthropology* 6 (4): 447–65.

1991b.   "The Misrule of Law: Land and Usurpation in Brazil." *Comparative Studies in Society and History* 33 (4): 695–725.

Forthcoming.   "Citizenship in Uncivil Democracies." In "Unsettling Citizenship: Disjunctions of Democracy and Modernity."

Holston, James, and Teresa P. R. Caldeira.

1998.   "Democracy, Law, and Violence: Disjunctions of Brazilian Citizenship." In *Fault Lines of Democracy in Post-transition Latin America*, ed. Felipe Agüero and Jeffrey Stark. Miami: University of Miami North-South Center Press, 263–96.

Howard, Ebenezer.

1902.   *Garden Cities of Tomorrow.* London: S. Sonnenschein and Co., Ltd.

Huggins, Martha Knisely.

1985.   *From Slavery to Vagrancy in Brazil: Crime and Social Control in the Third World.* New Brunswick: Rutgers University Press.

Human Rights Watch/Americas.

1994.   *Final Justice: Police and Death Squad Homicides of Adolescents in Brazil.* New York: Human Rights Watch

1997.   *Police Brutality in Urban Brazil.* New York: Human Rights Watch.

IBGE (Instituto Brasileiro de Geografia e Estatística).

1990.   *Participação Político-Social 1988: Vol. 1, Justiça e Vitimização.*
             Rio de Janeiro: FIBGE.

Jackson, Kenneth T.

1985.   *Crabgrass Frontier: The Suburbanization of the United States.*
             New York: Oxford University Press.

Jacobs, Jane.

1961.   *The Death and Life of Great American Cities.* New York:
             Vintage Books.

Jencks, Charles.

1993.   *Heteropolis: Los Angeles, the Riots, and the Strange Beauty*
             of Hetero-Architecture. London: Ernst and Sohn.

Johnson, Lyman, ed.

1990.   *The Problem of Order in Changing Societies: Essays*
             on Crime and Policing in Argentina and Uruguay, 1750–
             1940. Albuquerque: University of New Mexico Press.

Johnston, Les.

1992.   *The Rebirth of Private Policing.* London: Routledge.

Jones, David.

1982.   *Crime, Protest, Community and Police in Nineteenth-*
             Century Britain. London: Routledge and Kegan Paul.

Jornal de Alphaville,
     various issues.

Jornal da Pires,
     various issues.

Kling, Rob, Spencer Olin, and Mark Poster, eds.

1991.   *Postsuburban California: The Transformation of Orange Coun-*
             ty since World War II. Berkeley: University of California Press.

Kostof, Spiro.

1991.   *The City Shaped: Urban Patterns and Meanings through*
             History. Boston: Bulfinch Press Book, Little, Brown, and Co.

Kowarick, Lúcio, ed.

1989.   *Social Struggles and the City: The Case of São Paulo.* New
             York: Monthly Review Press.

Kowarick, Lúcio, and Nabil Bonduki.

1994.   Espaço Urbano e Espaço Político: Do Populismo à Redemocra-
             tização. In *As Lutas Sociais e a Cidade,* ed. Lúcio Kowarick.
             Rio de Janeiro: Paz e Terra, 147–80.

Kymlicka, Will.

1996.   "Three Forms of Group-Differentiated Citizenship." In

Democracy and Difference: Contesting the Boundaries of the Political, ed. Seyla Benhabib. Princeton: Princeton University Press, 153–70.

Lacarrieu, Mónica.
 1997. "El Dilema de lo Local y la Producción de la 'Feudalización.'" Unpublished ms..

Laclau, Ernesto, and Chantal Mouffe.
 1985. *Hegemony and Socialist Strategy: Towards a Radical Democratic Politics.* London: Verso.

Ladányi, János.
 1998. "Residential Segregation between Social and Ethnic Groups in Budapest during the Post-Communist Transition." Paper presented at the Conference "Social Geography of Divided Cities," International Center for Advanced Studies, New York University, February 26–27.

Lamounier, Bolivar.
 1989. "Authoritarian Brazil Revisited: The Impact of Elections on the *Abertura.*" In *Democratizing Brazil: Problems of Transition and Consolidation,* ed. Alfred Stepan. New York: Oxford University Press, 43–79.

Lane, Roger.
 1980. "Urban Police and Violence in Nineteenth Century America." In *Crime and Justice: An Annual Review of Research,* vol. 2, ed. Norval Morris and Michael Tonry. Chicago: University of Chicago Press, 1–43.
 1986. *Roots of Violence in Black Philadelphia, 1860–1900.* Cambridge: Harvard University Press.

Langenbuch, Juergen Richard.
 1971. *A Estruturação da Grande São Paulo.* Rio de Janeiro: IBGE.

Lara, Silvia Hunold.
 1988. *Campos da Violência: Escravos e Senhores na Capitania do Rio de Janeiro, 1750–1808.* Rio de Janeiro: Paz e Terra.

Lefort, Claude.
 1988. *Democracy and Political Theory.* Minneapolis: University of Minnesota Press.

Leme, Maria Carolina, and Ciro Biderman.
 1997. "O mapa das Desigualdades no Estado de São Paulo." *Novos Estudos Cebrap* 49:181–211.

Leme, Maria Carolina da Silva, and Regina Maria Prosperi Meyer.

1996.   "São Paulo Metrópole Terciária, entre a Modernização Pós-Industrial e a Herança Social e Territorial da Industrialização." Research Report no. 2. São Paulo: Cebrap.

1997.   "São Paulo Metrópole Terciária, entre a Modernização Pós-Industrial e a Herança Social e Territorial da Industrialização." Research Report no. 3. São Paulo: Cebrap.

Leme, Maria Cristina da Silva.

1991.   A Formação do Pensamento Urbanístico, em São Paulo, no Início do Século XX. *Espaço e Debates* XI (34):64–70.

Lemos, Carlos.

1978.   *Cozinhas, etc.: Um Estudo sobre as Zonas de Serviço da Casa Paulista.* São Paulo: Perspectiva.

Leps, Marie-Christine.

1992.   *Apprehending the Criminal: The Production of Deviance in Nineteenth-Century Discourse.* Durham: Duke University Press.

Lima, Roberto Kant de.

1986.   "Legal Theory and Judicial Practice: Paradoxes of Police Work in the Rio de Janeiro City." Ph.D. diss., Harvard University.

Linger, Daniel Touro.

1992.   *Dangerous Encounters: Meanings of Violence in a Brazilian City.* Stanford: Stanford University Press.

Lopes, Juarez Rubens Brandão.

1993.   "Brasil 1989: Um Estudo Sócioeconômico da Indigência e da Pobreza Urbanas." Núcleo de Estudos de Políticas Públicas da Unicamp, *Caderno de Pesquisa* 25.

Lopes, Juarez Brandão, and Andréa Gottschalk.

1990.   "Recessão, Pobreza e Família: A Década Pior do que Perdida." *São Paulo em Perspectiva* 4 (1): 100–109.

Mabin, Alan.

1998.   "The Creation of Urban Space: Contributions of South African Cities to Justice and Injustice." Paper presented at the conference "Social Geography of Divided Cities," International Center for Advanced Studies, New York University, February 26–27.

Machado, Marcelo Lavenère, and João Benedito de Azevedo Marques.

1993.   *História de um Massacre: Casa de Detenção de São Paulo.* São Paulo: Cortez and Ordem dos Advogados do Brasil.

Malkki, Liisa H.

1995.   *Purity and Exile: Violence, Memory, and National Cosmology among Hutu Refugees in Tanzania.* Chicago: University of Chicago Press.

Marshall, T. H.

1965 [1949].   "Citizenship and Social Class." In *Class, Citizenship, and Social Development.* New York: Doubleday.

Martins, José de Souza.

1991.   "Lynchings—Life by a Thread: Street Justice in Brazil, 1979–1988." In *Vigilantism and the State in Modern Latin America,* ed. Martha K. Huggins. New York: Praeger, 21–32.

Martins, Luciano.

1987.   "A Gênese de uma *Intelligentsia*: Os Intelectuais e a Política no Brasil, 1920–1940." *Revista Brasileira de Ciências Sociais* 4 (2): 65–87.

Massey, Douglas S., and Nancy A. Denton.

1993.   *American Apartheid: Segregation and the Making of the Underclass.* Cambridge: Harvard University Press.

McKenzie, Evan.

1994.   *Privatopia: Homeowner Associations and the Rise of Residential Private Government.* New Haven: Yale University Press.

Mello Jorge, Maria Helena P. de, and Maria Rosário D. O. Latorre.

1994.   "Acidentes de Trânsito no Brasil: Dados e Tendências." *Cadernos de Saúde Pública* 10 (1): 19–44.

Melo, Marcus C.

1995.   "State Retreat, Governance and Metropolitan Restructuring in Brazil." *International Journal of Urban and Regional Research* 19 (3): 342–57.

Metrô (Companhia do Metropolitano de São Paulo).

1989.   *Pesquisa OD/87: Síntese das Informações.* São Paulo: Metrô.

Miceli, Sérgio.

1979.   *Intelectuais e Classe Dirigente no Brasil, 1920–1945.* São Paulo: Difel.

Minayo, Maria Cecília de S.

1994.   "A Violência Social sob a Perspectiva da Saúde Pública." *Cadernos de Saúde Pública* 10 (1): 7–18.

Mingardi, Guaracy.

1992.   *Tiras, Gansos e Trutas: Cotidiano e Reforma na Polícia Civil.* São Paulo: Scritta.

Monkkonen, Eric H.

1981.   *Police in Urban America, 1860–1920*. Cambridge: Cambridge University Press.

Montoro, André Franco.

1982.   "Proposta Montoro." Electoral campaign program.

Morse, Richard M.

1970.   *Formação Histórica de São Paulo*. São Paulo: Difel.

Nedelsky, Jennifer.

1990.   "Law, Boundaries, and the Bounded Self." *Representations* 30:162–89.

Nelson, Sara.

1995.   "Paradoxo e Contradição nas Delegacias de Defesa da Mulher." *Comunicação e Política* 1 (2): 293–298.

Nepp (Núcleo de Estudos de Políticas Públicas da Universidade Estadual de Campinas).

1989.   *Brasil 1987: Relatório sobre a Situação Social do País*. Campinas: Unicamp.

1990.   "A Política do Governo do Estado de São Paulo na Área da Segurança Pública: Diagnósticos e Estudos Prospectivos— 1a. Parte." Campinas: Nepp/Unicamp. Research report.

Núcleo de Estudos de Seguridade e Assitência Social.

1995.   "Mapa da Exclusão Social da Cidade de São Paulo." Ms.

Ocqueteau, Frédéric.

1997.   "A Expansão da Segurança Privada na França: Privatização Submissa da Ação Policial ou Melhor Gestão da Segurança Coletiva?" *Tempo Social* 9 (1):185–95.

Ocqueteau, Frédéric, and Pottier, M. L.

1995.   *Vigilance et Sécurité dans les Grandes Surfaces*. Paris: IHESI-L'Harmattan.

O'Donnell, Guillermo.

1986.   "E Eu com isso? Notas sobre Sociabilidade e Política na Argentina e no Brasil." *Contrapontos: Autoritarismo e Democratização*. São Paulo: Vértice, 121–56.

Oliveira, Roberto Cardoso de.

1988.   *Sobre o Pensamento Antropológico*. Rio de Janeiro: Tempo Brasileiro.

1995.   "Notas sobre uma Etilística em Antropologia." In *Estilos de Antropologia*, ed. Roberto Cardoso de Oliveira and Guillermo Raul Ruben. Campinas: Editora da Unicamp, 177–90.

Ong, Paul, and Evelyn Blumemberg.

1996.   "Income and Racial Inequality in Los Angeles." In *The City: Los Angeles and Urban Theory at the End of the Twentieth Century*, ed. Allen J. Scott and Edward W. Soja. Berkeley: University of California Press, 311–35.

Paixão, Antonio Luiz.

1982.   A Organização Policial numa Área Metropolitana. *Dados* 25 (1): 63–85.

1983.   Crimes e Criminosos em Belo Horizonte, 1932–1978. In *Crime, Violência e Poder*, ed. Paulo Sérgio Pinheiro. São Paulo: Brasiliense, 11–44.

1986.   "A Etnometodologia e o Estudo do Poder: Notas Preliminares." *Análise e Conjuntura* 1 (2): 93–110.

1988.   "Crime, Controle Social e Consolidação da Democracia: As Metáforas da Cidadania." In *A Democracia no Brasil: Dilemas e Perspectivas*, ed. Fabio Wanderley Reis and Guillermo O'Donnell. São Paulo: Vértice, 168–99.

1990.   "A Violência Urbana e a Sociologia: Sobre Crenças e Fatos e Mitos e Teorias e Políticas e Linguagens e," *Religião e Sociedade* 15 (1): 68–81.

Paoli, Maria Célia Pinheiro Machado.

1982.   "Violência e Espaço Civil." In Maria Célia Paoli et al., *A Violência Brasileira*. São Paulo: Brasiliense, 45–56.

Pateman, Carole.

1988.   *The Sexual Contract*. Stanford: Stanford University Press.

Peirano, Mariza.

1980.   "The Anthropology of Anthropology: The Brazilian Case." Ph.D. diss., Harvard University.

Perillo, Sonia Regina.

1993.   "Migração e Mudanças: Uma Análise das Tendências Migratórias na Região Metropolitana de São Paulo no Período 1980–1991." *Conjuntura Demográfica* 22:1–13.

Pezzin, Liliana E.

1987.   *Criminalidade Urbana e Crise Econômica: O Caso de São Paulo*. São Paulo: IPE/USP.

Pietá, Elói, and Justino Pereira.

1993.   *Pavilhão 9: O Massacre do Carandiru*. São Paulo: Scritta.

Pimentel, Silvia, and Maria Inês Valente Pierro.

1993.   "Proposta de Lei contra a Violência Familiar." *Estudos Feministas* 1 (1): 169–75.

Pinheiro, Paulo Sérgio.
1981.   "Violência e Cultura." In *Direito, Cidadania e Participação,*
            ed. Bolivar Lamounier, Francisco Weffort, and Maria Vitória
            Benevides. São Paulo: TAQ, 30–66.
1982.   "Polícia e Crise Política: O Caso das Polícias Militares." In
            Maria Celia Paoli et al., *A Violência Brasileira.* São Paulo:
            Brasiliense, 57–92.
1983.   "Violência sem Controle e Militarização da Polícia." *Novos
            Estudos Cebrap* 2 (1): 8–12.
1991a.   "Autoritarismo e Transição." *Revista USP* 9:45–56.
1991b.   "Police and Political Crisis: The Case of the Military Police."
            In *Vigilantism and the State in Modern Latin America,* ed.
            Martha K. Huggins. New York: Praeger, 167–188.
Pinheiro, Paulo Sérgio, and Emir Sader.
1985.   "O Controle da Polícia no Processo de Transição Democrática
            no Brasil." *Temas IMESC* 2 (2): 77–96.
Pinheiro, Paulo Sérgio, Eduardo E. Izumino, and Maria Cristina Jakimiak
            Fernandes.
1991.   "Violência Fatal: Conflitos Policiais em São Paulo (81–89)."
            Revista USP 9:95–112.
PNUD-IPEA (Programa das Nações Unidas para o Desenvolvimento—
            Instituto de Pesquisa Econômica Aplicada).
1996.   *Relatório para o Desenvolvimento Humano no Brasil.*
            Brasília: PNUD-IPEA.
Queiroz, Maria Isaura Pereira de.
1977.   *Os Cangaceiros.* São Paulo: Duas Cidades.
Rabinow, Paul.
1989.   *French Modern: Norms and Forms of the Social Environment.*
            Cambridge: MIT Press.
Ribeiro, Luiz César de Queiroz.
1993.   "The Formation of Development Capital: A Historical View
            of Housing in Rio de Janeiro." *International Journal of Urban
            and Regional Research* 17 (4): 547–58.
Ribeiro, Luiz Cesar de Queiroz, and Luciana Correa do Lago.
1995.   "Restructuring in Large Brazilian Cities: The Centre/Periph-
            ery Model." *International Journal of Urban and Regional
            Research* 19 (3): 369–82.
Rieff, David.
1991.   *Los Angeles: Capital of the Third World.* New York: Simon
            and Schuster.

Rocha, Sonia.
1991.   "Pobreza Metropolitana e os Ciclos de Curto Prazo: Balanço
           dos Anos 80." *IPEA: Boletim de Conjuntura* 12.
1995.   "Governabilidade e Pobreza: O Desafio dos Números." In
           Governabilidade e Pobreza no Brasil, ed. Lícia Valladares and
           Magda Prestes Coelho. Rio de Janeiro: Civilização Brasileira,
           221–66.
1996.   "Who Are the Poor in Brazil?" IPEA. Research report.
Rohlfes, Laurence J.
1983.   "Police and Penal Correction in Mexico City, 1876–1911: A
           Study of Order and Progress in Porfirian Mexico." Ph.D. diss.,
           Tulane University.
Rolnik, Raquel.
1983.   "De como São Paulo Virou a Capital do Capital." In *Repen-
           sando a Habitação no Brasil*, ed. Lícia do Prado Valladares.
           Rio de Janeiro: Zahar, 109–34.
1994.   "São Paulo: Início da Industrialização: O Espaço e a Política."
           In *As Lutas Sociais e a Cidade*, ed. Lúcio Kowarick. Rio de
           Janeiro: Paz e Terra, 95–112.
1997.   *A Cidade e a Lei: Legislação, Política Urbana e Territórios na
           Cidade de São Paulo*. São Paulo: Fapesp/Studio Nobel.
Rolnik, Raquel, et. al.
n.d.   *São Paulo: Crise e Mudança*. São Paulo: Brasiliense.
Rutheiser, Charles.
1996.   *Imagineering Atlanta: The Politics of Place in the City of
           Dreams*. London: Verso.
Sachs, Céline.
1990.   *São Paulo: Politiques Publiques et Habitat Populaire*. Paris:
           Maison des Sciences de l'Homme.
Salgado, Ivone.
1987.   "Caracterização dos Promotores Imobiliários que Atuam
           na Cidade de São Paulo (1977–1982)." *Espaço e Debates* 7
           (21): 51–71.
Santos, Wanderley Guilherme dos.
1979.   *Cidadania e Justiça: Política Social na Ordem Brasileira*.
           Rio de Janeiro: Campus.
São Paulo—Emplasa (Empresa Metropolitana de Planejamento da Grande
           São Paulo).
1978.   *Pesquisa Origem-Destino/77: Resultados Básicos: Documento
           Bilingüe*. São Paulo: Emplasa.

1982.   *Sumário de Dados da Grande São Paulo: 82.* São Paulo: Emplasa.

1994.   *Sumário de Dados da Grande São Paulo: 93.* São Paulo: Emplasa.

São Paulo—Sempla (Secretaria Municipal de Planejamento).

1992.   *Base de Dados para Planejamento.* São Paulo: Sempla.

1995.   *Dossiê São Paulo.* São Paulo: PMSP/Sempla.

São Paulo—Seplan (Secretaria de Economia e Planejamento).

1977.   *Subdivisão do Município de São Paulo em Áreas Homogêneas.* São Paulo: Seplan.

Sassen, Saskia.

1991.   *The Global City: New York, London, Tokyo.* Princeton: Princeton University Press.

Scarry, Elaine.

1985.   *The Body in Pain: The Making and the Unmaking of the World.* New York: Oxford.

Scheper-Hughes, Nancy.

1992.   *Death without Weeping: The Violence of Everyday Life in Brazil.* Berkeley: University of California Press.

Schorske, Carl E.

1961.   *Fin-de-Siècle Vienna: Politics and Culture.* New York: Vintage Books.

Schwartz, Robert M.

1988.   *Policing the Poor in Eighteenth-Century France.* Chapel Hill: University of North Carolina Press.

Schwarz, Roberto.

1977.   *Ao Vencedor as Batatas.* São Paulo: Duas Cidades.

1992.   *Misplaced Ideas: Essays in Brazilian Culture.* London: Verso.

Sciascia, Leonardo.

1987.   *Portas Abertas.* São Paulo: Rocco.

Scott, Allen J.

1993.   *Technopolis: High-Technology Industry and Regional Development in Southern California.* Berkeley: University of California Press.

Scott, Allen J., and Edward W. Soja.

1996.   "Introduction to Los Angeles: City and Region." In *The City: Los Angeles and Urban Theory at the End of the Twentieth Century,* ed. Allen J. Scott and Edward W. Soja. Berkeley: University of California Press, 1–21.

448 References

eds. 1996. *The City: Los Angeles and Urban Theory at the End of the Twentieth Century.* Berkeley: University of California Press.

Scott, Joan Wallach.

1996. *Only Paradoxes to Offer: French Feminists and the Rights of Man.* Cambridge: Harvard University Press.

Seade (Fundação Sistema Estadual de Análise de Dados).

1990. *1990: Município de São Paulo.* São Paulo: Seade.

Various years. *Anuário Estatístico do Estado de São Paulo.* São Paulo: Seade.

Sennett, Richard.

1974. *The Fall of Public Man: On the Social Psychology of Capitalism.* New York: Vintage Books.

Serra, José.

1991. "A Boneca não Cobiçada." *Folha de S. Paulo.* 28 July 1991, 1–3.

Shearing, Clifford D.

1992. "The Relation between Public and Private Policing." In *Modern Policing,* ed. Michael Tonry and Norval Morris. Chicago: University of Chicago Press, 399–434.

Sigaud, Lygia.

1987. "Milícias, Jagunços e Democracia." *Ciência Hoje: Suplemento sobre Violência* 5 (28): 6–10.

Sikkink, Kathryn.

1996. "The Emergence, Evolution, and Effectiveness of the Latin American Human Rights Network." In *Constructing Democracy: Human Rights, Citizenship, and Society in Latin America,* ed. Elizabeth Jelin and Eric Hershberg. Boulder: Westview Press, 59–84.

Silva, Nelson do Vale, and Carlos Hasenbalg.

1992. *Relações Raciais no Brasil Contemporâneo.* Rio de Janeiro: Rio Fundo Editora.

Simmel, Georg.

1971 [1903]. "The Metropolis and Mental Life." In *On Individuality and Social Forms: Selected Writings.* Chicago: University of Chicago Press, 324–39.

Singer, Paul.

1984. "Interpretação do Brasil: Uma Experiência Histórica de Desenvolvimento." In *História Geral da Civilização Brasileira: 3, O Brasil Republicano; 4, Economia e Cultura (1930–1964),* ed. Boris Fausto. 211–45. São Paulo: Difel.

Singer, Paul, and Vinícius Caldeira Brant, eds.

1983.   *O Povo em Movimento.* Petrópolis: Vozes.

Skidmore, Thomas.

1974.   *Black into White: Race and Nationality in Brazilian Thought.*
             New York: Oxford University Press.

Soja, Edward W.

1989.   *Postmodern Geographies: The Reassertion of Space in Critical
             Social Theory.* London: Verso.

1992.   "Inside Exopolis: Scenes from Orange County." In *Variations
             on a Theme Park: The New American City and the End of
             Public Space,* ed. Michael Sorkin. New York: Noonday Press,
             94–122.

1996a.   "Los Angeles 1965–1992: From Crisis-Generated Restructur-
             ing to Restructuring-Generated Crisis." In *The City: Los
             Angeles and Urban Theory at the End of the Twentieth
             Century,* ed. Allen J. Scott and Edward W. Soja. Berkeley:
             University of California Press, 426–62.

1996b.   *Thirdspace: Journeys to Los Angeles and Other Real-and-
             Imagined Places.* Cambridge: Blackwell.

Sorkin, Michael, ed.

1992.   *Variations on a Theme Park: The New American City and
             the End of Public Space.* New York: Noonday Press.

Souza, Edinilsa R. de.

1994.   "Homicídios no Brasil: O Grande Vilão da Saúde Pública na
             Década de 80." *Cadernos de Saúde Pública* 10 (1): 45–60.

Souza, Edinilsa, and Maria Cecília de Souza Minayo.

1995.   "O Impacto da Violência Social na Saúde Pública do Brasil:
             Década de 80." In *Os Muitos Brasis: Saúde e População na
             Década de 80,* ed. Maria Cecília Minayo. São Paulo: Hucitec-
             Abrasco, 87–116.

Stavenhagen, Rodolfo.

1996.   "Indigenous Rights: Some Conceptual Problems." In *Con-
             structing Democracy: Human Rights, Citizenship, and Society
             in Latin America,* ed. Elizabeth Jelin and Eric Hershberg.
             Boulder: Westview Press, 141–59.

Stepan, Alfred.

1971.   *The Military in Politics: Changing Patterns in Brazil.* Prince-
             ton: Princeton University Press.

1988.   *Rethinking Military Politics: Brazil and the Southern Cone.*
             Princeton: Princeton University Press.

ed. 1989.   *Democratizing Brazil: Problems of Transition and Consolidation.* New York: Oxford University Press.

Stocking, George W.

1982.   "Afterword: A View from the Center." *Ethnos* 47 (1–2): 172–86.

Taussig, Michael.

1987.   *Shamanism, Colonialism and the Wild Man: A Study in Terror and Healing.* Chicago: University of Chicago Press.

1992.   *The Nervous System.* New York: Routledge.

Taylor, Charles.

1992.   "The Politics of Recognition." In *Multiculturalism and the Politics of Recognition.* Princeton: Princeton University Press, 25–61.

Taylor, William B.

1979.   *Drinking, Homicide and Rebellion in Colonial Mexican Villages.* Stanford: Stanford University Press.

Telles, Edward.

1992.   "Residential Segregation by Skin Color in Brazil." *American Sociological Review* 57 (2): 186–97.

1993.   "Racial Distance and Region in Brazil: Intermarriage in Brazilian Urban Areas." *Latin American Research Review* 41 (2): 231–49.

1995a.   "Structural Sources of Socioeconomic Segregation in Brazilian Metropolitan Areas." *American Journal of Sociology* 100 (5):1199–1223.

1995b.   "Race, Class and Space in Brazilian Cities." *International Journal of Urban and Regional Research* 19 (3): 395–406.

Tilly, Charles, ed.

1975.   *The Formation of National States in Western Europe.* Princeton: Princeton University Press

Tittle, Charles R., Wayne J. Villemez, and Douglas A. Smith.

1978.   "The Myth of Social Class and Criminality: An Empirical Assesment of the Empirical Evidence." *American Sociological Review* 43:643–56.

Turner, Bryan.

1992.   "Outline of a Theory of Citizenship." In *Dimensions of Radical Democracy,* ed. Chantal Mouffe. London: Verso, 33–62.

United Nations.

1995.   *Demographic Yearbook: 1993.* New York: United Nations.

United States Department of Justice. Federal Bureau of Investigation.
Various years. *Crime in the United States.* Uniform Crime Reports for
        the United States.

United States House.

1993.   Committee on Education and Labor. *Hearings Regarding
            Private Security Guards.* Serial no. 103–6, June 15 and 17.
            Washington, D.C.: U.S. Government Printing Office.

Vanderwood, Paul J.

1981.   *Disorder and Progress: Bandits, Police, and Mexican Develop-
            ment.* Lincoln: University of Nebraska Press.

Vargas, João.

1993.   "À Espera do Passado: As Transformações Recentes de São
            Paulo Vistas de seu Epicentro." M.A. thesis, Universidade
            Estadual de Campinas.

Velho, Gilberto.

1978.   "Observando o Familiar." In *A Aventura Sociológica:
            Objetividade, Paixão, Improviso e Método na Pesquisa
            Social,* ed. Edson de Oliveira Nunes. Rio de Janeiro:
            Zahar, 36–46.

1980.   "O Antropólogo Pesquisando em sua Cidade: Sobre Conheci-
            mento e Heresia." In *O Desafio da Cidade: Novas Perspectivas
            da Antropologia Brasileira,* ed. Gilberto Velho. Rio de Janeiro:
            Campus, 13–21.

1987.   "O Cotidiano da Violência: Identidade e Sobrevivência."
            Boletim do Museu Nacional 56.

1991.   "O Grupo e seus Limites." *Revista USP* 9:23–26.

Vidler, Anthony.

1978.   "The Scenes of the Street: Transformations in Ideal and
            Reality, 1750–1871." In *On Streets,* ed. Stanford Anderson.
            Cambridge: MIT Press, 27–111.

Wachs, Martin.

1996.   "The Evolution of Transportation Policy in Los Angeles:
            Images of Past Policies and Future Prospects." In *The City:
            Los Angeles and Urban Theory at the End of the Twentieth
            Century,* ed. Allen J. Scott and Edward W. Soja. Berkeley:
            University of California Press, 106–59.

Wade, Peter.

1993.   *Blackness and Race Mixture: The Dynamics of Racial
            Identity in Colombia.* Baltimore: Johns Hopkins University
            Press.

Weber, Max.
  1968.   *Economy and Society: An Outline of Interpretive Sociology.*
          New York: Bedminster Press.

Weinstein, Richard S.
  1996.   "The First American City." In *The City: Los Angeles and*
          Urban Theory at the End of the Twentieth Century, ed. Allen
          J. Scott and Edward W. Soja. Berkeley: University of California
          Press, 22–46.

Wells, J. R.
  1976.   "Subconsumo, Tamaho do Mercado e Padrões de Gastos
          Familiares no Brasil." *Estudos Cebrap* 17:5–60.

Weschler, Lawrence.
  1990.   *Um Milagre, um Universo: O Acerto de Conta com os*
          Torturadores. São Paulo: Companhia das Letras.

Wieviorka, Michel. 1991. *L'Espace du Racisme.* Paris: Seuil.
  ed. 1993.   *Racisme et Modernité.* Paris: Editions de la Découverte.

Wieviorka, Michel, P. Bataille, D. Jacquin, D. Martuccelli, A. Peralva, and
          P. Zawadski.
  1992.   *La France Raciste.* Paris: Seuil.

Wirth, Louis.
  1969 [1938]. "Urbanism as a Way of Life." In *Classic Essays on the Culture*
          of Cities, ed. Richard Sennett. New York: Appleton–Century
          Crofts, 143–64.

Wolch, Jennifer.
  1996.   "The Rise of Homelessness in Los Angeles during the 1980s."
          In *The City: Los Angeles and Urban Theory at the End of*
          the Twentieth Century, ed. Allen J. Scott and Edward W. Soja.
          Berkeley: University of California Press, 390–425.

Wolch, Jennifer, and Michael Dear.
  1993.   *Malign Neglect: Homelessness in an American City.*
          San Francisco: Jossey-Bass.

Wright, Winthrop R.
  1990.   *Café con Leche: Race, Class, and National Image in*
          Venezuela. Austin: University of Texas Press.

Young, Iris Marion.
  1990.   *Justice and the Politics of Difference.* Princeton: Princeton
          University Press.

Zaluar, Alba.
  1983.   "Condomínio do Diabo: As Classes Populares Urbanas e a

Lógica do 'Ferro' e do Fumo." In *Violência, Crime e Poder*, ed. Paulo Sérgio Pinheiro. São Paulo: Brasiliense, 249–77.

1985.   *A Máquina e a Revolta*. São Paulo: Brasiliense.

1986.   "Teoria e Prática do Trabalho de Campo: Alguns Problemas." In *A Aventura Antropológica: Teoria e Pesquisa*, ed. Ruth Cardoso. Rio de Janeiro: Paz e Terra, 107–126.

1987.   "Crime e Trabalho no Cotidiano Popular." *Ciência Hoje—Suplemento sobre Violência* 5 (28): 21–24.

1990.   "Teleguiados e Chefes: Juventude e Crime." *Religião e Sociedade* 15 (1): 54–67.

1994.   *Condomínio do Diabo*. Rio de Janeiro: Revan/UFRJ.

Zukin, Sharon.

1991.   *Landscapes of Power: From Detroit to Disney World*. Berkeley. University of California Press.

INDEX

ABCD region, 49, 50, 224, 234, 252, 409n70
Abdel Fattah, Ezat, 355
abortion, 353, 391n17. *See also* birth control
Abrevis, 204, 205, 400nn36,49
accidents, traffic, 315–16; children driving without license, 196–99, 257, 277, 316; death, 114, 117, 121, 126–27, 316, 317, 392n18, 412–13n24; impunity, 316, 412–13n24; physical injury, 117, 121, 126–27, 316, 317, 392n18
accountability, 208–9; police, 153–54, 160, 180, 397n15. *See also* courts
Adorno, Sérgio, 113
advertisements, 263; real estate, 12, 259, 263–75, 282–88, 305, 411n13
aesthetics: autoconstruction, 293*photo*, 332, 387n10; security, 291–96, 292–95*photos*, 329, 417n15. *See also* appearances; architecture; security features; social groups
age: adolescent crime, 126, 257, 276–77, 279–80; driving, 277; evil susceptibility, 91; homicide victims, 125–26; physical assault victims, 390n4; population distribution, 44, 45; worker, 63. *See also* children
aggressiveness: folk theory, 395n4; innateness of, 36, 207–8; in public space, 309–17. *See also* violence

Agueno, Maria Leonor Leiko, 412–13n24
AIDS, in prisons, 176, 177, 358
Aldeia da Serra, 253, 262, 272
Alphaville, 253, 262, 272, 277, 278–79, 411n9
Alto de Pinheiros, 14; housing, 14, 260; incomes, 408n60; interviews, 56, 66, 195–96, 362–63; streets, 311
Americas. *See* Latin America; North America
Americas Watch Committee, 159, 160
Amnesty Bill (1979), 341
Amnesty International, 159, 176, 179, 355
anthropologies: classic, 7, 381n4; and displacement, 5, 8, 11; Euro-American, 6, 7, 10, 381nn2,4, 382n11; imperial, 6, 7, 381n2; international, 5, 8–9, 10, 130, 381n2, 382n11; local, 5–6, 10; national, 5–10, 381n2, 382n11; and otherness, 6, 8–9, 141, 381n4, 382n7; peripheral, 7, 9, 381n2
apartment buildings, 216, 407nn53,54; advertised, 264, 282–88, 411n13; center, 224–29, 230*photo*, 241–43, 259, 285; circulation areas, 269–70; flats, 267; high-rise, 14, 224–28, 230*photo*, 241–48, 248*photo*, 254–61, 282–84, 416n13; luxury, 243, 407–8n55; and middle classes, 224,

Text: 10/13 Aldus
Display: Aldus
Composition: Integrated Composition Systems
Printing and binding: Data Reproductions Corp.